W9-BUY-991

## *By Guglielmo Ferrero*

---

**The Greatness and Decline of Rome**
**In Five Volumes**

Vol. I.—The Empire Builders
Vol. II.—Julius Cæsar
Vol. III.—The Fall of an Aristocracy
Vol. IV.—Rome and Egypt
Vol. V.—The Republic of Augustus

**Characters and Events in Roman History**
From Cæsar to Nero (60 B.C.–70 A.D.)

**Ancient Rome and Modern America**
A Comparative Study of Morals and Manners

**Between the Old World and the New**
A Moral and Philosophical Contrast

**A Short History of Rome**
In Two Volumes

**Problems of Peace in Europe**

# A SHORT HISTORY OF ROME

BY

GUGLIELMO FERRERO

AND

CORRADO BARBAGALLO

★ ★

## THE EMPIRE

FROM THE DEATH OF CAESAR TO THE FALL OF THE WESTERN EMPIRE

44 B.C.–476 A.D.

G. P. PUTNAM'S SONS
NEW YORK AND LONDON
The Knickerbocker Press
1919

---

Translated from the Italian by
GEORGE CHRYSTAL

The Knickerbocker Press, New York

# CONTENTS

CHAPTER XVI



CHAPTER XVII



CHAPTER XVIII



CHAPTER XIX

# A SHORT HISTORY OF ROME

## CHAPTER I

### THE THIRD CIVIL WAR

### (44–42 B.C.)

**1. The Amnesty of March 17th, and the Confirmation of Cæsar's Acts.** Cæsar had been assassinated on the morning of March 15th. In Rome his death made as it were a great void. The senate fled in terror. Cæsar's colleague in the consulship, Marcus Antonius, shut himself up in his house fearing lest the conspirators intended that he should share the fate of his friend. The conspirators threw themselves into the Capitol and fortified themselves there. During the whole of March 15th the city was left entirely to itself.

It was not until towards evening that Antony, who had been joined by Lepidus, Cæsar's *magister equitum*, ventured to leave his house and visit the *domus publica* where he took possession of the dictator's papers and money, while the conspirators, on their part, were endeavouring to get into touch with the more important members of the senate. On the following day, the 16th, the activity of both parties increased. Cæsar's soldiers and veterans, instigated by Antony, began to collect together and become turbulent. The leading personages of the dictator's party gathered round Antony, those of the senatorial party, including the conspirators, round Cicero. In both camps there were long discussions, and negotiations between the parties were commenced but led to no result. Meanwhile many of the troops and many veterans, having heard the news of the assassination, flocked into the city from the surrounding country. In the evening, as it was found impossible to arrive at an agreement between the Cæsarians and the conspirators, it was agreed to refer the matter to the senate which was convoked by Antony and met on the morning of the 17th in the temple of Dea Tellus. The senators proceeded to the meeting-place between two lines of soldiers stationed by Antony for the purpose, as he said, of maintaining order. Behind these lines thronged the crowd of Cæsar's veterans, the remains of Clodius's old *collegia* resuscitated for the occasion, and the humbler ranks of the populace whom the soldiers and Cæsar's friends had on the previous days done their best to excite against the conspirators.

The sitting was long. The question the senate had to decide was this:—Were the conspirators to be regarded as assassins and therefore to be brought to trial as the extreme partisans of Cæsar desired? Or, on the other hand, was Cæsar to be considered a tyrant who had richly deserved his fate; and were his murderers to be rewarded as liberators of their country as their ardent supporters contended? The conspirators, partly from fear of the veterans and partly owing to their distrust of Antony, had abstained from attending the sitting. It immediately appeared, however, that the majority of the senate was favourable, and openly favourable, to them, and consequently entirely averse from the first of the two alternatives before the House. Cæsar had struck too hard at the interests and had too deeply injured the susceptibilities of the aristocracy for it to be otherwise. But the senate was somewhat chary of adopting the other alternative, and in this attitude they were confirmed by the tempestuous murmurings and the cries of the crowd outside which, as time passed, began more and more loudly and vehemently to invoke curses on the heads of Cæsar's murderers. In the middle of the debate came a clever speech from Antony who in these early days must have shown himself a very different person from the caricature which Cicero was soon to hand down to posterity in the Philippics. Antony observed that the *damnatio memoriæ* of Cæsar which had been proposed and threatened would entail the rescission of all his acts. Consequently the senate would be decimated; several of the magistrates designate would lose their rank; the lands which Cæsar had given or sold would revert to their former possessors; the reforms he had carried out in Italy, in the provinces, or in the colonies would be annulled and likewise all the promises he had made, for instance those affecting his veterans. Was it possible that the senate really wished to decree such a universal upheaval, and to raise against them so formidable a coalition of interests which would unite their natural enemies with all their lukewarm friends and sympathizers?

The fact was that not a few of the conspirators owed their fortunes to Cæsar. The perplexity of the senate was, therefore, great and the discussion dragged on in uncertainty and confusion until Cicero found the solution of the problem by proposing the adoption of a judicial institution known as the amnesty, which had been invented by the Athenians, and which meant that both sides should reciprocally forget and forgive all that had been done contrary to the law. Cicero in short proposed on the one hand that the assassination of the dictator should not be regarded as a crime and that no one should be permitted to bring any accusation relating to his murder, and on the other hand that his acts, not merely those which had already been made public and had taken effect, but all the others that might be found indicated in his papers should, if reduced to official form, and if performed in virtue of the powers conferred on Cæsar by the senate and the comitia, be regarded as valid. This proposal was approved and in the evening the conspirators, protected by the immunity which had been so opportunely granted to them, were able, after much trepidation, to come down from the Capitol in which for three days they had been barricaded as refugees, to return in safety (so at least they thought) to their domestic hearths, and to take part in the affairs of the country.[1]

2. **The Funeral of Cæsar.** The sitting of the senate on March 17th, if it had not given a decisive victory to the group of irreconcilable Cæsarians, had at all events proved that the conspirators who had

[1] On the events of these three days *cf.* G. Ferrero, *The Greatness and Decline of Rome*, London and New York, 1908; vol. iii., Appendix A. Appendix A contains a minute analysis of the authorities bearing on these events and on the critical reconstruction of what happened.

killed the dictator were compelled to respect his work. Any other course was barred by the vested interests constituted by the civil war and by the dictatorship. It is, therefore, easy to understand why the Cæsarians took courage at the next meeting of the senate, which was held probably on the 19th,[1] and raised the question of the funeral of their dead leader. Piso, Cæsar's father-in-law, contended that his obsequies should be public, like those of all eminent citizens. This was a serious demand. To decree that Cæsar should have a public funeral was to admit that his death was a public affliction. And how was it possible to commend the murder of a citizen whose death was recognized to be a misfortune for the State? The good sense of many of the conspirators and Cassius's practical mind perceived the danger, and they tried to put a stop to the plan. But on the other hand how could this honour be denied to a man who had filled so many offices, against whom, while he lived, no kind of charge had been brought, and whose political work had been approved and confirmed after his death by the whole senate? The more moderate opinion, finally adopted by the ever extremely simple-minded Marcus Brutus, therefore prevailed. It was decided that Cæsar should have a public funeral.

The day, so much desired and so much dreaded, which must have been between March 20th and March 23rd, came at last. In the first place, Cæsar's will had been made known. In it he adopted as his son and made heir to the greater part of his private fortune his nephew Caius Octavius, and designated as secondary and eventual heirs certain of his own murderers. The principal heir was bound by a trust to distribute

[1] *Cf.* Ihne, *Römische Geschichte*, Leipzig, 1898; vol. vii., p. 265.

120 or 300 sesterces to every poor citizen of Rome. He bequeathed for the use of the public his immense gardens situate beyond the Tiber, together with the collection of works of art therein. During his lifetime, Cæsar had done greater things, but perhaps no act of his ever made so lively an impression on the lower ranks of the Roman people as his liberality, and the affection for so many of his murderers, to which his will bore witness.

The soldiers, the veterans, and the Roman populace were more and more deeply agitated; they lamented more and more deeply the death of the dictator; they invoked curses on his murderers with greater and greater fury and thus, on the day of the funeral, the forum, the temples and the adjacent monuments were invaded by an agitated and excited crowd ready for violence, vengeance and destruction. The ivory bier, covered with a purple pall edged with gold, on which Cæsar was sleeping his last sleep was borne on the shoulders of magistrates and ex-magistrates who had been friends of the departed. Before it, like a trophy, was carried the blood-stained robe and behind followed a long train of veterans, freedmen, and artisans, while through the funeral dirges repeatedly resounded a verse from an ancient tragedy.

"I had my death from those whom I had saved."

As at the obsequies of all noble Romans the funeral oration was to be pronounced in the Forum. Who was to be the orator? Who would recall to that excited and tempestuous crowd the figure of the great dead? The principal heir was absent; the other heirs were for the most part personages of small importance;

some of the secondary heirs had actually taken part in the conspiracy. There was no one but Cæsar's colleague Mark Antony who was also named in the will. His task was no easy one, for how was he to speak of Cæsar in the presence both of his veterans and of his murderers? Antony skilfully extricated himself from the difficulty by making public documents speak for him. He called upon a herald to read the decree whereby, in the early days of the year, the senate had conferred on Cæsar all honours human and divine. He made him read the words of the solemn oath in which the very persons who were so soon to slay him had pledged their faith to the dictator. He then added a few words of his own and left the rostrum. The cortège was preparing to resume its way to the Campus Martius when first some isolated voices and then others, more numerous and more insistent, cried out that the body should be burned there and then. In a moment the bearers of the bier were overpowered. Benches, stools, tables, faggots, collected wherever they could be found, together with doors torn from the neighbouring houses and public buildings, were heaped together and set on fire, and on this pyre was placed the body of the great Cæsar on which in an access of frenzy the women began to throw their necklaces, the veterans their arms, the trumpeters their instruments and some their very garments.

The burning of Cæsar's body could not fail to be the preliminary of a much vaster conflagration. From his pyre the infuriated mob rushed to set in flames the houses of Brutus and Cassius. There were riots in every quarter of the city and demonstrations against the tyrannicides and their partisans, some of whom were torn in pieces. Night failed to calm the fury and anger of the populace, and the agitation burst forth again on the following day. The demonstrations of the lower classes were now swollen by those of the very numerous foreigners sojourning in Rome who also flocked together to pay the last tribute of gratitude to the man who had begun the work of redeeming the provinces. It was a terrible scene of anarchy at which even the Cæsarians, or at least the more pacific and influential among them, looked on in terror. But it had the effect of annulling the amnesty of March 17th. Though the conspirators had been amnestied by the senate, the populace, the veterans, and the soldiers had not forgiven them. They called loudly for vengeance, and, when they could, they executed it with their own hands. The tumult did not work itself out as the days went by; on the contrary it persisted implacably, dying down at intervals only to flare up again more threateningly than ever, and making it impossible for the more prominent conspirators to leave their houses or to appear in public, thus preventing those who held office from performing their functions.

3. **The Son of Cæsar and his Struggle with Mark Antony.** These public tumults did what Cæsar's friends had not dared to do. They expelled the murderers of the dictator first from the senate and the magistracies and then from Rome itself. In a few days public life was practically paralyzed. It was all but impossible for the senate to meet, and, towards the end of the month, the conspirators, weary of living a threatened existence shut up in their houses, began to leave the capital and to seek refuge elsewhere. Their departure was followed by that of their friends and sympathizers; Cicero himself, the most influential

member of the senate, left for Puteoli (Pozzuoli) on the 6th or 7th of April. The senatorial party was breaking up, and little more than a month after Cæsar's death, Antony, without making the slightest effort was almost automatically left master of the State. There was no one who could oppose him. The conspirators were scattered over Italy. The senate was paralyzed. Almost all the holders of the magistracies had fled. The government of the State was vacant, and there appeared to be nothing left for Antony to do but to seize it for himself by securing the support of the troops and the veterans of Cæsar and by ingratiating himself with the populace who cherished the memory of the dictator. But suddenly an unexpected obstacle arose. This obstacle was Cæsar's heir, his nephew and adopted son Caius Octavius, a young man scarcely eighteen years of age who had been surprised by the death of his illustrious relative while staying at Apollonia on the Adriatic coast not far from Epidamnus, and who had returned to Rome while Antony was in Campania.

Octavius was born at Rome on September 23, 63 B.C., the year of the conspiracy of Catiline and the consulship of Cicero. His mother was a niece (the daughter of a sister) of Cæsar. He had lost his father when he was four years old and, his mother having married again, he had been brought up by Julia, his maternal grandmother. From his earliest years he had been a delicate, ailing, and nervous boy, but intelligent, sagacious and studious. Taken into favour by the dictator, he had been given some honorary office in spite of his extreme youth, and had been sent to Apollonia in order to prepare to accompany his uncle on the Parthian campaign. He had therefore as yet done nothing, and nothing was known of his views. But, if he had the ability and the ambition, it would be very difficult for him, the protégé and the adopted son of the dictator to renounce the task imposed on him by adoption and by the course of events, the task, namely, of defending the policy he had inherited from Cæsar and of taking vengeance on his murderers. On this ground his path and Antony's crossed, hence the quarrel which immediately arose between them. Octavius had at once claimed from Antony the money which must have been found in Cæsar's coffers. But Antony not only kept the money for himself but began to intrigue with the comitia curiata to induce that body to refuse or retard the ratification of the adoption of Caius Octavius into the family of the Julii. He relied on the absence of the majority of the more important senators, the humiliation of the rest, the strength he derived from the support of the veterans and the lower orders, to enable him to pass over Octavius altogether and to attain the commanding position at which he aimed by a few decisive and resolute strokes. On the 2d of June, he caused the comitia tributa to pass a law extending for five years, *i.e.*, until 39 B.C., the government of Macedonia, which had been assigned to him by Cæsar, as well as that of Syria which Cæsar had given to Cornelius Dolabella.[1] Shortly afterwards Antony's brother Lucius, a tribune of the people, brought forward a great agrarian law, the

[1] On the intricate question of the provinces assigned by Cæsar before his death *cf.* G. Ferrero, *The Greatness and Decline of Rome*, vol. iii., Appendix B. A final proof, however, that Macedonia and Syria had not been given by Cæsar to Brutus and Cassius may be found in the edict of Marcus Antonius, cited by Josephus, *Ant. Jud.*, xiv., 12, 4–5.

object of which was to prepare the way for a distribution among the veterans of all the remaining *ager publicus* in Italy and to acquire for the same purpose further land now in private possession. Finally he himself with Dolabella suddenly proposed to the people a law *de permutatione provinciarum*,[1] whereby Gallia Cisalpina, that most precious province which he meant to use for keeping Italy in subjection, was to be taken from Decimus Brutus, who had held it since April, and given to himself instead of Macedonia, from which he was to be allowed to remove the troops, a force amounting to about fifty or sixty thousand men.

His intention to succeed Cæsar in the predominant position in the State was clear. From Cisalpine Gaul Antony at the head of an army of such strength and with the support of the soldiers, would dominate Rome. In the senatorial order and among the upper class generally hatred of Antony was growing; but the support of the veterans and the absence from Rome of the most prominent and influential of the conspirators made his position exceedingly strong. In spite of some hesitation, caused by an attempt at opposition in the senate, the *lex de permutatione* was passed in the month of August. Antony, and with him the Cæsarian party, were therefore again masters of Gallia Cisalpina, of the army which was nearest to the capital and therefore of the State. The position of the conspirators and of all the party which supported them seemed desperate when this party obtained an unexpected ally in the person of Caius Octavius himself whose adoption had now been confirmed and who therefore had now the right to call himself C. Julius

[1] On this law *cf.* Ferrero, *The Greatness and Decline of Rome*, vol. iii., pp. 85 ff.

Cæsar Octavianus. The quarrel between him and Antony had become steadily more bitter. Resolved to carry out the obligations imposed on him by the testament of Cæsar and thus to create for himself a secure basis of popularity, Octavian, when Antony refused to surrender to him Cæsar's property, had sold all his personal possessions, had summoned to his assistance his relatives and the most faithful of Cæsar's friends, and had contrived to distribute to every poor citizen of Rome the legacy specified by his adoptive father's will. He then prepared and exhibited in honour of Cæsar's memory, and for the diversion of the veterans and of the people, games which he called *Ludi Victoriæ Cæsaris*, the Games of the Victory of Cæsar. When, however, in the course of these proceedings, which took place during the last ten days of July, he proposed to have Cæsar's gilded throne borne in state he was forbidden to do so by certain tribunes who had been suborned by Antony. Octavian appealed against them to the consul, but in vain. Not only did the consul support their action but he threatened Octavian with arrest if he persisted in carrying on an agitation among the people. A worse thing happened some months later. About the 4th or 5th of October all Rome was informed that Octavian had attempted to have Antony assassinated in his own house by hired murderers. Was this story true or false?[1] It is impossible to say. But, whether true or false, the fact that such an atrocious charge was made meant an open breach between Antony and Octavian, and this episode for the time decisively threw Cæsar's heir into the arms of the party of the

[1] On this obscure episode *cf.* G. Ferrero, *The Greatness and Decline of Rome*, vol. iii., p. 101.

conspirators. He was, in fact, acclaimed by them as their best defender now that Brutus and Cassius had gone to the East. Throughout all this Octavian had the intention of going himself to Campania so that he might recruit for himself among Cæsar's veterans a bodyguard which at the opportune moment might become the guardians of the conservative republic against Antony. In the middle of October he actually left Rome, taking with him all the money that he himself and his friends had been able to collect in order to attempt the most revolutionary enterprise which Rome had seen since the days of Milo and Clodius.

4. **The De Officiis of Cicero.** While Octavian was successfully pursuing his dangerous enterprise in Campania, Cicero, weary and disgusted at the many and ever increasing misfortunes of his country, was engaged at Puteoli in a loftier and perhaps a less feasible undertaking than Octavian, nothing less in fact than a moral regeneration of the people by which alone, in his opinion, the fortunes of Rome could be saved. Like all Romans since the second Punic War, he was much preoccupied with the tragic contradiction in which Italy had for the last century been entangled, the contradiction whereby culture was degraded into corruption, wealth into self-indulgence, the perennial and ever growing habit of war into a progressive obliteration of the all important military virtue of former ages, while the conquest and subjection of other countries was leading to the extinction of individual liberty in his own. For years he had been seeking the unattainable means of reconciling empire with liberty, comfort and riches with domestic and public discipline, culture with morality.

This was the theme of the *De Officiis*, the book he

was writing in these months, in which the compilations and translations he made from this or that Greek philosopher have not remained dead literary matter, but express very vividly the moral crisis through which the author was passing, and bear eloquent testimony to the political crisis of the time. In writing his book Cicero's chief object is to inquire what should be held to be the virtues required by the ruling class in a well governed State, and he discovers them to be all summed up in a single principle, which is as follows: Riches and power are not supreme goods, to be pursued and desired for their own sake, but rather heavy burdens to be assumed and borne for the good of all. As soon as the nobility and the rest of the ruling class grasped this principle they would know how to live with dignity but without pomp, spending thought and labour on their public duties, not in order to make fortunes and corrupt the people but to serve zealously the interests of the middle and poorer classes. They would undertake works of public utility such as walls, harbours, aqueducts, roads, and not mere monuments of luxury such as theatres, porticos, and temples. They would help the people in their necessities, but without ruining the public treasury, and would aid deserving debtors without using revolutionary methods to abolish debt. Finally they would distribute land to the needy, but without taking it from its rightful owners. In this way the good of all would become the supreme aim of government and its attainment by mankind would be secured by a scrupulous respect for the law, by the intelligent liberality of the great, and the general practice of virtue. Nor were the subject peoples in the provinces to be left out of this ideal reconstruction of the Roman polity. Even where they were concerned it was the duty of the republic to use her power with justice, seeking rather the good of her subjects than her own. She should abstain from acts of violent aggression like those of Cæsar and Crassus and from all useless acts of ferocious repression. She should abhor treachery and deceit, and war itself, except such as aimed at consolidating the national defence and preserving peace. She should prefer great orators, philosophers, and jurists to great soldiers, taking care, however, that in studying them the citizen should not be distracted from his own civic duty which ought to be the supreme end of all his efforts. Thus alone could be founded the true aristocratic republic, that is to say the State governed by its best men, without ambitious demagogues or violent conservatives, in which there should be no new Cæsar and no new Sulla. In writing thus Cicero, though he did not know it, was laying down the better and the more essential part of what was to be the programme and the secret of the Empire and the imperial policy. But he would not have recognized his plan in its realization. It was not his will or his teaching that were to bring that realization to pass, but rather the final exasperation of the crisis through which the State was to struggle for its existence for yet another ten years. For the moment he was merely preparing himself to look on at the first excesses of Caius Octavius, the man who was destined one day to embody in real life the political system of which he dreamed.

5. **The War of Mutina** (43 **B.C.**). Octavian's tour in Campania had been successful. By depreciating Antony as a somewhat luke-warm Cæsarian who was much more ready to come to terms with the enemy than to fight, and above all by spending enormous

sums of money, he succeeded in recruiting 3000 men (some say as many as 10,000[1]) whom he intended to use not for avenging Cæsar, but for a very different purpose. Meanwhile, by the agency of friends, he was secretly endeavouring to corrupt the Macedonian legions which Antony had brought to Italy, and which were discontented at being sent to Gaul instead of against the empire of the Parthians where they had hoped to secure much spoil. Antony was exasperated by all these intrigues so he sent three legions along the Adriatic coast in the direction of Cisalpine Gaul, led two into Latium and then went himself to Rome, determined to bring matters to a head with Octavian by prosecuting him for illegal armaments. It was a highly critical moment for Octavian. Had Antony succeeded in putting him on trial for *perduellio*, he would have had to choose between raising the standard of revolt and committing suicide. For a moment it really seemed as if he were lost. At the approach of danger the Pompeians who had hitherto encouraged him, left him to his fate. Even the veterans he had himself recruited, somewhat alarmed by the illegality of the situation in which they found themselves and rather disconcerted by his proud and ambiguous bearing, vacillated. He was saved by a miracle. At the last moment the two legions which Antony had brought to Latium, irritated by his severity, discontented with the gifts they had received, and, moreover, skilfully played upon by Octavian, mutinied and declared for the son of Cæsar. This mutiny reversed the situation to the disadvantage of Antony, whose danger was the greater as in the meantime Decimus Brutus, resolved not to recognize the

[1] *Cf.* Cic., *Ad Att.*, xvi., 8, 2; App., *B. C.*, iii., 40.

*lex de permutatione* was preparing to resist and was arming troops in Cisalpine Gaul. With the three legions which still remained faithful to him Antony was in danger of being caught between Octavian and Decimus Brutus. In order to avert this danger, and to defend and hold the threatened province at all costs, Antony, after hastily summoning the senate to discuss the question of the provinces which were still vacant, did not hesitate to leave Rome early in December, 44. He took with him all the veterans who were in Rome and who had rallied to his assistance immediately after the Ides of March; he summoned the sixth legion which had remained in Macedonia, to join him, and collected new forces as fast as he could. He pitched his camp at Ariminum (Rimini) and thence commenced operations against Decimus Brutus.

The consul's departure from Rome radically changed the political situation in the republic in favour of the party of the conspirators. Octavian, who was now definitely committed to opposing Antony, drew nearer and nearer to the Pompeians and opened negotiations with Decimus Brutus for common action. Decimus Brutus, finding himself supported at Rome, decided to resist Antony, notwithstanding the exiguity of his forces. His firm attitude infused courage into the party of the conspirators who began to hold their heads up again in the capital. The most significant sign of the new situation was the determined attitude assumed by Cicero. His relations with Antony had never been good. Several times during the preceding months the great orator had felt bound to take up his pen or to raise his voice against the audacity of the Cæsarian party. But he had not yet ventured upon resolute and continuous action, and after each effort he had fallen back into his fixed condition of weariness and lassitude. But from the 20th of December in that tragic year 44, from the day on which the senate met for the first time after Antony's departure, all his hesitation disappeared. At that sitting he made the speech known in his collected works as the third Philippic and for the first time openly declared himself an opponent of Antony. At the sitting of January 1, 43, when debate arose on the situation, he delivered the fifth Philippic, in which he roundly asserted that war should be declared on the consul without more ado. The mild and prudent man of letters had become the advocate of extreme measures. In the senate, however, there was a group friendly to Antony, and, above all, there were many who dreaded a new civil war. The debate was therefore long. Great honours were granted to Octavian, who in the senate was allowed to sit with senators of consular rank, and was authorized to stand for the consulship ten years before he was legally entitled to do so. As regards Antony, however, a middle course was adopted. War was not declared against him but a deputation of three senators was sent to invite him to surrender Cisalpine Gaul.

Antony, in the meantime, had forced Decimus to shut himself up in Mutina (Modena) which he besieged, though with no great energy, collecting new troops the while from all parts of Italy, even from the most Southern districts whither he had sent Ventidius Bassus, one of his officers, to raise three legions. The three envoys of the senate arrived, addressed him with the respect which was his due, and Antony entered into an amicable discussion with them. In the end he declared that he was ready to surrender Cisalpine

Gaul if he could he guaranteed Transalpine Gaul with six legions for five years and the confirmation of all his acts as consul. To many friends of peace this proposal seemed reasonable. Therefore, at the sitting of the senate early in February at which the report of the envoys was discussed, Cicero strove in vain to prove to his hearers that, as Antony had not obeyed the summons of the senate, they should at once declare him a public enemy (*hostis publicus*) and commence warlike operations against him. The majority in the senate, though unwilling to accept Antony's proposals, wished to keep a way to agreement still open, and, instead of declaring war it was merely decided to declare a state of *tumultus*, which meant no more than that public order was disturbed.

Moderate counsels thus prevailed in the senate, not only from love of peace but also because of the slender confidence which the party of the conspirators reposed in their own soldiers. The consul Hirtius, who had already left Rome, had taken command of Octavian's army and had begun to raise new forces. But neither he nor Octavian, nor even the besieged Decimus Brutus, though they disposed of a superiority of numbers, ventured to risk energetic measures against Antony because in their ranks there were too many of Cæsar's veterans who, they feared, would not fight against Antony and his soldiers. About the middle of February, however, a really remarkable piece of news was received at Rome. Marcus Brutus, who a few months earlier had fled from Rome almost as an exile, taking with him nothing but a few tens of thousands of sesterces which he owed to the generosity of a friend, had now, with the assistance of some of his companions in exile at Athens, contrived to carry to a successful conclusion a plan of supreme audacity. He had managed to get possession of the tribute which was being sent to Rome by the Governor of the province of Asia—a sum of no less than 16,000 talents. By using this money to corrupt the Roman armies in the East and to raise new levies, he had contrived to create an army sufficient to occupy the province of Macedonia, and, finally, to lay his hands on the great military magazines which Cæsar had prepared there for the projected oriental war. With a part of these forces he was now besieging in Apollonia Caius Antonius, brother of Marcus and governor of Macedonia. Thus the Pompeian party now had a great army and a war chest in the East, and, what was more, they now had proof that it was untrue that Cæsar's veterans would only fight for the Cæsarian party. The party of the conspirators decidedly recovered its ascendancy in the senate and the effects of this were immediately visible. Their former caution in dealing with Antony was succeeded by a new audacity; the same assembly which hitherto had been irresponsive to the stimulus of Cicero's fiery eloquence, changed its tone in a moment, and lent a reverent ear to his new oration against Antony (the tenth Philippic). They approved of all the more than revolutionary proceedings of Brutus in the East, and invested him with pro-consular command in Macedonia, Greece, and Illyria. What was still more important, they at the same time annulled all Antony's acts and all the laws passed on his initiative.

The senate had thus declared war on Antony, and the military operations which had hitherto been hesitating and uncertain, proceeded at a much more rapid pace. Antony began to besiege Mutina in earnest, and ordered Ventidius to join him with his legions as soon as possible. The senate on the other hand resolved to send effective aid to Decimus Brutus. On March 19th, the other consul Vibius Pansa, left Rome with four fresh legions and marched to effect a junction with the armies of his colleague Hirtius and of Octavian who were to attack Antony before Mutina and thus extricate Decimus. On the 14th or 15th of April, Antony, though in inferior force, attempted to prevent the junction of Pansa with Hirtius and Octavian by attacking the former on the march, while his brother Lucius, by a feint attack on the camp of Hirtius and Octavian, was to distract their attention from what was intended to be the main action. Hirtius, however, seeing through Antony's design, had sent twelve cohorts in good time to meet Pansa, and they succeeded in joining and accompanying the approaching army. Yet when Antony attacked Pansa's reinforced legions near Forum Gallorum (Castelfranco) he managed to defeat them, and Pansa himself being seriously wounded, had to abandon the field of battle. A messenger from the defeated army, however, succeeded in reaching the camp of Hirtius with an appeal for help, and Hirtius at once sent two legions of veterans to the rescue. Antony's twenty victorious cohorts, weary with the fight, were retiring to their encampment when they were attacked by the fresh troops of a new adversary and suffered a very serious reverse.

This was the first encounter and it was in no way decisive. Neither side had engaged more than a fraction of its forces and Ventidius was coming up by the Via Æmilia in the rear of Hirtius and Octavian. This circumstance, as well as the gravity of the situation of the army of Decimus Brutus, which was on the brink of starvation in Mutina, induced Hirtius, Pansa, and Octavian a week later to make an effort to break up the siege with the co-operation, which they trusted would be forthcoming, of a partial or general sortie of the invested garrison. Matters turned out as had been expected, and the battle—or rather the two battles—which had begun on both fronts of the investing army, raged furiously. Hirtius, fighting gallantly, perished in the mêlée, and Octavian, for the first time in his life had to fight simultaneously as a general and as a soldier. In the evening the forces of Decimus Brutus and those of Hirtius and Octavian were compelled to retire. But Antony's losses had been very severe, so severe that, fearing another attack on the following day, and before the arrival of Ventidius's reinforcements, he suddenly decided during the night to raise the siege and to retire into Gallia Narbonensis after sending messengers ordering Ventidius to join him there by way of Liguria.

**6. Triumviri Reipublicæ Constituendæ.** The news of Antony's retreat at first roused great enthusiasm in the senate. For a moment it was believed that the rebel general was lost, that the war was won, and the Cæsarians exterminated. At a memorable sitting held on April 26th, Antony and his partisans were finally proscribed. But the real state of the case was very different from these rosy illusions. Antony was abandoning Mutina with an army which, if it had not been victorious, had certainly not been beaten. He was moreover flying to meet a fresh and friendly army under the command of M. Æmilius Lepidus, governor of Gallia Narbonensis, and a friend of Cæsar, with whom during the siege of Mutina he had entered into successful negotiations and who had promised to help him. On the other hand, of the armies of the victors one, that of Decimus Brutus, was exhausted by the long agony of the siege, while the other was now without a general, for Pansa had also succumbed to his wounds a few days after the battle, and Octavian had no serious claims to that title, either on the ground of military experience or of natural ability. As a matter of fact Decimus found it impossible to persuade Octavian to cut off Ventidius Bassus who was now crossing the Appennines in order to descend into Liguria and thence to join Antony in Gallia Narbonensis. Octavian had made up his mind to fight Antony when Antony had wished to bar the path of his ambition; but now he could not be eager to sacrifice himself in order to secure the triumph of his father's murderers, a triumph which, without solid guarantees, would have meant his own political extinction. Moreover, even if he had been so blind to his own interests as to wish to take this course, it was clear that he would not be justified in completely trusting his soldiers. The hope of great rewards and the presence of an ex-Cæsarian like Hirtius as well as of Octavian himself had induced them to fight Antony. But it was difficult to suppose that Cæsar's old soldiers and officers would be willing to go to the length of exterminating one of Cæsar's old generals in order to found on his ruin the power of the senate and of the conspirators. To persuade them so far great inducements would be necessary—splendid and immediate donations, manifest guarantees in respect of the man who now led them. Was the senate good for so much?

The senate on their part immediately showed the hesitation usual in all assemblies divided into discordant parties at critical moments when resolute and thorough-going action is required. While Octavian remained at Bononia (Bologna) inert and apparently paralyzed, they decided after long hesitation that only the two legions which had mutinied against Antony were to receive any recompense, and they were only to get 10,000 sesterces per head and not 20,000 as had been promised. It was further decided, not indeed to deprive Octavian of the command as some had proposed, but to make a show of refusing to recognize his authority as in any way official, and to treat directly with the five legions under his command without any reference to him as their general.[1] Such methods were not calculated to exercise a favourable influence over his uncertain purpose.

At the time when Decimus Brutus with his weary troops was setting himself, unassisted and not without delay, to the difficult task of pursuing Antony, that general himself with four legions, other forces not yet embodied in formations and all his cavalry intact was proceeding by forced marches towards Gallia Narbonensis caring nothing for the fatigue or the roughness of the road. On April 23rd he swooped like a whirlwind on Parma, on the 25th he had reached Placentia (Piacenza), on the 28th Tortona (Dertona) from which, after resting for one day, his army had begun the ascent of the mountains which separated them from Vada Sabbatia (Vado). On May 5th and 7th he was joined with three legions by Ventidius Bassus whom Octavian had permitted to escape, and

[1] For a more minute account of the relations between the senate and Octavian after the battle of Mutina, and on the necessity for caution in accepting the accounts given by ancient historians *cf.* G. Ferrero, *The Greatness and Decline of Rome*, vol. iii., p. 152 ff.

the united force proceeded on its way to Gallia Narbonensis, arriving after eight days' march at Forum Julii (Fréjus) which was only twenty-four miles away from Lepidus whose camp was at Forum Vocontii (Vidauban). At the beginning of June, Rome learned that the troops of the governor of Gallia Narbonensis had fraternized with those of the routed pro-consul of Cisalpine Gaul, and that Antony and Lepidus were jointly in arms against the republic.

This was, in truth, an inevitable development. At Cæsar's death Lepidus was regarded as the most intimate of the dictator's friends, and he was also his *magister equitum*. In the evening of March 15, 44, he alone among the Cæsarians had hastened to Antony in order to decide what should be done in the critical situation of the party, and it appears to have been his opinion that the right course was to attack the Capitol with the forces at their disposal, and put the conspirators to death. Later, when the situation had become more complicated, he had been distracted between the two parties, until, making a show of having been compelled by his own soldiers, he had resolutely joined the side of Antony against the coalition of Octavian and the party of the conspirators. In any case Antony was now again master of a powerful army which could be used against that party and the senate. The senate immediately recalled to Italy from the East not only Marcus Brutus but also Cassius who, though with less celerity and good fortune than his friend, had also succeeded in raising an army in Syria where he had removed Dolabella from his path. They also recalled the legions stationed in Africa under the orders of Cornificius, and they placed in command of the fleet with the title of *præfectus classis et oræ maritimæ*, Sextus, the surviving son of Pompey, who had emerged from the hiding place in the extreme West of Spain which had sheltered him since Munda, and who was now granted powers similar to those held by his father during the war with the pirates.[1] An extraordinary contribution was levied all over Italy, and the command against Antony was entrusted to Octavius.

In the meantime Decimus Brutus was descending into Gallia Narbonensis by the Val d'Aosta and the little St. Bernard, and joined Plancus at Grenoble. Decimus and Plancus had between them fifteen legions, Lepidus and Antony fourteen. It would have been difficult for them to withstand a simultaneous attack by Decimus and Plancus on one side and by Octavian, who now had eight legions, on the other. Octavian had thus come to be the master of the situation since the party he joined would thereby acquire a decisive superiority of force in the West. Lepidus understood this so well that he at once opened negotiations with Octavian with a view to a reconciliation with Antony, appealing to the great name of Cæsar to whom they all owed so much. Octavian, however, understood the situation as well as Lepidus; he reflected that both consular offices were vacant by the deaths of Hirtius and Pansa, and he had formed the plan of profiting by the situation to be made consul with Cicero as his colleague.

A consul of nineteen years of age was a constitutional scandal the like of which had never been seen at Rome. But the times were so troublous, and the dangers so imminent that Cicero, who now personified

[1] This title is preserved on his coins. *Cf.* Cohen, *Monnaies romaines*, i., pp. 19 and 20.

Rome and the senate in the supreme struggle, was not disinclined to allow the young man the supreme honour in the State, himself participating. The senate, however, unanimously revolted against this monstrous illegality, and thereupon Octavian began to lend a willing ear to the proposals of Lepidus. A secret agreement was concluded, and immediately afterwards Octavian executed a sudden *volte face* and again presented himself to his soldiers as the son and heir of Cæsar. By vehement speeches he rekindled their admiration for his father, swore that if he had been made consul he would have given them all the rewards which Cæsar had promised, and persuaded them to send a deputation of centurions to Rome to demand from the senate the supreme authority for their general.

The senate refused and Octavian marched on Rome with his legions. On this the senate vacillated, and now hastened to concede what had before been vainly demanded of them, namely the grant of 20,000 sesterces per head to all Octavian's legions, his appointment to the commission appointed to distribute lands to the soldiers, and permission to stand for the consulship even though absent from Rome. But the news of the arrival of the legions from the province of Africa was enough to make the senate immediately withdraw all these concessions. Thereupon Octavian entered Rome with his army but without opposition or bloodshed, and the forces on which the senate had for a moment relied very soon declared for him. On August 19th, he was elected consul with Q. Pedius, another of Cæsar's heirs. Then came to pass what the Pompeians and the conspirators had been dreading for more than a year. After having secured the validation of Octavian's adoption by the comitia centuriata, and having paid part of Cæsar's legacy to the soldiers and the citizens out of the public treasury the two new consuls did what Antony had never ventured to do. They caused the comitia to pass a law whereby all the authors of Cæsar's death and their accomplices were to be brought before a special tribunal and condemned to the *interdictio aqua et igni* with the confiscation of all their property.

Cicero's masterpiece, the amnesty of March 17, 44, was shattered. Thanks to Octavian's incredible *volte face* the Cæsarian party had carried all before them at Rome and now had in their power a terrible weapon against the party of the conspirators. They were not long in making use of it. Octavian's friends divided the conspirators among them, each selecting the one whom he should accuse, and in a few days they were all condemned *in contumaciam*. Graver still was the effect of this triumph of Cæsar's party at Rome on the Western armies. Cæsarian enthusiasm, long repressed, burst forth in all of them, even in those serving under generals who remained faithful to the party of the conspirators, and drove them to rebel against the authority of the senate and to declare for the three new heads of the Cæsarian party. The army of Asinius Pollio in Spain, and in Gallia Transalpina the troops of L. Munatius Plancus which had been joined by those of Decimus Brutus, revolted. As for Decimus, when he endeavoured to lead his troops to Macedonia they gradually abandoned their general, at first in small bodies and then in large masses, until at last Decimus himself was captured and murdered by the chief of a barbarous Alpine tribe. With Decimus the senate and the party of the conspirators lost their last general in the West, where Antony, Lepidus, and

Octavian were victorious all along the line and came to a definite agreement for the partition of the empire, assuming the style of *triumviri reipublicæ constituendæ*. The two former quitted the province in which they were residing and Octavian left Rome, after securing the passage of a law annulling the double condemnation of Antony and Lepidus, and all three met not far from Bononia (Bologna) and the Via Æmilia on a little island at the confluence of the Rhenus (Reno) and the Lavinius (Lavino) where, after three long days of conference, they drew up the programme of the new government.

The first and most serious problem which faced the triumvirs was undoubtedly that of satisfying the pledges which they had made to their legions, which numbered forty-three, making 250,000 men to whom they had made many promises. In order to give effect to these promises they calculated that about 800 million sesterces would be necessary. But they were at the end of their resources. The treasury was empty; the richest provinces were in the hands of the conspirators, and Italy had proved very unwilling to submit to the extraordinary contributions which the senate had decreed shortly before. On the other hand it was necessary to take the offensive against the conspirators without delay and to conquer them before they had time to become too strong in the East. For this also ample means would be necessary, and where were they to be found? Under the stress of necessity the triumvirs decided to have recourse to a terrible expedient which had been unknown in the Roman world since the days of Marius and Sulla. This was the confiscation of property of the rich families who did not belong to the Cæsarian party and had been either hostile or neutral in the conflict between the Pompeians and the Cæsarians.

The power of the triumvirs placed at their disposal the means of doing this legally, for it had been made to include the power to make laws, penal jurisdiction without restriction, right of appeal or forms of process, the right to impose taxes, to raise levies, to command armies, govern provinces, appoint senators, magistrates and governors, the power to expropriate, to found colonies, and to coin money. Antony, Lepidus, and Octavian who successively arrived in Rome on November 24th, 25th, and 26th, each with one legion and its respective prætorian cohort, actually received this practically unlimited triumviral power on November 27th under the terms of the Lex Titia which conferred it upon them for five years, that is, until December 31st of the year 38.[1] Thereupon commenced the great proscriptions which served incidentally to gratify political vendettas and personal animosities, but aimed above all at dispoiling the richer classes of Italy for the benefit of the veterans and the troops generally. This explains the number of the victims who were not only robbed but condemned to death in order to prevent those who had suffered by the confiscations from swelling the ranks of the army of the conspirators. In a few days, by the mere operation of decrees issued by the triumvirs, and without the slightest pretence of a trial, a great part of the landed aristocracy and the higher ranks of the plutocracy of Italy was exterminated. The finest villas of Latium and Campania, an infinite number of properties all over Italy, the great domains of Magna Græcia and Sicily, the vast estates which senators and knights possessed in Cisal-

[1] Cf. *C. I. L.*, i., p. 466.

pine Gaul or outside Italy, the live stock, the *familiæ* of slaves, the objects of value, plate, statues, furniture, carpets, which adorned their fine houses in Italy together with the gold and silver found therein—all was seized and put up for sale. Among the victims the most illustrious was Cicero, whom Antony would not pardon.[1]

But the result which is usual in such cases followed. The property which the triumvirs accumulated was, in the mass, enormous, but the proceeds of the sale were, on the contrary, extremely meagre. Many did not dare to buy the goods of the proscribed, which they regarded as the seed of future feuds and future persecutions. The friends of the triumvirs who wished to seize for themselves whatever was going took care to frighten purchasers away. In short, amid the terrible disorder of the moment, capital was terrified and hid itself. The triumvirs were therefore compelled to suspend these forced sales, to wait for better days, and to think of some other expedient for raising money. They ordered the confiscation of the money deposited by private persons in the sacred temple of Vesta. All foreigners and freedmen who possessed as much as 400,000 sesterces were ordered to register the amount of their possessions and to lend to the State a sum equivalent to two per cent of the whole plus a year's income which, in doubtful cases, was to be reckoned at one-tenth of the capital.[2] Roman citizens possessing less than 400,000 sesterces were compelled to make a contribution equal to one-half

[1] On the proscriptions and their character *cf.* G. Ferrero, *The Greatness and Decline of Rome*, vol. iii., p. 182.

[2] This seems to be the result if we harmonize App., *B. C.*, iv., 34, and Dion Cass., xlvii., 16.

of a whole year's income, and the richest of the Italian matrons (to the number of about 1300) were invited to declare the value of their dowries. It was decided to confiscate the goods not only of the proscribed, but also of all who were in voluntary exile, the *émigrés* of that time. Then, and not till then, the triumvirs judged the moment opportune to leave Italy, which had been squeezed dry and bled white, in order to commence the final war against the conspirators. In the spring of 42, eight legions, the advance guard of the army of the triumvirs, crossed the Adriatic and moved in the direction of Macedonia.

7. **Philippi.** Marcus Brutus had meanwhile evacuated Macedonia and had betaken himself to Asia Minor with his whole army, perhaps with the object of collecting money and taking up winter quarters in a country which was richer and further from Italy than Macedonia. At Smyrna he had a conference with Cassius and they decided to unite their forces to fight the triumvirs. But, while Brutus would have wished to return immediately to Macedonia to drive out Antony's eight legions, Cassius was in favour of a more ambitious plan. This was in the first place to secure the whole of the East, and above all Egypt, where Queen Cleopatra remained faithful to the Cæsarian cause, next to seize the command of the sea in order to cut the communications between Italy and Macedonia, and then, and not before, to attack the army of the triumvirs in Macedonia. Without the command of the sea it would be impossible for the triumvirs to maintain a large army in Macedonia, and for the moment the sea was held by Sextus Pompeius, who, fortified by the senate's commission, had taken command of the naval forces of the republic

immediately after Antony's final defeat at Mutina, had occupied Sicily, and was now engaged in collecting ships, recruiting sailors, and organizing legions everywhere, raiding the Italian coast and intercepting the cargoes of grain which were being sent to Rome by sea. Cassius's plan was therefore adopted, and thereafter Cassius and Brutus separated. Cassius went to conquer Rhodes, to obtain money and shipping in Asia and to try to intercept the subsidies which Cleopatra was preparing for the triumvirate. Brutus went to undertake the conquest of the confederation of the Lycian republics.

These enterprises were successfully carried out and, at the end of the summer, Brutus and Cassius prepared to invade Macedonia and to overthrow the eight legions sent by Antony. On the other side Antony's first attempts to break up his opponents' plan came to nothing. Octavian, whom he had sent to Sicily against Sextus Pompeius, failed in his mission. Cleopatra's subsidies were scattered by a storm, and the fleet of Cassius under the command of a certain Statius Murcus, being thus freed from its task, at once sailed to Italy to blockade Antony in Brundusium at the very time when Brutus and Cassius were on their way to Macedonia, and Antony was preparing to take reinforcements thither in order to save his eight legions from the new catastrophe which was threatening them.

Antony was compelled to recall from Sicily the fleet commanded by Octavian and it was only by its assistance that he was able to compel Murcus to give him passage and to disembark twelve legions at Dyrrhachium (Durazzo). With these he joined the eight legions already sent and moved against Brutus and Cassius.

They were encamped at Philippi in a formidable position and had entrenched themselves in two camps, Brutus a little to the north, Cassius more to the south. Both camps communicated, by way of the great Via Egnatia, with the harbour of Neapolis where ships brought food and arms every day from Asia and from the neighbouring island of Thasus which the conspirators had chosen as their general depot. Antony succeeded in pitching his own camp directly opposite to that of the two conspirators, but not in bringing about the immediate and decisive battle he had come to seek.

The respective situations of the two armies themselves showed clearly which rôle was assigned to each. It was the business of the conspirators to assume the defensive and to await the day when hunger and sedition should have triumphed over an army more numerous than their own but encamped in an inhospitable country and (since Cassius had reinforced his fleet with a second squadron under Domitius Ahenobarbus) with no secure control of the sea. It was necessary on the other hand for Antony, and for Octavian who had accompanied him, to force the fighting with their enemy whose forces were weaker than theirs, to provoke him to battle and secure a decision as soon as possible. A desperate struggle therefore began, in the course of which Brutus and Cassius opposed an unwearied patience to Antony's daily provocations to battle. In the end Antony conceived the idea of constructing a road across the marsh which separated the camp of Cassius from the sea, thus menacing him in the rear. The danger was serious and accordingly, in the second half of October, Cassius and Brutus one day made a sortie, probably with the intention of interrupting this threatening operation. The right wing under the command of Brutus threw itself on Octavian's legions, the left under Cassius on those of Antony. A singular conflict ensued. The legions of Octavian, taken by surprise and not assisted by the presence of their general, who was forced to fly and to hide in a neighbouring morass, were completely defeated, and their camp was sacked. On the other hand, Antony's men threw themselves on Cassius's force and pursued them even into their camp. Neither of the victorious generals could extricate his troops from the confusion of plundering, and thus crown his victorious beginning with complete success. In the evening each army retired half-defeated to its own camp. But in the mêlée Cassius had perished—it is not clear how—and the army of the conspirators was thus deprived of its one real prop and stay.

The skirmish converted into a fierce encounter had nevertheless decided the war. Brutus had neither the energy nor the military ability of Cassius; he was both weak and weary. If he had had the strength to wait a little longer it is possible that the forces of his adversaries might have broken up, as they were in want of food and money, and the reinforcements of men and provisions which they expected from Italy had been sent to the bottom by the united fleets of Murcus and Ahenobarbus. But his officers, his principal oriental allies, and his troops themselves were impatient to finish the campaign, and cried out loudly for battle, threatening every day, like the Cæsarian veterans in the service of the coalition, that they would revolt or desert. Antony on the other hand, in view of the desperate plight of his army, spared no effort to provoke a final encounter and threatened a movement to cut his opponents' communications with the sea.

One day Brutus allowed the order for battle to be extorted from him and the final contest between Cæsarians and Pompeians, between the two great cliques which had divided the nobility, was decided in the plain of Philippi on a dismal day in the month of November, 42. Brutus was vanquished, and, having retired with a small group of friends to a little valley in the neighbourhood, the murderer of Cæsar took his own life with stoical serenity, assisted by a Greek rhetorician who had been his teacher.

## CHAPTER II

### THE VICISSITUDES AND THE FALL OF THE TRIUMVIRATE

**8. The War of Perusia (41–40 B. C).** The proscriptions of the year 43 and the massacre which followed the two battles of Philippi have an importance which transcends that of the political history of these months or the military results of these two engagements. For in them many of the most ancient and illustrious families of the Roman nobility either disappeared altogether or hopelessly declined, owing to the loss of some of their members. That nobility which had governed Rome for so many centuries and had managed to survive the great wars between Marius and Sulla, received in this final civil war a mortal blow from which it was not destined to recover. The whole of the confused history of the first century of the empire was nothing but the working out of the irreparable decadence of the nobility which had created the empire but which was now to have neither the men nor the families nor the resources nor the abilities which were necessary for its government, because all these had been swallowed up in the civil wars. The profound effects of this destruction, however, became apparent only by degrees. For the moment the proscriptions and the battles of Philippi seemed merely to abolish all opposition to the Cæsarian party. The handful of survivors who had escaped by sea, and even Sextus Pompeius with his fleet, could not hope to change the fortunes of war. Philippi had been an irrevocable confirmation of Pharsalia.

The Triumvirs, nevertheless, were confronted with terrible difficulties. They had in the first place to pay their innumerable soldiers the promised 20,000 sesterces per head, as well as the arrears of their pay, and they had no money. They had to disband a portion of the army, and, as regards the veterans of Cæsar, they had to carry out the old pledges given to them by the dictator and confirmed by the triumvirate. It was, moreover, necessary to re-establish their own authority and that of Rome in the East which had been turned upside down by the civil war, and which swarmed with pretenders who were waging war with each other. Finally they had to re-establish the authority of the triumvirate in Italy itself, where (a thing unheard of in the Roman world) Lepidus had surrendered the reins of government to a woman, Antony's wife, Fulvia.

It was decided to disband the eight legions of Cæsar's veterans, to reduce the army to 32 legions, dividing the whole between Antony and Octavian, the share of the former being seventeen and of the latter fifteen legions. By this arrangement Lepidus surrendered the three legions he had hitherto commanded. It was further agreed that Antony, in addition to the East, should have Gallia Narbonensis, while Octavian should take Spain which had hitherto belonged to Lepidus. Lepidus, therefore, because of his weakness and ineptitude and (it was added in justification of the treatment he received) because of certain alleged secret overtures to Sextus Pompeius,[1] was to be completely excluded from all share in the government of the provinces. Finally Antony was to leave at once for the East to bring about its pacification and to collect money, while Octavian was to betake himself to Italy to make war on Sextus, and to make a final distribution of land to his father's veterans. This was far from being an easy task, since it involved giving seven or eight thousand men two hundred *iugera* per head. This meant that he had to find eight or nine hundred thousand acres of good land in Italy, a country where hardly any public land was left. It was necessary once more to have recourse to violent measures, and it was decided to assign to the seven or eight thousand veterans land situated in the territory belonging to the eighteen finest and richest Italian cities, depriving each proprietor therein of a portion of his goods and compensating him with an indemnity to be fixed by the triumvirs themselves and to be paid when they were in a position to do so.

The plan was ingenious, and all that remained was to carry it out. No one could foresee that the gravest difficulties would arise from within the triumvirate itself. They did not come from Lepidus, a mediocre person, who was content to accept the secondary rôle which had been assigned to him, but from Antony's wife Fulvia, and from his brother Lucius, who was consul for the year. Lucius and Fulvia were now counting on being able to govern Rome and Italy without control or interference, the former as the brother, the latter as the wife of the man who had been the real victor of Philippi.

[1] *Cf.* App., *B. C.*, v., 3.

Thus it was that, when Octavian returned to Italy and tried to exercise his authority, violent dissensions immediately arose between the triumvir on one side and Lucius and Fulvia on the other. These dissensions rapidly became embittered and reached such a point that, when Octavian began to expropriate forcibly the Italian landowners in order to give their lands to the veterans, Fulvia and Lucius openly took the part of the expropriated possessors and affirmed that Mark Antony did not wish them to be deprived. Savage agitation thereupon ensued which ended in a new civil war. Fulvia and Lucius Antonius, by using the prestige of the triumvir's name and by promising money, contrived to raise an army among the landowners who had already been, or who feared to be expropriated, among the veterans of Cæsar and Antony, and among the survivors of the Pompeian and aristocratic party. Having done so they suddenly invited all Italy to fight with them for the destruction of the triumvirate which, now that Brutus and Cassius were no more, had lost its *raison d'être* and for the restoration of the free republic in accordance (as they affirmed) with the intention of Antony who was now restoring order in the East. Octavian, however, after various obscure vicissitudes, succeeded in shutting up and besieging Lucius in Perusia (Perugia) in the autumn of 41. In March of the following year Lucius was reduced to extremities and was forced to surrender to Marcus Vipsanius Agrippa, the general whom Octavian had charged with this siege, and who had hitherto been known only as one of the most implacable persecutors of the conspirators. Octavian did not wish to anger his powerful colleague and treated his brother kindly. He left Lucius at liberty, pardoned his soldiers, and merely put to death the *decuriones* of the city and some of the senators and knights who had been made prisoners, and abandoned Perusia to be sacked by his troops. Thus the most serious obstacle to the policy agreed upon after Philippi had been removed, but at what a price!

Fulvia embarked at Brundusium to join the triumvir in the East and with her went many eminent members of Antony's party who had been compromised in the last outbreak of civil war, among others Tiberius Claudius Nero, who in these terrible days sailed furtively from Naples with his wife Livia, the future spouse of Augustus and a little boy of about two years old who was destined one day to be the Emperor Tiberius. What was to be the end of this contest? Many feared a new and more terrible civil war. Antony, however, had never approved of the war against his colleague, which in fact had been an imprudent outburst against his own veterans, contrary alike to the pact of Philippi and to the general interests of the State. At that moment, moreover, he was revolving other plans in his mind, and was preoccupied with other difficulties. After reorganizing the East to the best of his ability he had gone to spend the winter of 41–40 at Alexandria as the guest of Cleopatra, who was trying with him the same scheme as previously with Cæsar. That is to say, she was endeavouring to persuade him to marry her, to become King of Egypt and to remove the seat of empire to Alexandria. It does not appear that Cleopatra had succeeded in winning him over. On the contrary it is probable that he was then thinking of resuming the design of Cæsar against the Parthians who, in the spring of 40 had made a great and dangerous raid on Syria at the instigation of an agent of Brutus and Cassius, Q. Labienus, the young son of Cæsar's lieutenant who had fallen at Ilerda. It was therefore not unnatural that, when, on his return from Egypt, he met Fulvia at Athens he severely rebuked the conduct of his representatives in Italy and disappointed all their hopes.

This would have been the end of the matter if Octavian, who shared the anxieties felt by all Italy about Antony's real intentions, had not taken advantage of the death of the governor of Gallia Narbonensis to intrigue for the transfer to his command of the legions stationed in that province which were under the orders of Antony. This act inevitably led to war. Antony, who wished to recover his legions, accepted the alliance of Sextus Pompeius and the help offered by Domitius Ahenobarbus, the former ally of Brutus and Cassius, who was under the ban of the lex Pedia, and who, like Sextus, had continued to command his fleet in defiance of the fulminations of the triumvirate. The forces thus united were concentrated for an attack on the Adriatic coasts of Italy and at once appeared off Brundusium.

**9. The Treaty of Brundusium and the Pact of Misenum** (40–39 **B.C.**). As a result of Octavian's imprudence, and as everybody had feared, there began yet another civil war. As before, however, the two belligerents were operating with soldiers who until the day before the conflict had been companions in arms and who, while they looked very much askance at a struggle between Antony and Octavian, were still less disposed to forward the ambitions and the interests of Sextus Pompeius and an ex-conspirator like Domitius Ahenobarbus. Their doubtful attitude was therefore sufficient to stop the nascent war and to impel the two competitors to an agreement. Antony, like Octavian, was forced to bow to the wishes of the troops who were against fighting. Thus it came about that, in the autumn of 40, the representatives of both sides met in the town of Brundusium and entered into a new convention whereby all the East, including Macedonia, Greece, Bithynia, Asia Minor, Syria, and the Cyrenaica, was given to Antony; the West, comprising Gallia, Transalpina, and Gallia Narbonensis, fell to Octavian; while Lepidus received only Africa as his share. On the other hand the armies were so distributed that Octavian had sixteen legions, Antony nineteen, with, in addition, the right to raise new levies even in Italy, while Lepidus got only six. Sextus Pompeius was abandoned by Antony, so that Octavian was able to declare war immediately against him, and finally the treaty of peace was sealed by a marriage. Fulvia had died during the brief resumption of civil war and Antony married Octavia, the sister of his colleague, who had recently been left a widow.

Sextus, therefore, was left to the vengeance of Octavian; but behind the triumvirs and the legions, labouring and suffering, hard hit by the ruin of so many of her richest families, there was still Italy, Italy from whom enormous taxes had been wrung, who had suffered terrible confiscations, whose public works were at a standstill, whose public buildings and private houses were going to ruin, and whose great roads were in disrepair. The country was seething with discontent and murmured against the policy of the triumvirate which had effected nothing but the distribution of lands to some thousands of veterans, and which had sacrificed everything—even the most legitimate interests of the possessing classes which had been foolish enough to allow themselves to be disarmed by Marius's military reforms—to the appetites of the soldiery. True, the general feeling of anger had hitherto been suppressed and contained because force was all on the side of the triumvirate. But the war against Sextus Pompeius which Octavian commenced immediately after the agreement of Brundusium at last provoked an outburst. When Octavian intimated that there would be war taxes on legacies and on slaves, there was a regular uprising of public opinion in favour of Sextus Pompeius. At Rome the infuriated populace tore down the triumviral edicts and made tumultuous demonstrations of all kinds in favour of peace. Such was their violence and obstinacy that not only Octavian but Antony himself was alarmed. Once more it became necessary to negotiate for peace. The negotiations between Antony and Octavian on the one side and Sextus on the other were long, but they ended in an agreement reached in 39 B.C. in the Gulf of Misenum. Sextus was to have Sicily and Sardinia as well as the Peloponnesus for five years; he was to have the consulship in 33; he was to be made a member of the College of Pontiffs and to receive seventy million sesterces as an indemnity for the confiscation of his father's property. In return he pledged himself to cease harrying the coasts of Italy, to deny any refuge to fugitive slaves and to put down piracy. There was also a condition of even greater importance. This was that the survivors of the proscriptions except those who had been condemned for the murder of Cæsar, and all deserters, were to be amnestied and part of their possessions was to be restored to them, while the slaves who had joined Sextus's army were to receive their liberty.

Peace therefore was re-established, and, what seemed even more remarkable, it had not been imposed by the swords of the veterans but by the invisible force of public opinion. Did Italy, then, still count for something? Was republican liberty still a living thing? Were law and the right of public criticism after all not crushed and wounded unto death by the swords of the legionaries? These were terrible questions which afforded Octavian, now the sole triumvir in Italy, food for profound and not unprofitable meditation during the next ten years.

**10. The Treaty of Tarentum (37 B.C.).** In the later months of 39 when Antony, leaving Italy so deeply disturbed, returned to the East, he found excellent news awaiting him on his disembarkation at Athens. The Parthians, who in the previous year had invaded Syria under the command of Labienus and Pacorus, the eldest son of their king, had been twice beaten by one of Antony's generals, first near Mount Taurus and secondly in a defile of the Amanus range at the northern entrance to Syria. The victorious leader was a man hitherto obscure, a certain P. Ventidius Bassus who had tried to bring aid to Antony in the war of Mutina. Following on these successes Antony had definitely resumed Cæsar's old plan for the conquest of Parthia and spent the whole winter of 39–38 in making his preparations. In the spring, however, he found himself unable to commence the expedition, either because his preparations were not complete or because the Parthians anticipated him by a renewed invasion of the empire, or because of the fresh quarrel between Octavian and Sextus Pompeius which had again led to war. He again despatched Ventidius Bassus to deal with the Parthians, and, on the anniversary of the battle of Carrhæ Ventidius inflicted on them a memorable defeat, Pacorus himself being slain in the battle. Antony next tried to impede the war between Sextus and Octavian but did not succeed, and in the summer of 38 Octavian lost the greater part of his fleet, partly in a battle and partly in a storm which followed the engagement. On the other hand the powers of the triumvirate expired at the end of the year 37, and Antony was becoming more and more attached to his plan of completing the conquest of Parthia which would make him master of the republic. He decided, therefore, to make use of all these contingencies to induce Octavian to give up to him a part of his army which he required for the conquest of Parthia, ceding in return a part of his own fleet which would be useful to his colleague for the war against Sextus Pompeius. In other words, his idea was to allow Octavian to wreak vengeance on Sextus on condition that Octavian helped him to conquer the Parthian empire and to prolong, on the pretext of the two wars, the powers of the triumvirate.

Octavian, however, much as he wished to conquer Sextus Pompeius, was by no means willing to weaken himself overmuch to the profit of his colleague. He demurred and temporized, set Agrippa to construct a new fleet, and haggled over every detail. Thus the agreement which Antony desired so ardently was only concluded at Tarentum in the spring of 37. The triumvirate was to be renewed by law for five years, counting from January 1, 37. Antony was to provide Octavian with 130 ships and was to receive in exchange 21,000 men. The agreements of Misenum with Sextus were cancelled and Octavian was to have a free hand against him.

11. **Antony and Cleopatra: the Nuptials of Antioch (36 B.C.).** After the agreement of Tarentum, Octavian returned to Rome to pass through the comitia the law prolonging the power of the triumvirate until January 1, 32, and also to make ready for war against Sextus. Antony returned to the East to make final preparations for the Parthian war, one of the greatest expeditions which the Roman and oriental worlds had ever seen. Antony's plan of campaign was identical with that which had been conceived and handed down to him by Cæsar.[1] But to carry out this vast undertaking, which was to secure Antony's power and glory, men, money, and munitions were needed in abundance. In order to procure these Antony decided on an act which was destined to have the gravest consequences. This was to accept the proposals of Cleopatra whom he had not seen for three years, and to become King of Egypt, marrying the queen in order to gain complete control of the treasures of the Ptolemies. At the beginning of the year 36 the nuptials of Antony and Cleopatra were solemnized with great pomp at Antioch. Antony became King of Egypt, and Cleopatra, in consideration of her alliance with the triumvir, was granted, in addition to the dominions of certain oriental sovereigns who were vassals of Rome, some portions of Roman territory which in former days had belonged to the empire of the Ptolemies. These were Cyprus, part of

[1] On this war see the study published by Kromayer in *Hermes*, xxxi., pp. 70 ff. *Cf.* also Bouché-Leclercq, *Histoire des Lagides*, Paris, 1904, vol. ii., pp. 258 ff.

Phœnicia, the fertile palm groves of Jericho, part of Cilicia and Crete.[1]

12. **The War against the Parthians and the War against Sextus Pompeius (36 B. C.).** This was a bold action, because it broke completely with Roman politics and traditions. Antony, indeed, did not assume the title of King of Egypt but retained that of *imperator;* he did not officially announce his marriage to Rome and he took good care not to repudiate his lawful wife, Octavia. He thus put himself in a dubious and equivocal position which was destined to be the cause of his ruin. For the moment, however, he might hope to secure the object of his wishes, for, with the help of Egypt, he could say at the beginning of 36 that all was ready for the Parthian expedition. In the spring of 36, while Octavian was commencing operations against Sextus Pompeius, Antony marched towards the frontiers of Media, sending forward his siege train, two legions, and the contingents from Armenia and Pontus under the command of Oppius Statianus, by the easier, if longer, route through the valley of the Araxes, while he himself with the mass of the Roman infantry took a shorter but much rougher and more difficult way. At the end of July he reached the boundary of Armenia Atropatene. Having reached this point Antony, we know not for what reason, made his first mistake. Without awaiting the army he had sent through the valley of the Araxes with his siege train, he invaded the country and

[1] *Cf.* Porphyrius Tyrius in Müller, *Frag. Hist. Graec.*, iii., p. 724 and Letronne, *Recueil des inscriptions grecques et latines de l'Égypte*, Paris, 1842–48, vol. ii., pp. 90 ff. On the whole legend of Antony and Cleopatra *cf.* G. Ferrero, *The Greatness and Decline of Rome*, vol. iv., Appendix.

marched on the capital, arriving under its walls, without meeting any resistance, at the end of August. Meanwhile in his rear Phraates, King of Parthia, attacked the other Roman army at Gazaca, succeeded in annihilating the two legions and the siege train, and forced the King of Armenia with his valuable cavalry —destined to be the most effective weapon against the Parthians—to return to his own dominions.

This was a serious blow. Antony had to choose between retreating or continuing the siege of the city with inadequate means. He chose the second alternative, hoping by threatening the capital to provoke the enemy to a pitched battle and so to destroy him. But the Parthians were not Gauls of the time of Vercingetorix, nor was Antony Cæsar, and his plan did not succeed. Meanwhile winter was at hand. The revictualling of the army became every day more difficult and dangerous; the besieged city resisted valorously. The soldiers suborned by the enemy murmured and averred that the Parthians were disposed to make peace. Antony had finally to make up his mind to retrace his steps, but, profiting by the experience of Crassus, and fearing he might be attacked on his retreat, he chose a route among the hills which was very difficult but inaccessible to cavalry, probably the road which now runs through Tabriz and ends at Iulfa on the Araxes. The retreat, though it did not end in a disaster, was most arduous. Before the army reached a place of safety it was exhausted by fatigue, by hunger and thirst, and by the incessant attacks of the enemy. It had marched for twenty-four days and had suffered great losses. The great undertaking, the idea of which Antony had inherited from Cæsar, was a failure.

In the year 36 Octavian, on the other hand, had at last succeeded in conquering Sextus Pompeius. Although on this occasion he disposed of superior forces both on land and sea, the commencement of the operations had not been fortunate. After various grave reverses, however, Octavian managed, at the end of July, to disembark an army in Sicily. Thereupon Sextus as a last resort attempted an attack on his adversary's fleet off Naulochus, although the latter was in considerable force. There followed a tremendous battle in which Pompey's son was defeated. A hundred and sixty of his ships were destroyed or captured. He himself fled, reappeared for a moment at Messina and thence set sail for the East, taking with him his daughter and his treasure.

13. **The Dissolution of the Triumvirate.** The success of the Sicilian expedition, more especially when compared with the failure of the Parthian enterprise in the East, greatly improved Octavian's position. An unwise attempt made by Lepidus to bring about a new civil war and to recover a position of equality with his two colleagues in the triumvirate, still further increased his power and prestige. The troops of Lepidus refused to obey him and deserted to Octavian, Lepidus had to retire into private life, and the youthful triumvir who was only twenty-seven, found himself suddenly at the head of forty-three legions, six hundred ships, and an empire which embraced a great part of northern Africa, Spain, Illyria, Gaul, and Italy, and invested with almost absolute authority in a republic which appeared to be sinking into the abyss.

The appearance, however, was very different from the reality. At this moment, at which his power seemed to be growing, the cruel tyrant of the previous ten years began to be transformed into the sagacious, merciful, moderate, and modest prince who was to be the Emperor Augustus. Immediately on his return to Rome on November 13th, he proclaimed a fiscal amnesty, remitting to the taxpayers the residue of the imports decreed by the triumvirs. Other taxes were abolished, one of the victims of the proscriptions was made a supplementary augur, and powers which had been usurped by the triumvirs were restored to certain of the magistrates. Octavian did his best to avoid new confiscations in distributing lands to the veterans, and all the slaves who were found fighting under Sextus Pompeius, as well as all the captured merchant vessels, were restored to their masters. He took measures for the suppression of brigandage throughout the peninsula and ordered public works on a large scale at Rome, in order that the proletariat of the eternal city might earn their bread. Finally in a solemn public oration he declared himself prepared to lay down the triumviral power and to re-establish the republic, now that the era of civil strife was ended and the *raison d'être* of the triumvirate had ceased to be.

How are we to explain this change which is little in accord with tendencies so usual and so profoundly rooted in human nature ever prone as it is to the abuse of good fortune? It was influenced no doubt by inner motives, but it was chiefly determined by political necessity. Notwithstanding the blood that had been shed, the outrages that had been committed and the destruction of republican traditions, the triumvirate had not managed to do any good either to Italy or the empire. Its greatest achievement had been the allotment of a little land and some donations to several thousands of soldiers. Its success depended on its armies and on the terror these inspired, and that these foundations were weak was made manifest by the circumstances that led up to the peace of Misenum. Moreover, the Cæsarian enthusiasm of the legions was cooling with the lapse of time, and was giving place to a spirit of sullen discontent caused by general disillusionment, by irregularities in issuing their pay, by the fatigues of the continual campaigns, by the failure after many years to carry out the pledges that had been given to them. The powers of the triumvirs might be increased but the power of the triumvirate was on the wane. The time had come to make concessions, to placate the public discontent, the moneyed interest, the conservative forces which were again gathering strength. Octavian who, notwithstanding the excesses of his earlier years, was a far-seeing, well-balanced, and prudent person, understood the position, and this was the chief cause of the extraordinary greatness to which it was his fortune to rise.

14. **The Donations of Alexandria and the Oriental Policy of Antony** (34 **B.C.**). While Octavian in Italy was trying to recover touch with the conservative elements in the State and to effect a reconciliation with the Latin and republican tradition, Antony in the East was becoming more and more entangled in a dynastic and Egyptian policy. As was natural he wished to retrieve the miscarriage of his Parthian expedition which had done him so much harm both in Italy and in the East, and he spent the whole of the year 35 in making plans for his revenge, while Octavian was engaged in an expedition into Dalmatia and

Illyricum. But although in this year he had enough to occupy him in repressing a revolt which the exiled Sextus Pompeius had raised against him, and though in consequence of this, none of his projects could be carried out, the influence of Cleopatra over him was growing. This was a fact of no small importance. The queen was a clever woman, Antony a violent rather than a strong man. On the other hand the more obstinately he set himself to secure a great triumph in the East the greater was his need of Egypt and its treasures. Italy, moreover, seemed at that time to be an irrevocably ruined country. It is easy, therefore, to understand with what force Cleopatra insisted on Antony laying aside more and more completely the dress of a proconsul and a Roman magistrate, and acting more and more as the husband of Cleopatra and the King of Egypt, on his divorcing Octavia and definitely deciding to found at Alexandria a new dynasty which would continue that of the Lagidæ and would reconstitute, with Egypt as its centre, a vast empire made up of provinces torn from the empire of Rome and territories now belonging to independent and vassal kings.

Antony, though ever more feebly, still resisted these suggestions, for he understood the danger of such a policy. In 34 he decided to conquer Armenia which would be the first step towards his second campaign against Parthia, and would avenge the treachery of the Armenian king in 36. He did in fact invade and conquer this kingdom, and secured possession of its treasures; but, having accomplished this enterprise, he determined to give Cleopatra the first great satisfaction of her ambitions. Not only did he celebrate his triumph at Alexandria and not at Rome, but immediately thereafter, at a solemn feast held in the Gymnasium, he proclaimed Cleopatra Queen of Kings. Cæsarion was proclaimed the legitimate son of Cleopatra and Julius Cæsar, and was made her colleague in the government of Egypt which was to be restored to its old boundaries and increased by the addition of Cyprus and Celesiria. Ptolemy, his own son by the Queen, who was a child of less than two years of age was made king of Phœnicia, Syria, and Cilicia. To Ptolemy's elder brother Alexander, who was now six, were given Armenia and Parthia, which had still to be conquered, and finally to Alexander's twin sister, the tiny Cleopatra, were assigned Lybia and the Cyrenaica as far as the great Syrtes.

The Roman triumvir was thus reconstituting the empire of the Ptolemies at the expense of the republic, and was trying to create once more in the East one of these great monarchical powers against which Rome had had to struggle through so many centuries of war. It goes without saying that he was doing this, not for the *beaux yeux* of Cleopatra but in order to become the head of this empire himself and to found an oriental dynasty like the generals of Alexander. Antony however did not yet finally and openly break with Rome and the Roman government. Not only did he, the consort of Cleopatra, assume no authority over the territories he had granted, but, immediately after the donation, he sent a report of the transaction to the senate and asked for approval of his own action. It is not difficult to see why he did so. In order to found the new dynasty he needed a powerful army and this army could be recruited only in Italy and commanded by Italian officers. For the moment, therefore, although in the East he might be regarded as the sovereign of Egypt, in Italy he must still remain the Roman triumvir.

This complicated policy, however, involved him in too many contradictions, all of which were full of dangers. Italy was displeased and Octavian disquieted. Antony had not only deserted his sister Octavia for Cleopatra, but he had declared Cæsarion the legitimate son of Cæsar, which might be construed to mean that Octavian had usurped the name and fortune of the dictator. Furthermore Antony had raised the number of his legions to thirty and had ordered new levies in Italy. Thus before long he would be at the head of a great army; of his own fleet and that of Egypt as well, master of the treasures of the King of Egypt and of the Ptolemies, and if he succeeded in conquering Parthia, he would be lord of an empire many times more powerful than the poor provinces of the West. Octavian had only one means of averting the danger and that was to embarrass Antony's menacing oriental policy in its beginnings by causing a conflict between him and the senate on the subject of the donations of Alexandria which were much blamed by public opinion. At the meeting of the senate, held on January 1, 33, Octavian himself as *princeps senatus* made a speech on the donations which he severely criticized. At the same time his friends and agents in Rome and Italy commenced a vigorous campaign against Antony, exaggerating his misdeeds, depicting in lurid colours his orgies at Alexandria, representing the Roman triumvir as the slave of Cleopatra, and revealing the presumptuous projects of the Queen which were so prejudicial to Rome and to Italy. This campaign and the attitude of Octavian made Antony so anxious that in the middle of 33 he resolved to suspend the new expedition against Parthia for which he had made great preparations, and to adjust the Italian situation once and for all by overthrowing Octavian. His plan was skilful. The triumvirate, now reduced to a duumvirate, expired at the end of 33. Antony accordingly intended to propose to the senate that he should lay down his office and restore the republic, provided that Octavian would do the same. He knew that Octavian, who did not trust him, would not accept this proposal and, by himself taking the initiative towards a republican restoration to which his colleague could not consent, he would counter the calumnies of Octavian and his friends, would have the air of being the real defender of the republic and of Italy, and would have an excellent pretext for declaring war on Octavian.

Antony and Octavian, in short, were publicly contending for the office of defender of the republic! On December 31, 33 B.C., the triumviral powers of both actually lapsed. Antony who was not in Rome, retained, according to the constitution, the command of his army as pro-magistrate until his successor should be appointed. Octavian, in order that he too might legally retain the command of his armies with the title of magistrate, had to leave the capital. He had hardly done so, however, when, on January 1, 32, the consul C. Sosius, who was a fervent partisan of Antony, as was also his colleague Domitius Ahenobarbus, profited by Octavian's absence to put Antony's plan in operation. He brought Antony's proposal before the senate and concluded his speech by making another proposal, which the ancient historians say was openly directed against Octavian, and which was probably a summons to him to lay down immediately the command of the armies which he continued to hold as pro-magistrate. A tribune friendly to Octavian interposed his veto, and several days of disputes, vacillation, and uncertainty followed. Finally Octavian, seeing that his inaction was encouraging his enemies, returned to Rome at the head of a body of soldiers and armed supporters, entered the senate, made a vehement speech against Antony and against the intrigues of the consuls, and concluded by promising on an early day, to establish by documentary proofs the charges he had made against Antony.

The sensation caused in the political world by this unexpected act was immense. Was this to be a new beginning of violence and *coups d'état*, the forerunners of civil war? Many were terrified, the consuls and numerous senators thought it better to leave Rome, and even Italy, and to fly to Antony who, in spite of the donations of Alexandria, was still the most powerful and the most admired of the triumvirs, and the one in whom the senate and Italy had most confidence. Antony in the meantime had arrived at Ephesus and had there collected from all parts of the East ships laden with grain, cloth, iron, timber, and with an extraordinary diversity of contingents sent by the kings, rulers, and tetrarchs of Asia to mingle with the soldiers of Antony's nineteen legions. The Egyptian fleet was also there under the command of the Queen herself who had brought with her much treasure and a great retinue. It is easy to imagine why Cleopatra had come. She did not wish Antony to become so deeply involved in this new civil war that he would be compelled to return to Italy to become head of the republic after he had won. She wished him to go back to Egypt, and to be the sovereign of Egypt at

Alexandria, the prop and stay of the new dynasty. But the senators who came from Italy wanted Antony to come back to Italy to calm the tumult there, either as the conqueror of Octavian or after having come to an understanding with him. This at once led to conflicts between Cleopatra and the most eminent of Antony's Roman friends, conflicts which caused Antony to hesitate. On the one hand he was coming more and more under the influence of Cleopatra, and his dependence on Egypt grew ever greater. On the other he had to take account of public opinion in Italy and of the aspirations of the senators who had come to him, for he needed Italy as much as he needed Egypt. The latter supplied him with money, it is true, but it was from the former that the best part of his army came.

The first great struggle between the Roman senators and Cleopatra had reference to Octavia. Cleopatra wished Antony to repudiate Octavia at any cost. The senators opposed this, but Cleopatra gained her point in the end. In the month of May in the year 32, Antony reached Athens with part of his army and it was from Athens that Antony sent Octavia his letters of divorce. This act made a bad impression and helped Octavian, who made use of it to hold up his adversary to the scorn of Italy as the demented victim of the love philtres of Cleopatra. He did not hesitate to compel the chief of the Vestal Virgins to hand over to him Antony's will in which he made new donations to the children of Cleopatra and directed that his body should be sent to the Queen of Egypt and buried at Alexandria. Octavian published this document and, in short, he profited by the impression produced by all these acts of Antony to provoke what was called the *coniuratio Italiæ*. What precisely this *coniuratio* was we do not know. It appears that, on the pretext that the senate was now reduced to a handful of members, Octavian's agents persuaded the magistrates of the chief towns in Italy to substitute themselves for the senate, to put Octavian at the head of the army, to direct him make war on Cleopatra, and to swear fidelity to him.[1]

**15. Actium (31 B.C.).** The expedient adopted by Octavian in order to secure a legal justification of his command was a trifle forced. But, however this may be, a new civil war had begun. Antony and Octavian were face to face, and each said that his object was the defence and restoration of the republic. Antony, however, was so much the stronger both in money, munitions, and prestige that he would certainly have conquered had not the policy of Cleopatra interfered with his plans. Cleopatra did not wish Antony to fight Octavian to a finish because the Egyptian empire which she dreamed of founding with Antony would have fallen to pieces, not only if Antony were to be conquered but even if he were to be victorious. In the latter case, Antony would have been forced to return to Italy to resume the government of the republic. She therefore wished Antony, instead of attacking Octavian in order to reconquer Italy, to return to Egypt, to abandon Italy to Octavian, and to wait until Octavian came to attack him in the East, if indeed he had the courage to do so. Her counsels were not in vain, and Antony did not in fact prepare

[1] Suet., *Aug.*, 17. Mon. Anc., v., 3–4: "*iuravit in mea verba tota Italia sponte sua et me bello quo vici ad Actium ducem depoposcit.*" On the whole question of the *coniuratio* cf. G. Ferrero, *The Greatness and Decline of Rome*, vol. iv., p. 84.

to attack Italy with the mass of his forces, but having left no less than eleven legions as a garrison for Egypt, he scattered a whole chain of naval and land garrisons over the Mediterranean from the Cyrenaica to Epirus in the autumn of 32. He occupied Cyrene, Crete, Cape Tænarus, and Methone. He disseminated his army over the whole of Greece, fortified Leucas, stationed the greater part of his fleet in the Ambracian Gulf and its advanced posts at Corpo. Having thus disposed his forces he devoted himself during the winter to intriguing in Italy, in order, by dint of promises and bribes to induce Octavian's armies to mutiny. It is clear that his object was to undermine the power of his rival without committing the whole of his superior forces to a real war. Cleopatra's counsels must have had much to do with this plan which is otherwise inexplicable.

The scheme, however, was so artificial that it suggested to Octavian, who was not the boldest of men, the idea of surprising and destroying Antony's fleet in the Ambracian Gulf in the spring. Early in 31, thanks to a skilful stratagem devised by Agrippa, Octavian succeeded in landing an army in Epirus, but he failed to surprise the fleet, because Antony was in time to recall his army from Greece and to concentrate it for the defence of the fleet in a vast camp on the promontory of Actium. Octavian, in his turn, was compelled to encamp and to anchor his fleet at no great distance. From this moment began a long and extremely singular war. Octavian did not attack Antony because he did not dare. Antony did not attack Octavian because Cleopatra would not let him. Overtures for peace were made but did not succeed. It was said that the two opponents would make neither peace nor war. The two armies, however, could not confront each other for ever. The Roman senators, who had joined Antony insisted that either peace should be made or that the war should be carried to a conclusion. Cleopatra wanted to go back to Egypt with the whole army intact. Discord raged round Antony more furiously than ever. In the end, towards the last days of August, Antony seemed to have made up his mind to fight a great naval battle. It was perhaps doubtful whether the war could be decided at sea but it is certain that the orders given for the battle by Antony were of the most extraordinary and equivocal character. He directed that 22,000 soldiers should be embarked in seventy merchantmen, that Cleopatra's treasure should be taken on board sixty Egyptian vessels, that the heavy and clumsy sailing ships intended only for long voyages should be loaded, while the lighter vessels, not excepting a part of the Egyptian fleet, which could not take part in the fight, should be burned. Did he mean to fight or to fly? There was such grave and acute doubt on this point that several influential senators, Domitius Ahenobarbus among the number, went over to Octavian some days before the battle.

At last, at dawn on September 2nd, the signal for battle was given and the fight went on during all the earlier part of the day. In spite of all, Antony's heavy turreted ships seemed to be prevailing over the faster but lighter and weaker cruisers of Octavian, when suddenly the great mystery of so many months' standing was unveiled. Immediately the north wind, which at this season blows down the Ægean every day, had arisen, the two startled armadas saw Cleopatra's sixty Egyptian vessels set sail, pass audaciously between the two opposing fleets, and sail off in safety towards the Peloponnese. At the same time Antony leapt into a quinquereme and followed the Queen. It was now clear that the battle had been a feint. Cleopatra had conquered. Antony was renouncing the struggle for the restoration of the republic in Italy and was retiring to his Egyptian empire with his Queen and her treasures and with part of his army. P. Canidius a trusted lieutenant had been assigned the task of bringing back the remainder of the army and of the fleet to Egypt.[1]

The plan was ingenious, but a difficulty, which no one had foreseen, caused it to fail most signally. The impression made on the army by Antony's flight was so bad that Canidius did not dare to reveal the instructions he had received and his charge to take the army back to Egypt. The party of Cleopatra and her ministers had triumphed in the tent of the general, but the Roman party was in the majority in the army and among the *émigrés* who had taken refuge with Antony. Canidius waited some days without coming to any decision while the army was left to itself without a leader. The soldiers fell into despondency and desertions began. First the more prominent Romans of Antony's following, next the oriental princes and the allied contingents, and finally, after seven long days of waiting, the stout legions of the land army and the fleet went over to Octavian. By September 9th Antony's army and his fleet had ceased to exist.

[1] On the battle of Actium and the reasons why its history has been reconstructed in this way *cf*. G. Ferrero, *The Greatness and Decline of Rome*, vol. iv., Appendix.

But, in spite of all, the soundness of the defensive plan of Antony and Cleopatra, had it been decisively and coherently carried out, was immediately made manifest after that date. Notwithstanding the fact that the triumvir and his Queen had lost nineteen legions and the whole of their powerful armada, that war had been openly declared on Cleopatra and that many Greek and oriental cities had now declared for the victor, Octavian did not venture to pursue his enemy or to attack him in his distant African refuge. On the contrary, as if he regarded the war as over, he disbanded a great part of his forces and directed Agrippa to bring the rest back to Italy.

This time, however, Octavian's prudence was destined to be overborne by the pressure of Italian public opinion. Italy could not endure that this ruinous civil war should remain unfinished with every prospect of breaking out again before long when Antony, as would soon have been the case, had recovered his strength. As little could she allow the Eastern provinces, the richest districts in the empire, to be taken from her with all their tribute and all their wealth. Neither, again, could she bring herself to renounce Egypt, her bitter enemy now apparently at her mercy. For all these reasons Italy demanded that Octavian should conquer the kingdom of the Ptolemies as an act of punishment and revenge, and with such insistence that he had to follow the course dictated to him by the sentiment of the whole people. A grave and significant incident which occurred in the winter of 31–30 must doubtless have confirmed him in this decision. The soldiers who had been disbanded without rewards filled Italy with disturbances and threatened serious disorders if they were not given the same pay as their comrades. It was clear that only the conquest of a rich country like Egypt could supply the means whereby all these grievances could be remedied!

Antony had prepared after a fashion for the defence of Egypt. With eleven legions at his disposal, an intact fleet with plenty of treasure, and time before him, he should have been able to make his enemy pay dear for his audacity. But the shock of Actium had bereft him of courage and authority, and had deprived his troops of confidence in their general whose equivocal position at Alexandria was now manifest. Octavian, therefore, was able to carry out successfully his advance on Egypt from Syria and Africa, and to march straight on Alexandria almost without opposition. There, under the walls of that fatal city, took place the last act of the great drama which developed from the death of Cæsar. On the 1st of August in the year 30 the army and the fleet which Antony had prepared for his defence betrayed him and deserted to Octavian.

All was now indeed lost. Antony committed suicide and on the same day Octavian entered Alexandria, where he ordered the execution (among others) of Cæsarion, the illegitimate son of Julius Cæsar, and of Canidius, who alone knew the secret of Actium. Cleopatra had shut herself up in her royal tomb, resolved either to continue her reign or to die. But when her last hope was gone the fragile woman, to whose fears a lying legend has ascribed the disaster of Actium, stoically took her own life and was found on her couch arrayed in the most sumptuous of her royal robes between two of her women, one of whom was dead and the other dying.

Egypt was not reduced to the status of a Roman

province. On his entering into Alexandria the conqueror had to recognize that Antony's oriental policy was not merely the caprice of personal ambition but was due, in part at least, to a political necessity. The national pride and the dynastic traditions of the land of the Pharaohs and the Ptolemies would not easily have brooked that their country should share the fate of Gaul or the kingdom of Pergamus. Octavian thought it best to feign, as Antony had done, that he was himself the new king of Egypt, the continuator of the extinct dynasty of the Ptolemies, and to govern the country he appointed, not a proconsul but a *præfectus*, who was his own personal representative. The first holder of this office was the Latin poet Caius Cornelius Gallus, an intimate friend of Virgil who dedicated to him one of the best of the Eclogues. All the Egyptians were made to pay a tax equivalent to a sixth part of their goods and further contributions were extorted from the richest among them. The immense treasure of the Ptolemies, a marvellous collection of finely worked objects in silver and gold was all brutally melted down and transformed into ready money. From this treasure were at last paid the officers and the soldiers who had fought in the recent campaigns and were still unsatisfied. From it also Octavian replaced the fortune he had lost and the friends of his evil days were given the great patrimonies which were to be a source of so much splendour and so much scandal in the coming days of the empire.

Octavian spent the remainder of the year 30 and the early part of the following year in the East. In the spring of 29 he finally returned to Italy, and on the 13th, 14th, and 15th of August his triumphal entry was solemnly celebrated at Rome.

## CHAPTER III

### THE AUGUSTAN REPUBLIC

**16. The Restoration of the Republic (27 B.C.).** After all these wars and catastrophes Octavian, the last survivor of the rivals who had fought for supreme power, remained master of the republic. All the legions recognized him as their general; the senate was unanimous in its admiration for him, and in its willingness to place the State in his hands; Rome and Italy acclaimed him as the saviour of the empire; the provinces, now subdued, obeyed him. At Rome no man had ever enjoyed so vast and so secure an authority. What use did he make of it?

The prevailing theory of all schools of thought during the nineteenth century was that Augustus availed himself of his good fortune to found a monarchy at Rome, but that he took the precaution to hide it under the outward forms of the old republic. This theory is, however, without foundation, either in the records of history or in what may be called the logic of the situation. We must go down as far as Dio Cassius, an oriental writer of the third century of the empire, before we find an ancient historian who speaks of Augustus as a monarch. Of the more ancient authors who were nearer to him in time not one appears to suspect that Augustus had hidden a monarchy under old republican forms. Nor is it difficult to show that Octavian had neither the power nor the resources with which to found a monarchy like those by which the peoples of the East had hitherto been governed. To found a monarchy meant to substitute the authority of himself and his family for that of the senate and the republican magistracies and therefore for that of the little group of great families who had founded the empire and, through a series of atrocious discords, had governed it up to that time. It meant replacing these families by a bureaucracy chosen from all classes and from all parts of the empire which would have recognized him as their sole chief and as the only source of authority. Augustus could have carried out such a revolution only if the public opinion of Italy had consented to it, for his power rested on the fidelity of the legions and the great majority of the legionaries were Italians. Had not Antony's disastrous end shown how dangerous it was to flout the sentiments and ideas which were rooted most tenaciously among the middle and lower classes in Italy? Now one of the strongest sentiments of Romanized Italy was veneration for the senate, for the ancient institutions of the republic and for the original aristocracy of Rome. Fierce as the struggles of Roman factions had been, they had not had the effect of increasing the spread of democratic ideas to any great extent among the masses. The leaders of the popular party, like those on the side of the senate, had been noblemen of ancient family, and, in the conflicts which had taken place, the middle and lower classes had aimed at securing material benefits rather than the right to rise to the highest offices in the State. Moreover, it did not occur to the populace or to those of middle rank in Italy that the armies should be commanded by any one not a member of the old aristocratic families holding senatorial rank. So much was this the case that all those persons of obscure origin who had succeeded in insinuating themselves into the senate during the disorders of the civil wars were exceedingly unpopular unless they possessed the outstanding personal merits of such men as Agrippa. In the very year (28 B.C.) in which Augustus is credited by modern historians with the intention of founding a monarchy he was obliged, in order to satisfy public opinion, to revise the list of the senate and to invite the resignations of no less than two hundred of its less distinguished members—precisely the people who would have been the most docile instruments of a monarchical régime. But if the Italian middle and lower classes would not be governed by persons drawn from their own ranks, can it be supposed that they would have accepted the rule of functionaries, some of whom would have been provincials and some even orientals? It is not likely! Indeed, more than four centuries were to pass before Italy could bring herself to submit to such an innovation as that.

The truth is that in these very years all Italy was agitated by a sort of traditionalist fervour of which her literature had preserved manifest traces. The immense confusion of the civil wars had brought men to their senses and had driven their terrified spirits back upon the past. It was at this time that Livy, destined to become Octavian's intimate friend, began to write his history of Rome, the object of which was to glorify on the one hand the ancient republican government and the men who, like Pompey, had perished in the struggle against the democrats and on the other hand to depreciate the leaders of the popular party, not excepting even Cæsar.[1] At this time also, the more ancient writers, such as Livius Andronicus, Pacuvius, Ennius, Plautus, and Terence were preferred to the most illustrious authors of more recent date. Epicureanism, so much in favour with the preceding generation, was losing ground, ousted by the doctrines of the Pythagoreans and the Stoics. Virgil was beginning to trace the outline of the poem which was to be the supreme moral and religious expression of the Roman spirit. And there had already been formed a party which was growing ever more numerous and more threatening, whose aim was to root out from Rome by means of savage penal laws what they described as "corruption," as well as the vices imported by conquest, orientalism, excessive riches, the immorality of women, and the complacency of their husbands, luxury and the love of pleasure.

In such circumstances not even a new Cæsar could have succeeded in setting up an absolute monarchy. It cannot be supposed that any such idea was ever entertained by a man like Octavian who was no great and ambitious general but a patient and methodical worker, an upright and prudent administrator, an adroit and sagacious politician, who moreover had just married Livia, the divorced wife of the fugitive Tiberius Claudius Nero, a lady of high character and great ability and an incarnation of the spirit and traditions of the old Roman nobility which a monarchy must needs have destroyed.

Octavian's political plan was therefore something much simpler and more modest than that attributed to him by the historians. It was to reconstruct, as

[1] *Cf.* Sen., *Qu. Nat.*, v., 18, 4.

far as he could and as well as he could, all that could still be preserved of the old aristocratic republic, to restore to the ancient Roman institutions the authority of which the triumvirate had despoiled them, seeking at the same time to correct the defects generated first by anarchy and then by the civil wars, the dictatorship of Cæsar and the triumvirate.[1] Among these defects two were especially serious. One was the division of military commands owing to which generals had often used their armies to forward their individual ambitions and had even made war on the senate to whose authority they were theoretically subject. The other was the system of electing to each office two annual magistrates with identical powers. This had on the one hand secured republican liberty but, on the other, had interfered with continuity of government or, worse still, had placed a potent instrument of disorder in the hands of the factions which, whenever they carried the election to an office, made use of the magistrate who was their successful candidate to obstruct all that was done by his colleague elected by their adversaries. While, therefore, it was necessary to restore the republic, to summon the comitia again, and to revive the old powers of the offices of State an authority had at the same time to be set up which would be sufficiently strong to control the

[1] The outline of this reconstruction of the political work of Augustus which entirely contradicts the incoherent doctrine of the "diarchy" maintained by Mommsen, has been filled in at great length by G. Ferrero, *The Greatness and Decline of Rome*, vols. iv. and v. The capital idea of this reconstruction had already been adumbrated by E. Meyer in a short study entitled *Kaiser Augustus* published in *Kleine Schriften*, Halle, 1910, pp. 441 ff., and by Fustel de Coulange, *La Gaule romaine*, Paris, 1901, pp. 147 ff.

factions, the magistrates, the generals, and the proconsuls alike, while leaving to the officers of the State the free exercise of their proper powers civil and military. Cicero, developing an idea borrowed from Polybius and Aristotle, had already demonstrated in his *de Republica* that in States which are distracted by civil discord it is necessary to appoint a single supreme magistrate, subject to the common law, and therefore republican, but invested with a longer term of power and with an authority of wider scope than that of ordinary magistrates, who in virtue of his personal and legal position would be able to prevent each institution or magistracy from invading the sphere reserved for the others and from neglecting its own proper business.

This is the cardinal idea—purely Latin and republican—which inspired the constitutional reform discussed by Octavian and the most eminent members of the senate during the year 28 B.C. and solemnly sanctioned on January 23, 27. Under the new reform, Octavian, by assuming proconsular power in all provinces in which there were armies, agreed to take command of all the armies so as to secure that all the soldiers and their officers were persons in whom he had confidence and were directly dependent on and responsible to him, instead of to the anonymous, intermittent, and feeble authority of the senate, as in past times. The provinces in which Octavian became proconsul in 27 were only three, viz. Syria with Cyprus, Gallia Transalpina, and Spain. The others were to be governed as before by proconsuls and proprætors. On the other hand, as it was necessary to have another authority in Rome itself to supervise the urban magistrates and, when necessary, to convoke and stimulate the senate, Octavian also consented to undertake this duty himself by becoming every year a candidate for the consulship. He was therefore to be at the same time consul and proconsul; through his lieutenants he was to govern from Rome the provinces assigned to him, and, if he had to go to the provinces, he was to continue to govern Rome in his capacity of consul. The combination of the two offices of consul and proconsul was undoubtedly rather a revolution than a reform in the old constitution, but it was not entirely a new thing, for, in 51, Pompey had held both. Octavian, moreover, was receiving these offices from the constituent authorities of the republic, and solely with the object of facilitating the working of the restored republican institutions, and, in short, he was placing himself at the head of the State *as first magistrate or president* (*princeps*) with legal and limited powers granted to him for ten years precisely as Cicero had advised in the *de Officiis*. At the same time he laid down all the powers with which, as triumvir, he had been invested by the lex Titia. Thus even this accumulation of exceptional powers on the person of the new president appeared to his contemporaries, who could not foresee the future, merely as a provisional system of government which was to last until the day on which the much damaged machine of the republic was once more in working order.

The conqueror could not have been more modest, and on January 16th he was richly rewarded. As if to imprint a sacred character on the new office created a few days before, the senate and people conferred on Octavian as a special honour the title of Augustus under which he has passed into history.

17. **The Reorganization of the Finances.** From

this moment begins the new political history of Octavian and the Roman republic, a history apparently modest and inconsiderable but, in substance and effect, of immense importance. One single idea dominates his whole policy—to satisfy as far as possible the new current of traditionalist opinion which wished to re-establish order in the State, in the family, in thought, and in manners, and to recreate the patriotism, the concord, the devotion, the simplicity of life, and the discipline of the most glorious days of the aristocracy. Cæsar's son, in a word, was seeking to establish a policy which was the antithesis of Cæsar's. The first measures of this policy which Augustus was to pursue uninterruptedly for more than forty years, were carried out in 28 while he was preparing the new republican constitution. In that year he had already reduced the army to twenty-three legions; he had set his hand to the re-establishment of discipline, beginning by excluding foreigners, freedmen, and provincials from the legions so that military service should remain, or rather again become, the privilege of the Italian citizen, and by restoring the strict system of rewards and punishments of former days. In the same year he had begun to reconstruct by means of donations the fortunes of many senatorial families fallen on evil days, with a view to restoring to them part of the influence they had lost, and to putting them in a position to help him in the government of the republic. Immediately after the republican restoration Augustus passed a law lowering the legal age qualifying for office and thus permitting young men to commence their political career early in life. The number of aristocratic families was so much diminished that it was impossible to fill all the important offices from the nobility without having recourse to the younger men. On the other hand it was a good thing to secure that youths should be occupied with public work at an age when they were most exposed to the temptations of idleness; this had, indeed, been the policy of the aristocracy itself in the second century B.C. when it was at the very zenith of its career.[1] He next passed a law the idea of which had already been conceived by Cæsar, which fixed salaries for governors of provinces and for all newly appointed magistrates. This was a necessary reform since a part of the aristocracy was too poor to support the expenses of public office, although it contravened the fundamental principle of the old republic that public service should be gratuitous. Finally and above all, he gave his mind to the reorganization of the finances.

Dilapidation, disorder, robbery, and malversation had been so rife that financial reform had become the problem of problems for the republic. Without solving it Augustus could not have carried on a war, or reorganized the public service or undertaken any public works. He therefore concentrated his forces on the financial question. And first of all he had to discover what precisely were the income and the expenditure of the republic. For this purpose he organized in his own service and for his own use a regular system of State accountants, choosing for the work the best educated and the most intelligent of his numerous slaves and freedmen. As head of the

[1] On this important point—important because it implies the republican character of the rapid careers of Drusus, Tiberius, and other members of the family of Augustus—*cf.* the more detailed explanations and proofs given in G. Ferrero, *The Greatness and Decline of Rome*, vol. iv., p. 174.

senate, as consul and proconsul of three great provinces, he had at hand all the necessary data, and was in a position to draw up a precise and complete balance sheet of the Roman State.[1] This balance sheet was even more exact and detailed than those prepared by the magistrates, and Augustus, without in any way infringing the principle of the autonomy of the existing financial organs of the State—the senate, and the *præfecti ærarii Saturni*—made a remarkably effective use of it in preparing bills for the reorganization of the finances, for censuring or recalling, or inducing the senate to censure or recall, magistrates who were guilty of useless expenditure or neglect in their provinces, and finally for exploiting the property of the State.

But knowledge was not enough. It was necessary to make provision for giving new life to the treasury, and with this end in view, he resumed in these years a plan of Cæsar's to take an inventory of the vast patrimony which the republic possessed throughout the empire and from which it had always derived great advantages, either directly, or by farming out contracts to the companies of *publicani*, though hitherto under a system which led to great waste and disorder. Augustus also took steps to increase the tribute from several of the provinces, especially those which in recent years had been less devastated than the others, and which by comparison with their condition fifty years before, showed the most manifest signs of progress. Such were Gallia Transalpina, and perhaps also the Illyrian provinces and some Alpine districts. He also did his best to put into circulation a greater quantity of coin to meet both public and private

[1] Suet., *Aug.*, 101.

needs. During the triumvirate a vast amount of gold and silver had been withdrawn from circulation in Italy as well as throughout the empire, owing to the terror inspired by the prevalent anarchy, and this had compelled the triumvirs to depreciate the coinage. To remedy the scarcity of circulating medium Augustus formed the plan of conquering some gold-producing territory, and, with this object he prepared the first war of his principate—that against the Cantabrians and the Asturians in the Iberian peninsula where the gold mines, after a revolt of the natives, had been abandoned during the anarchy of the preceding century. At the same time and for the same reasons he decided on the conquest of the valley of the Salassi (Val d'Aosta) which was equally valuable.

The reorganization of the finances, indeed, was a matter so near to his heart that in this very year (27) he determined to undertake a long tour of inspection, and in the first place to go to Gaul to establish the new tributes and then to proceed to Spain to conquer in person the Cantabrian and Asturian gold mines. Before this he had decided to undertake at his own charges, with the help of such of the richest of the senators as were willing to contribute, great public works in Italy, such as the repair of several roads, of many temples and public monuments as well as the complete reconstruction of other buildings. Having rapidly completed these arrangements in the last months of 27 he set out for Gaul and Spain.

**18. The First Difficulties of the New Régime and the Crisis of the Year 23 B.C.** The first stage of Augustus's journey ended at Narbona (Narbonne) where he had summoned all the notables of Transalpine Gaul to meet him, probably in order to announce to them a series of measures intended to prepare the way for a reform of the system of tribute in this province. Among these measures there was one providing for a general census designed to ascertain the changes of fortune which had taken place in Gaul during the period of nearly thirty years which had elapsed since the annexation. It was not by chance that Augustus had looked to the province conquered by Cæsar for an increase of tribute. During the last civil war, while Italy and the oriental provinces had been impoverished by depredations and exactions, Gaul had been growing rich. After the death of Cæsar the authority of Rome had been too weak to enable her to exploit the country very drastically. All she had been able to do was to impose a certain degree of peace and order by which Gaul had profited. No longer devastated by recurrent civil war, paying little or perhaps no tribute to the dominating power, freed from the turbulent nobles and the bands of robber knights and their dependents, who had been such a curse in the days of her independence, Gaul in the course of a single generation had been completely transformed. Many Gauls had become skilled labourers, others had taken to farming; others again had enrolled themselves as soldiers in the armies of the triumvirs, and had taken part in the plunder of the empire, bringing back to their own country the gold they had seized all over the world. In a country like Gaul, then as now, very fertile, covered with forests and rich in minerals, the effects of the new régime were everywhere apparent after thirty years. Mines were everywhere beginning to be sunk, gold was being looked for under ground as well as in the sands of the rivers, veins of silver were being discovered. New land was coming into cultivation and for the first time flax, hitherto cultivated only in the East, was being planted. In addition to this, the Gauls were making a prosperous beginning in industry—in the departments of textiles, pottery, and glass. They were endeavouring to imitate the products of the great industrial centres of the East and were making copies which were rougher, but also cheaper, than the originals. Rome, therefore, had a right to demand a higher tribute from Gaul than she had hitherto received.[1]

Augustus waited in Gaul until he had made the necessary preliminary arrangements for this augmentation of tribute and then went on to Spain to conduct the war against the Cantabri and the Astures while one of his lieutenants was conquering the valley of the Salassi. In the second half of the year 25 he was again in Rome. Two years had now passed since the solemn restoration of the republic, and the defects of that settlement were already manifest. In 25 there had not been a sufficient number of candidates to fill the twenty quæstorships. The public services in Rome and elsewhere continued to be carried on as badly as ever; the senate itself preferred to leave all decisions to Augustus, reserving only the right to ratify and approve what was done. All were ready to extol the aristocratic republic of the good old days, but few were prepared to make the sacrifices which were necessary to revive it. The historic families of the aristocracy who had the necessary prestige were no longer either numerous or rich enough or sufficiently public-spirited to undertake the whole administration of so vast an empire. In the equestrian order and

[1] On these tributes and the texts which relate to them *cf.* G. Ferrero, *The Greatness and Decline of Rome*, vol. iv., p. 214.

among the people there were indeed men who were sufficiently rich to serve the public disinterestedly and who had sufficient ambition to desire office, but these lacked the necessary training and the prestige of a great name. The people would not have obeyed or tolerated them, nor was the ancient nobility, whose pride had grown up again, disposed to admit too many new men into its ranks. Thus, between those who could have governed and would not and those who would have governed but could not, the administration of the republic had to get on as best it could, and Augustus was left to deal with all the difficulties. He had to think of everything and foresee everything, and the burden placed on his shoulders was so great that towards the month of June in the year 24 he fell seriously ill. He grew better, but in the following spring he had a relapse which was worse than the original attack. One evil day Rome learned that Augustus was dying and that he had already handed over to Agrippa and to C. Calpurnius Piso, his colleague in the consulship, his testamentary dispositions. It was a terrible moment for the whole capital, for who could say what might not be the political consequences of his death?

Augustus fortunately recovered, but when he became convalescent he declared that he must have absolute rest and expressed a wish to retire into private life. The consternation at Rome was indescribable. Every one believed that if Augustus went the civil wars would begin again. He was begged and prayed to remain at the head of the government. In the end he gave way when the senate—as perhaps he intended them to do—consented to a new constitutional reform which, while it left him immense personal power, had the effect of lightening the burden of his public duties. The princeps was to give up his annual consulship, thus abandoning the tedious and difficult business connected with Rome and Italy, and was to devote himself entirely to the provinces. In these he was to receive a supreme power of supervision and control. But, though the upper classes might be willing to be deprived of a powerful and benevolent consul like Augustus, the middle and lower classes were much less ready to consent to his giving up all share in directing the affairs of Italy. This no doubt was the reason why Augustus, though he was no longer to be consul, was willing to accept a new power or rather an abstract power—the *tribunicia potestas*—for life. This gave him all the ancient tribunician rights, the right of veto, the right of making proposals in the senate, the right of proposing laws to the people. It was a general power, unrestricted and at the same time indefinite, but it gave him power to intervene in the affairs of Italy, or rather to threaten intervention when required.[1]

This reform was passed about the middle of the year, and with it began the confusion of the conception of the restoration of 27 which had originally been so clear. Shortly after this, however, in the same year two events happened which demonstrated more completely than ever that the aristocratic republic, in spite of the efforts of Augustus and others to galvanize it into life, was in fact *in articulo mortis*. The first of these events was the arrival at Rome of a Parthian mission. For about ten years the Parthians had had no dealings of any kind with the Romans.

[1] On the true character of this constitutional reform *cf.* G. Ferrero, *The Greatness and Decline of Rome*, vol. iv., pp. 242–243.

It had happened, however, in the course of a dynastic war within the Parthian empire, that the eldest son of Phraates had been taken prisoner and handed over to the Romans, and that Tiridates, the rebel competitor, had taken refuge with them. The object of the Great King's embassy was to demand the surrender of both these princes—a serious matter because it reopened the most dangerous of the Eastern questions. The ambassadors came to Augustus, but he, as a zealous upholder of the constitution, referred them to the senate in whom under the constitution the control of foreign affairs was vested. The senate, however, after mature consideration sent them back to Augustus, recognizing that he knew better how to solve the problem than the supreme council of the republic. The other occurrence was a famine accompanied by a flood of the Tiber, which devastated Rome. The fact that Augustus had ceased for several months to be consul was enough to cause a revolt among the homeless and hungry populace against the negligence of the magistrates. They demanded that he should resume the consulship or that he should be invested with dictatorial powers as Pompey had been in 57, and should take charge of the victualling of the capital. The popular clamour was so great that Augustus had to assume plenary power over the corn supply. But this did not satisfy the people. Their confidence in Augustus was so great and their desire for a stronger administration was so keen that they demanded that he should at once assume the consulship for life or the censorship or the dictatorship—any form of power, in fact, whereby he could exercise an energetic, rapid, and absolute authority. Augustus demurred, for he knew by experience the dangers of dictatorship. But the situation was so serious that it was necessary to come to some agreement on the subject. The senate said nothing of the censorship or of a dictatorship but they gave him power to issue edicts exactly as if he were consul, when he thought it necessary in the public interest. In other words Augustus now received for Rome and Italy the discretionary power of supervision which he had so recently received in regard to the provinces. The old aristocracy was now incapable of sustaining the weight of government. A new social order which could replace it did not yet exist; all the burden of empire fell on Augustus and, whether he would or no, he had to shoulder it. In a single year, only a few months after Augustus had made a determined effort to retire into private life, the senate had abdicated in his favour their control of foreign policy and had granted him that power of issuing edicts which was to be the germ of the future monarchical despotism.[1]

**19. Augustus's Journey to the East (21–19 B.C.).** In the following year Augustus, as if to demonstrate by facts the provisional character of the government of the provinces which he had assumed in 27 B.C. and his firm resolve to restore them gradually to the republic as they were reduced to order, handed over Cyprus and Gallia Narbonensis to the senate. At the same time he prepared for his first tour of the Asiatic

[1] In the *lex de imperio Vespasiani* (*C. I. L.*, vi., 930, 17–19) we read: *utique quæcunque ex usu reipublicæ maiestate divinarum huma*(na)*rum publicarum privatarumque rerum esse censebit, ei agere facere ius potestasque sit ita uti divo Augusto. . . .* The reasons why we believe that it was at this particular juncture that this practically unlimited power was conferred on Augustus are set forth in G. Ferrero, *The Greatness and Decline of Rome*, vol. iv., pp. 248–249.

provinces which were still regarded as the most flourishing part of the empire.

From this journey Italy expected nothing less than the conquest of Armenia and Parthia. Augustus, however, had the more useful though more modest aim of reaching a final and honourable settlement of the Parthian dispute (on the subject of which he had been negotiating since the arrival of the ambassadors) and of confirming the authority of the empire even among the independent kingdoms of these parts. He left Rome in the spring of 21 and stopped in Greece whose ancient and deep-seated ills he sought to remedy. To placate national sentiment, he again separated Greece from the province of Macedonia, decorated it with the picturesque name of Achæa, and defined its territories so as to include Thessaly, Epirus, the Ionian islands, Eubœa, and several other islands of the Archipelago. Corinth was made the capital, and, by reorganizing the ancient Amphictyonic Council which met every year at Delphi, an attempt was made to establish a diet with annual meetings—a revised and enlarged imitation of the Achæan League—to which all the Greek cities were to send representatives. Autonomy was at the same time granted to several Greek cities.

From Greece Augustus went on to Asia Minor where he found the province of Asia busy with the establishment of a great temple in his honour, and in founding the cult of the new God on earth, Augustus. Antony had experienced something of the same sort at Alexandria. The adoration of dead monarchs in Asia and of living ones in Egypt had been one of the numerous expedients adopted by Hellenism in imposing its great schemes of economic and industrial domination on the native races of Asia and Africa. Now the cult was being timidly extended to the new magistrate who was arising at Rome amid so many uncertainties and contradictions, still wishing to be a republican official but finding it no longer possible. It was as if the Eastern peoples wished to tell Rome that it was her destiny also to fall under the same monarchical institutions by which they had been governed for so many centuries. Augustus accepted the dedication of the temple on condition that Rome was associated with his own person as an object of the cult. He then turned his mind to the solution of the Parthian and Armenian question. Armenia, which had been conquered by Antony, had again come under the government of a native monarch, whose policy was hostile to Rome and under Parthian influences. Augustus, therefore, had made up his mind to use great forces to recover the lost hegemony. But, in the winter of 21 and 20, while the Roman and allied forces were concentrating on the frontiers of Armenia, a revolution broke out. The king was overthrown and slain, and the insurgents declared for accepting the Roman supremacy. Augustus did not annex the country but gave it to Tigranes the brother of the late king, a prince friendly to the Romans, whom he had taken prisoner at Alexandria after Actium and whom he had caused to be educated at Rome in a manner befitting a king's son. Shortly afterwards Phraates, King of Parthia, carried out the agreement which had been concluded after long and difficult negotiations and sent back to the Roman camp the standards and prisoners taken at the time of the ill-starred expedition of Crassus accompanied by plenipotentiaries charged to conclude a definitive treaty of peace with Rome. This treaty was a very different thing from the conquest of Parthia of which many people at Rome had dreamed. It was a wise and reasonable compromise whereby Parthia definitely abandoned all participation in Mediterranean politics and surrendered Anatolia and Syria to Rome, while Rome on the other hand gave up the programme of Alexander, Cæsar, and Antony and pledged herself not to penetrate central Asia. But the advantages which accrued to Rome were great, for the treaty was to assure a century of peace between Rome and Parthia, a century during which Rome was to recover full liberty of action in Europe, and to be free to take up the policy of the Romanization of Gaul which was the source of modern civilization. This is why the treaty should be considered as one of the most signal of Augustus's services to Rome.

**20. The Great Social Legislation of the Year 18 B.C.** Augustus returned to Europe in the second half of the year 19 and found the capital full of agitation, discord, and disputes. The old families were more hostile than ever to the new men, the public service was as usual neglected, the populace was discontented, and there had been a great growth in public favour of the movement which began, as we saw, in the last days of the triumvirate, and which we described as traditionalist and puritan. This movement, headed at the same time by the old nobility and by a portion of the middle and intellectual class, had become bolder and demanded a purification of the senate, by which was meant the expulsion of all the intruders whom the revolution had permitted to enter it, the restoration of a timocratic constitution excluding from all office those not possessed of a certain fortune, and legislation which would impose a more modest and virtuous life on the rich, would repress the scandals of private life and put down the luxury of the aristocracy and what was called the corruption of women. The movement grew so strong that it became ever more difficult for Augustus to disregard it. It was, however, not easy to satisfy the agitators, still less so because the decennial powers assumed by Augustus in 27 expired with the year 18, and he had in mind a reform of the constitution which would relieve him of part of his cares and responsibilities. So little was Augustus thinking of setting up a monarchy that he proposed to divide his power with M. Vipsandus Agrippa who had recently married his daughter Julia. In fact Rome and Italy were expecting of Augustus a more strenuous government which would carry out great reforms, at the very time when Augustus had decided to share his powers with Agrippa. As always it was necessary on this occasion once again to arrive at a compromise. Augustus's powers were prolonged for another five years, beginning with 17, and Agrippa was placed by his side as his colleague with equal powers.[1] Thereupon Augustus with his new colleague carried out a *lectio senatus*, or in other words they took in hand the purification of the senate which the puritan party was loudly demanding. This having been accomplished with much prudence and consideration he proposed the measure which is known to history as the *lex Julia de maritandis ordinibus*, the first of a series of laws by which Augustus tried to restore the ancient moral-

[1] Dion Cass., liv., 12. Ferrero, *The Greatness and Decline of Rome*, vol. v., page 56.

ity of Rome. But the expedients that had to be used were complicated indeed!

The leading principle of the law was that marriage was a duty incumbent on all Roman citizens. It regarded not as marriage but as concubinage the union of a senator or of any of his descendants with a freedwoman and laid down that in the senatorial order only sons born of a free and virtuous woman should be regarded as legitimate and entitled to the privileges of their rank, and not such as had for their mother an elegant Syrian dancer or a fascinating Jewish freedwoman. Even in the case of plebeians the law did not recognize as valid marriage but regarded as concubinage, unions with prostitutes, procuresses, adulteresses, or actresses. This was all very well, but how were men and women to be compelled to marry? To attain this object Augustus invented an ingenious system of rewards and punishments to appeal to the selfishness of unmarried persons. Senators having wives and families received a regular scale of advantages laid down by the law. For instance among the magistrates he who had the most sons took precedence. Every citizen could anticipate the legal age for holding any office by the same number of years as he had sons. A woman who had been thrice fertile was by that fact alone entitled to enjoy practically an equality with men, and so forth. By analogy the law released from certain obligations to their former masters freedmen who had more than two sons. On the other hand those who obstinately remained single were to be excluded from all public festivals and spectacles, and were deprived of the right to receive legacies from any one not related to them, at any rate in the sixth degree.

The law, as it is easy to see, was both conservative and revolutionary, for, in order to restore ancient manners, it subverted several immemorial principles of the Roman law. It recognized marriages between plebians and freedwomen; it limited the rights of the *patronus* over his *libertus* and the freedom of bequest. It is not surprising, therefore, that it required the support of other and complementary enactments. How, indeed, could it be pretended that an honest and serious-minded man should be compelled to marry if he had no means of restraining the prodigality, the luxury, or the frivolity of his wife? The *lex de maritandis ordinibus* was accordingly followed by two other new laws, one a *lex sumptuaria*, the other the famous *lex Julia de pudicitia et de coercendis adulteriis*. The first clearly aimed at restraining the luxury of women, of banquets, and of the whole private life of the citizen. The second authorized a father, as in ancient times, to punish with death an adulterous daughter and her paramour. It authorized the husband in certain circumstances to kill the paramour but not the wife, and further it obliged the husband or, if the husband were unable or unwilling, the father, to denounce the wife or daughter guilty of adultery to the prætor or the *quæstio* within sixty days. If he failed to discharge his duty anybody was at liberty, after the lapse of sixty days, to lay an information. Those guilty of adultery were declared *iudicia publica*, as in the case of parricides, and the penalties were very severe—banishment for life for the two guilty parties and, in addition, for the man, the confiscation of half of his property and, for the woman, the loss of her dowry and of a third of her own property.

Laws of such a character may appear to us so

terrible as to be inexplicable. It is, however, easy to explain them when we remember that they applied only to Roman citizens and in reality were aimed merely at senators and knights whose riches and fame were alone sufficient to tempt accusers by the hope of what they might make out of the goods of the accused. This consideration reveals to us the real character of the laws, which aimed less at a general increase of the Roman birthrate than at a restoration of the aristocracy by an economic and moral reorganization of the families of the old nobility; that is of the old nursery of generals and diplomatists who had made the empire and created the glory of Rome. Here again Augustus took a course exactly opposite to that which the founders of absolute monarchies invariably follow, aiming as they always do at the break up of existing aristocracies. This is confirmed by two provisions, one in the *lex de adulteriis* itself and the other in a law passed at the same time. By the first of these provisions, the object of which was to consolidate the economic basis of wealthy families, Augustus forbade a husband to sell or pledge in any way his wife's dowry. By the second he forbade citizens possessed of an income of less than 400,000 sesterces to aspire to public office. Thus the portals of the public service were again closed to the poorer classes and the timocratic constitution was solemnly re-established. The son of Cæsar reconstituted from its foundations the aristocracy against which his father had struggled so long, and did all he could to restore the very class which, willingly or unwillingly, his father had half destroyed.

**21. The Development of Gaul and the Conquest of Germany (12–8 B.C.).** The passing of these great social laws was celebrated in the year 17 by a solemn ceremony, the *ludi sæculares*, first instituted in 509 B.C. at the beginning of the republic and repeated in every century though not at precisely fixed anniversaries. It was for this ceremony that Horace composed the *carmen sæculare*, the most harmonious of Roman hymns. Sung in the temple of Apollo on the Palatine by twenty-seven youths and twenty-seven maidens, it begged the gods to bestow on Rome peace, power, glory, prosperity, fertility, and virtue. But while at Rome these laws were being passed and these festivals observed, a great storm was arising in the European provinces, so recently and so imperfectly subdued, that is to say in the valleys of the Alps, in Gaul, and in Pannonia. This was to a large extent one of the consequences of the peace and good government introduced by Augustus. With the coming of peace had ceased the frequent military levies for the Roman civil wars which had been a perfect godsend to all the idle adventurers of the last generation. Augustus's good administration was beginning to result in a strict and regular collection of the taxes. And so it came about that in the early part of 16 B.C. a storm burst on the frontiers of Italy. Transalpine Gaul was in a ferment. In the Alps the Vennonetes (who inhabited the Valtellina and perhaps also the valleys of the Adige and the upper Inn) and the Camuni, who lived in the Val Camonica, flew to arms. The Bessi revolted in Thrace against King Rimetalces who had been imposed on them by the Romans. Macedonia was invaded by several barbarous tribes, the Dentheletæ, the Scordisci, and perhaps also the Sarmatians. Pannonia and Noricum, hitherto under the protection of Rome, rebelled and invaded Istria. The conflagration spread rapidly, especially in the Alps. The Trumpli in the Val Trompia and the numerous tribes of the Lepontii who lived in the Italian and Swiss valleys leading to the Lago Maggiore and the Lago di Orta, the Rhætians and the Vindelicians who extended from the Grisons country across Bavaria as far as the Danube, the inhabitants of the Cottian Alps, and, finally, the Ligurians of the Maritime Alps, had risen in rebellion. Practically the whole of the great mountain chain in which survived the last remnants of the races which had once inhabited the plains—the Iberians, the Celti, and the Etruscans—was in flames. At the same time a Germanic horde invaded Gaul and defeated Marcus Lollius, the Roman legate.

Augustus could not remain at Rome drafting laws and celebrating festivals when the fate of the whole of the Western Empire seemed to be trembling in the balance. It was clear that military operations on a great scale as well as a thorough reorganization of these provinces would be necessary in order to consolidate the authority of Rome. By good fortune the German invasion of Gaul was not serious. The mere appearance of Augustus was enough to secure the recoil of the wave. After the retreat of the Germans the most serious revolt was that in the Alps which threatened to cut off Italy from her western provinces. Augustus decided in the first place to commence a series of methodical operations in the chief Alpine valleys in order to subdue their populations once and for all. He entrusted the conduct of these operations to three generals, P. Silius, who shortly before this had freed Istria from the Pannonians and the Noricans, and to the two young sons of his wife Livia—Tiberius, the prætor of the year, who had already accompanied

Augustus in Spain and in Armenia, and his younger brother Drusus, then twenty-two years old, who had been elected quæstor for the year 15. The young Drusus had excellent qualities. He had all the energy, the courage, and the pride of Tiberius, but conjoined with such amiability that in him the traditional Roman virtues seemed to become agreeable and attractive, and he was universally popular. All this, however, was not enough in itself to justify Augustus in nominating a mere quæstor as his lieutenant in a war of such importance. There must have been more serious reason; perhaps the lack of capable men whom the prince could entirely trust. It is clear at any rate that the appointment of Drusus was a violent departure from the strict republican tradition, for, according to the principles of Roman public law, Drusus was too young for a command of such importance.

The operations of Silius against the Lepontii and those of Drusus and Tiberius against the Rhætians and the Vindelicians were entirely successful. The two young men carried the frontiers of the empire as far as the Danube and conquered Noricum (15 B.C.). Not long afterwards the insurrections in the Cottian and Maritime Alps were subdued, the male population was enslaved, the property of the tribes and of the rich families of the country was confiscated, and their territories divided among the towns of Cisalpine Gaul. In Noricum the native dynasty was abolished and a provincial régime similar to that in Egypt was established. That is to say the country was thenceforth governed by a *præfectus*. In the Cottian Alps also the native dynasty lost the royal title but the chief continued to govern the country under the title of *præfectus*. On the other hand Rhætia, Vindelicia and all the country from the crest of the Alps to the Danube and from Lake Leman to the frontier of Noricum was made into a province. Finally Augustus conceived the plan of opening up great strategic routes between the new provinces and the valley of the Po so that, without creating new military units, the legions stationed in that valley could be rapidly moved to the defence of any threatened point.

By these expeditions Augustus completed a work the effects of which have lasted to this day; for he opened up this famous chain of mountains to civilization. The task was heavy, but Augustus intended it to be merely a preparation to a still more vast undertaking, which was to be of even greater consequence in the history of civilization. The years following 16 B.C. which, owing to the demands of the war were spent by Augustus in Gaul or in its neighbourhood, were decisive both in his history and in that of the ancient world, for they were the years in which he and the Roman government came to see that Gaul, the barbarous, chilly, poverty-stricken Gaul of tradition, was an extremely rich province which was rapidly growing richer, a veritable Egypt in the West, which might be as valuable to Rome as Egypt itself and which it was as much Rome's interest to defend as the richest province of the East. The consequences of this discovery were destined to be formidable. So far Rome had looked above all (and almost solely) to the East as the seat of civilization, riches, and culture. Hence she was always in danger of being absorbed by the East and of being transformed into an Asiatic empire. From this moment she became a power, half Asiatic and half European, in whose empire Gaul formed the counterpoise of Egypt and Syria, and Italy was well placed in the midst for becoming the arbitress and the sovereign of the Orient and the Occident alike. From this moment also Græco-Latin civilization overcame the obstacle of the Alps and penetrated the European continent; there was a real beginning of the history of Europe, hitherto a barbarous continent except for its southern coasts, and the Roman Empire became a mixed empire, half occidental, half oriental, united under the hegemony of Italy. Had it not been for the growing riches of Gaul, it is clear that Rome would not have been able to remain for long the capital of an empire whose most important provinces and whose greatest interests were in Asia and in Africa and that, sooner or later, Italy would have been absorbed by her Asiatic and African conquests. In other words the unity of Rome's Mediterranean empire and the predominant position of Italy depended on the possession and on the development of Gaul.

If these, however, were to be the momentous historic consequences of the conquest achieved by Cæsar, the immediate effect of the material progress of Gaul was that Rome had to turn her attention to the defence of that country against the Germans, always restless and warlike, and all the more inclined to attack Gaul because she was no longer defended by her ancient military aristocracy. Thus the German danger was no longer, as in the time of Cæsar, a Gallic question, but a question vital to the Roman Empire. But how was Gaul to be secured against the incursions of the Germans if not by subduing them and conquering their country? Such is the logical result of all colonial conquests. The disturbances in the western provinces and the discovery, more and more confirmed by the course of events, of the immense importance of Gaul, led Augustus in these years to substitute for the dream of conquering Persia, which had been cherished by every Roman, the idea of a conquest of Germany. Rome was becoming a European and an occidental power.

Before committing himself to this enterprise Augustus was anxious to remove all possible chance of anti-Roman agitations in Gaul itself. The territorial divisions which Cæsar had found in the country still existed. The more powerful peoples such as the Ædui and the Arverni still preserved, as allies of Rome, their clientèle of small *civitates* directly under their government. Gaul, however, had now become a commercial and industrial country and the client communities under the control of the Ædui and the Arverni were either useless except for the preservation of ancient privileges and for the support of fictitious pretensions of superiority, or were actually dangerous to Rome, inasmuch as they might be made to serve as nuclei of new nationalist coalitions.

Augustus, therefore, placed all these subordinate communities under the direct authority of Rome, and indeed, on the basis of the results of the census, divided all Gaul into sixty *civitates*, of about equal size and all possessed of equal rights. As this increased the powers and responsibilities of the Roman government of Gaul, he partitioned the country into three provinces: Aquitania, Lugdunensis, and Belgica (the *Tres Galliæ*), each of which was to be under a lieutenant of the governor-general of the province. In this partition Augustus took no account of the ethnic diversities or affinities or the immemorial historic unities of the country, except in so far as he made each administrative unit a mixture of the three diverse elements—Celtic, Iberian, and Celto-germanic—of which the population was composed, in order to extinguish the ancient and traditional spirit of nationalism, to impede understandings between kindred tribes, and to bend the country thus denationalized to the purposes of Roman policy.

Before entering on his great undertaking Augustus felt that it was necessary to reorganize the army. He therefore passed a law settling certain of the more important conditions of service hitherto regulated only by vague tradition. The term of service was fixed at sixteen years for the legionaries and at twelve for the prætorian guard of the *imperator*. It was further laid down that, when their engagement came to an end, both legionaries and prætorians should receive as a gratuity not land but a sum of money, the amount of which is unknown to us. This having been settled, preparations for the expedition were begun on an adequate scale, and a highly ingenious plan of invasion was worked out in which the hand of Agrippa may probably be traced. It was decided to attempt the penetration of Germany, which was no easy task, from the North Sea by the two great river lines of the Ems and the Weser. Following these rivers two armies were to work their way into the heart of the country. On each of the rivers was to be constructed a great entrenched camp which would serve as a base of operations for completing the conquest of the interior. Simultaneously another army, having crossed the Rhine, was to be directed towards the Ems. The army of the Ems was to advance slowly and endeavour to join hands with the force coming from the Rhine and that approaching from the Weser. Thus by a widely sweeping operation flanked by fortifications the Rhine was to be linked with the Ems, the Ems with the Weser and perhaps even with the Elbe. The plan was excellent for it reduced to a minimum the risks to which the invading armies were exposed. But, as the Roman river flotillas would have been too long exposed to the storms of the North Sea, it was decided to open a canal between the Rhine and the Yssel so that the Roman fleet could safely enter the Zuiderzee (Lacus Flevo) and thence, through the communicating channel, the North Sea itself.

This great expedition, which was to be the cause of so many sorrows to Augustus, commenced under the shadow of a great bereavement. Augustus had easily obtained from the senate the prolongation for another five years of the powers accorded to himself and to Agrippa which expired at the end of the year 13. He was actively pushing on the preparation for the war in Germany when, in March in the year 12, a few days after Augustus's election as *pontifex maximus* on the death of Lepidus, Agrippa died in Campania at the very moment when the invasion of Germany was to be begun. The loss of such a coadjutor was serious, both because Augustus, who had hoped to share the cares and responsibilities of power with him, was now again forced to assume the government of the republic alone, and because, on the eve of an expedition of capital importance, Rome was deprived of the most experienced soldier on whom she could rely. The death of Agrippa seems, in fact, to have induced Augustus to postpone the war with Germany. For the moment, he contented himself with sending Tiberius to put down a revolt which had broken out in Pannonia. It was not till late in the year that he resolved to resume the larger plan, and charged Drusus, then a youthful prætor of 26, with its execution. Following Agrippa's long meditated design, Drusus with part of his troops descended the course of the Rhine and entered the Zuiderzee, thus penetrating into the heart of the country of the Frisii (the modern Holland). Thence he emerged into the North Sea with the fleet and sailed up the Ems, disembarking a portion of his forces at a certain point on the river. He then redescended the river, and appears to have tried to repeat on the Weser the operations he had already carried out on the Ems. This time, however, he did not succeed, and in fact narrowly escaped shipwreck. At the end of the year 12 he was again in Gaul.

These operations were merely the preliminaries of the real campaign which was to commence in the following year and, according to Augustus's plan, was to consist in a slow, methodical, and gradual invasion. In the spring of 11, Drusus was to ascend the valley of the Lippe on the right bank with his army and was to join the other forces already disembarked on the banks of the Ems, which in their turn were to progress towards the upper course of that river. At the confluence of the Lippe with a river which the ancient historians call the Aliso he was to construct a great fortress which was to be connected with the Rhine by a new system of roads and a chain of minor forts. This was the programme set before Drusus for the year. He victoriously ascended the valley of the Lippe and effected his junction with the army which had ascended the Ems, but immediately afterwards he risked a departure from the prudent and methodical plan of Augustus and Agrippa. Finding the Germanic tribes at war among themselves he judged that an audacious stroke would at this point be more effectual than a long and cautious campaign. Hastily collecting provisions, he traversed the country of the Sicambri, which was deserted because the male population had thrown themselves on the country of Catti, and invaded the territory of the Tencteri who submitted to him in terror. Then, as if gaining new courage from his own audacity, he advanced on the country of the Catti and compelled them and their Sicambrian opponents to recognize the overlordship of Rome. Want of provisions, however, and the natural sterility of the country very soon compelled him to retire towards the Lippe. On his return march he fell into an ambuscade and was very nearly annihilated with all his army. Escaping, as if by a miracle from this great peril, he regained the Lippe where he resumed the plan of Augustus and gave directions for the construction of the *Castellum* which was called Aliso. He then returned to Gaul and decided to build another fortress on the Rhine which in all probability occupied the site of the future Coblenz.

The third year of the war—10 B.C.—seems to have passed quietly without important incident. Probably the Germans were quiescent and the Romans were busy with the construction of the two fortresses which had been begun the year before. It is at any rate certain that Drusus was able to go to Rome in this year and to stand for and be elected to the consulship for the year 9. Before the end of the year, however, and before he could take possession of his high office, Drusus was compelled to leave the capital and to return in all haste to Germany where the Sicambri, the Suevi, and the Cherusci had coalesced for an attack on Gaul. In the following year (9 B.C.) the war entered on a new phase, and, whether because Drusus had convinced Augustus of the necessity of striking a great blow in order to terrify Germany or because he had been convinced of this necessity by the ambitious projects of the Sicambri, the Suevi, and the Cherusci, Germany was in this year invaded in earnest. We do not know by what routes or in what force Drusus conducted this invasion but he fought his way first to the Weser and then to the Elbe. His bold move succeeded; the Germans did not dare to attack him in mass, and Drusus was able to work his will in Germany until early in August, when, owing to the advance of the season, he decided to return. On the way back he broke his leg owing to a fall from his horse, and died a few days later as the result of this accident. The death of Drusus was a serious loss to the republic, but more especially to Augustus, who, after the death of Agrippa, was now deprived of another trusted coadjutor at a time when among the senate and the aristocracy there was a growing reluctance to assume high office and the number of competent men was decreasing. The young men, in particular, were unwilling to leave Rome and to pass long years in the provinces in a severe apprenticeship in the business of leading armies. It appears, in fact, that Augustus once more formed the intention of retiring into private life at the end of the year 8, when his quinquennial powers expired. He had now governed Rome as *princeps* for twenty years since the restoration of the republic, and he had earned the right to repose. But who was to be put in his place? Would not the whole administration of the empire fall to pieces if the man were to retire who fulfilled all the duties for which the senate and the republican magistrates failed to provide? The irremediable decadence of the aristocracy made the personal power of Augustus indispensable to the State. He was therefore compelled, whether he would or not, to accept a further prolongation of his powers for ten years, and, to deal with Germany, he summoned his other stepson Tiberius who for three years had been fighting in Pannonia and Dalmatia, and charged him with the task of completing the conquest of that country. Tiberius had now also become his son-in-law, for, in the year 11 Augustus had compelled him to repudiate his wife who was a daughter of Agrippa, and to marry Agrippa's widow who was his own daughter Julia. In the year 8 Tiberius had merely to cross the Rhine at the head of an army to receive the submission of all Germany. The march of Drusus had borne fruit. Within four years Germany had been, or at least appeared to have been, conquered from the Rhine to the Elbe, and the great enterprise first attempted by Cæsar had been successfully accomplished by his son.

# CHAPTER IV

## THE STRUGGLE FOR THE SUCCESSION OF AUGUSTUS

**22. The Retirement of Tiberius to Rhodes (16 B.C.).** At this point a very grave crisis arose in the State which may be said to have lasted until the death of Nero, that is to say, until the fall of the Julio-Claudian family. Augustus had governed the republic as princeps for twenty years. In the course of that period the clear and distinct conception which inspired the restoration of the year 27 B.C. had become much blurred. The authority of the princeps which in the original design of the reform, was to have been temporary, and was merely to have served to control the ancient institutions of the republic, had now acquired a life tenure and had been transformed into a real and indispensable directing force which was more and more displacing the antiquated and decadent senate. But no one complained of this. In the course of these twenty years Augustus had behaved with so much tact, had rendered so many services to the State, had now become so necessary, had gained so much prestige by restoring peace to the empire, that no one was aggrieved by the power he possessed. Augustus, however, was not immortal and was already nearly sixty. What was to happen when he died? The question was already in the public mind. Some thought that then indeed, the ancient republic would really and finally be restored without a princeps, but these were few. Men of sense and experience understood that without a capable and energetic chief, the senate and the republic would come to a standstill. But who was capable of being the second princeps? If the most competent, active, and experienced man in the State was to be chosen, it was clear, after the death of Agrippa and Drusus, that Tiberius was that man. Tiberius, however, had many enemies. He was not merely a haughty Claudius, of obstinate and severe temper; he was also an extreme traditionalist, a man of the old stamp, who would have liked to see Rome governed by an austere, parsimonious, energetic, zealous aristocracy such as that of the third century B.C. In the new generation, on the contrary, there was a growth of luxury and riches and of the taste for pleasure. The refinements and the vices of the East were becoming more and more widely spread, and with these there was an increasing indifference to political events and an ever greater distaste for military service. At Rome there was, therefore, a party against Tiberius, and all those who did not wish the supreme office of princeps to become the appanage of a single family (and there were not a few who held this opinion) very naturally reinforced this opposition.

This state of matters was aggravated by the marriage with Julia which Augustus compelled Tiberius to contract after the death of Agrippa. This marriage was one of Augustus's greatest mistakes. The characters of Tiberius and Julia were antipathetic. Julia, an elegant, fashionable woman, fond of splendour and courtly observances and of a free way of life, represented the new generation. Tiberius, stiff, unbending, and an implacable enemy of all the weaknesses of the *jeunesse dorée*, represented the old. Discord soon broke out between the spouses which arose not merely from incompatibility of temper but implied also a serious political antagonism, the antagonism in fact, between the party of the young nobility and the party of antique tradition which was now beginning to grow serious. It appears that Julia ended not only by betraying her husband but also by putting herself at the head of a regular *côterie* of young noblemen who were plotting to exclude him from eventually succeeding Augustus. They used every means in their power to effect this object. They calumniated him to Augustus and to the people, they alienated his friends from him and, finally, they tried to set up rivals against him. Agrippa and Julia had had several sons, of whom the eldest was then fourteen. Having been adopted by Augustus he was called Caius Cæsar. The party against Tiberius cast their eyes on this youth as a possible rival heir, and, after having tried to poison his mind against his step-father, certain members of the party proposed a law to the comitia enabling Caius Cæsar to be made consul on his attaining the age of twenty. The young man, as Agrippa's son and the adopted son of Augustus, was much beloved by the populace which was now quite accustomed to rapid elevations of this kind in the family of the princeps. Tiberius's enemies counted on this sentiment to enable them to secure the acceptance of their proposal. Augustus began by opposing it with all his authority, for he understood the danger that lurked behind this manœuvre. But it was not difficult to excite the people, who loved the Claudii little and the Julii much, in favour of Caius. Julia on her part was not idle, and in the end, Augustus gave way, and permitted Caius Cæsar to be elected consul five years in anticipation of his assuming office. He hastened, however, to give Tiberius the great compensation of conferring on him the tribunician power for five years, thus making him his own colleague as Agrippa had been. Tiberius, however, was a true Claudius and the compensation did not induce him to swallow the affront. He refused the honour, asked Augustus to allow him to retire into private life, and in spite of Augustus's entreaties that he should remain, he betook himself to the island of Rhodes where he lived in voluntary exile (6 B.C.).

23. **The Struggle between the Julii and the Claudii.** The departure of Tiberius was a great disaster to the State. Augustus remained alone at the head of the republic, without the assistance of a capable and trusted colleague, and the result was that the administration rapidly fell back into the negligence and confusion of previous times. Such order as had been secured by the exhausting labour of twenty years disappeared. The finances again became so disordered that the treasury could no longer keep up the payments required for the army. Augustus, however, could not make up his mind to prepare, or cause to be prepared, a reform of taxation, and preferred in his weariness and disillusion, to live from day to day, charging his own personal fortune with a large part of the public expenditure or allowing government services to lapse. His social laws were every day less observed, and those who had been condemned under the *lex de adulteriis* left their places of exile and dispersed themselves throughout the luxurious cities of the East and the West, leading a life of pleasure. The

*lex de maritandis ordinibus*, which had struck so hard at obstinate celibacy, was easily evaded by a great number of childless marriages against which the law had not provided. The army also was disintegrating. Recruiting in Italy became every day more difficult, for the natural growth of the riches of the country was such that free men easily found a more remunerative occupation than war. It was, therefore, necessary to increase continually the number of auxiliary corps by recruiting an even greater number of provincial Gauls, Germans, and Syrians. These, however, still further impaired the moral unity of the forces, while other causes—among them the absence of a leader who should be imperator in fact as well as in name—were productive of much indiscipline among the soldiers.

The most miserable spectacle, however, was that of the senate, into which Augustus could no longer instil even a semblance of vitality. How often had he not tried, and what means had he not used to make it work as an organ of the State? Now he had filled it with new elements drawn from the equestrian order, threatening that he would exclude them from the number of the knights if they would not consent to enter the senate. Again he had punished with increasing fines those who did not regularly attend the sittings, had decided to reduce the number of obligatory meetings, and had reduced the required quorum at those held during the months in which all Rome was in the country, or during the vintage. Finally, he had set up within the senate itself a small committee of senators chosen by lot to discharge the current business, their decisions being ratified later in plenary session. But in spite of these expedients the senators did not come, and any affair of importance was always discharged on the now weakened shoulders of the aged and weary prince.

The internal crisis had its counterpart in an external one. Germany, after being conquered, had been left to itself and no one seriously thought of organizing and consolidating the Roman dominion there. In the East, however, the peace which had with such difficulty been re-established in the first years of the principate was again in peril. In Judæa, after the death of King Herod in 4 B.C. the nationalist party had resumed its agitation, and the governor of Syria, Quintilius Varus, had had to bring great forces to pacify the district. In the Parthian empire Phraates who died in 3 B.C. had been succeeded by Phraataces who, unlike his father, had inaugurated an anti-Roman policy, had occupied Armenia, and had expelled the monarch recognized and protected by Rome.

There is no doubt that Tiberius hoped that all these difficulties would compel Augustus to recall him to Rome. But Augustus, who seems always to have had more esteem than affection for Tiberius, had been much irritated by his retirement, and after his departure had got into touch with the young nobility who were against Tiberius and the traditionalists, and were trying to govern the empire with their aid and without Tiberius's help. He had loaded Caius Cæsar with honours, had accelerated his career, and had granted the same distinction and privileges to his brother Lucius, thus ostentatiously showing that he considered these two youths as his only assistants and collaborators. The traditionalist party of which Livia, Tiberius's mother, seems to have been one of the most active members, did their best on the other hand to combat the growing power of their adversaries and to secure the recall of Tiberius. All this led to intrigues, quarrels, cabals, and scandals one of which, in 2 B.C., caused the ruin of Julia. It appears that the traditionalist party, seeing that Tiberius would never return to Rome until Julia was driven out, had contrived to procure proofs of her adultery, and that a member of the party denounced her under the provisions of the *lex de adulteriis* which Augustus had proposed and passed in the year 18. By this law, when the husband was unable or unwilling, the father was bound to punish the adulteress. Tiberius, the husband in this case, was not in Rome and Augustus was compelled in virtue of his own law to strike down his own child whom he banished to Pandateria. In spite of this, however, he did not reconcile himself with Tiberius, and, finally, in the year 1 B.C., when he decided to send an army to the East to try to effect an agreement with the Parthians he gave the command to Caius Cæsar in spite of his youth and inexperience, and sent with him as tutors and advisers men who were bitter enemies to Tiberius.

Thus the fortunes of Tiberius seemed to be hopelessly compromised by his fatal error in leaving Rome in 6 B.C. His opponents, with Augustus on their side, were as powerful as they were implacable. It was not until the year 2 A.D. that, through the intercession of Livia, he obtained permission to return to Rome, and then it was on condition that he should live in retirement and lead a strictly private life. At this point, however, fortune, which had persecuted him for eight years, again turned in his favour. In this very year Lucius Cæsar fell ill and died, and sixteen months later, at the beginning of the year 4,

Caius also died in the East as the result of a wound. These premature deaths were too useful to the cause of Tiberius not to be ascribed by many to the hand of Livia, but their suspicions had no serious foundation. Even the greatest families have never been exempt from paying their debt to nature in untimely deaths. However this may be, after the exile of Julia the party opposed to Tiberius lost the two leading figures on whom they relied. Augustus was again left alone without any effective assistance. The oriental situation once more became grave, and, what was worse, revolts began in Germany. Tiberius's party began to hold up their heads again, and openly demanded the recall to the head of affairs of the man who was the best general and, after Augustus, the most experienced statesman of his time. Augustus, however, still resisted, and finally, when rebellion broke out more threateningly than ever in Germany, the party of Tiberius lost all patience and seems to have actually gone so far as to form a conspiracy to overcome the obstinate reluctance of the old man whose presidential powers had in the previous year been prolonged for another ten years. This was the famous conspiracy headed by Cornelius Cinna, a grandson of Pompey. We do not know what its real aims and character were, but we do know that when it was discovered Augustus hastened to pardon the conspirators and to recall Tiberius to the government. On June 20th of the year 4 A.D., Augustus adopted him as his son and caused the comitia to confer the tribunician power upon him for ten years. The republic, therefore, again had two heads as it had had during the lifetime of Agrippa. Of these the younger and more active was a Claudius, the most uncompromising representative of the tradionalist and conservative party.

**24. The Government of Augustus and Tiberius (5–14 A.D.).** It is really from this moment, and not from the death of Augustus, that the government of Tiberius, destined to such a melancholy celebrity, begins. The clear proof of this is the contrast between the period which closes and that which begins at this point. The ten years now commencing saw an exemplification on a grandiose scale of Tiberius's idea of what the government of the republic ought to be. With great resolution he at once took in hand two enterprises, the reform of the army and the repression of the Germanic revolt. The former of these was subordinate to the latter but the military reform involved a reorganization of the finances, for it was certain to be very expensive. Where was the necessary money to be obtained? The two presidents formed the idea of giving the screw of the social laws another turn, and of withdrawing from Italy her ancient privilege of immunity from tribute. This policy had a moral as well as a fiscal significance. By a *lex Julia caducaria* married persons without children (*orbi*) were given the same treatment as unmarried persons and made liable to the same legal inferiority. Moreover, inheritances left to them illegally were now to devolve not upon the other heirs but on the public treasury.[1] Finally the announcement of a census of all citizens possessing more than 200,000 sesterces began to prepare Italy for a new impost.

Contemporaneously, however, the army was rein-

[1] On this law *cf.* G. Ferrero, *The Greatness and Decline of Rome*, vol. v., p. 295.

forced by two new legions;[1] the old and expensive military law of Augustus was rescinded, and for it was substituted the old term of service of twenty years for the legionaries and fourteen for the prætorians, after which period both were to receive a gratuity in cash and a pension for which a special fund was established (5 A.D.).

After this, Tiberius, who had already made a preliminary tour in Germany, returned to that country having made up his mind to repeat the great expedition of Drusus. Following the plan which had been settled (and which was in substance the old plan of Agrippa) the fleet went down the Rhine and through Drusus's canal to the North Sea, coasted along the inhospitable peninsula of Jutland, the ancient seat of the Cimbri, entered the estuary of the Elbe and began to ascend that river. Meanwhile the land army marched from the Rhine to the Elbe, sometimes receiving the homage of the peoples through whose territory it passed, sometimes fighting and subduing the more hostile such as for example the Langobardi. Finally the fleet and the army joined hands, and the barbarians who had massed threateningly on the right bank of the river, preferred, in the face of so powerful a demonstration, to come to terms with the invaders.

Tiberius was able to return to Rome to settle the taxes made necessary by the new law as to the army. Nor was his presence superfluous. Up to the time of his arrival all attempts to obtain money had been vain, but after he came the two presidents having paid into the new fund 170,000,000 sesterces of their

[1] *Cf.* Pfitzner, *Geschichte der römischen Kaiserlegionen von Augustus bis Hadrianus*, Leipzig, 1881, p. 14.

own money, succeeded in enacting a law imposing a tax of five per cent. on property passing by inheritance to Roman citizens, the proceeds of which were to be paid to the military pension fund. This was an excellent measure, all the more because it provided for the exemption of small estates and of legacies to the poor. But the discontent which it excited among the richer classes was great, and it was all directed at Tiberius who was known to be the real author of the law. Tiberius, however, as usual paid little attention to these murmurs and, early in the year 6 he returned to Germany to carry out the latter part of his plan. Several years previously the Marcomanni, in their flight before the invasion of Drusus, had migrated into the modern Bohemia and there, under their king, Marbod, had formed a powerful State which had persisted in refusing to recognize the Roman supremacy, and which was in any case capable of becoming a dangerous centre of resistance to the Roman arms. Tiberius wished to subdue this people or to bring them under Roman suzerainty and threatened them with invasion from two sides—from the West across the country of the Catti, and from the south across Pannonia. Hardly, however, had this undertaking been set on foot when Tiberius was informed that the Pannonians and the Dalmatians had again risen in fierce rebellion and had driven out the few Roman garrisons in the country together with the foreigners who had already begun to penetrate the country for commercial purposes.

**25. Varus meets with Disaster in Germany.** The Pannonian and Dalmatian insurrections were therefore a serious matter enough; but at Rome the danger seemed tremendous. Tiberius, however, was not a man who easily lost his head. He did not break off the enterprise on which he was engaged, but he gave up all idea of conquest and contented himself with concluding a treaty with Marbod. He then turned back towards Pannonia. His intention was not to shatter the revolt by a single stroke as the strategists of the forum were loudly demanding at Rome, but in accordance with the nature of the country, the enemy and the forces at his disposal, to counter the guerilla tactics of the natives with a guerilla warfare waged by Roman legionaries drawing their supplies from outside the country.

These tactics led to the pacification of Pannonia towards the end of the year 8. But the effort had been great. Rome had had to enrol veterans, freedmen, foreigners, and, ultimately, slaves taken from private persons but still maintained at their masters' charges. Tiberius had had to stifle the insurrection in its own centre with this amorphous mass of largely inferior troops, and it is not surprising that the process took some time. But hardly had the news of his victory reached Rome and honours and triumphs were being showered upon him, when most terrible tidings of disaster came from the banks of the Rhine.

The resolute policy of Tiberius and his firm intention, revealed by his return, to Romanize Germany had roused the country. Germany had found her Vercingetorix in the person of a certain Arminius who had been a friend of the Roman General Quintilius Varus and a Roman citizen to boot. By skilful manœuvres the Germans had induced Varus to advance into the heart of the country and there, in the mysterious Teutoburg forest, between the Lippe and the Weser (where a colossal but excessively vulgar monument has been raised in our time to commemorate not so much Arminius's exploit as the triumph of Germanism), Varus was overwhelmed, and his legions—the flower of the Roman army—literally massacred. Varus himself committed suicide rather than live a prisoner in the hands of the enemy (September or October 9 A.D.[1]).

**26. The Death of Augustus (14 A.D.).** The defeat of Varus was not in itself an irreparable catastrophe. So great an empire could lose a few legions without being shaken to its foundations. Tiberius in fact, having hurried to the Rhine, was at once able to show would-be disturbers of Gaul that if the Germans were able to surprise and destroy some Roman garrisons they could not presume to cross the Rhine or to attack the most flourishing provinces of the empire. But the disaster to Varus greatly weakened, if it did not entirely destroy, the purpose of the Roman government to extend its dominions beyond the Rhine and the Danube. So, as Rome had not the strength to cross the Danube and the Rhine to subdue the Germans, she was destined to see the day when the Germans would themselves cross these two rivers to destroy the empire! But neither Augustus nor Tiberius could see so far into the future, and their judgment had to be guided by the necessities of the moment. In the light of these necessities it seemed prudent not to demand too great an effort of Italy and to restrict the boundaries of the Western Empire to the Rhine and the Danube. Be this as it may, the defeat of

[1] On this catastrophe the most recent books are Gailly de Paurines, *Les legions de Varus*, Paris, 1911, and W. A. Oldfather and H. Vernon Canter, *The Defeat of Varus and the German Frontier Policy of Augustus* in *University of Illinois Studies*, 1915.

Varus was the last great sorrow of Augustus's long life which was now drawing to its close. In the year 13 the quinquennial powers of Augustus and Tiberius lapsed and were renewed once more and for the last time. In the following year, 14, Augustus died at Nola at the age of 77.

How is his policy to be judged? His plan of restoring the aristocratic republic after having, as triumvir, contributed so greatly to its destruction, undoubtedly failed. The republic into which he wished to infuse new life mummified under his hands in an equivocal and self-contradictory form of government which was at once feeble and rigid, and in which his own person and prestige had become the principal prop of its authority. At the end of his life the institutions of the republic, from the senate to the comitia had become a mere fiction. This is sufficiently shown by the fact that in the year before his death the senate had decided that twenty of their number should be chosen and that all decisions taken by Augustus in agreement with these twenty together with Tiberius, the consuls designate, his adoptive sons, and any citizens Augustus might think proper to consult, should have the force of senatorial decrees! The senate, in fact, had in its weariness and decadence abdicated all its powers. Must it therefore be concluded that Augustus's work was useless? By no means. It had two great effects, one on internal policy, the other on foreign affairs. In Italy, if it did not succeed in reanimating the decrepit body of the republic, it helped to preserve for another three centuries the principle which in the course of history was to be the great creation of the Roman Empire in its best days—the principle that is to say, that the empire was not, as in the case of the old monarchies, the property of a dynasty, but belonged, one and indivisible, to the Roman people. The government of the empire was to fall into the hands of men and of families who made a good or bad use of their power for a longer or a shorter time; but for several centuries to come it may be said that no man and no family could say that the empire was his or their chattel. They all had to recognize that the power entrusted to the emperor was a delegation from the Roman people. How important were the consequences of this principle and how from it the Roman senate, which at the death of Augustus seemed mummified, was able to draw a strength which renewed its youth, will be seen in the subsequent parts of this history.

In his foreign policy Augustus had the great merit of reaping the fruits of the conquest of Gaul achieved by Cæsar and of grasping the fact that the future of the empire lay more in the West than in the East. We have seen that, up to the time of Cæsar, Roman policy looked to the East, to Parthia, and aimed at a reconstitution of the empire of Alexander. Into this abyss Antony's policy and Antony himself had plunged. Augustus abandoned great oriental ambitions, and, after some hesitation, turned his forces resolutely towards the Rhine and the Danube; he conquered the Alps, solidly established the frontiers of the empire on the two great rivers, and promoted the Romanization and the development of Gaul and Spain, particularly of Gaul. If any policy can be said to have had a world-wide effect it is this policy of Augustus; for one of its consequences was that Europe entered into the history of civilization, hitherto entirely monopolized by the East and by the small

States at the extreme southern points of the European continent. Moreover, between the decrepit civilization of the East and the nascent civilization of the West, Italy and Rome managed, thanks to this policy, to preserve for another three centuries the crown which had been won at the cost of so many wars. It is, in fact, clear that without the vigorous development of the western provinces, and principally of Gaul, the centre of the empire would have been displaced towards the East. Rome and Italy, as outposts on the verge of barbarism could not for centuries have remained, one the capital and the other the dominant nation in an empire whose richest, most flourishing, and most populous provinces were in Asia and Africa.

## CHAPTER V

### TIBERIUS[1] (14–37 A.D.)

**27. The Election of Tiberius as Emperor and its Motives (14 A. D.).** On the death of Augustus, and during the dismal interval before the senate decided who should be his successor, the man whose duty it was to carry on the government of the State was of course Tiberius, Augustus's adopted son and colleague in the empire. This, however, by no means necessarily signified that he was to be the man who would continue his father's office and functions in the Roman republic. It was the expectation of very many that he would do so, but others had in mind more acceptable names, and he himself knew his fellow citizens

[1] The chief source for the history of the government of Tiberius is the *Annals of Tacitus*, which, however, magnificent in point of literary form, are less an impartial history than a vehement and passionate diatribe against the earlier Cæsars. Tiberius has been much mishandled by Tacitus, but modern criticism has now rated at its true value the dark legend which the historian has handed down as the true story of the second emperor. One of the first to bring out the contradictions and improbabilities in Tacitus's account was the great French historian V. Duruy in a Latin thesis, composed in 1853 and republished with the author's *Histoire des Romains*, Paris, 1882, vol. iv., pp. 271 ff. There followed on the same lines, Merivale, *History of the Romans under the Empire*, London, 1865; G. B. Sievers, *Studien zur Geschichte der römischen Kaiser*, Berlin, 1870; Stahr, *Tiberius, Leben, Re-*

and contemporaries too well, and was too well aware of his own character and of the difficulties of the office not to view with much anxiety the moment when the whole burden of empire was to fall on his shoulders. The friends and partisans of Julia, the whole party which had laboured to set up Caius Cæsar against him, the classes which had been hit by the social and financial legislation, those who knew him to be an angular, haughty, and uncompromising person, entirely wanting in the indulgence and the flexibility which had made Augustus so popular,—all these could not but look forward with terror to the day when the power of the defunct should pass to his surviving colleague. To govern in the face of this latent and tenacious opposition was no easy matter, and it is not surprising that Tiberius himself hesitated to assume the empire.

There was one circumstance, however, which inevitably drove the senate, in spite of their reluctance, towards Tiberius and drove Tiberius towards what he called the "untameable monster" of empire. That was the international situation. The German question was not solved but only in abeyance, and the one

---

*gierung, Charakter*, Berlin, 1885; T. Gentile, *L'Imperatore Tiberio e la Moderne Critica Storica*, Milan, 1887; Ihne, *Zur Ehrenrettung des Kaisers Tiberius*, Strassburg, 1892. The ancient historian who best understood and described Tiberius is Velleius Paterculus, who has been unjustly regarded as a flatterer for his pains. Velleius had been an officer under Tiberius's command and therefore knew him personally. Gratitude and admiration may have prevented him from seeing some of the defects of his chief, but his judgment is candid, well weighed, and well supported, and in these qualities forms a contrast with that of Tacitus who wrote a century later and relied on second-hand documents and traditions which originated in preconceived animosity and rancour.

man who could take it up again and deal with it effectively was beyond all doubt the adopted son of Augustus. The "German question" did not merely mean the war beyond the Rhine. Pannonia and Illyria were—or remained—imminent and threatening dangers for Italy. The same was true of the East. For several years Roman influence in Armenia had been going to pieces. The kings who were friendly to Rome were invariably overthrown and murdered by their discontented and turbulent subjects; nor, in view of the quarrels about the succession in Parthia, could it be said that that great and dangerous power was more a friend than an enemy of the Roman people. In Asia, as in Europe, the empire was confronted with grave difficulties of foreign policy. But the one irreplaceable person who had the profoundest grasp of the two questions was Tiberius. Finally the empire required a disciplined army. And who could keep the whole army to its discipline better than Tiberius, who was the greatest general of his time, who bore the name of Cæsar, and to whom after the long administration of Augustus the soldiers were well affected?

For these definite reasons, notwithstanding the sullen hostility of part of the senate, and his own sincere reluctance,[1] the powers of Augustus were handed over to Tiberius. One innovation, however, was made which was intended by the new ruler to bring the hour of his liberation nearer and to free the electors from a pledge which circumstances might make both useless and intolerable. The duration of the new imperial election was not fixed. Tiberius's term of office, as he himself put it, was to be limited by the

[1] *Cf.* Vell. Pat., ii., 124; Tac., *Ann.*, i., 11–13; Dion Cass., lvii., 2.

necessities of the situation and even more by the imminence of old age. As always, however, the new arrangement was destined to produce effects which were not intended, and the imperial dignity which, as the senate believed, could be taken away, was henceforth to last as long as the lives of the men who assumed it.

**28. The First Years of the Government of Tiberius —their Republican and Aristocratic Character.** Tiberius was a traditionalist and an aristocrat who would have been delighted to carry out a reform of Rome comparable to that of Sulla. The first acts of his reign prove this. Ancient historians, even those most hostile to him, who have done most to establish the legend of his monstrous tyranny, tell us that in his early days he did nothing without consulting the senate, refused all extraordinary titles and honours, respected scrupulously the laws of the republic, and in word and deed showed at all times that all he wanted to be was first among Roman noblemen—*primus inter pares*. Indeed one of the first reforms carried out under his government was the transfer of the right to appoint magistrates from the comitia to the senate. Tiberius did what Sulla had not dared to do. The people practically ceased to exist as an organ of the constitution, and the senate, that is to say the aristocracy, became the arbiter of all the offices of State. But the fact of the matter was—and it is necessary to grasp this point if we are to understand this strange figure and his still stranger history—that this Roman noble of the old stamp who wished to reconstitute the ancient power of the aristocracy had to deal with a very different type of aristocrat from those of the older generations. During the long and paternal ascendancy of Augustus, many of the great families had re-established their fortunes. Others of more recent date had become illustrious. Peace, power, and security had fomented in them the sentiments natural to all dominant classes, more especially those who govern by hereditary right—namely pride, a spirit of criticism and reciprocal jealousy, together with a proneness to discord and litigation. The Roman nobility had respected Augustus, though they felt that he had ruled long enough, but Tiberius could not hope for a similarly benevolent attitude. He lacked the prestige assured to Augustus by long years of rule, by his re-establishment of peace in the empire and the salvation which he had seemed to bring to Rome in her hour of danger. Nay, precisely because he himself proposed not to be, and not to wish to be, considered more than one noble among the rest, his peers thought themselves entitled to criticize and scan narrowly his every word and deed, to see in every exercise of his supreme authority an abuse of power, a manifestation of secret ambition, of crooked plans, of acts contrary to the public good and to the spirit of the republican constitution.[1] Their acrimony was all the greater as they were all compelled to recognize that this supreme authority was a necessity. From the moment of Augustus's death there arose among the Roman nobility a kind of latent and implacable opposition to the supreme power of the princeps, which was the last desperate protest of aristocratic pride against the historic necessity which was throwing all things in

[1] *Cf.* the passage of Tacitus (*Ann.*, i., 75) which is practically an admission of this: *multaque eo coram adversus ambitum et potentium preces constituta; sed, dum veritati consulitur, libertas corrumpebatur.*

Rome into the hands of a single family. But, though the aristocracy looked askance and with ill-concealed jealousy on the princeps and his power now that Augustus was gone, they were none the more willing to second his endeavours to revive the ancient republican institutions, which would have been the best way of making the new supreme office merely transitory as they all still hoped it was to be. The tradition whereby the great Roman families had for centuries been regarded as schools of generals and statesmen was too much weakened by the force of circumstances, by new needs and customs and also by new ideas. A system of moral philosophy—Stoicism—was beginning to spread among the Roman upper classes which taught that the truly happy man is not the King of Persia with all his treasures but he whose conscience is free; which affirmed that the individual was in subjection to no earthly power but only to God; which encouraged men to judge the great exactly in the same way as the rest of mankind, and declared it not only a right but sometimes a duty to rebel against the orders of the prince; which inculcated that exile, death, and misfortune might be accepted with as much satisfaction as honours and riches, and that there was no punishment on earth more terrible than the condemnation of one's own conscience. This doctrine, which set the individual conscience above all exterior authority, produced heroes under the principate and covered with a superb mantle of moral beauty many things which in themselves were of small account. At the same time, however, it was destined to be a serious embarrassment both to the new imperial régime and to the restoration of the old aristocratic republic. The princeps who, as Tiberius was soon to learn by experience, had ceased to possess the influence enjoyed by Augustus, could not fail to irritate the aristocracy, whether by his efforts to restore the ancient constitution by overcoming aristocratic selfishness, or by actions at variance with the spirit of the constitution to which he was compelled to resort by the decadence of old institutions produced by the growing apathy of the nobility. What was still worse, this perennial discontent would not dare to show itself in open and resolute opposition—for no one seriously thought of overthrowing the principate,—but in a kind of perpetual and insistent *fronde*, dividing the senate into a number of bitterly hostile groups. These inevitably tried to exploit the quarrels within the family of the princeps, and in the senate and in the presence of the army and the people, to oppose to his person and his policy that of some other member of his family. *Nec totam servitutem pati possunt nec totam liberatatem*—the Tacitean epigram[1] describes this state of mind with admirable lucidity.

Thus the act whereby Tiberius transferred from the people to the senate the right to elect the magistrates of the republic, does not seem to have earned for the new princeps any particular gratitude from the senate, where he had many enemies dating from the days of Rhodes. Moreover, Tiberius, in passing this reform had not aimed at the gratification of the senate but at the good of the State. The comitia during the previous twenty-five years had been scenes of disorder, tumult, faction fighting, and corruption. Augustus, with all his influence and with his power of recommending selected candidates, had had the greatest difficulty in keeping them in order. Tiberius, who wished the

[1] Tacit., *Hist.*, i., 16.

magistrates to be competent and honest, handed over the elections to a safer body in which the prince could more easily exercise the right of *commendatio* which throughout his life he was to use with impartiality and entire self abnegation. It is not improbable, on the other hand, that the lower classes received with little favour this serious diminution of their privileges which had been consecrated by centuries, and that Tiberius had to describe it as the pious accomplishment of a plan conceived by Augustus.[1] However this may be, the senate, after this reform, found itself during the first two years of the principate of Tiberius, stronger perhaps than it had ever been since the time of Sulla, both because its powers had been notably increased and because the new prince, feeling his authority to be weak, and anxious about the responsibilities which weighed upon him, asked for nothing better than that the great council should act with all the authority that law and tradition allowed to it. But out of this situation, so favourable to its pretentions, the senate could make nothing better than a stupid and violent quarrel, in which the authority of the princeps and its own were alike weakened.

**29. The War of Revenge in Germany (14–16 A.D.).** This did not happen at once, however, for the two first years, which were years of transition, were prosperous enough. Foreign troubles, moreover, were the chief preoccupation of this period. Immediately after the death of Augustus the legions of Pannonia and Germany mutinied, demanding pay at the rate of a denarius per day, instead of ten asses as heretofore, ten years' service, and the punctual payment of pensions. This grave revolt was subdued

[1] Vell. Pat., ii., 124.

partly by concessions and partly by severity, and thereafter (if we are to believe many ancient and modern historians), Germanicus, son of the ill-fated Drusus (and therefore nephew of Tiberius) who was in chief command of the legions in Germany, led them across the Rhine to wage a war of revenge against the Germans. According to this account this youth of twenty-five, as the sequel to a military rebellion, took it upon himself to decide on a new adventure into that mysterious Germany which had been the grave of his father and of Varus, in order that his legions might be led out of temptation! This explanation is improbable, for what he was attempting was no mere raid of brief duration but a dangerous expedition which lasted nearly three years and involved enormous expense to the imperial treasury as well as a new levy which fell on the provinces.

The true reason was different and by no means difficult to conjecture. The German expedition five years previously had been suspended but not finally abandoned. It is probable that Augustus himself had not renounced the hope of reconquering the country some day when the memory of the disaster had faded into the past, when Italy had overcome her reluctance to undergo new sacrifices and a favourable opportunity presented itself. All these conditions were now fulfilled. Arminius at the head of the warlike Cherusci was fighting his father-in-law and rival Segestes who implored the aid of the Roman legions. On the other hand the election of Tiberius was primarily due to the dangers of the external situation of the empire and to his own military qualities, and it was natural that he should desire to bring to a happy consummation a task which had been very near to the heart of Augustus.

Moreover, was not continuous military expansion an essential part of the policy of the republic? To these considerations were of course added the aspirations and personal ambitions which were more than legitimate in a young man like Germanicus. We must therefore think of this resumption of the German campaign as initiated by the common intention of the prince and the young commander-in-chief of the armies of the Rhine and carried out in accordance with a plan previously settled by them in concert.

Germanicus, who had begun hostilities towards the end of the year 14 by ravaging and burning the country of the Marsi (between the rivers Ruhr and Lippe), now, several months later, made a new thrust into Germany, crossed the territories of the Catti, entered those of the Cherusci further to the north, liberated Segestes and captured a great number of prisoners among whom was Tusnelda herself, the wife of Arminius then pregnant with a boy—a precious hostage. After this, he commenced his great expedition, resuming the plan conceived by Agrippa and followed by Drusus. Germany was again invaded, partly by land and partly by water, by a force sent up the Ems, in such a way that the enemy was both attacked in front and taken in reverse. These operations were successfully carried out. The Germanic tribes which did not submit were beaten as in the case of the Bructeri, and Germanicus was able to clear a way to the Teutoburg forest, the scene of the massacre of Varus's army six years before. There were found the battered remains of the last position occupied by the Romans, the bones of slain men and animals whitened by time, confused heaps of weapons and human skulls hanging from the trees. Germanicus and his troops raised a mound in pious memory of the slain, so that their bones, now avenged, might at least find a permanent resting place secure from wind and rain. But there was little time for delay. Arminius reappeared on the flank of the Romans, always present and always out of reach, endeavouring to repeat once again the blow which had fallen at Teutoburg, and winter was at hand. Germanicus, though he had not won a decisive success, decided to return. He himself with four legions was to descend the course of the Ems, partly by water and partly by land in order not to overload the ships. The other half of his army, amounting to another four legions, under the command of his courageous lieutenant Aulus Cæcina was to regain the Rhine by land, following the road called the *Pontes Longi* built on embankments and piles, which, sixteen years before had been driven through the vast marshland then extending from the Ems to the Rhine. But while the legions of Germanicus marching by land towards the estuary of the Ems were caught and severely damaged by one of the terrible tides prevalent in the North Sea at that time of year, the land army under the orders of Cæcina reached Castra Vetera after a narrow escape which they owed entirely to the imprudence of the enemy, the intrepidity of the general, and the valour of the soldiers intensified by the memory of Varus to a desperate courage (autumn 15).

The cost of the campaign, therefore, had been greater than its achievement, but neither Germanicus nor Tiberius regarded this as a sufficient reason for giving up the war. A larger force was necessary and this was to have been provided in the following year. The plan for this new invasion of Germany was somewhat different from its predecessors. The dangers of

Cæcina's retreat had been too serious for the commander-in-chief to risk them a second time. To invade by water was no doubt the best plan, and therefore the winter of the years 15 and 16 was devoted not only to increasing by new levies the forces which were guarding the Rhine but also to increasing the fleet. A thousand vessels and eight legions, in addition to a great number of auxiliaries, were prepared in the spring of 16. Germanicus, after securing the line of the Lippe against possible incursions by the enemy, led his great army by sea to the mouth of the Ems, and, disembarking on the banks of the river, moved in the direction of the Weser against the enemy whose force was this time not wholly composed of Cheruscans but of troops representing several Germanic tribes. He pitched his camp on the banks of the Weser, crossed the river, and, on the plain of Idistavisto, probably not far from Minden, where the Weser makes a sudden bend to the left in the middle of its course, he discovered the enemy and inflicted on him a severe defeat. Arminius himself escaped from the field, disguising his well-known features with the blood of his own wounds. Shortly afterwards he in vain tried once more the fortune of arms, hoping to intercept the Romans on their return journey and so to raise the fortunes of his people. Arminius had repeated the error of Vercingetorix and of all barbarian armies flushed with the pride of an initial success by abandoning the guerilla tactics which had proved so effective and by risking a pitched battle, and the second encounter resulted in a second and even more serious defeat for the Cherusci.

To all appearance Germany was again subdued, and for the moment it was possible to make the return march through a terror stricken country. Germanicus decided that on this occasion he would not put himself at the mercy of the tides which were likely to be more dangerous than ever owing to the approach of the equinox. He therefore sent away a good part of his army by land while he himself with the remainder rejoined the fleet which awaited him at the mouth of the Ems. The unpleasant experience of the previous year, however, was destined to be as nothing compared with the trials which now awaited the thousand ships of Germanicus. It was not the tide this time but a storm which dispersed and sank these small vessels which were assuredly not intended to sustain so rough a shock. Many men and horses were engulfed for ever in the depths of the German ocean. Others were cast away far and near on the northern coasts, and it was long before Germanicus, who had gone to the country of the Cauci, could collect the survivors and resume his return journey. This new disaster had had its effect in Germany. The country again flew to arms and all the sacrifices of the campaign were in danger of having been made in vain.

A new and violent campaign against the incorrigible Cherusci and an expedition against the Marsi, who lived between the upper Lippe and the upper Ruhr, were necessary before the weary Roman legions could finally retire to the winter quarters for which they longed and which they had so hardly earned.

**30. The German Policy of Tiberius.** Germanicus had carried out in Germany some of the finest campaigns in the military history of Rome. In particular the expedition of the year 16 by reason of the number of troops involved, the great scale of the preparations, the difficulties overcome, the enormous extent of territory covered, and the victories that were won, was undoubtedly one of the greatest military undertakings in ancient history. It proves that the military power of the empire was still very great. Teutoburg was avenged, but could Germany be said to be conquered? For Germanicus and for the whole court of friends and flatterers who surrounded the young general, now regarded by most people as the colleague and successor if not actually the rival of Tiberius, there could be no doubt about it. A little more persistence and Rome would conquer another vast province in the West. Tiberius, however, was of a different opinion. These expeditions to Germany demanded great armies, great sacrifices of men, and enormous expenditure The enemy was brave, obstinate, and mobile, and easily recovered from every defeat, while his country was poor and sparsely populated This being so was the game really worth the candle? Would it not perhaps be better to abandon the country to its present inhabitants and to rule it indirectly by holding the balance of its fierce internal struggles which could be kept permanently inflamed by the manifold resources of diplomacy? Would it not be better to protect Gaul, a very much more valuable country, by strengthening the frontiers of the province rather than by conquering Germany? Tiberius accordingly abandoned the idea of adding a new and vast province to the Western Empire. He decided, now that the prestige of the Roman arms had been re-established by the expeditions of Germanicus, to evacuate Germany; he separated the military command of the line of the Rhine from the government of the Gallic provinces; divided the Celto-germanic Rhine country into two districts—provinces in name rather than in fact—

under the names of Upper and Lower Germany; charged his son, who also bore the name of Drusus, to keep an eye on Germanic affairs from Pannonia; and directed Germanicus to return to Rome to celebrate his triumph.

Thus in the West also Tiberius followed the policy of caution and patience, more ready to use diplomacy than arms, which was one of the oldest traditions of the Roman aristocracy. The aristocracy of his own time, however, which recollected its traditions only when they served to satisfy its rancour, showed him no gratitude for this. The abandonment of Germany, on the contrary, aroused discontent at Rome, especially among the nobility; and in this they found their first pretext for venting their latent ill-will against Tiberius. It was whispered that Tiberius had recalled Germanicus because he was jealous of his successes, and, in order to spite the princeps, his nephew was overwhelmed with admiration and praise. Other causes contributed to increase public discontent. Tiberius's method of adminstering the empire, which was gradually growing firmer, was not calculated to win him the sympathies of the majority whether of the upper or the lower classes. This system, to which he adhered until the end of his life, consisted in an endeavour to ameliorate the public and private life of his time not by passing far-reaching laws but by daily good government, of which the life and conduct of the prince were to be the first and most brilliant example. The law was to be respected at any cost and was to be equal for all, whether the case affected the lowest of the citizens or the dearest friends and relations of the prince. Impartiality was to be the first principle in administration and in courts of justice. Manners were to be purified and made more austere, and to this end were to be abolished all the noisy popular festivities which characterized the last days of the republican period, in which the great had delighted to mingle, and towards which even Augustus had shown some indulgence. There was, therefore, no longer to be a superabundance of public games with the idleness which they brought in their train; there were to be no more largesses to play actors. Clamorous demonstrations were no longer allowed in the theatres nor were any spectacles permitted which could in any way injure public morals. In compensation the finances were to be administered with firmness but without parsimony, especially when it was a question of the real and proper needs of the State. Agriculture, particularly the production of such necessaries of life as grain, was encouraged in every possible way. Rome and Italy were urged to make every effort not to depend on the provinces for bread. The luxury of the upper classes, above all the importation of gems and costly fabrics from the far East (India and China) was discouraged as far as possible as being morally and financially calamitous. At the same time Tiberius's policy did what was possible to secure the safety of villages and country districts. His firmness and authority restored in the armies the discipline which had been so seriously shaken at the time of his accession. His sense of justice, his wisdom in the choice of governors, and his severity in dealing with them compelled a proper treatment of the provinces. He was never tired of reminding his governors that a good shepherd may shear but should never flay his flock. He ruled, in short, like a Roman noble of the old school, gifted with intelligence and public spirit, with dignity and firmness; but the people began to grumble that the prince was "mean," the nobles that he was harsh and tyrannical, and everybody turned to Germanicus, attributing to him all the virtues opposed to the vices which, rightly or wrongly, they saw in Tiberius.

**31. The Mission of Germanicus to the East (17–19 A.D.).** Meanwhile Germanicus had returned to Rome where, in the month of May, 17, he celebrated one of the greatest triumphs that the history of the Roman republic had ever seen. So little truth was there in the accusations of jealousy against Tiberius! Shortly afterwards he was sent to the East on a mission at the same time important and honourable. New political complications there required the presence of an energetic and capable person who enjoyed the full confidence of the prince. The Parthians had driven out their king, Vonones, who was favourable to the Romans and had substituted for him Artabanus, a warlike person whose manners and sentiments were more nationalist in character. The change in Parthia had reacted on Armenia. There Vonones on his expulsion from Parthia, had at first succeeded in getting himself proclaimed king but had finally been forced to fly before the threats of Artabanus. Thus the influence of Parthia had begun to predominate in Armenia. Furthermore Cappadocia had lately been annexed to the empire and required to be organized. Anatolia the independent part of Cilicia, and Commagene, a new kingdom composed of parts of Cappadocia and Syria, had lost their kings. Both were under Roman suzerainty and were now a prey to internal quarrels which necessarily concerned Rome. Syria and Judæa were protesting against the burden of the tribute. All this necessitated the presence of a trusted envoy who would study the many problems on the spot and would put them in the way of the solution which was best for Roman interests. Tiberius wished Germanicus to be this envoy. A decree of the senate invested him with the governorship of the oriental provinces but with an authority (*imperium maius*) superior to that of all Roman governors whether senatorial or imperial (17 A.D.).

If, however, Tiberius prized highly many of Germanicus's qualities he believed that some of his other characteristics required to be moderated and curbed. In the East it was no mere question of fighting barbarians as it had been in Germany; it would also, and above all, be necessary to manage with the finest arts of diplomacy peoples of ancient civilization and courts proficient in every kind of intrigue. An older and more experienced man could be of the greatest assistance to Germanicus. In agreement with the senate, therefore, and perhaps at the senate's suggestion, he sent out as governor of Syria a man from whose voluntary co-operation with Germanicus he had every reason to expect good results. No one at this time could have said that he was sending a favourite, a secret agent or even a personal friend. Cn. Calpurnius Piso on whom his choice had fallen was the descendant of one of the most illustrious families of the Roman aristocracy, the son of a man who sixty years before had taken the side of the Pompeians against Cæsar, and had applauded the murder of the dictator on the Ides of March. Piso was proud of his ancestry, and, some time before, had raised a question in the senate which above all others was calculated to affirm the rights of the senate as against those of the princeps.

He had affirmed—and had invited the senate to discuss—the right of that assembly to meet for its ordinary deliberations and for the despatch of public business even in the absence of the princeps who usually presided. Thus, in choosing or accepting the choice of this man as the counsellor and guide of Germanicus, Tiberius was certainly not consulting his own personal interests but those of the empire. In any case he wished to show his respect and deference for the ancient aristocracy by placing Germanicus, his young nephew, his probable successor and the hope of the Empire, under the tutelage of one of the most authentic and noble families of Rome. And yet, by a disastrous concatenation of events, the most terrible consequences were destined to flow from an act the motives of which were so reasonable and unexceptionable.

Germanicus first went to Greece, and after making some stays at Athens, proceeded to Eubœa whence, via Lesbos and Thrace, he crossed to Asia Minor and there eagerly devoted himself to the settlement of the intricate affairs of the East. On the throne of Armenia he placed Zeno, son of Polemon, king of Pontus, who took the Armenian name of Artaxes. He was a prince friendly to Rome and, through his mother, related to the Imperial house;[1] but in the eyes of orientals he had also the advantage of having remained by custom and inclination an oriental himself. Cappadocia, Cilicia, and Commagene were annexed to Syria. Finally, the effect of Germanicus's presence

[1] He was a grandson of Antonia, daughter of the triumvir Mark Antony. Cf. *Ephem. Epigr.*, i., 270; and V. Strazzulla, *La famiglia di Pithodoris regina del Ponto* in *Bessarione*, 1901, pp. 80 ff.

and the fame of his exploits and good fortune spread so rapidly that Artabanus, the new king of Parthia, sought an interview with him and promised to renew the alliance, provided that Rome did not contest his sovereignty in the name of the rights of Vonones. Germanicus next proceeded to Egypt where he intended to travel without guards and dressed after the easy fashion of the oriental Greeks, rather as a private person than in the character of the imperial representative.

These many-sided activities, however, soon gave rise to differences with Piso which rapidly grew more acute. We cannot say exactly what were the real causes of the quarrel or who was in the wrong. Perhaps Piso, who hardly admitted the superiority of Tiberius himself, thought that, as a Roman of ancient senatorial family, he had the right to impose his will on one whom he considered as after all only an inexperienced youth and merely an emissary of the princeps. Perhaps Germanicus, being a spoilt young man proud of his own merits and his own origin, committed some imprudence and thought that he could transgress the methods and traditions of Roman governors or even the law itself, as he undoubtedly did when he went to Egypt without the imperial sanction, and also when, to remedy a famine in that country, he distributed to the people the contents of the imperial granaries reserved for the use of Italy. It may also be that the two men held different views on some of the great political problems of the East. It appears, indeed, that Piso did not wish to throw over the old king of Parthia, Vonones, as Germanicus had done, in order to secure the friendship of Artabanus. Whatever may be the truth of all this, the fact remains that before long there was a rupture between Germanicus and Piso and, what was more serious, because it now happened for the first time at any rate openly, not only between them but between their respective wives. Germanicus had gone to the East, as he had gone to Germany, accompanied by his beloved consort Agrippina, the daughter of Julia and Agrippa, who had never been able to forget that her mother's exile was largely due to Tiberius and Livia. The wife of Piso, who had also accompanied her husband to the East, was Plancina, a very close friend of Livia, the mother of Tiberius. The presence and the quarrel of the two ladies profoundly aggravated the dissensions of Germanicus and Piso. When Germanicus returned from Egypt he not only found letters from Tiberius reproving him for transgressing the imperial order to which he owed obedience by going there, but also discovered that many of his directions had been cancelled by Piso, that the loyalty of the troops to him had been undermined, and that the East was, as it were, divided into two parties, one favourable to him and the other to Piso.

**32. The Death of Germanicus (19 A.D.) and the Prosecution of Piso.** There was a violent altercation between the two men—so violent that Piso decided to leave his province. He had hardly departed, however, when Germanicus became suddenly ill and, after repeated alternations of improvement and relapse, died in the flower of his manhood at the early age of 34 (October 12, 19).

This melancholy event, which was an accident of nature of a by no means unusual character—for there are many young men who die before their time—was destined to kindle a tremendous conflagration. His friends, his partisans and admirers, Agrippina, the opponents of Livia and Tiberius and of his policy, would not admit that Germanicus had died or could have died, a natural death. He had been killed by one of those poisons which were so skilfully prepared in the East, and he who had prepared it was the man whom Livia and Tiberius had placed by his side. Accusations began to be made loudly and openly against Piso; cautions and covert allusions were made to Tiberius as having ordered the commission of the crime, and in short all Rome and all Italy mourned as a public calamity the untimely death of Germanicus and clamoured for vengeance. Grief for Germanicus was merely a means for ventilating the discontent which was felt against Tiberius and his government. All the sincere republicans who believed that it was merely the will of Tiberius that prevented the restoration of the ancient republic; all those whose ambitions were not satisfied, the enemies of Tiberius and Augustus, the sincere friends of Germanicus; the lower classes who were discontented with the austerity of the government and were greedy for spectacles and profuse donations—all these gave themselves up to violent and clamorous manifestations of sorrow when Agrippina arrived in Italy from Syria bringing with her the ashes of Germanicus. Matters came to such a point that Tiberius, mindful of the customs of the old republic, thought it right to moderate these transports by the publication of a noble manifesto: "Many illustrious Romans," he said, "have died for the republic, but none has been mourned with such deep sorrow. This redounds to his honour and to the honour of all, but it is right that due measure should not be exceeded, and what might be suitable to a modest family or a small city would be out of place among great men and in a sovereign people like the Romans. . . . We must return to the ancient spirit of fortitude shown when the divine Cæsar lost his only daughter and the Emperor Augustus his grandchildren. . . . How often has not the Roman people had to support with firmness the destruction of whole armies, the deaths of great generals, and the annihilation of noble families! The great are mortal; only the republic is eternal. . . ."[1]

The people were silent, but Agrippina and her own and her dead husband's friends kept up the struggle, until one day some of them formally charged Piso with poisoning. Piso, on hearing the news of the death of Germanicus, had immediately returned to take possession of his province. But he had been compelled to give up this intention because the governors appointed by Germanicus and the friends of the latter in the East had withstood him by force of arms. There had thus been a beginning of civil war in the East which had still further excited the anger of Piso's enemies. It may easily be imagined in what an atmosphere the trial of Piso was conducted on his return to Rome! Among all the judicial dramas of which the history of Rome is so full, this was assuredly the most terrible. The people were persuaded that Piso had poisoned Germanicus; many added *sotto voce* that he had poisoned him by order of Tiberius, that Piso had the letters in which the order was given and would produce them at the trial—as if such orders, supposing them to have existed, would be given in writing! In the senate before whom the trial was to take place, the enemies of Tiberius and all the party of Germanicus were determined to secure Piso's

[1] Tac., *Ann.*, iii., 6.

condemnation at any cost. Of those who were impartial most were afraid of being considered corrupt if they judged according to their consciences. The charge was absurd; Tacitus himself, in spite of his hostility to Tiberius, says so. But what could Tiberius do either for himself or for justice? Every step he took in favour of the accused would have been interpreted as a proof of his complicity. Public opinion was so adverse and the senate so prejudiced against Piso that after a few sittings he committed suicide to escape an inevitable condemnation. Tiberius and Livia were thus able at least to save his wife and his sons and the family fortune.

33. **The Political Effects of the Trial of Piso.** This trial is not to be regarded as merely a judicial incident, however terrible; it was a real political catastrophe which was to have the gravest consequences both for Tiberius and for the empire. From it arose in the imperial family an incurable discord; for Agrippina, who was not appeased by the death of Piso, implacably persisted in accusing Tiberius of having caused the death of Germanicus. After this trial, too, charges of offences against the emperor and condemnations under the *lex de maiestate* began to grow more frequent —the charges and condemnations for which Tiberius, and after him all the princes of the Julio-Claudian house, were to acquire so melancholy a celebrity. It should, however, be remembered that the *lex de maiestate* was in no way the work of Tiberius. It had been passed in a fit of anger a hundred years before the Christian era by Saturninus, a democratic tribune of the people, in order to defend the republic against the intrigues of the great. It should also be remembered that the initiative in applying it to the punishment of

offences against the emperor did not come from Tiberius; that Tiberius, as Tacitus admits, did what he could to limit its application; that the senate, which tried these cases, was not in Tiberius's time an assembly of slaves but was on the whole against the emperor as the case of Piso had shown, and that, therefore, the frequent condemnations must have had some more serious motive than fear of Tiberius. Finally we must bear in mind the fact that the emperor was now the mainstay of public order throughout the empire. It could not be otherwise, because the loyalty of the legions depended on the devotion of the soldiers to his person and on the oath which they had sworn to him. Now the emperor, the head of the army, was being unjustly accused every day by his own relations in his own house, by a whole powerful party in the senate and in the upper classes, of having through jealousy, poisoned his nephew, a young general much beloved by the soldiers, that is to say of having committed a crime which in the eyes of all Romans, would have justified a mutiny of the armies! The Italians who formed the greater part of the army were not yet disposed to respect the authority of a chief who caused members of his family to be assassinated in order to gratify a caprice. It is therefore clear that Agrippina and the friends of Germanicus by their foolish charges were weakening the authority of Tiberius and therefore endangering public peace and order. We cannot be surprised if serious-minded persons with the public good at heart thought it impossible to leave the emperor exposed to these calumnies, more especially as Tiberius had not—and could not have—the authority and the prestige of Augustus. The growing frequency of cases under the *lex de maiestate* represents the natural reaction against the increasing perils of the internal situation which arose from the factions and irrational opposition carried on by part of the senate and aristocracy, and part of the family of Augustus against Tiberius's government.

This reaction was the more justifiable as under the prudent and sagacious control of Tiberius the situation of the empire had notably improved. About this time, for example, the German policy of the emperor began to bear fruit. The Marcomanni and the Cherusci mutually weakened each other by constant wars, and the Cherusci tore each other to pieces in atrocious civil conflicts, in one of which Arminius himself had perished. The storm which had been gathering for many years on the northern frontier was dispersed. With equal good fortune Tiberius's lieutenants in Africa repressed the dangerous forays of a Numidian adventurer named Tacfarinas. The insurrection of certain Thracian tribes was also quelled, and in Gaul some more or less violent agitations, alleged to be due to excessive taxation, were no less firmly dealt with (21 A.D.). As for internal administration, even so antipathetic a historian as Tacitus is forced to admit that up to this point the government of Tiberius had been a model, that all the most serious concerns of the republic were referred to the senate and were discussed with entire liberty by that assembly, that honours were distributed among the men who were best qualified by birth and merit to receive them, that the offices of State were restored to their pristine dignity and the laws applied with good sense and impartiality, that the departments controlled by the prince were entrusted to capable persons, that the provinces were laid under contribution with moderation, and that the law and the courts of justice were above all men even the prince himself.[1] It is not surprising that there were people who thought that, since the law of Saturninus existed, it was right and wise to use it for the defence of so excellent a prince against so injudicious an opposition; it would have been strange had it been otherwise.

**34. Tiberius at Capri and the Struggle between Agrippina and Sejanus (26–31 A.D.).** But the *lex de maiestate*, applied as it had to be applied in a society in which private prosecution was the only organ of the law, could only check without eradicating the evil from which the empire was suffering—all the more because Tiberius showed great weakness. Whether it was due to old age or to weariness, to his growing detestation of mankind or to the uncertainties of his position, the fact remains that this man, who was destined to pass into history as an unbridled tyrant, betrayed extraordinary irresolution to all who viewed his actions from close at hand. Not only did he allow Agrippina and the old party of Germanicus which had now gathered round her, complete freedom to calumniate him and to excite the people against him, but he actually permitted them to bring forward Nero, the elder son of Germanicus who was fourteen years old in 21, as his possible antagonist and successor. When, in 23, his own son Drusus, who after the death of Germanicus had become his principal collaborator and who in the previous year he had caused to be invested with the tribunician power, died in his 38th year, he reconciled himself with Agrippina and in a noble speech

[1] Tac., *Ann.*, iii., 60; and above all *Ann.*, iv., 6. This appreciation of the government of Tiberius, coming from Tacitus, is of capital importance.

presented Nero and his younger brother to the senate as the future hopes of the republic. Thus Tiberius took the initiative towards a reconciliation, and concord in the imperial family might have been re-established if Agrippina had been a wiser woman, and if the old quarrels had not been envenomed by the intervention of a new personage, Ælius Sejanus, the commander of the guard.

Sejanus belonged to the equestrian order and was what we should call a permanent official. He had acquired, more especially since the deaths of Germanicus and Drusus, the complete confidence of the emperor. He was Tiberius's daily helper in the difficulties of administration, the only man of experience with whom he could discuss the complicated questions which never ceased to arise. But Sejanus feared that he might be supplanted by the sons of Germanicus in the favour of the prince and therefore made use of every imprudence committed by Agrippina and her party to aggravate the discord by which the imperial house was rent, and, in a word, Rome and the senate were disturbed by a ferocious struggle between the party of Sejanus and the party of Agrippina and the young Nero. Intrigues, scandals, prosecutions, and calumnies were the weapons commonly used in this conflict. As usual Tiberius looked on as an almost inert spectator until, in the year 26, he crowned his irresolute course of conduct by a culminating act of weakness. Disgusted by all these quarrels which he could not control, the prince ended by forsaking Rome and Latium, and retired into a second, and this time irrevocable, exile at Capri, the wildest and most rugged of the Parthenopean islands, where he gave himself up to communion with nature since mankind seemed incapable of understanding him.

In spite of this Tiberius did not lose hold of the government of the empire. The solitary of Capri was still a conscientious ruler. But henceforth he could communicate with the empire only through his trusted prætorian prefect whose power and authority rapidly increased in Rome. In the absence of Tiberius, Sejanus gradually became the real emperor, because now the decisions which governed the empire from Capri depended mainly on what he thought and what he advised. Sejanus managed to compass what Tiberius had been unable or unwilling to do. He freed Rome from the presence of Agrippina and her son. The catastrophe did not come until the year 29 A.D. after the death of Livia at the age of 86. So long as Livia was alive Sejanus had not dared to attack the son and the widow of Germanicus. But immediately after the disappearance of their last protectress Agrippina and Nero were accused of conspiring against Tiberius and condemned to exile. Nero soon afterwards committed suicide. It is impossible to say how far the charge was well founded and the condemnation just. It is difficult to believe that Agrippina herself formed a conspiracy under the eyes of Sejanus, and it is more likely that the prosecution made skilful use of the imprudences and the unwise speeches to which Agrippina was particularly prone. Ancient Rome, both under the republic and under the empire, suffered from the two irremediable evils of espionage and delation. A public department for prosecutions, as we now know it, did not as yet exist, and private delation and accusation was considered a meritorious action and, in case of success, was very profitable, as part of the fortune of the condemned passed to the informer. It is easy to see, therefore, that, after the death of Livia, the departure of Tiberius from Rome and the establishment of the omnipotence of Sejanus who wished to drive out Agrippina, volunteers could easily be found who would rush in from every side to furnish the information and the proofs necessary to secure the ruin of the imprudent lady under the penalties of the *lex de maiestate*.

However this may be, even if, as is probable, the punishment which fell upon Agrippina was greater than she deserved, this sentence sent into exile an eccentric woman who had done nothing but create embarrassments for a responsible government seriously occupied in serving the public. That the government of Tiberius continued zealously to follow this course is explicitly stated by a contemporary who strikingly confirms what we have already read in Tacitus: "Good faith was recalled to the Forum, sedition, intrigue, and favouritism were driven from the Campus Martius and discord from the senate. A rebirth of justice, equity, and industry, which seemed to have disappeared for ever, was seen in Rome. The magistrates again acquired respect for their duties; the senate recovered its ancient dignity, the courts their solemnity. There were no more riots in the theatres, the citizens by choice or necessity were again brought to see the necessity for industry and good conduct. Virtue was honoured, vice punished; the small respected but did not fear the great; the superior took precedence of his inferior but did not despise him. The cost of living was moderate; men enjoyed the blessings of peace. Diffused from one end of the world to the other from the West to the East, from the North to the South this *pax Augusta* guaranteed complete security everywhere. . . . Cities were restored in Asia; the provinces were freed from the despotism of their governors, honour was bestowed on merit; punishment was rare but, when needed, prompt and opportune. Justice and virtue drove out favouritism and intrigue, for the best of princes taught his fellow citizens to do good by his own practice and, though he was in authority superior to all, he was still more superior by the example of his own conduct."[1]

35. **Culmination and Fall of Sejanus (31 A.D.).** But an even more terrible storm was brewing at Rome. With the condemnation of Agrippina the power of Sejanus reached its culmination. Honours of all kinds were showered upon him by Tiberius and by the senate. In 31 he received what appeared to be the supreme recompense of his long service. He, the obscure knight, was raised to the consulship with Tiberius as his colleague, and, soon afterwards, there was talk of an engagement between him and Tiberius's granddaughter, the divorced wife of Nero. What more could be desired by a man born in the equestrian order?

Sejanus, however, did desire more. He wished to succeed Tiberius in the supreme position; but Tiberius, who was a true Claudius, could not suffer that a knight should become the head of the Roman nobility. In this very year, indeed, his thoughts and affections seemed to be turning in a special manner towards Caius the youngest of the sons of Germanicus. Though Caius was not yet twenty, he made him a Pontiff and, what was of more importance, in the official reports which from time to time the emperor had occasion to send to the senate he manifested for Caius the same

[1] Vell. Pat., ii., 126.

sentiments as he had shown towards his elder brothers nine years before. At this point Sejanus seems to have reflected that if he continued to serve Tiberius, old, unpopular, even detested as he was, he would gain nothing but the certainty of falling a victim at the emperor's death to the accumulations of hatred which were being heaped up against him, and to have decided to come to an understanding with the enemies of Tiberius, who were so numerous in the senate, with a view to overthrowing the prince and taking his place. We cannot say with certainty what the constitution and importance of this conspiracy may have been. It is certain that on one terrible day at Capri, Tiberius was made aware of the machinations of Sejanus and that his informant was his relative, the gentle Antonia, daughter of the triumvir, one of the few people who had remained faithful to him through his days of glory and of sorrow, and who was honoured as the widow of the great Drusus and the mother of Germanicus whom Tiberius was said to have poisoned. It must have been a terrible blow to the old emperor. After having lost, one after the other, his dearest relatives and collaborators, after having been persecuted and tormented by his own family, was he now to be deceived by his most trusted friend, whom he had never doubted for a single instant, who owed everything to him, and to whom, as the supreme proof of his confidence, he had entrusted the command of his personal bodyguard? Was he now to be at the mercy of his own prætorians, corrupted and incited to mutiny?

Tiberius, however, though long suffering, was not a man who would let himself be tricked without taking steps to defend himself. Without loss of time and with consummate skill he began to isolate Sejanus, without allowing him to suspect what was happening. By satisfying some disappointed ambitions, by conferring some favours, by accentuating his affection for Caius, by repudiating some of the less laudable features of the work of his prætorian præfect, he undermined the position of his crafty minister, the fortunate *parvenu* whose power and reputation were due entirely to the favour of his prince. Then, on October 18, 31, when he thought the moment opportune, Tiberius secretly deposed Sejanus from the command of the guard which was given to a certain Macro. One of the *cohortes vigilum* was entrusted with the defence of the senate house and then, at a sitting of the senate the emperor caused a letter to be read in which he explicitly accused his ex-prefect and some others of high treason. The sensation produced was tremendous, and, if the rapidity with which the senate condemned Sejanus may be imputed to the servility of that assembly, the vehement demonstrations of public feeling which took place at the time showed clearly the confidence in the rectitude of the emperor which at least part of Rome still cherished.

The condemnation and execution of Sejanus was followed by many others. It would be rash on the strength of the documents known to the ancients to affirm that the absent prince was more responsible for these than the senate whose attitude had contributed so much to encourage the ambitions of Sejanus.[1] From the very brief and summary accounts of a few of the cases amid the flood of prosecutions, it is im-

[1] *Cf.* Suet., *Cal.*, 30: *Sæpe in cunctos pariter senatores, ut Seiani clientes . . .* [*Caligula*] *invectus est, prolatis libellis quos crematos simulaverat, defensa que Tiberii sævitia quasi necessaria, quum tot criminantibus credendum esset.*

possible to say how often justice and truth were vindicated and how often both were outraged. Tiberius would have been more than human if he had shown mercy this time, for in these very days he was struck to the heart by a blow more terrible than all the rest. The first wife of Sejanus, whom he had divorced in order to ally himself with the imperial family, committed suicide, but not before she had revealed that the death of the emperor's son Drusus was due to poison administered to him by Sejanus himself and by Drusus's unfaithful wife Livilla, daughter of Antonia. It is practically certain that this was an atrocious calumny invented by a jealous woman who wished to be revenged. But everybody believed it, and a new and even more terrible scandal broke out which was followed by a new tragedy. Innocent or guilty, Livilla in order to escape an accusation which she could never have disproved, starved herself to death.

**36. The Last Years of Tiberius (31–37 A.D.).** These were months of black terror. The Roman aristocracy had been bled once more, and they revenged themselves, as the weak always do, by bespattering with atrocious calumnies the solitary life led at Capri by the aged prince now over seventy and in feeble health. To judge of these abominable inventions it is enough to ask whether they are likely to be true of a man of that age, and how the historians came to know all the details which they so picturesquely recount. As before, Tiberius repeatedly intervened to check the universal delirium of persecutions, servility, mutual vengeance, espionage, and suicide which was sometimes heroic but more often the desperate refuge of the guilty. All these horrors, were, however, confined to Rome, which was a small corner of the world.

The remainder of the empire knew only the excellent administration of Tiberius which was full of firmness and good sense, and uniform in good and evil fortune. Italy was regularly provisioned. The provinces were tranquil and provided with good governors who grew old at their posts, and taught the provincials that proconsulships and proprætorships were not positions created in order to enable them to make money or pursue enjoyment, but offices which must be administered for the public good.

Peace reigned everywhere on the frontiers. In the last years of Tiberius's reign the Armenian question showed signs of reawakening, but the diplomatic skill of the prince soon restored calm. For though Tiberius was now 78 and his physical forces were declining, his intelligence was still alert. A few days before March 16, 37, he had gone to Misenum for a change of climate, and there a friend of his, who was a physician and had come to greet him, observed the feebleness of the emperor's pulse and informed Macro the commander of the Prætorian Guard. Tiberius understood that his last hour was at hand and, wishing to honour the anxious friend whom he would never see again, he insisted on ordering a banquet and on remaining at table longer than usual. Two days later one of the greatest of the Roman emperors died suddenly, alone at the last without a friend at his bedside—a death as lonely as his life had been (March 16, 37 A.D.)[1]

[1] The account of Tiberius's death may, it seems, be thus reconstructed by combining what Tacitus (*Ann.*, vi., 50) tells us with the testimony of Seneca quoted by Suetonius (*Tib.*, 73). The hatred of his enemies surrounded even his deathbed with inventions the object of which was to put it about that his death had been violent.

## CHAPTER VI

### CALIGULA AND CLAUDIUS

(37–54 A.D.)

**37. The Election of Caligula and the Reasons for it (37 A.D.).** Unlike Augustus, Tiberius died sole emperor without a colleague. The senate, therefore, was free either to continue the experiment of the principate or at once to attempt a complete restoration of the republic. It does not appear, however, that they spent much time in considering the latter alternative, and this is also a clear proof that the "tyranny" of Tiberius is an invention of the ancient historians. The authority of the prince was now too useful to be dispensed with, even though the holders of the office had been unpopular in many quarters.

It was at once recognized, therefore, that a new princeps must be put in the place of the deceased. The question was, who should it be? If a successor was to be found in the family of Augustus there was not much room for choice. The surviving male members of that family were three: Tiberius Claudius Nero, the brother of Germanicus; Caius Caligula, the son of Germanicus, the only male who had been spared by the storm which had destroyed his father's house; and Tiberius the son of Drusus, whom the

Emperor Tiberius had adopted by his will. Of these the last was a boy of seventeen and the first though of mature years, was looked upon as a half crazy imbecile, the butt of women and freedmen. For this reason he was kept in seclusion and had in fact occupied no office. Thus there remained only Caius Caligula. Caius was twenty-seven. He was probably born in Germany during his father's campaigns,[1] and it is certain that he was brought up there among the soldiers. While still a little boy he had worn the soldier's dress and had donned the military boots (*caligulæ*) whence he acquired the *sobriquet* by which he is known to history. Later he had accompanied his father to the East, and after the death of Germanicus had lived first with his mother, then with his grandmother Livia, and finally with his paternal grandmother Antonia. He was intelligent, eloquent, a lover of the arts, and a man of taste. But he was clearly anything but well balanced; being irritable, impulsive, and almost insanely attached to the ideas by which he was from time to time possessed. He had, in short, both qualities and defects, and he was, moreover, still very young to become the head of a great empire. His defects however were not known to most people; and after all there was no other suitable member of the family.

It was therefore necessary to be content with him unless it was intended to seek some one outside the descendants of Augustus. This would not have been impossible, and would have been quite legal, for a hereditary principate had not so far been even distantly adumbrated in the constitution. Any senator

[1] Tac., *Ann.*, i., 41. Others, however, say at Tibur or Antium; *cf.* Suet., *Cal.*, 8.

might have become the successor of Tiberius. There was, however, an important consideration which must have had its effect in inducing the senate to prefer a member of the family of Augustus. For at least fifty years the barbarians and the army had identified the Roman Empire with the Julio-Claudian house. The army, in particular, cherished for the members of that family an attachment beyond all comparison. Among the soldiers, especially those stationed on the Rhine and on the Danube, the name of Germanicus's son was most popular. From the military and political point of view Caligula's appointment presented great advantages and he was accordingly elected (March 18, 37 A.D.).[1]

**38. The First Acts of Caligula.** According to the ancient historians the government of the new and youthful emperor had the happiest beginning. Amid universal jubilation Caligula declined to propose divine honours for Tiberius as had been done in the case of Augustus. He burned, or made a show of burning, all the political papers of his predecessor, forbade accusations of *læsa maiestas*, and granted a general amnesty to all who had been accused, condemned, or exiled. The people once more had donations in profusion. The soldiers received gratuities which doubled the legacies left to them by Tiberius. Italy was exempted from some of the recent taxation. The theatres began to reopen and public games were held with a frequency to which the citizens had for many years been unaccustomed. Caligula restored to the comitia their full electoral powers and did his utmost to distinguish clearly the powers of the senate from those of the prince. He restored the obligation

[1] Cf. *Acta fratrum Arvalium*, in *C. I. L.*, vi., 1, 202, p. 467.

of the prince to give an account of public expenditure ordered by him, annulled the sentences pronounced against his mother and his brother and gave solemn burial to their ashes, and on July 1st, at the inauguration of his first consulship, he made a great speech in the senate, which was intended to be the political programme of his reign, and in the course of which he declared that his chief model would not be Tiberius but the divine Augustus. All hearts were thrilled with the most joyous expectations.

**39. The Volte Face of Caligula and his Attempts to Orientalize the Empire.** After eight months of power if we may believe the ancient historians, Caligula was suddenly seized with illness and from the wreck of a good and kind emperor there emerged the mad and cruel tyrant who tormented the Roman world with his perversities until the beginning of the year 41. But ancient historians in writing of the Cæsars have been much too fond of dividing their administrations into two parts, the first admirable, the second detestable—as, for instance in the case of Tiberius, Nero, Domitian, and Commodus. The fact as regards Caligula is that several of his earliest acts must necessarily have put on its guard any people less inclined to self-delusion than the Romans. The young prince had begun by depriving the one surviving senatorial proconsul (of Africa) in the empire who, since the days of Augustus, still held the *imperium militare*, of the two legions under his command. What was even worse, he had conferred on his grandmother Antonia and on his sisters the privileges of the Vestal Virgins and had directed that the names of his sisters were to be mentioned in all the prayers that magistrates and priests offered every year for the prosperity of the emperor and the people. Though he affected to call himself the great grandson of Augustus he had re-established the memory of Mark Antony and had suppressed the annual festival which Augustus had established to commemorate the victory of Actium. He had officially established the cult of the Egyptian divinity Isis, and he himself lived surrounded by Egyptian domestics, while the most faithful and influential of his freedmen was an Alexandrian, a certain Helicon. Finally we know that, on the eve of his illness, Caligula, who had become a widower, had the intention of marrying and making his colleague in the empire his own sister Drusilla, to whom, moreover, in a will made while he was ill, he had left the empire as a legacy as if it were a thing of which he could dispose!

The truth is that from the very beginning Caligula showed signs of what historians have called his "madness," and which must have appeared to the Romans to be such. That his conduct was partly due to insanity we may agree, but it was only partly, for the idea which inspired his policy, though chimerical in the circumstances to which Caligula wished to apply it, had in itself a certain logical consistency giving a meaning and a coherency to many of his acts which at first sight look like the wild caprices of a disordered brain. Indeed, if we set aside some of the more absurd stories handed down by the ancients, which are less damaging to the young prince than to the historians who have believed them and their readers who have accepted them, we shall find it possible to discern in Caligula's proceedings a clear and distinct purpose which was to orientalize Roman society and government by force, and to found in

Rome a monarchy analogous to that which until sixty years previously had existed on the banks of the Nile. Caligula was an orientalizer who repudiated and wished to destroy all Roman traditions and to set up at Rome in a single day a monarchy like that of Egypt. Hence his mania for self-deification and his violent efforts to impose on the Romans and on the provincials, even on the Jews who were most recalcitrant, the cult of himself and of his family. Hence too his assumption of the title of Brother of Jove, his affecting to call his fellow citizens his "subjects" and himself their "master," the new etiquette and customs of his court, the desire to implant in the mind of everybody and at any cost the idea of his omnipotence, the official rehabilitation of Antony who had wished to continue the dynasty of the Ptolemies at Alexandria, the oriental splendour of the festivals with which he sought to dazzle the people, and the marriage with his sister, projected as an attempt to introduce at Rome the dynastic custom of the Ptolemies and the Pharaohs which countenanced marriages between brothers and sisters in order to preserve the purity of the royal race. Hence, finally, the will in which he left the empire, which he looked upon as his own, to Drusilla, and the temples he erected and the divine honours which he paid to her when she died.[1]

The same tendencies which inspired his home policy are visible in his foreign policy as well. In the East his object was not the Romanization of the provinces, but their complete Hellenization, not conquest but the formation of a ring of friendly client states. With this in view he reconstituted the kingdom of Commagene

[1] On this interpretation of the government of Caligula, *cf.* G. Ferrero, *The Women of the Cæsars*, New York, 1911, pp. 212 ff.

in the first year of his principate and even added to it a strip of the coast of Cilicia, restoring it to the son of Antiochus whom Tiberius had deposed together with his consficated patrimony. In the same year, 37 A.D., Caligula separated northern and western Palestine from the province of Syria to which it had been attached since 34, and assigned it, together with some neighbouring territories such as Celesiria and Abilene to Herod Agrippa, the nephew of Herod the Great, who was then living at Rome. Similarly he restored to his throne the king of Nabatæans, gave Ituræa an Arabian king and a Thracian monarch to Armenia Minor and a portion of Pontus. Nor can it be said that his oriental policy was imprudent or dangerous except in Judæa, where he attempted to impose the "innate divinity" of the emperor on a people which made bold to prefer their own single and universal God. In vain did the prince order the troops of Syria to enter Jerusalem to compel the synagogues to admit the statues of the new Roman deity. All he accomplished was to fan the first sparks of the conflagration which was destined to break out thirty years later.

The West, on the other hand, was regarded by Caligula as the source from which to replenish the treasury which had been emptied by his prodigalities. Between 39 and 40 he attempted a raid on the gold and other riches of the Gallic provinces which he intended to continue in Spain, Germany, and Britain. But his forces were too small for such great designs, and in the West his policy was much more feeble than in the East. His invasion of Germany remained an unfulfilled aspiration, his conquest of Britain was cut short by the arrival of an embassy bringing many gifts and verbal promises of submission;[1] the raid on Gaul was interrupted or at least seriously disturbed by a conspiracy formed by Cn. Cornelius Gætulicus, one of his generals, in concert with some of his own relations (39 A.D.).

**40. The End of Caligula (Jan. 24, 41 A.D.).** This attempt to divert the turbid streams of the Nile and the Euphrates into the current of Roman life seemed unheard-of madness to the Romans. But, once the principle is admitted, many of Caligula's apparently insensate acts explain themselves. His insanity, therefore, consisted less in the strangeness and violence of his individual actions than in the idea from which these actions came, the idea that by the will of one man the republic could be transformed into a monarchy like that of the Ptolemies.

Caligula in fact soon became highly unpopular even with the lower classes who profited largely by his profuse expenditure. Rome and Italy were still so much attached to the past that the monarchical and oriental craze of the young prince excited the contempt and disgust of all classes in the community. Tiberius had been hated for his too great attachment to tradition; Caligula was not less detested because of his too manifest revolt against it, for in those days men could neither live entirely in accordance with tradition, nor yet abandon it altogether. In order to impose his oriental dreams on his subjects and to lessen the resistance with which he was faced, Caligula was compelled

[1] On the subject of this expedition the ancients have handed down to us a story which may be described as a caricature too absurd to be taken seriously. *Cf.* Suet., *Cal.*, 46. If this story is true the prince was much less mad than those must have been who obeyed him.

to have recourse to condemnations for *læsa maiestas*, to proscriptions and executions. As the finances were in ruins, he proceeded to confiscations and new forms of oppression of every sort. The rabble of Rome, dazzled by his prodigality, supported him, but in the imperial family, in the senate, among the officers of the prætorian guard and of the army, and generally among the upper and middle classes, disgust and aversion rapidly increased. Rome was not yet ripe for Asiatic despotism. The excesses and eccentricities of his extemporized tyranny reawakened republican sentiments everywhere, even among the prætorians who were charged with his personal safety, and on January 24, 41, he was assassinated by a certain Cassius Chærea, a prætorian tribune, in one of the corridors of his palace as the result of a conspiracy in which persons of considerable importance were concerned.

**41. The Election of Claudius (Jan. 24–25, 41 A.D.).** On the news of Caligula's death the senate met, honoured Chærea and his accomplices with the ancient title of "Restorers of Liberty," and proceeded to discuss what was to be done. This time the party which desired to abolish the principate and restore the old republic was more numerous than it had been on the occasion of the deaths of Augustus and of Tiberius. The violence and extravagance of Caligula had reawakened in many minds the latent hatred of the new régime. But could the senate, weakened, discredited, divided as it was, govern the empire itself without a prince? Many, however reluctantly, doubted the possibility of this. On the other hand if an emperor was a necessity, it was not easy to find one. Of the family of Augustus, Claudius, regarded as imbecile and incapable, alone remained, for Tiberius, the son of Drusus, was now also dead. It appears that several senators more or less openly became candidates for the vacant dignity. If, however, the influence of members of the Augustan family was now questionable and uncertain, how was a senator unknown to the provinces and the army to govern the empire without the prestige of that family which had been prominent and powerful for so many years? It is not surprising that the senate spent two days in discussions which reached no conclusion. While these discussions were going on, however, the soldiers of the prætorian guard, scouring the imperial palace, discovered the imbecile Claudius in a corner where he had hidden himself in terror. Recognizing in him the brother of Germanicus, they acclaimed him as emperor. It was a solution, for an energetic decision, even if lacking in prudence, is often worth more than the most prudent hesitations. The senate, not knowing what to decide, accepted and ratified the solution of the problem which the prætorians offered on the point of a sword. Claudius, the imbecile, was emperor.

**42. The First Three Years of the Reign of Claudius: his Merits and his Weaknesses (41–43 A.D.).** Tiberius Claudius Germanicus was born at Lugdunum (Lyon) in 10 B.C. His parents were Drusus and Antonia, daughter of Mark Antony the triumvir. He was therefore the younger brother of Germanicus. He was not an imbecile, as he was said to be, and as he appeared to many who judged him superficially. He was on the contrary an excellent Greek scholar, a good speaker, a studious and erudite person by no means wanting in originality and acumen. He had, in fact, quite enough ability to make a figure in the world beside the other and more illustrious members of his family, but unfortunately his brilliant qualities were obscured by strange lapses and weaknesses. His mother described him as "a man half made" and perhaps it is the best description that can be given of him. His timidity and *gaucherie* were incredible; he was quite unable to make himself respected; his slaves and freedmen treated him as if they were the masters and he did not dare to protest. He was often the slave of the women with whom he lived and had no idea how to behave in society, often saying things which were extremely *mal à propos*, partly from shyness and partly from a kind of boyish inattention. This must have been the reason why Augustus kept him in the background. He had therefore lived a solitary life almost entirely in the company of slaves and freedmen, banned by all that was smart, polished, or aristocratic in society, and entirely occupied with his favourite historical and philological studies. He had been a pupil of Livy and devoted himself to writing history and to spelling reform, at the same time not denying himself the pleasures of love and of the table, for Claudius, if we may believe the ancients, was almost brutishly gluttonous and sensual. It is not surprising that among the Roman aristocracy such a person should have passed for an imbecile, though he was not wanting in the intelligence of a scholar and a man of letters, he lacked firmness, courage, and self-control, that indefinable quality without which a man cannot command the respect of others or take the lead, however clever he may be.

Being a man of intelligence, a Claudius, and an archæologist into the bargain, the new emperor was not long in bringing back the government to the great tradition of Augustus and Tiberius. Once more the senate was frequently convoked to decide even on matters directly under imperial control. He honoured the magistrates in the old fashion, often summoned the comitia to exercise their ancient electoral and legislative functions, limited the grants of citizenship which had been so lavish under Caligula and revoked those which had been made to provincials who had not learned to speak Latin. He laid aside all personal pomp, affected a desire to be regarded as a mere senator, declared that he would not appoint any one to the senate whose great grandfathers at least had not enjoyed Roman citizenship, and re-established the cherished distinctions of the orders which Caligula had purposely confused. He repressed the disorders of the populace at public spectacles where under Caligula discipline had been much relaxed, and did his best to re-establish the finances on a sound basis and to restore the ancient forms of religion.

**43. Claudius and his Freedmen—the Conspiracy of 42 A.D.** Thus the beginnings of the new reign were excellent. Rome, it seemed would again be able to breathe freely! But instead there began almost at once a new period of turbulence and disorder. In spite of all his efforts Claudius failed to conquer the hostility shown him by one part—and that the strongest—of the Roman aristocracy. The new prince had been injured above all by the manner of his election. Claudius was the first emperor to be imposed on the senate by the military, by an open breach of the law, and the nobility were all the more unwilling to pardon the innovation because the *coup d'état*, by which the emperor had profited had come at a moment when the aristocracy was fondly imagining that they would reconquer all their ancient privileges and when more than one of their leaders had hopes of at once seizing the empire for himself. The weakness of the prince aggravated the discontent which had been thus aroused. Claudius might, it was true, govern in the traditional way, but he did not surround himself with knights and senators. On the contrary he kept about his person the servants and companions of his youth and early manhood, that is to say, his slaves and, still more, his freedmen. In this way these men gradually secured an influence and an ascendancy which deeply offended the aristocracy, the more so because Claudius did not know how to keep them in their place and allowed them to flaunt their power and insolence by his side. Among his freedmen were some of much intelligence and capacity who were of great assistance to him in the business of government. Such were Polybius, Narcissus, Harpocrates, Pallas, and even the eunuch Pasides. But though these freedmen helped Claudius to rule according to the great traditions of the aristocratic republic, the Roman nobility could not endure that on occasions of public ceremonial Polybius should appear with the consuls, that Harpocrates should traverse Rome in a litter and be the giver of spectacles, that Narcissus and Pallas should receive the insignia of quæstor and prætor by the wish of Claudius who proposed these honours in the senate. The jealousy felt by the old and decadent order for new men and the exclusive spirit of the ancient Roman world were reviving, and well as Claudius governed, he governed in such a way as to make himself ridiculous and lacked all prestige and authority.

This singular contradiction explains the great conspiracy of 42, the object of which was to procure the deposition of the emperor, who was the creature of the prætorians at Rome, through the instrumentality of the legions of Dalmatia. The leader of the conspirators at Rome appears to have been a senator named Annius Vinicianus who on the death of Caligula was said to have put himself forward as a possible emperor. Furius Camillus Scribonianus, the governor of Dalmatia, who had three legions at his disposal, acted with him. The good sense of the soldiers and their attachment to the Julio-Claudian house defeated this movement. The legions, led away for a moment, soon repented and slew their traitorous general; but the attempt was so serious and on such a scale that on the first news of the mutiny, Claudius had been on the point of abdicating. He recovered himself and pardoned the soldiers, but Rome was once more devastated by one of the storms of judicial savagery envenomed by private feuds and interested accusations which from time to time deluged the capital with blood.

**44. The Conquest of Britain (43 A.D.). The New Policy in the Provinces and the New Social Legislation.** This conspiracy left behind it a legacy of terror in the mind of the emperor. Claudius surrounded himself with guards. No one could now come near him without being personally searched. No one could entertain him without having his house minutely examined beforehand. But, if the government of Claudius was weak it did not lack a certain determination (due either to the intelligence of the prince, to the ambition of his freedmen or to both) to struggle against its weakness and to strengthen itself by attempting great reforms and important enterprises. A British chief driven from his country by civil war had come to

Rome and for some time had been trying to persuade the Roman government to invade the great island. Was this chief clever enough to persuade Claudius that the undertaking would be easy? Or did Claudius, in the first moment of his recovery from the shock of the Dalmatian conspiracy, understand that what had injured him above all was the fact that he, the son of Drusus and the brother of Germanicus, was without military renown? However that may be, the fact remains that in the year 43 (and according to the historians on Claudius's own personal initiative) a great army consisting of several legions landed in Britain and successfully commenced the enterprise which Cæsar had barely attempted and of which Augustus and Tiberius had deliberately repudiated all idea.[1] The moment had been well chosen. The population of the southern regions of Britain was at that time weakened by wars and revolutions, and the legions, in the course of a rapid and successful campaign, were able to conquer, at any rate for the moment, a great part of the island. Claudius himself went to Britain, crossed the Thames at the head of his legions and for the first time in his life was present at a military operation, the result of which was the occupation by his army of Camulodunum (Colchester). He then returned to Gaul, declared Britain a Roman province and came back to Rome where the senate conferred great honours upon him.

The conquest of Britain was in truth only begun. Ten more years of sanguinary fighting were needed before some parts of the island at least could be called Roman. But in Rome and Italy, where the public had for long been casting covetous eyes on Britain as

[1] *Cf.* Strab., ii., 5, 8. Tac., *Agr.*, 13.

the natural complement of Gaul, Claudius's bold move gave great satisfaction. In the same year Lycia, in which disturbances had broken out, was annexed to the empire and attached to the prefecture of Pamphylia. Claudius, in fact, was initiating a vigorous foreign policy, and for a moment it seemed that his government might derive from these successes something of the strength and the prestige of which it stood in need. Between 43 and 48 there ensued a period in which, though it made mistakes it showed great activity and intelligence, and even a new and increasing largeness of view both in foreign and in domestic policy. In this unusual broad-mindedness, must we not recognize the influence of the freedmen, intelligent persons who were naturally very little constrained by ancient Roman tradition? It is a probable explanation, but in any case, the policy of Claudius, though in its main lines it remained faithful to the Roman tradition, nevertheless introduced many administrative and judicial novelties which the times required. In 46 the emperor, abandoning the purely exclusive and restrictive system followed by Augustus and Tiberius, granted Roman citizenship to whole tribes of the inhabitants of the Alps, such as the Ananes in the Trentino, the Tulliassi, and the Sindones.[1] Two years later, in 48, he openly affronted in the senate the opposition of the old intransigent spirit of Roman nationalism by securing the concession of the *ius honorum* (that is, the right to be made senators) in its entirety to the rich men belonging to Transalpine Gaul, in the first instance to the Ædui, who were already citizens.[2]

[1] Cf. *C. I. L.*, v., 5050.

[2] On the text of the speech made in the senate by the prince on this occasion cf. *C. I. L.*, xiii., 1668; Tac., *Ann.*, xi., 24.

This was the first time that this right was explicitly given to the upper classes of a province, and it is not unlikely that Claudius was moved to take this bold step not only by a desire to reinforce the senatorial aristocracy but also by the expedition against Britain. As he wished to conquer Britain he had to make every effort to secure the loyalty of Gaul, which was the base of his operations against the island. Many indeed were the changes of which this reform was destined to be the seed! We may note in passing certain legal reforms due to Claudius in which for the first time appears something of a universalizing spirit in marked contrast with the hitherto narrow and formal character of the Roman law.

45. **Messalina—History and Legend.** In the year 47 Claudius assumed the office of censor, which for many years had been in abeyance, and carried out its duties in scrupulous accordance with the tradition of the old republic. He began by issuing many *notæ censoriæ*, by expelling unworthy senators, forcing indigent senators to resign, and filling the gaps by creating new patrician families.[1] On the proposal of one of the consuls with the assent of a majority of the assembly, he received the title of *pater senatus*. Rome should have been content at last! On the contrary, however, neither good government nor the senate's applause could allay the opposition which persistently smouldered and every now and then flared up in Rome. Claudius might conquer provinces and make excellent laws but Rome could not tolerate that the emperor, who should have been supreme in all things, was unable to secure obedience in his own house from his

[1] *Cf.* Tac., *Ann.*, xi., 13; xii., 52; and *C. I. L.*, iii., 6074; xiv., 3607.

freedmen and his wife. The conduct of the empress was another and equally serious cause of discontent. Claudius had first married a certain Plautia Urgulanilla whom he had had to repudiate, secondly Ælia Pætina whom he also divorced, and, thirdly and lastly, a young lady of great beauty and very ancient lineage. Classical historians have described Valeria Messalina as licentious beyond belief, as cynical, cruel, and greedy. But if she was all this, it is difficult to explain some of her characteristic acts, and impossible to understand not only why her presence was tolerated so long in a house like that of Claudius, but also why she enjoyed (as she did) no small consideration among the Roman aristocracy of her time, which was certainly not a society of abandoned men and women, and why, finally, she never lacked, up to the disaster which finally overtook her, the friendship, the affection, and the help of one of the most important of the Vestals against whose good name no ancient writer has dared to suggest a shadow of suspicion.

A more balanced judgment will conclude that Messalina was neither a Livia nor an Antonia, but that, at the worst, she may have been a Julia. That is to say, she was a woman like so many others of the Roman aristocracy of the day, young, beautiful, capricious, frivolous, fond of pleasure and luxury and sumptuous entertainments, prone to confound the affairs of her family with those of the empire, and rash in presuming on her husband's weakness, even in matters which concerned the State alone. This led her to interfere in public affairs in the way women will, and thus too often the weakness of Claudius allowed her likes and dislikes to vitiate correct principles of public administration and the strict observance of justice. Too often she took it upon herself to violate the *leges sumptuariæ* which Claudius had re-established, and too often, also, it appears that she abused her position in order to make money; for, according to the ancients, she was both very avaricious and very prodigal. In Rome, however, there still prevailed the strong Latin tradition against the open participation of women in public business, and public opinion required that the emperor's consort should be a matron who, like Livia, was a model of all the ancient Italian virtues. Though a section at least of the nobility, being inclined to modern manners, was indulgent to Messalina, the Roman middle class thought it outrageous that so scandalous an example should be set in high places.

**46. The Conspiracy of Messalina and Silius (48 A.D.).** The weakness of Claudius, his perpetual terrors, the hesitation and uncertainty of which they were the cause, the excesses and the financial corruption of Messalina, the peculation and the presumption of the imperial freedmen, nullified the effect of all the zeal and energy with which he conducted the affairs of State and the wise and sagacious legislation by which he sought to remedy abuses. Discontent grew apace in the senate and among the people. Everyone cursed Messalina and the freedmen, and laughed at Claudius. Among the senators the number grew of those who hoped to be able to take the emperor's place. Every day there were rumours of conspiracies and of imminent revolts among the troops, and every now and then there were popular outbreaks. In 46, there had even been a plot the leading spirit in which was no less a person than Asinius Gallus, half-brother to Drusus the son of Tiberius, who had persuaded himself that he was strong enough, with the support of the popular discontent, to deprive Claudius of the empire. This atmosphere of discontent, conspiracy, and menace added to the terrors of Claudius, who was no lionheart, and made him more than ever dependent on his freedmen whose power grew in direct proportion to their master's fear. Little by little there came about a strange and paradoxical situation such as had never before been seen at Rome. It was as if the Romans did not know whether they wanted or did not want their rulers. These rulers had done excellent things, but they were threatened on every side and had fallen into extreme discredit. It looked as if they might fall at any moment; every morning the catastrophe was expected to come before night, and many were prepared to take up the succession. Yet the government successfully resisted every conspiracy against it and—with difficulty—it went on. The truth was that, if between the time of Augustus and that of Claudius the government had weakened, the opposition was also much less strong and energetic than it had been in the days of Tiberius. The aristocratic cliques which attacked the government of Claudius were at variance among themselves, were unskilful, feeble, and rash rather than bold. Public discontent spent itself in speeches; but the army remained faithful to the son of Drusus. Thus the government was able—with difficulty—to limp on its way.

In 48 and 49, however, a new danger arose—this time from within. We have now arrived at the most startling episode in Claudius's history. Everyone has heard how Messalina fell in love with a young senator named Silius, how she was not content that he should be her lover but would marry him although she was the wife of Claudius, how in 49, while her husband was at Ostia, she solemnly celebrated her nuptials with Silius, carrying out all the religious rites in the presence of a horrified and alarmed people, and how finally, when Claudius was informed, he ordered her to put an end to her life. Tacitus, Suetonius, and Dio Cassius agree in this account, which is repeated by almost all the modern historians of Rome, great and small. Yet, in the form in which the ancient writers have handed it down to us, this story is incomprehensible. To explain such an outrageous incident, we should have to suppose not only that Messalina was mad herself (which is possible enough), but also that many other people, including Silius himself, all the magistrates who met together to carry out the marriage ceremonies, and all those who assisted at this sacrilegious travesty were equally demented. This makes a quite improbable number of lunatics, and no one who knows the superstitious veneration of the Romans for all ceremonial, especially ceremonial of a religious character, will believe in it for a moment. If Messalina and Silius publicly solemnized their marriage with the venerable rites of their religion, this must mean that they were in a position to do so, that is to say, that Claudius and Messalina had been divorced. This supposition is indirectly confirmed by Suetonius who says that Claudius had assigned a dowry to be given to Messalina on this marriage.[1] Now, if Claudius assigned a dowry to Messalina he must have consented to the new marriage and therefore have divorced his wife and handed her over to Silius—an arrangement which, as we know, was anything but uncommon at that time among the Roman aristocracy.

[1] Suet., *Claud.*, 26 and 29.

Claudius then had ceded Messalina to Silius and, therefore, had divorced her. But why? What was behind the divorce and the new marriage? We can only answer this question by conjectures, the most probable of which seems to us to be that made by an Italian writer Umberto Silvagni, more especially if a few necessary modifications are made in it.[1] Silvagni observes that Silius, the new husband of Messalina, belonged to a noble family celebrated for its devotion to the party of Germanicus. Silius's father had not merely been one of Germanicus's most intimate friends, but owing to the intrigues of Sejanus, had been charged with high treason, and had been obliged to commit suicide. His mother, Sosia Galla, was a devoted friend of Agrippina, the wife of Germanicus, and for this friendship had been condemned to exile. Starting from these considerations, Silvagni reaches the hypothesis that the marriage of Silius and Messalina in its turn concealed a conspiracy the object of which was to oust Claudius and put in his place Silius who was an important personage and consul-designate for the ensuing year. The sequence of events might then be reconstructed somewhat as follows. Messalina feared that Claudius's government would inevitably be upset one day or another as the result of some revolt or conspiracy. She was not unaware that she was much more hated than Claudius, and that if he were overturned by any successful rebellion she would afterwards herself be eliminated. There was only one way of meeting this peril, and that was for her to remove Claudius, and herself to take the initiative in substituting another emperor for him. Such a

[1] Silvagni, *L'impero e le donne dei Cæsari*, Torino, 1909, pp. 338 ff.

substitute could not be found in the family of Augustus for in that family there was only one other male person, namely, Britannicus, her own son by Claudius, who was at that time a little boy of seven. She had therefore to direct her choice elsewhere and, as the troops were so much attached to the memory of Drusus and Germanicus, the best she could do was to select a family famous for its devotion to this branch of the Claudian house for which it had shed its blood. By marrying Silius and making him emperor, she would at once be enabled to resume her place as empress by the side of a stronger ruler than Claudius.

Some such hypothesis as this seems alone capable of supplying a reasonable explanation of this extravagant episode in Roman history. And if it is a true explanation it places beyond doubt that of all the plots against Claudius that of Silius was the most dangerous. It was hatched in the emperor's own house by an intelligent, energetic, and unscrupulous woman, who had an enormous influence over Claudius, who was feared by the most powerful of his freedmen, and who had friends, clients, and pensioners in every department of State. It is not surprising that Messalina was able to come to an understanding with many high officers of State and influential personages, or that she could lay her plans by patient and skilful manœuvres without raising the emperor's suspicions and without any of his faithful freedmen daring to put him on his guard. Who could have predicted the issue of the struggle between the weak and discredited emperor and the energetic and all powerful empress? There was, however, one possibility of difficulty and danger in this cunningly contrived plan. How was Claudius to be persuaded to divorce his wife without rousing his suspicions? On this point also the ancient historians are very obscure. Suetonius seems to say that Claudius was induced to sign the deed granting Messalina a dowry for her second marriage by a trick,[1] and from the very confused account given by Tacitus, it would appear that no one was more surprised than Claudius when he learned that Messalina was no longer his wife. However this may be, Messalina contrived to make her husband sign the letters of divorce and, as soon as the divorce was secured, hurried to Rome to celebrate her marriage with Silius, which was to be immediately followed by the deposition of Claudius.[2]

The plan was bold, but it might have succeeded if it had been supported by the freedmen of the emperor, and we know that they hesitated up to the very last moment. Claudius was at Ostia. Messalina had already celebrated her marriage at Rome with great pomp, as if to present the new master to the people. Claudius's most faithful freedmen could not yet make up their minds and remained uncertain. It was not till near nightfall that Narcissus decided for Claudius against Messalina and hastened to Ostia. We do not know, and shall never know, what he said to Claudius or what proofs he gave of the conspiracy.

[1] Suet., *Claud.*, 29: . . . *inductus, quasi de industria simularetur, ad avertendum transferendumque periculum, quod imminere ipsi per quædam ostenta portenderetur.*

[2] That there was in fact behind this marriage a political conspiracy to change the emperor is also hinted by the very romantic account given by Tacitus. Cf. *Ann.*, xi., 26: *se (Silium) cælibem, orbum, nuptiis et adoptando Britannico paratum; mansuram eamdem Messalinæ potentiam, addita securitate* . . .; xi., 30: *ni propere agis, tenet Urbem maritus* . . .; xi., 31: *satis constat eo pavore offusum Claudium, ut identidem interrogaret; an ipse imperii potens? an Silius privatus esset?*

It is certain, however, that Claudius, thoroughly dismayed, returned precipitately to Rome, and that once again there burst forth one of those storms of judicial vengeance which from time to time filled the capital with bloodshed and mourning. Silius, Messalina, and a great number of their friends and adherents were charged with high treason, conspiracy, adultery, and a hundred other crimes; some committed suicide and the rest perished by the hands of the executioner.

**47. The Last Years and Death of Claudius (48–54 A.D.).** Claudius was left a widower. While still suffering from the first shock of the catastrophe, he made a speech to the troops in the course of which he declared that, after such a melancholy experience, he would never marry again. But Claudius's intentions, even when most solemnly announced, were never taken very seriously. The old emperor was immediately surrounded by a new series of plots and intrigues the object of which was to make him again enter the bonds of wedlock, for everyone knew that whoever succeeded in giving him a new wife would through her acquire great influence over him. The disastrous end of Messalina, however, had not been without its uses. The public was nauseated by the many scandals and disorders and by the social chaos of recent days. There was a universal cry for a more serious, a stronger, and a more reputable government. Even in the *entourage* of Claudius, among the most powerful of his freedmen there were some intelligent persons who understood that it was impossible to irritate public opinion beyond a certain point and that Rome must be satisfied by the choice of a consort for the prince who would cause Messalina to be forgotten and would, to some extent at least, remind the Romans of the revered figure of Livia. The leader of the party holding this view seems to have been the freedman Pallas whose choice fell upon Agrippina, the daughter of Germanicus and Agrippina the elder, whom Caligula had exiled and whom Claudius had recalled.

Agrippina was then about thirty-three years of age. She was the widow of Cn. Domitius Ahenobarbus by whom she had had a son—the future Nero. She was a well-educated, clever, and energetic woman of unblemished character, the very type of the antique Roman matron, simple, active, and parsimonious. As a mother, says Tacitus, she was *trux et minax;* that is to say, she brought up her son in the ancient severe manner and not in accordance with the more modern and softer notions which were beginning to be imported into Roman houses from the teachings of humanitarian philosophers. The daughter of Germanicus might well be at last the empress dreamed of and desired by the Romans, who would worthily continue the tradition of Livia and restore to the imperial authority something of the prestige it had lost owing to the scandals of recent years.

There was, however, one obstacle. Claudius was Agrippina's uncle. Marriage between an uncle and his niece was not absolutely forbidden, but was regarded by the Romans with a certain distaste. Pallas, however, by skilful argument and action was able not only to persuade Claudius but to remove the difficulty altogether, and the senate was asked by its special authorization to permit the marriage between Claudius and Agrippina. It cannot be denied that the choice was a happy one and that the author of the idea rendered a real service to the empire. The last five years of Claudius's reign were very much more peaceful and fortunate than the first six, and this was due, at least in part, to the influence of Agrippina. The marriage, moreover, came at a favourable moment. The public was weary, as we have said, of scandals, disorders, State trials, and accusations. The parties, or rather the cliques and coteries which, ever since the days of Augustus, had struggled so fiercely in the senate and in the bosom of the imperial family itself were now exhausted. On every side the one desire of the people was for a little rest. And Agrippina—energetic, intelligent, and virtuous—was able to satisfy these aspirations as far as was possible by exercising an influence over the feeble Claudius which was as great as that possessed by Messalina but much more beneficial, and by imparting to his mind something of the firmness and coherence which it lacked. There is no doubt that in his later years the finances were better administered, that peculation was checked, that the arrogance and interference of the freedmen were kept within bounds, and that treason trials and condemnations were less frequent. Part at least of the credit for this happy change is due to Agrippina, and this is sometimes openly admitted and more frequently indirectly admitted by the very historians who, like Tacitus, have bespattered her memory with so many calumnies.

Agrippina, indeed, soon became extremely popular with that part of the people whose only desire was to be governed with honesty and vigour, and who had no preconceived hatred or inexorable rancour against the family of Augustus. There can be no other explanation of the fact that the senate decreed extraordinary honours to Agrippina, such as even Livia had never received. She was authorized to drive up to the capitol in a gilded chariot (*carpentum*) like that reserved for the sole use of the priests and the images of the gods. During her lifetime she received the title of Augusta, and her name was given to the town recently founded in the territory of the Ubii on the Rhine, which was destined to become the famous city of Cologne. All this cannot be attributed to the servility of the senate, for, servile as it may have been, it was decidedly hostile to the imperial house, and Messalina, who was much more ambitious and intriguing than Agrippina, never received such honours, which were, in fact, due to and demanded by the high opinion which the public had formed of the new empress. Still the small clique in the senate which hated the imperial family did not lay down their arms, nor were the ambitions appeased of those who had hoped to overthrow Claudius, and take his place. Indeed the ranks of this party were swelled by the many whose opportunities for dishonest gain had been restricted by the greater strictness introduced by Agrippina's influence into the management of the finances of the State. And all these, while in the senate they acquiesced in the decrees proposed in her honour, murmured against her under their breath, put the worst construction on all her actions, calumniated her best intentions, distorted the significance of all she said and did, and thus created the legend which Tacitus afterwards accepted blindly. But how easy it is, even after all these centuries, for an impartial historian to discover the contradictions and the falsehoods of the traditional story! Agrippina, as we have seen, had had a son by her first husband Domitius Ahenobarbus. She had brought him up very strictly, and had given him the most distinguished preceptors, from whom was Seneca. In the year 50 she procured his adoption by Claudius and caused him to assume the name of Nero which had acquired such glory on the banks of the Metaurus on the day which was perhaps decisive of the great conflict between Rome and Hannibal. In securing the admission of her son into the family of Augustus, she sought to secure both the interests of that family and those of the State. Had not recent events shown how difficult it was to find an emperor outside the Augustan line? If Claudius, in spite of his many weaknesses, together with Agrippina, who was but a woman, had managed to keep the State going was it not partly due to the prestige of their name? But if the family were to retain the supreme power it was necessary that it should possess a certain number of male members from whom an emperor might be chosen. Claudius was an old man, and the only other man in the family was Britannicus, his son by Messalina, then a boy of nine. In 50 the son of Agrippina was thirteen—also a mere child though somewhat older—and if Claudius were to die at that moment there would be no possible successor in the family. It was indeed to be hoped that Claudius might yet live many years, but it was only prudent to prepare the son of Domitius Ahenobarbus for the succession by giving him an illustrious and venerated name. Had not Augustus simultaneously prepared first Drusus and Tiberius, and then Germanicus and Drusus son of Tiberius? Precisely because the office was not yet in any way hereditary it was desirable to leave the senate a certain liberty of choice and to make provision for all eventualities. And what if Britannicus should die young like Drusus and Germanicus?

The enemies of Agrippina, however, did not construe her action in this way. According to them she introduced her son into the imperial family out of hatred for Britannicus, in order to deprive him of his position and prevent him from succeeding his father. Agrippina was so far from wishing to persecute the descendants of Messalina that she betrothed her son to Octavia, Messalina's daughter by Claudius, an excellent young lady, strictly brought up according to ancient principles. In spite of this, it was said that Agrippina was keeping Britannicus in the background, was preventing him from seeing his father, was interfering with his education, and was doing all she could to injure him. It appears also that attempts were made to influence the boy and to poison his mind against Nero and Agrippina, and in fact to recommence the old game of sowing discord among the members of the imperial family. No attempt, however, was made to make a quarrel between Claudius and Agrippina. An empress was practically invulnerable. Messalina had been able to hatch a plot on a vast scale and to carry it to the very point of execution before any one dared to accuse her to the emperor; it was therefore useless to attempt any direct machinations against Agrippina who enjoyed a certain popularity. All the same, sinister rumours were cautiously circulated in whispers in order to discredit her. She was the mistress, some said of Pallas, some said of Seneca. She was insatiably avaricious, proud, domineering, and vindictive. She tyrannized over Claudius and had carefully isolated him. Woe to any young and good-looking woman who tried to go near the emperor!

Meanwhile Claudius's government, feeble, undermined, and discredited, followed its curious destiny and, largely owing to the vigorous support of Agrippina, went on in spite of all. But, suddenly, in the night of October 12–13, 54, Claudius fell a victim to a sudden illness and died. This abrupt end of his curious reign was an event of such grave consequence that it is necessary to examine closely the rumours, the stories, and the fictions to which it gave rise.

# CHAPTER VII

## NERO

**48. The Story of the Poisoning of Claudius and the Election of Nero (Oct. 13, 54, A.D.).** Tacitus relates that Agrippina, disquieted by the preference which Claudius had for some time been showing for Britannicus, poisoned her husband by drugging a dish of mushrooms. Claudius, however, though he felt ill, did not die and, on this, the empress summoned Claudius's physician Xenophon who was devoted to her, and he, on the pretext of curing the emperor, spread a deadly poison on his throat.[1]

This tale is so strange that Tacitus himself when he comes to the final and most improbable incident, that of the doctor, finds it necessary to shield his responsibility behind a "*creditur*." But if, on Tacitus's own admission, the episode of Xenophon is

[1] Tac., *Ann.*, xii., 66–67. It is to be noted that Suetonius (*Claud.*, 44) says that there were many different accounts of the way in which Claudius had been poisoned. He gives several versions entirely different from that followed so confidently by Tacitus. It is also noteworthy that Flavius Josephus (*Ant. Jud.*, xx., 8, 1), a contemporary writer, explicitly declares that the account of the poisoning was a story told by some people. These two facts confirm the supposition that this is another of the many cases of defamatory tales invented against the Julio-Claudian family.

doubtful, what is left of the whole story? Moreover Tacitus himself, in the chapter containing this romantic account, states that Claudius had been ailing for some time, so much so that he had gone to Sinuessa for a cure. Is it not then simpler to suppose that the old emperor, being already ill, succumbed unexpectedly to his malady? The motive assigned by Tacitus for the commission of the crime is absurd. It is more than probable that Claudius, in his heart at least, preferred Britannicus to Nero. Britannicus was his own son, Nero only his step-son. But, even admitting that Agrippina desired her son to succeed Claudius, what danger could she see in this affection? The imperial authority was not hereditary, and the choice of each new emperor, which it fell to the senate to make, depended on many quite uncertain conditions among which the most important was the support of the army. If Agrippina indeed desired that Nero might be the successor of Claudius she must have ardently desired that Claudius might live some years longer. Nero was not yet seventeen and was therefore below the age at which his mother might hope to make him emperor.

Nor is the account more probable which Tacitus gives of Agrippina's intrigues, during the night on which Claudius died, to prevent Britannicus from being chosen emperor and to bring about the election of Nero. If we remember that Britannicus was then only thirteen years of age we shall see how absurd the charges made by Tacitus are. Britannicus was excluded by the mere fact of his age. A boy of thirteen could not be put at the head of the legions and of the empire. On the other hand, if we keep in mind the respective ages of Britannicus and Nero, and admit that Claudius died a natural death, it is not difficult to reconstruct the situation at this critical moment. Britannicus and Nero were the only two male members of the family of Augustus. On the death of Claudius, when the elder of the two was only seventeen, had it not become necessary to seek for Claudius's successor in another family as had already been attempted after the death of Caligula? Was it possible to make the senate elect and to impose on the legions a stripling like Nero who was inexperienced and timid, and still, as it were, at school? On the other hand to seek for a successor in another family was obviously not an expedient which could be very pleasing either to Agrippina or to the freedmen who had become so rich and powerful owing to the favour shown them by Claudius. To attempt such a change might, moreover, be dangerous. And yet if it was to be avoided there was only one thing to be done and that was to confront the senate with the candidature of Nero and to ask them to place at the head of the greatest empire and the greatest army that had yet been seen a mere boy!

Agrippina and her friends must have been in great perplexity during the hours which preceded and followed the death of Claudius. The two alternatives were equally dangerous. It was finally decided to stake all on the candidature of Nero. The move was a bold one because strong, and perhaps insuperable, opposition was to be expected in the senate, if the senate were allowed to discuss the question freely. It was therefore clear that recourse must be had to the same weapon as had conquered the senate's hesitation on the occasion of the election of Claudius. That weapon was the army. Accordingly during the night the prætorian cohorts were warned and prepared by Seneca and Afranius Burrus, the commander of the guard. The great name of Nero—then still the most glorious in Roman history—and the memory of Drusus and Germanicus had their wonted effect on the soldiers. On the morning of the 13th the gates of the imperial palace were thrown open, and Nero, accompanied by Burrus, presented himself to the cohorts of the guard. Acclaimed by them he was placed in a litter and conducted to the camp of the prætorians who in their turn acclaimed him as their chief. Shortly afterwards the senate was convoked and received the official intimation of the death of Claudius, after his successor had already been indicated by the troops. What was to be done? With a bad grace and with many muttered remonstrances the senate ratified the choice. And the senators returned to their homes shaking their heads over an empire which had been entrusted to a boy. Never had there been such a degrading scandal, never such a dangerous situation. To what depths had the great State of Scipio, Æmilius Paulus, and Sulla now descended? What would be the end of it all?

**49. Agrippina and the Restoration of the Republic.** Immediately after the funeral of Claudius, however, the impression of the senators was dissipated by a joyful surprise. Nero appeared in the senate and, in the course of a modest and polished oration, asked their indulgence for his youth and inexperience and invited their counsel and assistance in the performance of his heavy task. He declared that he would restore to them all the civil, judicial, and administrative powers exercised by his predecessors, retaining for himself only the command of the legions.[1] In other words he was to carry out that almost complete restoration of the republic for which the malcontents in the senate had been crying out for so many years, and the senate was once more to have, in all but the military sphere, all the powers it had possessed in the greatest days of the republic.

There can be no doubt that this unexpected restoration of the republic was a skilful move of Agrippina and her friends to mitigate the natural discontent which the election of such a mere boy inevitably caused in the senate, and to make them forget the violence offered by the prætorians to the great assembly. On the other hand the government of a boy of seventeen must necessarily be weak, especially during the early years in which the emperor would be serving his apprenticeship. The support and goodwill of a body which, in spite of its decadence, had still much influence would be of immense assistance to him in that phase of his reign. It was an extremely adroit manœuvre and it was successful. The senate was conquered by the concessions offered to them; they ceased to grumble, and the first two years of the new reign were entirely successful. Nero kept his word and allowed the senate to exercise its functions without interference while he, obediently following the counsels of Seneca, of Burrus, and of his mother, occupied himself entirely with the army. It seemed to everybody that Nero was showing an example of modesty and self-restraint remarkable in itself and still more so in so young a man.

[1] Tac., *Ann.*, xiii., 4: *teneret antiqua munia senatus: consulum tribunalibus Italia et publicæ provinciæ adsisterent: illi patrum aditum præberent: se mandatis exercitibus consulturum.*

But this was an illusion. Nero's contemporaries mistook for modesty and self-restraint what in fact was idleness and indifference. In all aristocracies in which deference to family tradition is considered to be the most sacred duty rebellious spirits every now and then arise who feel compelled to do all that tradition forbids and not to do all that it requires. Nero was one of these rebels of high descent, and his personality and his fate will remain a mystery to us if we do not firmly grasp this point. He was glad to leave to the senate the control of many departments of State, not because of his respect for the constitution but because he found war, law, public affairs—all the pursuits, in fact, which tradition indicated as most worthy of a Roman nobleman, tedious and distasteful. His predilection was for the fine arts, more especially poetry, music, singing, and dancing. He indulged this predilection much more than was thought fitting in a noble Roman, taking much more trouble to cultivate these accomplishments, and in particular to perfect himself in singing and playing, than he did in learning to play his part as the head of the army and the empire. It is easy to see that this was bound to lead very soon to a breach between Nero and his mother. Agrippina was a devotee of tradition and would have had her son devote himself to military affairs, to the administration of the law and the concerns of diplomacy, and not to musical studies. Thus, though Nero was universally popular at Rome both with the senate and with the people, Agrippina was far from satisfied. Riches, power, and adulation soon developed the young man's natural but hitherto latent inclinations, and Agrippina soon saw her son to whom she had so faithfully imparted a severe and thoroughly Roman education, growing into an effeminate fop full of exotic caprices, who lived only for pleasure. She did her best to correct these tendencies; but an emperor cannot be ruled like a son, her efforts soon led to differences of opinion and, owing to an incident which occurred about a year after Nero's election, finally ended in an open rupture.

**50. The Beginning of Family Quarrels—The Death of Britannicus (55 A.D.).** Nero, as we said, had married Octavia, a perfect type of the Roman matron. But he soon showed his foreign tastes by taking a fancy to a beautiful freedwoman named Acte. So violent was his passion that for a moment he thought of repudiating Octavia and putting Acte in her place. This was madness, for the *lex de maritandis ordinibus* made marriage between a senator and a freedwoman impossible. Agrippina opposed the repudiation of Octavia and succeeded in preventing it; but, in spite of her protests, Nero retorted by ignoring Octavia and openly living with Acte as his wife. Once more, this time owing to an amorous caprice, discord had entered the house of the Cæsars. As had always been the case since the days of Augustus, people were not wanting who were ready to turn the quarrels of the imperial family to account by envenoming the dispute. Agrippina, as we have seen, had many enemies. Nero was soon surrounded by a clique who, by flattering his vanity and pandering to his evil passions, hoped to set him against his mother and through him to overthrow her power in the State which they so much detested.

Meanwhile the senate, to which Nero had restored practically all its powers, had begun to govern the empire once more, but in a manner which was feeble and incoherent indeed. The senate had become a senile assembly wanting in powerful leaders, lacking both activity and energy. The authority of an energetic and sagacious prince was now necessary to a State which without it always erred either by excess or defect. But the boy on whom chance had devolved this office thought of nothing but his own amusements and his musical successes. There remained Agrippina who was a resolute woman and had the support of a small but powerful party composed, as Tacitus tells us, of the oldest families of the aristocracy. Since Nero neglected his duties and separated himself from her party, Agrippina drew nearer to Britannicus, the other male member of the family on whom the hopes of the most ancient and conservative nobility were also set. It was, however, in vain, for towards the end of the year 55, Britannicus was suddenly seized with illness during a banquet and died shortly afterwards. It was at once said that he had been poisoned by Nero and this charge has since been repeated by the historians.

This is more probable than many other similar accusations which we find in Roman history, for there was at least an obvious motive which may have induced Nero to get rid of Britannicus. We can hardly venture to say, however, that the case is proved, for several details in the story suggest doubts. Be this as it may, the rumour spread rapidly and was believed, by Agrippina among others, and, whether true or false, it had the effect of still further exasperating the empress mother. Though the death of Britannicus had deprived her of her most potent weapon, Agrippina did not give up the struggle. She drew closer the bonds which united her to the great families. She used all her efforts to stir up among them an opposition which would control Nero, and her agitation was pushed forward with all her usual energy. Nero took alarm, deprived his mother of the bodyguard which had been assigned to her in the time of Claudius, compelled her to leave the palace and take up her abode in the house that had belonged to her grandmother, the mother of Germanicus and, in fact, did what he could to isolate her. She resisted these measures and the conflict between mother and son was embittered.

**51. Nero's Oriental Policy.** Though the senate was inactive and Nero neglected public affairs there was a group of men about the emperor, headed by Seneca and Burrus, who, particularly in military matters, were able to give to the policy of the government the impetus which should have come from Nero himself. This is shown by a great scheme of political activity in the East which was begun early in 55. The preceding emperors had occupied themselves much with Gaul, Germany, and Britain, that is to say with the western provinces, and but little with the East where the Parthians had again put themselves forward to the detriment of Roman power and prestige. At the accession of Nero Armenia was under the government of Tiridates, the brother of Vologeses, king of Parthia. The country was therefore entirely swept clear of Roman influence, and this caused discontent among the Roman public. Nero's government, that is the counsellors by whose opinion he was guided, therefore decided that Eastern affairs, too much neglected by Claudius, must immediately be taken in hand and dealt with more firmly. As Ummidius Quadratus, the governor of Syria, had shown himself incapable, L. Domitius Corbulo, who had distinguished himself some years before in Germany, was sent to the East with considerable forces. The vassal sovereigns were directed to prepare auxiliary contingents, and at the same time negotiations were opened with the King of Parthia to induce him to evacuate Armenia. Vologeses was probably caught unprepared by this threat, and in 55 he made a show of yielding. He asked for peace and gave hostages to Rome, but Tiridates did not leave Armenia. On the other hand, though the troops at Corbulo's disposal in Syria were enough for a military demonstration they were insufficient for a serious war against the Parthian empire. For this it was absolutely necessary to restore discipline among the soldiers, whose moral had been relaxed by life in the East and by the long continuance of peace. It was also necessary to re-arm them and to transfer to the scene of action some of the seasoned legions of the Western provinces. Foreseeing that the agreement of 55 would be a mere truce preparatory to a decisive conflict, and, wishing to reach a stable settlement in the East, those who governed in Nero's name while he lived in discord with his mother gave Corbulo the means of carrying out a reorganization of the Eastern armies.

**52. Poppæa Sabina and the Assassination of Agrippina (March, 59 A.D.).** Thus between 56 and 58 while the discord between Nero and Agrippina was reaching a pitch of frenzy, while the party of the younger nobility and the party of tradition whose struggles had disturbed the State ever since the days of Augustus were regrouping themselves respectively about the emperor and his mother, an army was being prepared in the East which was to be much stronger than any which Rome had maintained in that region for some time. After 58, however, the struggle between the mother and the son took a disastrous and indeed a fatal turn. It was then that Nero, who had forgotten Acte, became enamoured of Poppæa Sabina, the woman who was destined to ruin his life and the whole fortune of the Julio-Claudian house. Poppæa belonged to a wealthy and prominent Roman family; she was very beautiful, highly cultivated, and attractive, and, like her husband Otho, she belonged to that section of the nobility which admired and imitated the manners and customs of the Orient. Her husband was the most distinguished of all the young aristocrats of Rome for his elegance and luxury. It is easy to see what followed when Nero fell in love with Poppæa and in order to have greater freedom, despatched Otho on an honorary mission to Lusitania. Poppæa remained in Rome with the emperor, and, perceiving that her power over him was continually growing, conceived an audacious scheme which was no less than to secure a divorce from Otho and to become the wife of Nero.[1] The emperor was visibly changing his habits, manners, and ideas. In place of his former indifference to politics he now displayed a sudden desire to leave his mark on public affairs. One day, for instance, he appeared without warning in the senate and proposed nothing less than the

[1] Tacitus tells the story of Nero, Poppæa, and Otho in two different ways in *Ann.*, xiii., 45, and *Hist.*, i., 13. We have followed the version given in the *Annals* because it is much simpler, clearer, and more probable than the romantic narrative given in the *Histories*, although Suetonius (*Otho*) and Plutarch (*Galba*, 19) approximate to the latter.

abolition throughout the empire of all the *vectigalia*, that is of all the indirect taxes. These imposts were a great burden to the lower orders and the small traders, and it is therefore impossible to imagine a more popular proposal. But the senate was much disconcerted, because if such a measure were passed the finances of the empire would be bankrupt. There was a long discussion, and, in the end, Nero was persuaded to desist, but he insisted on doing at least something for the people by an edict abolishing many of the abuses which aggravated the burden of these taxes and by exempting soldiers from paying them.[1]

It is possible that Poppæa had something to do with this sudden concern of the prince for his people. Nero was more and more inclined to marry her, but in order to do so it was necessary to repudiate Octavia. Now public opinion would never have tolerated without scandal and protest the divorce of Octavia who was a model of Roman virtue, in order that the emperor might marry a frivolous and immoral woman like Poppæa. In view of the hold which the principles of the traditional Roman puritanism still possessed over public opinion, if not over the private lives of individual citizens, it would be a bold and dangerous step to attempt such a divorce. Nero therefore had to prepare one way to the attainment of his wish by acquiring popularity with the soldiers and the mass of the people. Soon, however, it became clear to Nero and Poppæa that there was another obstacle in the shape of Agrippina. Agrippina had made the marriage between Nero and Octavia, and she had declared that, so long as she was alive, Octavia should not be repudiated.

[1] *Cf.* Tac., *Ann.*, xiii., 50.

In spite of the isolation in which her son had condemned her to live, the empress mother had still sufficient energy and prestige to give the emperor pause in a matter in which she was certain to have the support of public opinion. Nero, moreover, was timid, weak, and vacillating in his methods, and it is not surprising that he became alarmed by his mother's opposition. What followed? We have now reached the most terrible moment in the life of Nero, at which he took the decisive and irrevocable step on the path which was to lead him to ruin and infamy. Was it the effect of Poppæa's seductions that nerved Nero to matricide? Was she assisted in her aims by the many enemies of Agrippina in Rome and in the palace? Did Nero finally convince himself that unless his mother were removed he could never freely enjoy the empire which he regarded more and more as an instrument of pleasure and of luxury? We cannot answer these questions with certainty, but there is no doubt that in the year 59 Nero made up his mind to have her assassinated in accordance with a plan prepared by the freedman Anicetus, the commander of the fleet, by which it was hoped that secrecy would be assured. Nero was not so foolish that he did not know that at Rome even an emperor could not with impunity stain his hands with his mother's blood. Anicetus, therefore, had contrived a vessel with a secret trap-door, and, if Nero could persuade Agrippina to embark, it would be easy to arrange for her to be sent to the bottom, thus burying the secret of her death in the sea.

The account by Tacitus of this infamous murder is too well known to require detailed repetition. In the spring of 59 Nero, who was at Baiæ, pretended to desire a reconciliation with his mother, and invited her to come from Antium, where she then was, to visit him at his villa. He received her with respect and tenderness and when Agrippina, glad and reassured, prepared to return in the ship prepared for her by Anicetus, Nero accompanied her on board and affectionately embraced her. The ship set sail on a fine spring evening; the sea was calm and threatened no danger. Agrippina, reclining on a couch, enjoyed the beauty of the night. But when the sailors opened the trap-door the ship, whether owing to a defect in the machinery or to want of skill or courage on the part of the murderers, did not sink as rapidly as had been expected, but merely heeled over. Agrippina had time to throw herself into the sea, while in the confusion the assassins were killing one of her attendants whom they mistook for herself. At dawn, shortly after the murderers had brought to Nero the news that Agrippina was at the bottom of the sea, there arrived at the emperor's villa one of her freedmen who announced that the ship had been wrecked owing to an accident, but that the empress herself had been able to swim ashore safely, was now at one of her own villas in the neighbourhood, and had sent to reassure her son as to her safety. She had certainly understood the true reason of this extraordinary shipwreck in a calm sea, but she pretended that she had not understood, for this was her last and only chance of escape. What could she do against an emperor who did not recoil from matricide?

Nero, however, was dismayed. He feared that Agrippina would hasten to denounce his crime to the senate and people, and would raise the legions against him. What would happen if the soldiers knew that he had planned the assassination of the daughter of Germanicus? Mad with terror, Nero ordered Seneca and Burrus to be summoned. They had certainly known nothing of his infamous project, but he now told them the whole truth and asked for their advice and assistance. If Tacitus has not over-coloured the picture, the scene which followed was highly dramatic. It appears that at first the two counsellors did not know what to advise. Then Seneca is said to have asked Burrus what would be the consequence if the prætorians were ordered to complete the work which had been commenced. That is to say he hinted, in the form of a question, the advice that Agrippina should be killed. Burrus, however, who did not wish to take such a responsibility upon himself, is said to have replied at once that the prætorians would never kill the daughter of Germanicus, and to have added that, if it had indeed come to that, Anicetus and his sailors, who had begun the work, might perhaps be able to carry it to a conclusion. He also therefore, gave the same advice as Seneca, but he too only hinted it, and left the responsibility with Nero. Nero sent for Anicetus and begged him to save him and give him the empire a second time. And Anicetus, who, if Agrippina were spared, ran the risk of bearing all the blame for the sanguinary imbroglio which had arisen, had no hesitation in sending a party of sailors to murder Agrippina at the villa where she had taken refuge.

53. **The War with Armenia and Parthia (58–60 A.D.).** The irrevocable deed had been done. But the death of Agrippina was an event of such consequence and had happened in such circumstances, that it could not be concealed. It was necessary to give

an account of it that would disarm suspicion. Nero and his advisers sent the senate a report which stated that Agrippina had been discovered conspiring against the emperor and had committed suicide. Her friends however were faithful to her memory. In the version given by the emperor, the account of the conspiracy and her suicide sounded awkward in conjunction with the story of her extraordinary shipwreck to which it had been necessary to allude as everyone knew about it. The official account was not believed; strange rumours were soon in circulation, and through much that was invented and fanciful, the public divined the truth. It made a terrible impression. No doubt the people of Rome and Italy had become very corrupt, but they were not so degraded as not to be horrified at matricide, even when committed by an emperor. Nero was terrified; he postponed the divorce of Octavia and his marriage with Poppæa to a more suitable opportunity, and for several months did not dare to return to Rome. But there were no serious consequences. The horror felt by the public did not manifest itself in any open and irrevocable act. The legions did not move and the senate pretended to accept the official version of Agrippina's death. Though Agrippina, who in her later years had been thoroughly detested, now became an object of universal commiseration, Rome had no means of expressing its sorrow more effectively than in sterile lamentations.

The news which about this time came from the East helped Nero to overcome the dangers of the first and most perilous moment when the impression produced on the mind of the people was fresh. In the spring of 58 Corbulo, as we have seen, had commenced the reconquest of Armenia. The Roman general, by exciting internal troubles in Parthia, had prevented the king from coming to the aid of Tiridates. Nevertheless the conquest of Armenia had proved no easy task. Tiridates had known how to combat the large Roman armies by an implacable guerilla warfare which compelled his adversary to scatter his forces. By the end of 58 Corbulo managed to occupy and burn Artaxata but had not succeeded in destroying Tiridates who reappeared in the following spring to obstruct Corbulo's further advance from Artaxata on Tigranocerta. Guerilla tactics were recommenced but, thanks to superior organization and generalship and at the cost of much hardship, the Roman army succeeded in occupying Tigranocerta in the autumn of 59, and shortly afterwards Corbulo placed on the throne of Armenia Tigranes, a descendant of Herod the Great and of King Archelaus, who had for long lived at Rome. The outlying districts of the country were given to Pharasmanes king of the Iberians, to Polemon king of Pontus, to Aristobulus king of Armenia Minor, and to Antiochus king of Commagene.[1]

**54. The Insurrection of Britain (60 A.D.).** The news of this successful campaign caused great joy at Rome, and helped to mitigate the painful impression produced by the tragedy of Misenum. Since the

[1] On the relations between Rome and Armenia in the time of Nero, *cf.* Furneaux, *The Roman Relations with Parthia and Armenia from the Time of Augustus to the Death of Nero*, in *The Annals of Tacitus*, vol. ii., Oxford, 1896, pp. 96 ff.; W. Henderson, *The Chronology of the Wars in Armenia, A.D. 31–63* in the *Classical Review*, vol. xv., (1901); A. Abruzzese, *Le relazione politiche tra l'impero e l'Armenia da Claudio a Trajano* in *Bessarione*, 1912, pp. 22 ff.

days of Augustus there had never been such a glorious victory in the East. The era of Pompey the Great seemed to have returned; festivals and honours to Nero were lavishly decreed, as if the Eastern question had been settled for ever instead of only for a few months, as turned out to be the case. Nevertheless this elation, though very temporary, helped Nero and was not disturbed by the less agreeable tidings which soon afterwards came from Britain. In the year 60, while Suetonius Paulinus, the governor of that province and the best general in the empire after Corbulo, was engaged in extending the Roman conquest in the western part of the island, and endeavouring to seize the islet of Mona (Anglesey), a venerated sanctuary of the Druids, the whole of the Romanized portion of the country rose in rebellion in his rear. The imposts and levies, the influx of Italian traders, the economic, moral, and political disturbances produced by the conquest had provoked this primary reaction in Britain as in so many other regions. The revolt was serious, but, fortunately for Rome, Suetonius Paulinus by rapid and energetic action was able to subdue it in the course of the year.

55. **Nero and Orientalism; the Emperor's Growing Excesses (60–62 A.D.).** At Rome, meanwhile, Nero now free from the influence of Agrippina, reassured by the oblivion into which his crime had been allowed to fall, and encouraged by his successes in the East, took a bolder step in the direction of his new oriental inclinations. Personal predilection and political motives combined to drive him into this path. He wished to help the people to forget Agrippina by giving Rome and Italy the easy-going, splendid, and generous government which corresponded to the aspirations of

the most numerous and least opulent classes in the State. In 60, therefore, he founded at Rome the *Ludi Neroniani* at the expense of the State, which to some extent resembled the ancient Olympic Games. Like these, they were to take place every five years, and, in addition to athletic contests and chariot races, there were, it appears, also to be competitions in music, singing, eloquence, and poetry. In all these contests the emperor of course took part, accompanied by a train of those who were now called his *augustani*, chosen by himself from among the youth of the Roman nobility on the same principle as the courts of the Hellenistic successors of Alexander the Great. In addition, however, the members of the highest classes, the whole of the *jeunesse dorée* of the capital, were also expected to participate, and did in fact participate, while the *élite* of the spectators on the great occasions attended in Greek costume. The *collegia juvenum* which Augustus had founded in Rome and Italy to be schools for training in citizenship and in the national religion became under Nero the organs of an education half sporting and half theatrical, whose methods and curriculum were wholly Greek.[1] Nero squandered money, was profuse in largesses and spectacles, and commenced great public works at Rome. He opened his house to the most elegant and dissipated young noblemen, and assumed the position of their head and master. Every day there was a feast, now in the house of one, now in the gardens of another. And at these gatherings the last descendants of the families which had conquered the

[1] On the changes imported into public education by Nero *cf.* Barbagallo, *Lo stato e l'istruzzione pubblica nell' impero romano*, Catania, 1911, pp. 61 ff.

world vied with one another in singing and dancing and strove for victory in chariot races. All this was no great novelty for the Romans. Both Rome and Italy had long been familiar with what Nero prized above all things. They had seen the interminable retinues of servants, mules shod with gold and silver and their drivers attired in costly wool, outriders adorned with necklaces and bracelets, golden nets for fishing, luxurious baths, travelling carriages by the thousand, silken garments embroidered with gold, musicians, actors, and gladiators extravagantly paid, sumptuous banquets, magnificent litters, houses resplendent with gilding and marble, crammed with bronzes and pictures, lakes bridged, seas filled up, and mountains levelled to give pleasure to the great ones of the earth. The last century of the republic and the first seventy years of the empire had seen all these things. But at Rome there had never yet been any official encouragement of such tastes and such manners which the Latin West, while it received and tolerated them, had never ceased to regard with diffidence and alarm. The effects of the imperial encouragement on a society hesitating between two paths and two civilizations was necessarily profound. A morbid desire to repudiate the traditions, obligations, and prejudices of their rank seemed to invade the youth of the great families. Dancing became a craze, and skill in this art a higher title to preferment than ability to command the legions. Nero had now cast aside all restraint. His one ambition was to be a great singer, and all earthly glories seemed to him insipid in comparison with success on the stage. The example that he set in fact precipitated the moral crisis in the Roman upper class which had been slowly maturing for two centuries. The dam of ancient puritan tradition seemed to be swept away in a moment by a torrent of luxury, pleasure, and dissipation of which the emperor set the example.

**56. New Difficulties in the East: the final Agreement with Parthia on the Subject of Armenia.** Such a revolution, however, could not but produce a new reaction. Tradition was still very strong, and the mere will of Nero and his young friends was not enough to destroy it all in a few years. In all classes, high and low, there were many who disapproved of these innovations, and murmured against them. It was in these years, between 60 and 62 that the first libels were published against the emperor and his court and the first prosecutions in Nero's reign (which were still mild) for *laesa maiestas* were launched. The death of Burrus, which took place in 62, made the situation worse. His successor was a certain Tigellinus, with whom history has perhaps dealt hardly, but who was at any rate a very faithful servant of Nero. The significance of the appointment was clear. The emperor had freed himself from the last of the restraints imposed on him by his mother and was officially inaugurating his own personal policy. From this moment, indeed, Seneca's influence was finally paralyzed, and early in this year (62) Nero finally divorced Octavia in order to marry Poppæa. A preference for another woman was not yet, however, a sufficient ground for divorce in the eyes of the public, at any rate for an emperor, and a charge of adultery was accordingly trumped up against the unfortunate empress. This, however, gave rise to agitation and disturbance, for the populace openly took the part of Octavia, who was a descendant of

Drusus, against Poppæa whom they regarded as an interloper. Nero, encouraged by Poppæa, held his ground, and in the end Octavia was first condemned to exile and then killed. Poppæa took her place, but the people cherished a lively and affectionate memory of Octavia which was destined one day to be useful to the enemies of Nero, who were becoming ever more numerous.

While Nero's government was producing such alternations of hope, praise, criticism, and hatred at Rome, grave events were developing in the provinces. The successes in Armenia which had caused such rejoicings in 59, had been of short duration. In 61 the King of Parthia sought his revenge. Having allied himself with the King of Adiabene he sent the latter with part of his army to invade Armenia, while he himself prepared to attack Syria, thus repeating the double manœuvre attempted so often by the Parthian kings in their wars against Rome. This time, however, the move seemed to Corbulo to be so threatening, that he left Tigranes with only two legions, collected all the rest of his army in Syria, wrote to Rome asking that an army under a new general should be sent to Armenia as his own was barely sufficient to defend Syria, and opened negotiations with the King of Parthia to induce him to suspend the war and send ambassadors to Rome, allowing it to be understood that a settlement would not be difficult. Meanwhile the King of Adiabene had unsuccessfully attempted to attack Tigranocerta and had been defeated by Tigranes with the two Roman legions and the other forces at his disposal. The King of Parthia was therefore prepared to listen to Corbulo's advice and sent the ambassadors. Hostilities were, accordingly, suspended, but at Rome

Corbulo's prudence, his suggestion that a new army should be sent to Armenia and his negotiations with the Parthians had been very badly received. As has so often happened to sagacious and prudent commanders, Corbulo was accused of cowardice and incapacity by irresponsible persons who formed their opinions in peace and security on the banks of the Tiber. The embassy from Parthia was sent back without an answer. Another general was sent to Armenia as Corbulo had requested, but the selection fell on a certain Cæsennius Pætus, who boasted loudly that he meant to follow a different plan from that of Corbulo who, he said, was a timid fellow. It cannot be doubted that the appointment of Pætus was dictated by hostility to Corbulo who, however, was not removed from Syria.

Pætus arrived in Armenia with his army, apparently in the second half of the year 61, and commenced a bold offensive while Corbulo devoted himself to fortifying the line of the Euphrates. In the following year, however, Pætus seems to have allowed himself to be surprised with part of his troops by an attack delivered by strong hostile forces at a place named Randeia on the river Arsanides, a tributary of the Euphrates. Having by a skilful feint induced Corbulo to mass the best of his troops on the Euphrates, the Parthians had delivered their attack in Armenia. Corbulo had to rush his forces to the assistance of Pætus who was besieged at Randeia, but he was too late. Before Corbulo arrived Pætus had surrendered, and, in order to save his army, had pledged himself to evacuate Armenia, which thus again fell into the hands of the Parthians. In spite of his pledge, Pætus is said to have wished to invade Armenia with his own and Corbulo's united armies, but Corbulo refused, and as the King of Parthia had sent to demand the withdrawal of the garrison posted beyond the Euphrates, negotiations were again opened and it was agreed that the Roman armies should retire behind that river, but that the King of Parthia should withdraw from Armenia.

Armenia thus became once more free both from Rome and from Parthia, and, though at first an attempt was made to claim this result of the war as a triumph for Rome, the truth was soon apparent. All efforts to gain a solid footing in Armenia had failed. Nero consulted all the most eminent persons in the empire and it was decided to make another attempt. Pætus was recalled and Corbulo was placed in sole command of a strong force. Faithful to his original method Corbulo in 63 used the powerful army entrusted to him as an instrument of intimidation with a view to reaching an agreement. Rome and Parthia were, in fact, equally weak in Armenia, and thus it was possible this time to come to terms. Tigranes was definitely set aside. Vologeses obtained what he had asked for in 61, the investiture of his brother Tiridates as King of Armenia. But the brother of the Great King had to submit to receiving his regal diadem from Nero's hands, and had to go to Rome for that purpose. A Parthian prince was to sit on the throne of Armenia as a vassal of Rome—such was the effect of this tedious transaction.

Meanwhile the revolt of Britain had not exhausted itself. The very energy of Suetonius's repressive measures seemed to add fuel to the flames. The prince therefore found it necessary to order an inquiry to be held on the spot and finally entrusted the province to a new governor (62). But while it had become necessary to send reinforcements from Germany to Britain and to raise new levies for drafts to fill up the gaps in the decimated legions, the empire on the line of the Danube had to deal with a series of small and intermittent attacks by the tribes living beyond the river and had to undertake regular campaigns against the Sarmatians and the Scythians,[1] the success of which raised the question whether a great Caucasian expedition was not necessary.

**57. The Burning of Rome (July, 64 A.D.).** At Rome, in the meantime, Nero seemed to take a pleasure in flouting even more audaciously that section of public opinion which was most attached to tradition. It was about this time, in the year 64, that Nero did the maddest thing he had done since the murder of his mother—he appeared on the stage in the theatre at Neapolis, before a regular audience, as a public singer. He had not chosen Neapolis as the scene of his artistic début by chance, for Naples was then a Greek city where Roman prejudices were unknown. Nevertheless it is easy to imagine what were the feelings of Italy and of Rome on hearing of this extravagant proceeding on the part of the son of Agrippina. The Romans regarded the stage as an infamous profession, however necessary it might be to the pleasure of mankind. That a Claudius, the descendant of the most ancient and illustrious family of the Roman nobility, should condescend to appear on the stage in the dress of a player and solicit the applause of an audience of Greeks was a scandal which in a

[1] There is no mention of these wars in the ancient writers, but they are vouched for by the evidence of inscriptions, cf. *C. I. L.*, xiv., 3608.

sense was worse than a crime! A crime might excite horror; an action such as this excited merely contempt and disgust. For men who have to rule over their fellows it is better to inspire neither horror nor contempt nor disgust, but of the three evils to inspire horror is the least.

The effects of this caprice, however, were not immediately visible, for a great calamity shortly afterwards occurred which distracted public attention from it. This was the fire, famous in all history, which broke out in Rome in July, 64, and devastated the city for ten days, destroying, practically completely, ten of the fourteen districts into which it had been divided by Augustus. Immediately on hearing of the disaster, Nero returned hastily to the capital where, however, he was unable to prevent the destruction of his own house. He did all he could to mitigate the irreparable loss which had been sustained. He opened the public buildings and his own gardens to the people who had been made homeless; from the neighbouring towns he sent for everything necessary for the repair and equipment of these temporary shelters as far as that was possible, and he took energetic measures to provide against the still greater calamity of famine.

All the emperor's zeal, however, could not prevent a strange rumour, as to the cause of the fire, spreading among the people more swiftly than the flames which had destroyed the city. A whole library has been written on this question, so many are the hypotheses, as ingenious as ill-supported, which have been framed to account for this memorable conflagration. There is indeed no means of proving that Rome was burned by Nero, or that the fire was started by the Christians or by the friends of Piso with whom we shall shortly have to deal. The most simple and probable explanation will always be that Rome was burned by accident like so many other cities. Americans know that the burning of an entire town is unfortunately a catastrophe which is anything but uncommon in countries where most of the houses are still built of wood, and such was the case in Rome at that time, especially in the poorer quarters. On the other hand it is clearly much more probable that in the hot season a fire which began accidentally in a few houses would spread to whole quarters, especially if the fire brigade was deficient, than that a single man or a group of men should conceive the extraordinary idea of burning a whole city and should succeed in their design. But the first impulse of men when stricken by a great disaster is to attribute it to their own kind. When there is scarcity they blame speculators in food; when their armies are defeated they suspect treason; when there is an epidemic they say that they have been poisoned. So in those days the Roman people became convinced that the city had been maliciously set on fire. But by whom? We must not forget that Nero by his excesses, his prodigalities and his crimes, by his easy and free-handed government at once attracted and terrified the popular mind. It is therefore not surprising that the burning of Rome appeared to the masses as a divine punishment for the new and illicit pleasures which for ten years the prince and his people had together enjoyed, and for all the excesses to which he had given himself up and into the vortex of which the people had been swept. From this state of mind, in which they were ready to believe in any criminal origin of the fire, it was but a step to the conviction that it had been deliberately contrived by the emperor himself. The story was in fact that Rome had been burned by Nero's orders and, though (as Tacitus himself admits) this was absurd, it was believed by many.

**58. The Christians and " the First Persecution."** The belief that the fire was the work of criminals was so general that the authorities had to institute an inquiry for the purpose of discovering the guilty parties. The conclusion of this investigation laid the responsibility for the conflagration at the door of the Christians, a religious sect the name of which was for the first time publicly pronounced on this occasion. This sect had come into being about forty years previously in Judæa in the bosom of Judaism. For centuries the Jews had expected that God would send them a Messiah who would rescue the people from servitude and restore them to their pristine glory and independence, and would make them, in return for their perfect observation of the divine law, the chosen people on earth. Towards the end of the eighth century after the foundation of Rome the Messiah had appeared in the villages and townships of Judæa declaring himself to be the Son of God, but proclaiming, not a national revival but the approaching end of the world and the near advent of the Kingdom of God. On this great day the Messiah would appear in the clouds surrounded by angels, his disciples would sit round him on thrones, the dead would arise and the Messiah would proceed to judgment. The good and the elect clothed in light would participate in the eternal feast prepared by Abraham, while the condemned would be sent to Gehenna. Men should prepare themselves for the Kingdom of God which was imminent, by listening to the Messiah, by freeing religion from all the external forms and fetters by which Judaism had, as it were, shackled it, and by practising a system of morality of sublime nobility and purity. The supreme law of the spirit, was to be love, fraternity, peace between master and servant, between man and woman, between Jew and Roman, between citizen and foreigner, and hatred against the negation of all these things, the hypocrisy of the Pharisee, the avarice of the rich, the pride of the great. It was to be a spiritual hatred, however, not the violence of rebellion; for the beginnings of the Kingdom of God were in the souls of those who were converted.

The herald of God's Kingdom found in Judæa a certain number of devoted disciples, but his work was soon cut short by the persecutions of the decadent Jews. After the death of Jesus, however, the new sect, persecuted in Judæa had crossed the borders of that country under the guidance of the first and most faithful disciples and had gradually diffused itself over the whole empire among Jews and pagans alike, multiplying its little communities in great cities and small. For the original announcement of the Kingdom of God, of the end of the world, and the Last Judgment which was to follow the appearance of the Messiah, had been substituted—and to this had greatly contributed Paul of Tarsus a remarkable man converted to the sect after the death of Jesus Christ—the doctrine of the redemption of mankind from original sin and from evil which had been achieved by the blood of Jesus Christ the Son of God who had sacrificed Himself on the cross. To the moral system of Jesus, which above all inculcated brotherly love, was added—this too partly as a result of Paul's work—the doctrine that the love of Christ required men to repress the strongest passions known to Græco-Roman society, which were sensuality and cupidity. Thus the new Christian sect had entirely separated itself from Judaism and had even abandoned circumcision, one of its most ancient and venerated rites. For thirty years it had been slowly propagating itself in the Roman Empire and had penetrated into Rome itself, where it had made many converts, especially among the lower classes—slaves, freedmen, and foreigners of oriental origin. Perhaps too in the time of Claudius, its growing importance had given rise to a violent reaction against it on the part of the numerous Jews living in the capital.[1]

It would be difficult to say what led the Roman government to charge with the burning of Rome this sect which had devoted itself to elaborating a system of the most sublime morality. It is possible that the wild excesses of Nero and the burning of Rome seemed to many Christians to be the very calamities which, according to Jesus, would precede the end of the world and the advent of the Kingdom of God. Moreover, among the pagans in the city, there was much distrust of the secret ceremonies and singular practices of the Christians and, what was more serious, the Jews and the Christians at Rome, as everywhere else, were at daggers drawn. It is therefore not improbable that the satisfaction or indifference which many Christians showed about the fire which was the beginning, so they said, of the end of all things, were promptly accepted as evidence of their guilt, that the vague suspicions which were current were at once diverted from the prince who required a scapegoat on whom the public could wreak vengeance, and that the

[1] Suet., *Claud.*, 25.

charge was brought home to the Christians by the calumnious delation of the Jews and by the confessions extracted by torture from the weaker of those who were first accused.[1] Thus began what is known as the first persecution of the Christians, which, however, is incorrectly so described because, though the Christians were the victims of persecution, they were not persecuted because they were Christians.[2]

**59. The Rebuilding of Rome; a Great Financial Crisis Throughout the Empire.** The fire had been a calamity but not an irreparable one. It was left to Nero to aggravate the loss by his ambition to build at once on the ruins of the old city a new one of surpassing beauty. The city which had been destroyed was the old town which had been hurriedly rebuilt on the ruins caused by the fire at the time of the Gallic invasion. It had grown up, century by century, as chance dictated. It had been embellished as far as was possible by Agrippa and Augustus, but in the mass it was a rude city if contrasted with the great capitals of the East. Nero wished to give the empire a capital whose beauty and magnificence were equal to the empire's power and glory. His idea was not wanting in greatness and nobility, but enormous sums of money were required in order to carry it out rapidly, and to procure these Nero had recourse to the most perilous expedients. Most of the sudden condemnations and confiscations in cases of treason, the fines for new and strange offences, the whole long

[1] Tac., *Ann.*, xv., 44; *primo correpti qui fatebantur*.

[2] On the burning of Rome as on all insoluble historical problems, a whole library has been written. One of the most recent studies is that of C. Pascal, *L'Incendio di Roma e i primi cristiani*, in *Fatti e leggende di storia antica*, Firenze, 1903.

series of pecuniary penalties which contemporaries and posterity alike have attributed to the unexampled ferocity of the prince and his ministers, were really due to this want of money. But, as these sources proved insufficient, the empire was bled white. From the most famous sanctuaries, from public buildings and private houses were torn the precious offerings of the faithful, the images of the gods, the most valued statues. Public offices and contracts were again put up to auction, and governors were once more compelled to make money out of the subject populations. The burden of taxation was made heavier and there was a revival of the most pedantic methods of extortion. Nor was Italy immune from the scourge. Immediately after the fire Nero ordered a general contribution to meet the most pressing needs of the city and the people of Rome. In addition to this he began in the same year to depreciate the coinage by issuing light money. The *aureus* which, as coined by Augustus, had been practically pure, fell from an average of 7.64 to 7.36 grammes, and the fine silver *denarius* of the first days of the empire was reduced from 3.90 to 3.40 grammes while the percentage of alloy rose from 5 to 10 per cent. It was Nero who commenced the bad currency policy of the empire which was destined to have such evil results.

**60. The Conspiracy of Piso (65 A.D.).** All these circumstances explain why the two years which followed the burning of Rome were the most critical in Nero's reign, and why in the year 65 there was a great conspiracy among the aristocracy against the emperor. The head of this movement, C. Calpurnius Piso, belonged to one of the noblest Roman families. With him participated in the plot senators and knights, plebians and republicans of the straitest sect, officers of the prætorian guard (among whom was actually one of the two præfects, Fænius Rufus the colleague of Tigellinus), the poet Lucan and, finally Seneca, Nero's old tutor. It appears that the object of the conspirators was to kill Nero and make Piso emperor in his place. The plot was discovered by a mere accident and, as might be expected, was punished with merciless severity. Trials and condemnations lasted through all the year 65 and went on into the following year. Lucan, Seneca, and C. Petronius, whose work is so much appreciated nowadays, and a great number of senators and officers fell victims. And after the conspiracy was suppressed, as often happens in such cases, Nero, whether intoxicated with his own power or exasperated by the terror he had suffered, far from reforming his ways, went from bad to worse and abandoned himself entirely to his unbridled passions.

**61. Nero's Journey to Greece and the Revolt of Judæa.** Towards the end of 66, the emperor left Italy for Greece accompanied by a crowd of Augustani, admirers and *claqueurs*, an army large enough—it was said—to take the field against the Great King. Nero intended to take part in the contests of the periodic Greek Games which he had ordered to be performed together all in one year! Never had a prince been seen to degrade himself, according to Roman ideas, in a manner so indecorous in the presence of his oriental subjects. A prince who was an actor was for the Romans the last and worst disgrace.

Nero had scarcely arrived in Greece, however, when news reached him of grave events in Judæa. That country had suffered from a prolonged crisis ever since the time when within its narrow borders the Syrian

Hellenism of Græco-Macedonian colonists, with its cosmopolitan tendencies, its scepticism, and its material sensualism had come face to face with the native Mosaic religion. That religion was at the same time the most living and the most exclusive of oriental creeds, and a body of rites and rules of piety, of purity, and of conduct in practical affairs which knit together like the links of a coat of mail the life of each individual Israelite with the entire national life. Its exclusive spirit had strengthened the national aversion from foreign government, and *vice versa*, as had been proved by the history of the Seleucid monarchy which owed its tragic fall in great part to this circumstance. Roman policy had profited by the critical state of the country, but Rome had soon found herself face to face with the same difficulties—that is to say she had to govern a country in which religion fomented political discontent, and political discontent with a foreign rule exacerbated religious fanaticism. Little by little, while the Roman rule was being consolidated in Judæa, the country was invaded by Italians and Greeks who, with the aid of the government, exploited the country as best they could. As the pressure of the tribute to which the country was subjected under the Roman government gradually increased, the religious intransigence of the masses became more ferocious; once more announcements of the imminent arrival of the Messiah who this time was to liberate Judæa and not establish the Kingdom of God, had begun to agitate the minds of the people. An anti-Roman party—the so-called Zealots—as implacable against their luke-warm compatriots as against the foreigner, had inaugurated a veritable reign of terror in Judæa, justifying the habits of brigandage common among certain tribes in Palestine by religious and nationalist enthusiasm. For many years the cities and the country of Judæa had been distracted by murders and fighting in which religious fanaticism and hatred of greedy and domineering foreigners found expression along with the anarchical instincts latent in so many individuals and peoples. The situation became more serious in 65 and 66 owing to the question of the administration of Cæsarea which the Jews wished to be Jewish and the Greeks Greek. After much disorder, rioting, and negotiation, rebellion openly broke out towards the middle of 66. At the end of September in that year the small Roman garrison which had barricaded itself in the three forts dominating Jerusalem capitulated and was put to the sword, and the troubles in Judæa spread to the whole of the south of Syria, as far as Egypt, where, in the larger and smaller cities the Jews made attempts at revolutionary movements. Cestius Gallus, the governor of Syria, hastily collected an army and resolutely invaded Palestine, having decided to annihilate the insurrection by a single blow. At the price of heavy sacrifices Cestius succeeded in entering Jerusalem, but could not manage to take the temple, within whose walls the rebel army had fortified itself. Being unable to maintain himself in the hostile city he decided to leave Jerusalem and encamp in the vicinity, but during his retreat was attacked by the revolutionary troops, suffered serious losses, and was compelled to withdraw as far as Antipatria.

**62. Titus Flavius Vespasianus.** The impression made at Rome may easily be imagined. All Nero's enemies loudly demanded what was to be the end of the emperor's much vaunted foreign policy. In

Armenia, after tremendous efforts a peace had been first refused and then accepted which implied the final renunciation of Armenia itself.[1] In Britain peace had been purchased at the price of conceding the demands of the natives,[2] and there were ceaseless wars with the Trans-Danubian and Caucasian tribes. Now, in addition to all this, they had to contend with a rebellion in Judæa! The emperor, it must be admitted, met the danger promptly and energetically by finding the man who was needed, not among the illustrious descendants of ancient families. That man was T. Flavius Vespasianus, a senator whose nobility was of very recent origin. His grandfather, Titus Flavius Petronius, came from Reate and was a modest plebian who had fought at Pharsalia as a centurion under Pompey and had afterwards been pardoned by Cæsar. Flavius Sabinus, the son of the centurion, had grown rich as a tax farmer and banker, first in Asia and then among the Helvetii. He had two sons both of whom had taken up a political career (being the first members of their family to do so) and had entered the senate. Of these Vespasian was the younger. He had occupied the whole series of public offices, including the consulship, had campaigned in Britain under Claudius, though without any special distinction, and had kept himself safely apart from the serious dangers of intervening in the struggles by which Rome was distracted at that time. To this obscure senator Nero now entrusted the direction of the war in Judæa, and

[1] These criticisms may be traced rather in the authors followed by Eutropius than in Tacitus, *Eutrop.*, 7, [*Nero*] *imperium romanum et deformavit et diminuit. . . . Armeniam Parthi sustulerunt.*

[2] *Cf.* Tac., *Ann.*, xiv., 38 and 39.

placed at his disposal immense forces collected from all parts of the empire.

63. **The War in Judæa (67 A.D.).** The Jewish war was destined to be one of the most terrible in the history of Rome. True, the Hebrews lacked the concord and organization which alone make it possible to carry on war against a powerful State possessed of powerful forces. The upper classes, though they desired independence, thought the Romans invincible, and had a horror of the religious and nationalist fanaticism from which the rebellion had taken its rise, and in which they clearly perceived the germs of a social revolution. The rebels, therefore, were unable to find among the classes which alone could supply them, a sufficient number of trustworthy leaders who could co-ordinate the national forces and discipline the popular fanaticism. But this fanaticism was so intense and so highly stimulated by the Zealots, among whom were to be found enthusiasts of all classes, that, even without a supreme control to co-ordinate their forces, the resistance of Judæa, scattered though it was over a great number of centres, was terrible. When in 67 Vespasian entered the rebellious province at the head of 60,000 men, he had to reconquer it city by city, village by village, at the cost of unheard-of slaughter. It took a whole year to reconquer Galilee. It was not until 68 that the Roman general was able to enter Judæa proper and even then it was not to march straight on Jerusalem, which was the main centre of resistance, but to conquer in the first place the minor centres which were numerous. Although dissensions had broken out, between the Zealots and the Moderates, who had lost hope and wished to treat with the

Romans, Vespasian had a desperate struggle, especially before the walls of Jericho. And when Jericho fell at the end of May, and his way to Jerusalem lay open, grave events in the West jeopardized the whole result of this long and sanguinary conflict.

**64. Preparations for a Great War in the Caucasus and the Revolt in the West (67–68 A.D.).** Nero had gone to Greece in 67 squandering money, seeking to revive the customs and traditions of the past and busying himself with games and feasting. These however did not quite exhaust his activities for Nero who, as we have repeatedly said, was not without a certain largeness of view in public affairs, formed the plan of cutting through the Isthmus of Corinth and was preparing another expedition to the extreme eastern boundaries of Europe which Pompey alone, in the course of his weary pursuit of Mithridates, had seen and known, to the so-called *Portæ Caspiæ* in the region of the Caucasus. This expedition was undoubtedly intended to dam up once and for all the insistent and annoying raids of the Scythian and Sarmatian tribes into the most easterly European provinces. The emperor had been meditating this enterprise for years, but his plan had been frequently postponed and it was only now that he had definitely made up his mind to carry it into execution. He had taken important steps with this object, had raised two new legions, and had detached numerous units from all the legions of the eastern and western armies. The levies of citizens from the provinces had been made more strict, Italy herself had had to furnish a contingent of her own, a *legio Italica* which was denominated the *Phalanx Alexandri* and was destined to be placed under the orders of the new Alexander the Great.[1] But in the midst of these plans and dreams, in the midst of the feasts and the excursions to which he gave himself up during the winter of 67–68, the emperor was informed that the situation in Italy was giving cause for concern. He therefore returned thither at the beginning of 68 just in time to hear that an insurrection had broken out in Gaul.

The governor of Gallia Lugdunensis who had taken the initiative in this revolt was a Romanized Gallic nobleman of Aquitania named C. Julius Vindex. That a Roman of such recent date whose ancestors had been Celtic barbarians should have been the first to feel it his duty to rise in rebellion against the unbridled orientalism of Nero was no mere accident. It is the first instance of a phenomenon the historic importance of which we shall soon see—the force which Roman ideas and sentiments had acquired among the upper classes in the western provinces. In northern Italy, in Spain, and in Gaul there were rich families which, though they had been Romanized for only a few generations, were more fervid in their attachment to the traditions of the aristocratic republic than the ancient families of the Roman nobility. However that may be, the attempt of Vindex does not seem to have been in itself very dangerous. Not having an army he had tried to collect one secretly among the Gauls, and had at the same time endeavoured to excite against Nero several generals whom he believed to be at variance with the emperor. But only one of these lent an ear to his solicitations and that was Servius Sulpicius Galba,

[1] On this design *cf.* Pfitzner, *Geschichte der Kaiserlegionen*, Leipzig, 1881, pp. 39 ff. Henderson, *The Life of the Emperor Nero*, London, 1903, pp. 226–227.

the governor of Hispania Tarraconensis. He was a serious, energetic person, a rich man of very ancient lineage, by family tradition little inclined to the Julio-Claudian house, and like all the serious portion of the nobility, disgusted by Nero's misgovernment. On the death of Caligula he had been spoken of among others as a possible emperor. Thus when Vindex raised the standard of revolt he found himself alone, and Nero, without very much anxiety was able to direct the governor of Germania Superior, Lucius Virginius Rufus, to repress this attempt at rebellion. Virginius in fact beat Vindex, who committed suicide, in a short battle at Vesontium (Besançon). But Nero had no cause to rejoice at the victory, for the victorious army had proclaimed Virginius emperor on the field of battle, and this was followed by the revolt of Galba and the Spanish legions.

**65. The End of Nero and the Fall of the Julio-Claudian House (June, 68).** Nero tried to resist his fate. He caused the senate to declare Galba a public enemy. He ordered the forces which had been despatched to the *Portæ Caspiæ* to turn back, and directed that the sailors of the fleet at Misenum, the former murderers of Agrippina, should be organized in legions and kept ready to embark for Spain. He sent couriers to the legions in Illyria with orders to proceed to Aquileia. He decreed a special war tax, armed slaves, public and private, and, emboldened by the gravity of the situation, he deposed the consuls whom he did not trust and declared that he himself would lead his legions against the rebels. But his fate depended on the loyalty of the army, more especially on that of the prætorian guard, and by his crimes, his excesses, and his extravagances Nero was too much discredited even in the opinion of the mass of the population and therefore of the soldiery. Encouraged by the growing signs of a breakup of the government, the senators hostile to Nero and the friends of Galba did all they could to undermine this loyalty. It seems certain that they succeeded in coming to an understanding with Nymphidius Sabinus, one of the two præfects of the prætorians and the colleague of Tigellinus, and through him with some of the officers and part of the guard itself, even it is said with a Germanic cohort which was specially charged with the personal safety of the emperor. When, however, Nero understood that he was faced with a conspiracy on a larger scale than Piso's, that his own prætorians were betraying him, he completely lost his head, and with a few friends and some soldiers, who, he believed, would be faithful to the last, he fled for refuge to the *Horti Serviliani* on the *Via Ostiensis* which had already sheltered him during the conspiracy of Piso.

The prince having disappeared, the government automatically reverted to the senate, but the majority of Nero's enemies did not agree among themselves. Some wished to restore the republic forthwith. Others desired to entrust the defence of the State to Galba, others to make Virginius Rufus emperor. On the other hand, the leaders of the movement among the prætorians, though inclined to depose Nero, had absolutely decided not to give up any of the privileges which the empire had procured for them and in particular the right to make a profit out of the new transfer of the imperial dignity. Nymphidius Sabinus cut the knot of these uncertainties by convoking the prætorians and persuading them that, as Nero had disappeared, their only course was to unite themselves with the Spanish legions and proclaim Galba emperor. The energy of the soldiers once again overbore the hesitations and discord of the senate.

The senate was now no longer free to choose. If they decided against the proclamation of the prætorians, they were setting themselves up in opposition to the forces in Spain and at Rome, and again raising the chances of the Neronian minority. If on the other hand they accepted the decision of the prætorians, they were abdicating their own will. There was a sharp struggle and a long discussion in the senate. The coalition of various opposition groups easily secured a decision in favour of the deposition of the reigning prince and of his being declared an enemy of the State (*hostis publicus*) but in spite of this it was found impossible at a single sitting to decide who the new emperor was to be. Indeed the people believed that the republic was at once to be restored and prepared great demonstrations of joy such as Brutus and Cassius had vainly hoped for a hundred and ten years before on the fatal Ides of March. But the republic could not be ruled without force. The senate had no arms and the generals whom they believed to be most faithful to the republic such as, for example, Virginius Rufus were far away. A second sitting decided the fortune of the State. They had no alternative but to concur in the election of Servius Sulpicius Galba.[1]

The empire was safe but Nero was lost. He had

[1] There were certainly two sittings (Zon., xi.–13) though in Zonaras neither the programme assigned to each nor the interval between the two is correctly given. On all this question *cf.* C. Barbagallo, *La catastrofe di Nerone*, Catania, 1915.

left his hiding place which he had finally felt to be unsafe, and, after an adventurous journey by night, had succeeded in reaching the villa of a faithful freedman outside the Porta Nomentana. On the way he had heard the shouts of the prætorians acclaiming Galba and cursing his own name. In this house he had lived several days until the morning of June 9, 68—the date is a probable but not absolutely certain conjecture—and on the arrival of the soldiers who came to lead him to execution he finally killed himself with his freedman's aid. He was not yet 31!

The Julio-Claudian family was extinct. The last of its members had disappeared after making for ever infamous the name of Nero which, since the days of the second Punic War, had been one of the most glorious in Rome.

# CHAPTER VIII

## THE FIRST GREAT CRISIS IN THE HISTORY OF THE EMPIRE

**66. The Reign of Galba (June 9, 68–January, 69 A.D.)**[1] The new emperor intended that his government should be the very opposite of Nero's, simple, economical, full of respect for tradition and deference to the senate and firm without being arbitrary. These were excellent ideals but hard to realize in these troubled times. Galba, moreover, did not possess the qualities necessary for success in such a difficult enterprise. He was old, rich and parsimonious, severe and narrow-minded, violent and weak, obstinate and maladroit as noblemen often are. He showed this at once by committing a series of errors which caused a rupture between him and those who had at first been his supporters. On his journey through Gaul he ill-treated the cities which had opposed Vindex, sowing discontent everywhere and offending the legions from Germany which had crushed the revolt raised by the Gallic noble. He added to this affront by depriving them of their general Virginius Rufus, to whom the legions had in vain offered the empire, and

[1] On the reign of Galba *cf.* C. Barbagallo, *Un semestre di impero repubblicano* in *Atti della R. Accademia d'Archæologia lettere, etc.*, Napoli, 1913.

by substituting for him another officer without prestige or authority. Next he quarrelled so violently with Nymphidius Sabinus that the offended prefect tried to organize a new conspiracy among the prætorians to have himself elected emperor in place of Galba. The plot was discovered and suppressed and Nymphidius and several officers perished, but from this moment the prætorian guard ceased to be faithful to Galba. In revenge Galba refused to pay the prætorians the donation promised by Nymphidius, which naturally aggravated the difficulties of the situation. Difficulties and discord arose also with the senate, and particularly with the party which dreamed of a complete restoration of the old republic. Many were disappointed with the dictatorial and sometimes positively violent manner in which Galba exercised his supreme authority. Finally he was much damaged by the measures which he took to re-establish the finances of the empire, more especially by the commission he appointed to investigate the expenditure of Nero, and the donations he had made. The gifts Nero had given had been sold, left as legacies, given away again, divided, improved, increased, and mixed with other property so that it was now impossible to go back on the past without an infinity of litigation, contestations, and complaints. Moreover, Galba tried to reintroduce into the administration of the empire the old republican parsimony which Nero had cast aside, and had suppressed all festivals and other unprofitable expenditure. It was a wise move, but it alienated from him many people, especially among the lower classes, who were accustomed to live comfortably at Rome on the money scattered by Nero. Thus many of those who under Nero had cursed the mad prodigality of the emperor were now ready to murmur against the meanness of Galba.

For all these reasons, Galba's government soon caused much discontent at Rome which the friends of Nero, the partisans of Nymphidius who had escaped punishment, and the disappointed republicans did not hesitate to foment as much as they could. It was not long before some began to lament the disappearance of Nero. This opposition would not however have been very dangerous had there not been added to the difficulties of the moment another difficulty which had hitherto been evaded or circumvented, but which now for the first time appeared in all its force. That difficulty was the great uncertainty which existed as to the legal principle from which the supreme authority of the emperor was derived. This is a point of such vital importance in the history of the empire that it is necessary to understand it thoroughly. Little by little, under the pressure of circumstances, the supreme imperial authority had arisen, had become consolidated in the ancient aristocratic republic and was now an absolute necessity owing both to the growth of the empire and the internal changes which had taken place in the State. The legal principle however on which this authority was based was, as we have seen, election by the senate and not hereditary right, which was an oriental and dynastic principle repugnant to Roman ideas. We have also seen that from Augustus to Nero the emperors were all chosen from the same family, but that this was due to political necessity and not to any family right. The senate had always asserted its right of election very feebly, either because the assembly no longer possessed its ancient prestige, or because it was lacerated by internal discord, one party being too much interested in maintaining the new authority, the other averse to it on principle and anxious for its abolition. This weakness had given an opening for the intervention of another power, the military, in the choice of emperors. Claudius and Nero had been imposed on the senate by the prætorians and Galba by the Spanish legions. It is easy to imagine how these precedents in troubled times like those succeeding the death of Nero, when the empire and the army were not controlled by a firm hand, might give rise to the assumption in the rude minds of the soldiers that the legions had the right to elect the emperor. The example set by the legions of Spain in proclaiming Galba had been especially serious. If these legions had elected the emperor and the senate had recognized the election why should not the other legions have the same right? The *esprit de corps*, the natural emulation and the desire to imitate, which were so strong in all the armies, were bound, in the existing great uncertainty as to the legal principle of the supreme power at a moment of civil disturbance, to lead each army out of *amour propre* to desire to have its own emperor.

**67. The Revolt of the Legions of Germany and the Fall of Galba (January 1–15, 69 A.D.).** It was in fact the legions of Germany which gave the signal. They had been offended by Galba as we have said, and they nursed their resentment throughout the year 68. Excited by the news from Rome and by the lively discontent throughout Gaul, which was due to Galba's ill-treatment, badly led (at least as regards the legions of Germania Superior) by the weak general sent to them by Galba, driven by a kind of madness which was shortly to infect almost all the armies, and exalted by every sort of chimerical hope, the legions of Germania Superior and Germania Inferior proclaimed Aulus Vitellius, governor of the latter province, emperor in the early days of January, 69 amid the greatest popular enthusiasm. This revolt was enough to bring about the collapse of Galba's government at Rome within a very few days. When he received the news Galba decided to carry out a plan which had for some time been mooted of strengthening his government by choosing a younger colleague whom he was to adopt as his son. It appears that this measure was due to a desire to make up for Galba's many shortcomings and also to avoid new difficulties about the succession at his death. Effect had not yet been given to the suggestion because among Galba's friends and advisers there were different opinions as to who should be chosen. Some wished for Nero's old friend Otho, who had been Poppæa's first husband, while others had set their hearts on divers other candidates. The news from Germany precipitated a decision, but Galba did not choose Otho, perhaps because he had been too much Nero's friend. His choice fell upon L. Calpurnius Piso Licinianus, a man who represented an entirely opposite tendency, who by family tradition and personal inclinations belonged to the most conservative branch of the Roman aristocracy and who was an enemy of Nero and one of the last living examples of the old school of manners. The meaning of this selection was clear, and Otho after the adoption of Piso did not hesitate to form a conspiracy among the prætorians for Galba's overthrow. The guard were discontented with the emperor, because he had refused to give them the donation promised by

Nymphidius, because he had been imposed on the senate not by themselves like Claudius and Nero but by the legions of Spain, and finally because he had endeavoured to make even their discipline more rigorous. It was a troubled time; men's minds were in a state of agitation and Rome in chaos. On January 15th Galba's reign came to an end. A military revolt which began among a single maniple of the guard spread to the whole of the troops stationed in Rome and to a great part of the civil population, who were angered by the parsimony of the new government. M. Salvius Otho was proclaimed emperor and Galba and Piso were murdered.

**68. Otho and Vitellius: Italy Invaded by the German Legions (January 15–April 16, 69 A.D.).** When Otho returned on the evening of that fatal day from the senate which had unanimously ratified the proclamation of the prætorian guard he was saluted by the cheering crowds that thronged the streets by the name of Nero. Galba's government had already caused many to forget the vices and crimes of his predecessor. Otho showed no repugnance to this title. He caused Nero's statues to be set up again, and some ancient historians even affirm (though it is not certain) that he actually assumed Nero's name in his first official acts. He did his best at any rate to restore to Rome and to the empire, weary of Galba's harsh and avaricious reign, the easy-going and generous type of government at which Nero had aimed, but accompanied by greater moderation, coherence, and good sense. It cannot be said that, on the whole, Otho governed badly. He granted an amnesty to all those who had been accused under his two predecessors. He treated the prætorians with generosity and tact, allowing them to elect their own prefects. He did his best to conciliate and reassure the senate. He resumed the great building operations in Rome commenced by Nero, and tried to avoid violence, confiscation, and repression. Otho, in short, became popular in Rome and his government seemed also to be consolidating itself in the provinces. Chiefly because his election had been ratified by the senate he was recognized by the legions of Syria and Judæa, by those of Dalmatia, Mœsia, and Pannonia, by Egypt, by all the oriental provinces, and by all Africa. Gaul and Spain, on the other hand, after some hesitation, and owing to the powerful attractive force of the legions of Germany, declared for Vitellius. The legions of Britain seem to have remained outside the conflict. On the total reckoning Otho had on his side a part, though the smaller part, of the western provinces, Italy, all the East, and all Africa: enough perhaps to bring the rebellious legions in the West to their senses. Nevertheless, Otho wrote privately and repeatedly to Vitellius urging him to spare the State the scourge of a new civil war and assuring him a prospect of power and riches and a most splendid and pleasant retirement. Undismayed by initial rebuffs he continued the negotiations. He pledged the credit of the senate itself and endeavoured to resume directly with the armies of the Rhine the *pourparlers* for an honourable compromise, to which their leader had refused to listen. Otho, in short, wished to avoid war and, if war proved inevitable, not to appear responsible for it, for all Italy was terrified, and not without reason, by the storm which lowered on the horizon. Italy had enjoyed precisely a century of peace and quietness, tranquilly cultivating her fields and adorning her cities. She had forgotten what war, and especially civil war, was like, and, lo, all of a sudden it was again suggested that a torrent of armed men would descend upon the face of the country destroying everything in its course.

All Otho's endeavours, however, were in vain. Vitellius was now the prisoner of his own legions. Exalted by a mistaken sense of honour, by mad hopes of recompense and booty, and by a kind of delirium which had taken possession of them, they would hear of nothing but invading Italy at any cost, and imposing their own emperor on the world. They would have murdered Vitellius if he had insisted on making peace. The only result of the parleying which had taken place was to impel Vitellius and his generals to take the offensive before Otho could send for the legions of the Danube. Profiting by the hesitation and delays of their adversary, they occupied during the winter the Alpine passes which Otho had left unguarded, and thence they invaded Italy with two armies. The first of these, under Fabius Valens, having crossed Gaul was to enter Gallia Narbonensis and from there by way of the country of the Allobroges and the Vocontii was to debouch on the plain of the Po through the Cottian Alps. The other, commanded by Alienus Cæcina, was to invade Italy through the country of the Helvetii and the Pennine Alps. The two forces were to effect a junction in the valley of the Po. The revolt in favour of Vitellius of a body of cavalry stationed in that valley precipitated the execution of this plan. Cæcina, who had reached the territory of the Helvetii, hastened to cross the Alps in midwinter with his army and, probably as early as February, the valley of the Po was in the hands of Vitellius.

Otho was now also forced to take arms. After the loss of part of the valley of the Po he sent the fleet to disembark troops in Gallia Narbonensis to threaten the flank of the army of Valens and to try to prevent its arrival in Italy. While he awaited the coming of the Danubian legions he collected and armed other forces, and, on March 14th, he left Rome with all the troops for the moment at his disposal and with most of the magistrates and ex-magistrates and some of the equestrian order.

It had been decided that, pending the arrival of the legions from the Danube, the line of the Po was to be defended. An attack by Cæcina on Placentia (Piacenza) was in fact vigorously repulsed by Otho's generals. Unfortunately, however, the force Otho had sent to Gallia Narbonensis to detain the army of Valens beyond the Alps had not succeeded in its task. Valens had crossed the Alps and was on the point of joining Cæcina in the valley of the Po. On this Suetonius Paulinus, the father of the historian and Otho's best general, had abandoned the defensive south of the river, and had crossed to the northern bank in order to seek battle with the enemy before Valens should arrive. Not far from Cremona, at a place called Locus Castrorum, he succeeded in inflicting a serious defeat on Cæcina but not in enveloping and destroying him. Thus, although he was defeated, Cæcina contrived to escape and join Valens who had already reached Ticinum (Pavia). Otho then called a council of war at which Suetonius expressed the view that, as it had been impossible to prevent the junction of Aulus and Cæcina they should postpone giving battle until the arrival of the legions of the Danube. Another plan, however, was adopted concerning which the details given by ancient writers are very obscure. It appears that Otho meant, by a flank march to north of Cremona, to transfer to a point west of that town at the confluence of the Adda and the Po, the forces which he had at Bedriacum east of Cremona, so as to cut the communications between Vitellius who was crossing the Alps and his army at Cremona. Otho was himself to remain at Brixellum (Brescello) and wait for the army which was coming from Aquileia. With this army and that which had passed west of Cremona he was to encircle the enemy and compel him to surrender before the Vitellians could arrive. If this was Otho's plan, its success depended on his flanking force reaching its objective. But, whether because the enemy were informed of his design or because his generals, several of whom were opposed to the plan, did not properly execute the emperor's orders, the Vitellians succeeded in barring the way and attacked Otho's army on the march outside Cremona. A battle followed—known as the battle of Bedriacum—which resulted unfavourably for Otho's army. The defeat however was in no way decisive, and Otho would easily have recovered himself if he had but awaited the arrival of the great forces which were on the point of joining him. On the news of the reverse, however, the emperor committed suicide, not so much, we may legitimately conjecture, because he had lost a battle as because of his despair at the stupendous disorder into which the empire had fallen. Otho was a refined and intelligent person and, in spite of his defects, no ordinary man. He must have seen that Nero's government of which he had been a supporter had brought the empire into a situation so critical that he did not feel he had strength to extricate it. He had in fact collapsed under the burden of his position.[1]

**69. Vespasian and the Revolt of the Eastern Legions (July, 69).** After Otho's death Vitellius, who had not yet crossed the Alps, remained master of Italy. Otho's soldiers still attempted to resist and offered the empire to Virginius Rufus who refused it. Finally, however, as they had no head and were assured of pardon, they resigned themselves to acknowledging the victory of the German legions and swore fidelity to the victor. The senate, having returned hastily to Rome, ratified the proclamation of Vitellius as emperor, and the images of Galba, crowned with laurel and with flowers, were carried round the city. Thus Italy in her anguish turned once more on her bed of thorns, and, after having identified the government of Nero with the clement and sagacious rule of Otho, now tried to regard the government of Vitellius who had meanwhile arrived in Italy with the third army which, like the other two, was in great part composed of Gallic and German mercenaries, as a continuation of the régime of Galba. Italy was now for the first

[1] On this war and on the wars between the Flavians and the Vitellians *cf.* B. W. Henderson, *Civil War and Rebellion in the Roman Empire, A.D. 69–70*, London, 1908. The explanation we have given of Otho's plan of campaign is that which Mr. Henderson has worked out in this book with much ingenious argument. It is still somewhat obscure and open to objections, but it remains the most satisfactory explanation for any one who is not content with the incomprehensible account of Tacitus. Mr. Henderson's conjecture depends on two main arguments: (1) the fact that Tacitus (*Hist.*, ii., 40) explicitly says that Otho's army was directed *ad confluentes Padi et Adduæ fluminum;* (2) that it is necessary to find some military reason for the emperor's presence at Brixellum instead of the romantic one which satisfied Tacitus,

time to learn what it meant to possess an army of which the components, whether legionaries or auxiliaries, were to such a great extent non-Italian. On its way across Italy towards Rome the army pillaged the country and was swollen as it went by a nameless crowd of new-found friends, followers, and admirers; senators, knights, idle plebians, parasites, athletes, strolling players, charioteers, gladiators—in a word, all the rabble of which in Nero's time the city and the court were full, and which now crowded about the chariot wheels of the conqueror in order to pick up fragments of the spoil amid the general confusion.

Vitellius, like many other emperors, was better than his reputation. When he arrived at Rome in July he did his best to reduce the terrible confusion of public affairs to some kind of order. In choosing his ministers he replaced freedmen by knights whom moreover he forbade (as a class) to appear as performers in the theatre or the circus. In the senate he made a point of being treated merely as an ordinary senator. He disbanded the old corps of prætorians. He was anxious to send the legions back to their provinces and tried to mitigate the bitter rivalry which separated the Othonian and the Vitellian troops. At the same time he caused the statues of Nero to be raised again in order to please the multitude, another proof of the persistent popularity of the last of the Claudii among certain classes in the community. He did not however, entirely devote himself, as was afterwards alleged, to the giving of sumptuous feasts, but tried his best to restore some measure of peace to the weary empire. It was hoped indeed for a moment that the tempest was over, but suddenly it recommenced more violently than ever. After the West the East was now in motion, and the legions of Judæa, Syria, and Egypt took the field.

We left Vespian in the spring of 68 on the point of commencing the siege of Jerusalem. The disastrous end of Nero shortly afterwards checked his activities. It appears that, not wishing to commit his army to such a serious enterprise while things were so uncertain, he contented himself with holding the most important positions in the neighbourhood of the city, suspending meanwhile the active prosecution of the siege. His legions, therefore, were permitted to enjoy some degree of rest while the whole empire was in flames. At first they did not abuse this privilege. Partly owing to their greater distance from Italy and partly because among them the non-Italian element was represented by orientals, the legions of Judæa, like those of Syria and Egypt, were at first content to remain inactive spectators of the conflicts which were developing in the West. But, as time went on and the struggle became more complicated, they too began to be invaded by the madness which had infected all the other legions. Why should the legions of Germany impose an emperor on the senate and enjoy all the advantages of such a power, any more than the legions of the East? Were they of less account than the others? The oriental provinces, it must further be remembered, and therefore the legions stationed there, had, for obvious reasons, been much more favourable to Nero than Italy and the West. This explains their prompt recognition of Otho. But now Otho was gone and the legions which for two years had been fighting the most obstinate enemy of the empire were invited to accept the caprice of the soldiers of Germany or of the unwarlike Roman senators who had overthrown

Nero's lawful rule! With these sentiments were mingled apprehensions of a more practical sort. How would the new princeps treat those, whether soldiers or generals, who in the civil war which was so recent had declared for his rival? Thus, from the earliest days of the reign of Vitellius there had been negotiations between the East and the West, between the legions of the Danube which had not had the opportunity of fighting against Vitellius, and the legions of Syria, Judæa, and Egypt, with the object of finding a new emperor who could be set up against the emperor of the German legions. Their first choice was Mucianus, the governor of Syria, a man of much merit and of the most illustrious descent, but as he refused, Vespasian was finally selected. Vespasian lacked both high birth and ambition, but the times were critical and his army, his son Titus who was both bold and intelligent, and Mucianus himself who had previously been far from friendly, all insisted. On July 1st, in the year 69, therefore, the præfect of Egypt proclaimed T. Flavius Vespasianus emperor at Alexandria. Some days later the armies of Syria and Judæa swore fidelity on the images of the new prince, and a little later the legions of Mœsia, Pannonia, and Dalmatia, which had had no opportunity of fighting either for Nero or for Otho, also swore allegiance to Vespasian. The oriental princes of Sophene, Commagene, and the independent part of Judæa also declared themselves adherents of the new candidate. Even the King of Parthia undertook not to molest the empire during the war which would be necessary in order to establish the new emperor.

**70. The New Civil War and the Victory of Vespasian (July–December, 69 A.D.).** Titus was to carry the siege of Jerusalem to a conclusion while Vespasian was to go to Egypt to take secure possession of the granary of the empire, so as to be able to starve Rome out if necessary. Mucianus was to take part of the army and assume command of the legions of Pannonia, Mœsia, and Dalmatia with which he was to invade Italy. Such was the plan which Vespasian and his generals concerted at Berytus in Syria. It was a vast, but at the same time, a skilful and prudent combination, which aimed at securing its object slowly but surely. The impatience of the Pannonian legions substituted for it without the knowledge of their leaders another plan which was more summary as well as more dangerous. The commanding officers of the legions stationed in Pannonia partly because recent news from Italy showed that an immediate attack would take the Vitellians unprepared, and partly because they wished to be the first to divide the honour and the spoil of the undertaking, met in council at Petovio (Pettau) on the Drave in upper Pannonia, and, on the proposal of Antonius Primus, decided to invade Italy at once without waiting for Mucianus. Antonius Primus, who in the time of Nero had been expelled from the senate to which he was re-admitted under Galba, was undoubtedly a bold and valiant soldier as was shown by this audacious initiative on his part. The Vitellian army was really in a condition, no doubt transitory, of disorganization and reorganization. The general to whom had been entrusted the defence of eastern Italy was Alienus Cæcina who had had but little success in the preceding campaign. Operating with a slackness (which might easily be mistaken for treachery) in spite of his superiority of numbers he allowed Antonius Primus to reach the line of the Adige with considerable forces. There, hearing that the fleet at Ravenna had gone over to the enemy, he made up his mind that further resistance was useless and proposed to his soldiers that they should desert also. Indignant at such treason the legions put their general to the sword, decided not to yield and retreated on Cremona with a view of joining their comrades there and resisting to the last. Antonius Primus however, with lightning rapidity, followed them towards Cremona. Between Redriaco and Cremona and almost under the wall of the latter town was fought an exceedingly violent action which lasted a day and a night and ended in the complete defeat of the Vitellians. The best army which Vitellius had in Italy was thus practically destroyed and, on hearing of this defeat and of the treachery of the fleet, Fabius Valens, the other Vitellian general, fled to Gaul where the Narbonese province had also declared for Vespasian. Shortly afterwards, when all the Alpine passes had been barred by Antonius Primus against the threat of reinforcements which might have come from Germany, the fleet at Misenum also joined the rebels. Mucianus in his turn arrived in Italy with the legions he had brought from the East, and his army, like that of Antonius Primus, was advancing through central Italy on Latium.

On this the Flavian party at Rome which consisted of the old Neronian and Othonian party together with Vespasian's few personal friends, led by T. Flavius Sabinus the præfect of the city who had been appointed by Nero and reinstated by Otho in that office, persuaded Vitellius to yield and to abdicate, thus making the renunciation which he had refused to make in January, 69. Now, however, as before, Vitellius was not master of his destiny. He belonged to the legionaries of Germany from whom he had selected the new prætorian cohorts, to the maddened soldiers who had rushed back to Rome from the line of the Po, to his own friends and even to the rabble of the city desperate after a year and a half of civil war. This time, as before, he was compelled to resist. And the resistance on the part of his friends and supporters was obstinate and ferocious. The city had to be taken by storm and conquered, quarter by quarter, house by house, garden by garden, by the rebel army converging from three different directions. The Capitol was burned. Sabinus was slain and Vespasian's younger son, the future emperor Domitian, escaped as if by a miracle from the fire and the carnage. Finally, however, on the evening of December 21st, after long and ignominious tortures, Vitellius himself was thrown into the Tiber.

## CHAPTER IX

### THE FLAVIANS (69–96 A.D.)

**71. The End of the Crisis.** As soon as Rome had fallen into the hands of Vespasian's generals the senate hastened to recognize the victor. We possess part of the text of the law by which the comitia ratified the senatus consultum which conferred the empire on Vespasian.[1] In this law are enumerated the powers which, having first been conferred on one or other of his predecessors, were now handed over to him. We do not know with certainty whether a similar *lex de imperio* had been passed in previous cases. Perhaps however it is not an accident that the fragment of this law which has been handed down to us engraved on a bronze tablet, should relate to Vespasian. It is clear that in engraving this enactment on bronze—and not merely in Rome—it was intended to publish as widely as possible the legal credentials of the new emperor's authority. Vespasian was the first emperor not belonging to the family of Augustus who really ruled. His name, therefore, was not enough, as in the case of Claudius and Nero, to serve as a subsidiary title for his authority side by side with his more or less free election by the senate. And, as the terrible crisis

[1] The *lex de imperio*, or rather the fragment of it which has been preserved, is to be found in *C. I. L.*, vi., 930.

through which the State was passing sprang from the wavering uncertainty of the legal principle on which the supreme power was based, it is easy to see why it was desired to emphasize, by engraving it on bronze, the most important title to the empire possessed by the man who had hitherto been no more than an ordinary and very obscure senator, namely, the will of the people and of the senate who had elected him.

There was, moreover, no time to be lost. The crisis was anything but over. The new emperor was in Egypt and his friends in Italy were confronted by difficulties of every kind. The surviving forces of the Vitellians gave, it is true, less cause for anxiety than the remnants of Otho's army had lately given to the Vitellians, but they were not altogether to be despised. Mucianus was compelled to postpone the reorganization of the army until the arrival of the new princeps and had to content himself with temporary expedients. On the other hand he had to take immediate measures in Gaul, where an insurrection commenced among the Batavi, a Germanic tribe, who lived near the mouth of the Rhine, with a view to helping Vespasian against Vitellius, had gradually spread to other tribes in the neighbourhood, involving all the fighting auxiliaries of the legions stationed on the Rhine, and several Gallic populations, such as the Treviri and the Lingones, hitherto most faithful to Rome. The movement was led by four men of great capacity and valour, the Batavian Julius Civilis, Julius Classicus, and Julius Tutor of the Treviri, and Julius Sabinus of the Lingones. Under their influence the revolt against Vitellius had been converted into a national movement tending to separate Celtic, and Celto-Germanic Gaul from the Roman Empire. Assisted by the remnants of the Vitellian forces on the Rhine, the insurrection had made such progress that Mucianus had to send a considerable force against the rebels, amounting to seven legions under Q. Petitius Cerialis. Gaul was easily reduced to submission but the war with the Batavians was much more difficult and was only ended, partly by force of arms and partly by diplomatic negotiation, in the autumn of 70. At the same time there were raids by Sarmatians and Dacians into Mœsia which was empty of troops. Troubles and forays distracted Africa, and the Jews within the walls of besieged Jerusalem were offering a desperate resistance to Titus the emperor's son. It was not until August 29th of this year that the temple was burnt out, and not until a month later that the upper city shared the same fate. The figures given by the ancients of the losses sustained by the Jews are certainly exaggerated, but the carnage must have been terrible. The slaughter, such as it was, was not enough to tranquillize the country, for sporadic groups of desperate men resisted for more than a year longer.

The terrible crisis in the history of the empire caused by the fall of the Julio-Claudian house and the uncertainty of the legal principle of the transmission of the supreme authority was not really terminated until 72, when the revolt in Gaul, the revolt in Judæa, and the minor troubles of the empire were definitely disposed of, and when it was made clear to all that Vespasian, who had come to Italy in 70, could exercise seriously and in its entirety a universally recognized authority, and, in a word, that the empire really had a princeps again. All now depended on how the new ruler would govern.

**72. The Government of Vespasian and Titus.** Vespasian, as we have seen, was the grandson of a centurion, and the son of a publican. He and his brother had been the first of their family to enter the senate and to reach high office and high military rank. He was therefore a *homo novus* like Cicero. This was a serious source of weakness in dealing with the historic Roman aristocracy who were so proud of their ancestors. But Vespasian was an intelligent, sensible, and well-balanced person who had been tempered to the difficult duties of command by a long apprenticeship of obedience in minor offices. With the aid of these qualities improved by time he discharged his difficult mission with striking success. One of the first things he did was to imitate Augustus by making his son Titus his colleague in the empire. On July 1, 71, the conqueror of Judæa received the tribunician power and the consulship which from this year were periodically renewed to him and to Vespasian. Titus, therefore, from this date onwards found himself in the same relation to Vespasian as Tiberius had been to Augustus in the last ten years of his reign. Thus what is usually called the government of Vespasian should more properly be termed the government of Vespasian and Titus, so impossible is it to distinguish in the complex achievement of Vespasian which is the father's share and which the son's.

The objects and the advantages of this appointment, which the services rendered by Titus in Judæa amply justified, were several. First and foremost Titus, being a young man, after being his father's colleague would in the natural course of events become his successor, as Tiberius had been the successor of Augustus. Vespasian might therefore hope that the appointment of Titus would eliminate from the selection of his successor the uncertainty which had been so disastrous at the time of the death of Nero, and also that he would thus be enabled to leave the succession to his son without introducing the oriental and dynastic principle of hereditary right into the constitution. Moreover, Vespasian, who was old, in this way secured a young and energetic collaborator in the work which awaited him, a vast and difficult work which had three main objects: the reorganization of the army, the readjustment of the finances, and the renovation of the senate.

**73. The Military Reforms of Vespasian and Titus.** As regards the army Vespasian fixed the number of the legions at 29 or 30; the exact figure is uncertain. Many veterans were discharged and provided with lands. Certain legions which, like the 8th and the 16th German legions, had been too seriously compromised in the revolt in the provinces, were disbanded and replaced by others newly formed. The civil war had shown the danger of having legions containing too large a proportion of provincials who had been made Roman citizens, and the still more serious danger of having numerous auxiliary bodies all drawn from the subject peoples. But this was an evil which Vespasian could not remedy, for Italy in her progress towards riches and civilization could not furnish a sufficient number of soldiers. Now even the sons of small proprietors were unwilling to enlist unless they were made centurions. Italy in a word was more and more restricting herself to furnishing the armies with their complements of officers.[1] Italy alone, on the other

[1] On the military reforms of Vespasian *cf.* Pfitzner, *Die römische Kaiserlegionen*, Leipzig, 1881, pp. 68–73.

hand, furnished the imperial guard whose political importance had so much increased that Vespasian entrusted its command to his own son. In this way the danger of a new Sejanus or a new Nymphidius Sabinus was obviated, but the concentration of power in the hands of a single family acquired a dynastic character.[1]

**74. The Rearrangement of the Finances.** Far more imporant, however, were the financial reforms. In the history of Roman finance Vespasian is of capital importance because he was the first who ventured to increase and multiply taxes of all kinds throughout the empire. Since the time of Augustus one of the fundamental principles of Roman finance had been to interfere as little as possible with the existing system of taxation, alike in Italy and in the provinces, to avoid increasing imposts as far as possible, and, whenever it could be done, to reduce them. This prudent and conservative financial policy had been one of the reasons for the continual embarrassments in which the imperial government had found itself, embarrassments which each emperor had tried to meet by expedients—some good and avowed, others bad and unavowable. Under Nero, for example, one reason for the many unjust prosecutions of rich men involving the confiscation of their property was the fact that the imposts did not bring in enough to carry on the administration of the empire in accordance with its growing necessities. Thus the finances were constantly in disorder and the public services neglected. The civil war had made matters worse; so much so that Vespasian on his accession to power, after a rapid examination of the situation had declared that the empire required at least four milliards of sesterces if it was to be put de-

[1] *Cf.* Suet., *Vesp.*, 25.

finitely on a proper footing.[1] Not wishing to raise this money by spoliation and violence, he reduced to the position of a province many countries which the generosity of his predecessors had left at liberty, as well as several small States hitherto autonomous, though in a state of perpetual vassalage to Rome. Such were Achæa which Nero had liberated, Lycia, Rhodes, Byzantium, the kingdom of Commagene, and such parts of Thrace and Cilicia as still remained independent (73). He set up a rigorous and universal survey of the empire which enabled him to discover numerous places and persons who had in one way or another escaped paying tribute or had never been subjected to it. It seems that he also contrived to secure for the State a share in the improper but now, owing to long prescription, inevitable gains which many magistrates made out of their public functions. Finally—and this was his main reform—he re-established all the imposts that had been abolished, increased all the existing ones and augmented, sometimes even doubling, the direct tribute payable by the provinces.[2]

It is easy to understand why the empire endured these new burdens without excessive complaints. Italy and the provinces had been greatly enriched by

[1] Suet., *Vesp.*, 16: *professus quadragies millies opus esse, ut respublica stare posset.* Others read *quadringenties millies.* But four milliards of sesterces seems a more probable sum than forty milliards. We must not forget that, in its totality of wealth, the ancient world was very much poorer than the world of today.

[2] Suet., *Vesp.*, 16: *Non enim contentus omissa sub Galba vectigalia revocasse, nova et gravia addidisse, auxisse tributa provinciis, nonnullis et duplicasse. . . .* This passage is of capital importance in the history of the empire, for it proves that Vespasian introduced the fiscal system by which the empire was brought to ruin.

the century of peace and quietness of order and secure communications which they had enjoyed. In every district agriculture, industry, mines, and commerce had developed. The population had increased. The East was flourishing again and the West was beginning to prosper. Vespasian—to his great credit—understood that the empire could stand an increased pressure of taxation. By imposing this pressure he did the empire a great service, for he thereby furnished the means of doing the great things which made the age of the Antonines illustrious in peace and war. Nevertheless it was he who initiated the policy of great expenditure and increasing taxation which, growing from generation to generation, ended by making the Roman treasury the ruin of the empire.

75. **The Great Reform of the Senate** (73 **A.D.**). Of even greater moment was Vespasian's reform of the senate. The weakness of the senate had been one of the chief causes of the crisis which followed the death of Nero. Vespasian, though he was an Italian recently ennobled, could not take the view that this evil might be remedied by substituting a new authority for the senate. In his eyes, as in those of Augustus, Tiberius, and Claudius, the destinies of the senate were the destinies of Rome itself. But he was a sensible man, and therefore could not conceal from himself that the customary procedure which had been used since the days of Augustus was quite inadequate to effect the regeneration of an institution so much enfeebled by age. This was especially the case after an atrocious civil war, in the course of which so many senatorial and equestrian families had been destroyed. Taking advantage, therefore, of the severe shock which the great crisis had given to the pre-

judices, the doubts, the inertia, and the selfishness of the ruling cliques and classes, he ventured on a measure which many people had for long recognized to be necessary, but which no one had dared to carry out from fear of the rigid exclusiveness of ancient Roman ideas. In 73 he caused himself to be elected censor, and not only expelled unworthy members from the senate, but at least effected a vigorous infusion of new blood into the senatorial and equestrian orders. Carrying out on a great scale and with much more vigour the policy which Claudius had already timidly adumbrated, he introduced into the two orders about a thousand new families, already, of course, possessed of Roman citizenship, choosing them not only in Italy, but also among the richest, most highly respected and most influential inhabitants of the provinces.[1] From the names of these families which are known to us we may conclude that the greater number came from Northern Italy, Spain, and Gaul, and some from Africa, while the East supplied a much smaller number. The reason for this difference is clear. In the western provinces, which when conquered were still barbarous, many families had grown rich during the past century and had adopted the ideas and the manners of Rome, which to them was a model of high culture and civilization when compared with the rudeness of their own country. In the East, on the contrary, the new families which had risen to opulence and culture since

[1] Suet., *Vesp.*, 9: *amplissimos ordines . . . purgavit; supplevitque recensito senatu et equite, submotis indignissimis, et honestissimo quoque Italicorum ac provincialium allecto;* Aurel. Vict., *Cæs.*, 9: *lectis undique optimis viris mille gentes compositæ.* Here *gentes* simply means "families." These two passages are of the highest importance in the history of the empire.

the time of Augustus had become Hellenized rather than Romanized. Thus in the space of a century there had grown up in Spain and Gaul a local aristocracy with some grasp of public affairs which had not only learned to speak good Latin and to admire Rome in the immortal work of Livy, but had also learned in the schools from the great books of Virgil, Horace, Cicero, and Varro, all the ancient virtues of the Roman aristocracy. To these virtues, which the Roman aristocracy had itself now almost entirely lost under the influence of Hellenism, and of which the chief were economy, simplicity, subordination, respect for tradition and public spirit, they added a certain moderation and humanity and a largeness of view derived from the new spirit of the time. Such were the families to whose care Vespasian confided the empire when he summoned them to Rome to take part in the government.

This renovation of the senate by the addition of elements drawn from the Romanized provinces of the West, an event of capital importance to which historians have not yet given its due prominence, was the most important consequence of the tremendous crisis through which the empire passed after the death of Nero. After this trial the tenacious opposition offered by the narrow selfishness of the old senatorial families to every proposal for the reconstitution of the old assembly disappeared. Vespasian was able to do what Claudius had timidly attempted. But it is his immortal glory to have been able to carry out this reform when it was most needed, for it supplied precisely that reinforcement of the Roman element to which was due the peace and prosperity enjoyed by the empire for a century—that is to say, throughout the so-called age of the Antonines. By means of this reform the West was once more to save Rome and all Rome stood for. Just as the conquest of Gaul had prevented the centre of the empire from being displaced from Italy towards the East, so the Romanized nobility of the occidental provinces preserved for another century in the institutions of the empire a republican and a Latin character. Vespasian understood so thoroughly that Rome must seek new strength from her European provinces that his censorship culminated in the grant of Latin citizenship (*ius Latii*) to Spain, one of the oldest and most completely Romanized of the provinces (74).

**76. Hellenism and Romanism under Vespasian.** It cannot, however, be said that Vespasian was a traditionalist emperor like Tiberius. In a certain sense his policy was self-contradictory; indeed, on its contradictions its fruitfulness depended. Thanks to the circumstances of his time Vespasian is distinguished as the emperor who succeeded for a moment in balancing the eastern and the western provinces of the empire. He was not an avaricious emperor according to the Latin tradition like Tiberius and Galba, nor a prodigal emperor of the Asiatic type like Nero. He resembled Tiberius in being sparing in his personal expenditure and strict in levying taxation, but he was the first of the emperors who were wise enough to spend largely, having grasped the fact that the new generation would not tolerate a parsimonious government such as Augustus, Tiberius, and Galba had given them, and that, in view of the increased needs and the higher aspirations of the people, such a policy was henceforth impossible. His expenditure on public works was therefore large. The roads in Italy and in the provinces and the aqueducts were repaired.

The archives in the Capitol were rearranged and the Capitol itself rebuilt. Throughout the empire cities which had been destroyed by fire or earthquakes were restored. On the frontiers Vespasian constructed military roads and traced powerful lines of fortifications, especially on the Rhine and on the Danube. He formed great intrenched camps, such as those of Vindobona (Vienna) and Carnuntum (Petronell). He strengthened the fleet on the Danube and founded numerous military colonies. He also spent much money on festivals, banquets, spectacles, and ornamental buildings. At Rome he repaired the theatre of Marcellus and began the construction of the Flavian Amphitheatre now known as the Colosseum, which remains the most grandiose of the monuments of ancient Rome. Like Augustus and Tiberius he was generous in giving assistance to noble families fallen into want, and zealous in repairing ancient temples and restoring the most archaic forms of traditional religion.[1] But he was ready to move with the times and, recognizing that the people had a right to be amused, he gave splendid money prizes to actors and musicians. He was the first to give State protection to the arts, by assigning allowances, amounting to a million sesterces, to certain of the most celebrated Greek and Latin rhetoricians (among whom was Quintilian) who taught at Rome. Similarly he granted rewards of various sorts to poets, sculptors, and architects, but he expelled from Italy not only the astrologers but also those philosophers whose doctrines and discussions seemed to him to be contrary to good sense. It appears, moreover, that he required the heads of the

[1] Cf. *C. I. L.*, vi., 934, in which inscription Vespasian represents himself as a conservator of ancient rites.

different philosophical schools in Greece to be Roman citizens.[1] In a word he presented a harmonious blend of Nero and Tiberius, and, while he held fast to the vital elements of Roman tradition, he recognized the claims of the invading Hellenism.

He died in peace on June 24, 79, at the age of sixty-nine after a term of power which had been threatened by few conspiracies and stained by few acts of repression, leaving behind him no such infamous and extravagant legend as has persecuted the memory of Tiberius and Claudius. Historians have attributed this to the humanity of his character which doubtless was great, but which was not the only reason. Tiberius and Claudius also endeavoured to restrain accusations and prosecutions for treason, but without success. How was it that Vespasian succeeded? It was because both the times and the senate had changed. After the critical period of the civil war when the haughty, quarrelsome and purely Roman element with its rancorous feuds, had been tempered by the new ingredients from Italy, Spain, and Gaul, a more exalted spirit of concord and a more noble sense of the dignity of the assembly began to prevail. Hence the terrible gusts of mutual hatred and recrimination of former days were not so easily aroused.

**77. The Government of Titus (79–81 A.D.).** Immediately on the death of Vespasian his son Titus assumed the title of Augustus which was confirmed by the senate. As a matter of fact the reign of Titus did not begin but ceased from this moment. As we have seen, he had been his father's colleague since 71. When Vespasian died his difficult task was completed.

[1] *Cf.* Barbagallo, *Lo stato e l'istruzione pubblica nell'impero romano*, Catania, 1911, pp. 108–109.

Titus, moreover, though scarcely forty years of age, was in a very bad state of health. His sole tenure of the supreme office was therefore brief and in the nature of a tranquil epilogue to that of Vespasian. Titus spent money like his father, but even more lavishly, on festivals, donations, and public works. He inaugurated the Flavian amphitheatre with grandiose ceremonies; he did his best to please everybody and to injure no one; and after twenty-six months of single rule he died suddenly, passing to posterity adorned with the title of *amor ac deliciæ generis humani* (September 13, 81). During his brief reign there had been no conspiracy, and the *lex de maiestate* had been idle.

**78. Domitian's Accession to the Empire (September 14, 81 A.D.). The Conquest of Britain (77–84 A.D.). The First Wars in Germany (83 A.D.).** Titus had a brother, T. Flavius Domitianus, then a young man of thirty. The emperor had not breathed his last before Domitian galloped from his villa at Reate to the camp of the Prætorians at Rome to receive their first salutations as successor in the empire. The senate was invited to acquiesce in this revolutionary form of election and once more, though this time with greater repugnance, they accepted the *fait accompli* to avoid worse. On September 14, 81, Domitian became princeps.

Domitian was undoubtedly a man of intelligence, fond of literature and of books, himself a poet and a lover of the fine arts, a patron of scholars and of libraries—in a word a Hellenist. But he was not, at any rate at first, a second Nero. He took the supreme power with the intention of continuing his father's policy of countenancing the advance of Hellenism, while at the same time, reinforcing the Latin tradition by every possible means. Following Vespasian's example he spent large sums of money on entertainments, buildings, and the patronage of art and artists, but in the administration of justice and in religion he tried to renew the severity of ancient times. For example, he insisted on re-establishing the former very severe penalties imposed on Vestal Virgins who proved false to their vows. The impartiality and the severity of his judicial administration are acknowledged and praised even by those authors who are his bitterest opponents.

Domitian, however, lacked the patience, the coolness, and the invariable good sense that had distinguished his father, and the senate was no longer what it had been in the days of Claudius and Galba. The reforms of Vespasian were beginning to bear fruit. The new families from Italy and the western provinces had at last infused into that weary assembly the vigour which seemed to have been extinguished for ever. The senate raised its head again, became once more conscious of its rights and of its duties, and again claimed to assert itself and to act. For this body, remodelled as it had been by the hand of Vespasian, the manner in which Domitian had secured his election was a source of incurable distrust and rancour. Nevertheless the first years of the new reign were tranquil enough. Important military events monopolized public attention during this period, among others the conquest of practically the whole of Britain.

In 77, Cn. Julius Agricola, by origin a Gaul and one of the most illustrious members of the new aristocracy, had been sent to Britain. By the time of Domitian's accession Agricola, pursuing the difficult task of his predecessors had not only firmly occupied the island of Mona (Angelsey) but had advanced to the southern borders of Caledonia (Scotland) where the island contracts between the two estuaries of Bodotria and Clota (the Forth and the Clyde). He had fortified the boundaries of the new province and was preparing to invade Hibernia (Ireland) and Caledonia itself. But the difficulties of the undertaking, revolts which had broken out in the parts of the island which had already been conquered, and serious troubles which had arisen in Germany obliged Rome to give up this project. Agricola was recalled, an act which was severely criticized in senatorial circles at Rome, though it is difficult to admit that it was due to Domitian's jealousy of Agricola's successes.[1]

Domitian took the affairs of Germany in hand personally. In 83, on the pretext of rebellious movements on the part of the Chatti, one of the most warlike of the German peoples, the emperor in person led an expedition to Germany which was of course well supplied both with men and material. Assisted by good generals and advisers Domitian won notable successes,[2] but the aftermath of the expedition was even more remarkable. This was the construction of the colossal line of fortifications known as the *limes germanicus*, completed in the second century, which was to traverse the hundred and twenty miles between the Rhine and the Danube and bar that part of the frontier which was not covered by these two rivers.

**79. Domitian Censor for Life: His Rupture with the Senate** (**85 A.D.**) Already during these relatively

[1] This appears even from the biography of Agricola composed by Tacitus; *cf.* Tac., *Agr.*, 39 ff.

[2] Front., *Strat.*, i., 1, 8.

peaceful years there had been several collisions between the emperor and the senate. The senate, for instance, in 82 had tried without success to establish the immunity of its members from the jurisdiction of the princeps. Their relations, however, did not become at all strained until towards 85, after the German expedition, when Domitian, like his father, assumed the censorship, and particularly when he caused himself to be appointed to that office for life. In order to understand Domitian's government, the struggles by which it was distracted, and the catastrophe in which it ended, it is necessary to understand fully the meaning of this act. The censor, the most exalted but also the most dreaded, of Roman magistrates, had among other powers that of appointing new senators for exceptional reasons and of ejecting from the senate persons who already held the rank of senator. He was in a sense the judge and arbiter of the senate. For this reason there had been a time when all parties in the State came to an understanding that no more censors should be appointed. So heavy was the responsibility of the office that the emperors themselves, even the most powerful such as Augustus and Vespasian, had accepted the censorship unwillingly, and only as a temporary measure dictated by the pressure of public opinion and circumstances of exceptional gravity. Vespasian, for example, did so after a tremendous civil war which had necessitated a reconstruction of the assembly. The senate was a body which renewed itself practically automatically, for all who had served the office of quæstor became senators by right at the end of their term, and once a man had become a senator he could not be dispossessed of his rank except as the result of a trial. Now the assumption of the censorship in perpetuity by Domitian meant that the emperor wished to resume the power of expelling from the senate all those whom he considered unworthy or dangerous, and in fact to bring the assembly entirely under his control. The senate which Vespasian had reinvigorated with new energy revolted against the imperial pretensions, which even Augustus and Vespasian had not ventured to put forward, and from this moment began an implacable conflict between the new aristocracy and Domitian.

80. **The Dacian War (85–89 A.D.).** In the years 85–86 grave external events supervened to complicate the internal struggle. The Dacians, who had for long been seated in the plain now inhabited by the Hungarians and the Rumanians, had been threatening the right bank of the Danube since the time of Nero. This threat had become more serious during the recent civil war, when Antonius Primus had emptied Mœsia of troops. But (shortly, it would seem, before Domitian's accession) an even more notable development had taken place—the union of these scattered tribes in a single State under an extremely able chief named Decebalus who on the one hand did all he could to civilize his people and on the other armed them powerfully and entered into close relations with his neighbours. In 85, Decebalus suddenly crossed the Danube, surprised and defeated the governor of Mœsia, and invaded the province. The accounts given by ancient historians are so imperfect that it is impossible to relate the events of the war that followed or to estimate Domitian's conduct of the campaign. We are told that Domitian hastened from Rome to the invaded province where he gave orders for

the concentration of several legions, but did not take part in the military operations, that he provided for a reorganization of Mœsia,[1] and afterwards returned to the capital to inaugurate the Capitoline Games in the year 86. These games, like the *Ludi Neroniani*, consisted in musical and poetical recitals, contests of eloquence, races and sports of all sorts in which even women took part. While the emperor by these festivities was rendering the most solemn homage ever hitherto officially given at Rome to Hellenism his generals were successfully driving back the Dacians across the Danube,[2] which seems to show that his return to Rome was not due to frivolity or negligence but to the fact that his presence was not required in the field. When however, Cornelius Fuscus his prætorian præfect tried to cross the Danube and invade the country of the Dacians in the spring of 87, he was defeated and slain, which made people think that the expedition had been somewhat carelessly prepared. Be this as it may, Domitian did his best to repair the reverse, and prepared a third campaign, the conduct of which was to be entrusted to Calpurnius Julianus. Though it is difficult to form any clear judgment of Domitian's conduct and generalship in this campaign, there can be no doubt that all these vicissitudes and oscillations of fortune stimulated the senate's discontent with the perpetual censor. They began to accuse him of endangering the prestige of the empire, and the effects of their attitude were soon visible. One conspiracy was discovered in the autumn of 87[3],

[1] *C. I. L.*, iii., 4013; xi., 571; G. Corradi, *Domitianus* in De Ruggiero, *Dizionario epigrafico*, p. 2010.

[2] *F. H. Gr.*, iv., p. 185; Dio Cass., lxvii., 7.

[3] *Acta Arv.*, p. cxx. ed. Hensen, *C. I. L.*, vi., 2068.

and immediately afterwards steps were taken towards an insurrection, the object of which was nothing less than to place the army of Upper Germany in the hands of the opposition. This rebellion, it appears, broke out in 88, and failed because the legionaries refused to follow the mutinous general who received little support from the governors of other provinces. The senatorial aristocracy nevertheless continued to murmur against the methods and results of the Dacian War and against Domitian who was directing it. The emperor sought in vain to secure some definite and unquestionable success which would silence all his enemies. In the spring of 89, Julianus had inflicted a serious defeat on the army of Decebalus, but now Decebalus had succeeded in raising the Quadi, the Marcomanni and, it seems, also the Suevi, against Rome and Julianus was forced to arrest his advance and the emperor to negotiate for peace. Decebalus consented to restore all the spoil he had taken both in arms and prisoners, to regard himself as a client of the empire, and to defend the neighbourhood of the Danube on behalf of Rome, for which purpose he was to receive means and men with which to organize the necessary force. This acceptance of the collaboration of barbarians is a policy which great States have adopted in all ages in relation to the small potentates established on the frontiers of their colonies. But the senatorial aristocracy reproached Domitian as if he had been guilty of treason and even went so far as to say that he had made the Roman Empire a tributary of Decebalus! The emperor, however, once freed from the embarrassment of the Dacian campaign, was able to turn all his forces against the Quadi and the Marcomanni, who were in the end beaten and compelled to make peace.[1]

**81. The Catastrophe (89–96 A.D.).** The discord between the senate and the emperor, however, was now incurable. The settled hostility and implacable criticisms of the senate could not fail to irritate more and more a suspicious, haughty, and violent man like Domitian, and naturally drove him to the adoption of more and more arbitrary measures. These in their turn inevitably exasperated the resistance of a body which, like the senate, had recovered something of its old energy owing to the new blood transfused into it by Vespasian. The critical state of the finances aggravated a situation which was already bad. The prodigality of Vespasian and Titus, which Domitian had continued, the numerous wars, and the increase by three *aurei* of the pay of the legions had disorganized imperial finance. Money had to be found somehow. Domitian's government, already inclined to violence, soon became rapacious as well.[2] Once more there was an outbreak of the legacy-hunting which in his early days Domitian had so much deplored, the *lex de maiestate* was once more used as a means of raising money and the collection of the taxes was carried out with increasing severity. The senate in particular had to lament the continual growth of the scope of the imperial *fiscus* at the expense of the *ærarium* of the republic. At Rome there was another storm of delations, State trials, scandals, and conspiracies which exasperated Domitian's violent and suspicious temper and in the end appear really to have

[1] Euseb. Hieron., *Chron.*, ed. Shoene, pp. 160–161. Aurel. Vict., *Epit.*, xi., 2.

[2] *Cf.* Suet., *Domit.*, 12.

deranged his mind. A kind of tyrannic frenzy seems to have taken possession of him, and to have impelled him to imitate Caligula by proclaiming himself a god, after the fashion of the ancient kings of Egypt. But Rome was not Alexandria, and there was as yet no room within her walls for a despot who desired to be worshipped. Domitian's principate dragged on till 96, the prince ever more gloomy, violent, and suspicious. In the latter year, a vast intrigue in which several of his ministers and finally his wife and both the prætorian præfects took part, at last quelled his despotic spirit. On the eighteenth of September, Domitian was despatched by the dagger of an assassin in his forty-fifth year after ruling for fifteen years and five days.

# CHAPTER X

## THE REPUBLIC OF TRAJAN AND THE LAST SPLENDOURS OF THE ROMAN SPIRIT

**82. Nerva (September 18, 96–January 27, 98 A.D.).** This time the conspiracy had been well prepared. Its object had not been merely to kill Domitian but also to anticipate the soldiers by procuring the immediate election of his successor by the senate. The conspirators were ready with a candidate, and the senate were both more adroit and more resolute than they had shown themselves on similar occasions in the past. Domitian had scarcely breathed his last when, without hesitation or discussion, the senate elected as emperor M. Cocceius Nerva, an elderly member of their own body who was an eminent lawyer.

The energy and the harmony of the proceedings in the senate on this occasion, and perhaps also the renewed prestige of the assembly, overawed the soldiery. The prætorians at Rome and the legions in the provinces murmured a little and showed some inclination to protest. On the Danube and in Syria there were some disturbances. But after some harmless mutterings the storm passed off without bursting. The fact that the Flavian family came to an end with Domitian, and that the legions and the prætorians were thus without a candidate to oppose to Nerva, facilitated the victory of the senate. In any case the empire for the first time had a head who had not been imposed on it by circumstances, like Augustus and Tiberius, or by the soldiers, like Claudius, Nero, and Vespasian, a princeps who had been freely elected by the senate and who might be regarded as possessing the confidence of that body.

This was an important event the consequences of which were soon apparent. Nerva hastened to realize the most cherished aspirations of the senatorial aristocracy. He pledged himself not to condemn any senator to death. He restricted to the senatorial order all the old offices of state. He forbade slaves and freedmen to appear as witnesses against their masters and patrons. He prohibited trials for treason, persecuted the informers who had been the feared and hated instruments of Domitian's government, recalled the exiles, left unpunished the attempts which were made to conspire against him, and drafted a scheme for supplying cheap food to the necessitous population of Italy which was to be perfected by his successor. Further he did his best to restore the finances and to resume the ancient tradition of the republic by distributing land to the poorer citizens of Rome. He occupied himself much with public works, and in a word, he aimed at decent government. But he was old and feeble and therefore his energy did not always correspond to the goodness of his intentions. He tried to do more than he could and thus often displeased even those whom he wished to help. He was, moreover, a lawyer and not a soldier, and thus had little prestige in the army, a fact which increased the uncertainty and insecurity of his rather weak government. Because of this weakness the menace of a mutiny always hung over him like the sword of Damocles, for all his wisdom and honesty. The danger was so serious that in October, 97, the emperor, in full agreement with the senate, followed the precedents of Augustus, Galba, and Vespasian, and adopted M. Ulpius Traianus, governor of one of the two Germanies (whether of Upper Germany or Lower is uncertain) and one of the most illustrious soldiers of his time. As in the days when Augustus and Agrippa had been colleagues, the empire now had a military and a civil chief. This, however, did not last long. Three months later, in the early days of 98, Trajan received at Colonia (Cologne) the news that the emperor who had appointed him his colleague was dead, and that the senate had entrusted the empire to him alone, vesting the supreme office in its entirety in his person.

**83. The First Years of Trajan (98–101 A.D.). The New Aristocracy and the Republican Renascence.** To the letter from the senate which recognized him as sole emperor Trajan replied with noble simplicity. He thanked them and renewed the pledge given by Nerva never to be judge in a capital charge against any senator. Leaving the senate to govern the republic in the meantime he remained for two years longer on the Rhine in order to carry out the military mission entrusted to him by Nerva. It was not until the year 99 that he returned to Rome, when, renewing the tradition of antique republican simplicity in his very act and deed, he entered the capital on foot, passed without pomp among the holiday crowds, took up his abode in a modest house where he lived without splendour or ceremony, and received and spoke familiarly with all who approached him. He neither was nor wished to be more than the most powerful of the senators, and his policy corresponded to his manner of life. The senate was frequently consulted even on questions relating to foreign affairs. The ambitions and the vanity of the nobility were satisfied; treason trials were things of the past; informers were severely punished. The aristocratic character of the government was respected, for all the highest offices of State were reserved for the senatorial order. In return the senate showed the new emperor, though with sincerity and without loss of dignity, the respect which was his due as *primus inter pares*, and for the first time the empire saw perfect concord between a prince who was a model of all the ancient republican virtues and the senate in which the feuds of cliques and cabals by which it had been so long distracted were now finally extinguished in a new spirit of harmony. Two things which had seemed irreconcilable—liberty and the principate—were now at last reconciled. Rome at last had an emperor whom the nobility unanimously admired. To the republic of Augustus had succeeded the republic of Trajan, and how much more tranquil and better ordered was the latter than the former!

This was such an unexpected phenomenon that contemporaries were amazed. Yet it was no miracle but merely the result of the great reform of the senate accomplished by Vespasian which was now bringing forth its fruit, and of the definitive accession to power of the provincial nobility which once more, and for the last time, revived the traditions and the institutions of the old republic. The families from northern Italy, from Gaul, Spain, and Africa of which it was composed had been refined by an education in rhetoric and literature based chiefly on the great writers of the age of Cæsar and Augustus. They were animated by a spirit of admiration for Rome and of sincere gratitude to the power which had drawn them from the depths of their provinces and set them on the summit of power and worldly glory. Thus the ancient Latin spirit lived again with a sincerity and a seriousness which had long been unknown to the ancient Roman nobility, tempered at the same time by a humane breadth of view which had been infused into the new generation by philosophic culture, the spirit of the age, the greatness of the empire, and the variety of the elements of which it was made up. At Rome the senatorial aristocracy was no less rich, but it was much simpler in its way of life than in the days of the Julio-Claudian dynasty.[1] They were very proud of their rights and privileges, but they were also conscious of their duties to the empire. They were not without learning, but they did their best to cultivate not only their minds but the virtues needful to the ruler. They were inspired by the high moral ideal formed by the ancient Roman tradition, by the influences of literature, and of the better part of Greek Philosophy. They no longer knew the ferocious spirit of discord and the terrible jealousies which had lacerated the Roman nobility during the last centuries of the republic. They were in fact an aristocracy superior in every way to that which had been so sorely tried by

[1] *Cf.* Tac., *Ann.*, iii., 55, gives an account of the luxury of Rome which is a document of capital importance. That the aristocracy established by Vespasian was simpler in its habits is very clearly stated: *novi homines e municipiis et coloniis, atque etiam provinciis, in senatum crebro adsumpti domesticam parcimoniam intulerunt, et quamquam fortuna, vel industria, plerique pecuniosam ad senectam pervenirent mansit tamen prior animus. Sed præcipuus adstricti moris auctor Vespasianus fuit, antiquo ipse cultu victuque.*

civil war, political strife, and the sudden development of Hellenism at Rome between the second Punic War and the accession of Augustus. Tacitus is the historian who represents this new aristocracy and its aspirations, and the works of Quintilian the first holder of the chair of Rhetoric established by Vespasian, give us some idea of the spirit of the education by which it was formed.

Trajan was the great figure and the ruling representative of the new nobility. He came of a Spanish family, that is to say one of the Romanized provincial stocks with which Vespasian had reinforced the declining senate. His father, after having served with honour in the army, had become a senator in the time of the Flavians, but it was chiefly the military side of the old Roman tradition which was exemplified in him. Trajan was above all things a soldier after the fashion of Scipio and Æmilius Paulus. Hence after satisfying the civil aspirations of the senatorial order he prepared to gratify another ambition which had been revived in the new aristocracy by a study of the past and the worship of tradition. This was the ambition to bring about a new flourishing of the military glory of Rome. It seemed to these aristocrats, who regarded the century between Augustus and Domitian as a time of decadence, that the honour of the Roman army had been compromised during that period. The peace concluded by Domitian with Decebalus was looked upon as the last of the many humiliations produced by the foreign policy of Rome, and from all sides there came a cry for a great warrior who would renew the glories of the great days of the republic.

**84. The War against Dacia (101–102; 105–106 A.D.).** Trajan was the great captain for whom they were longing. His first sojourn at Rome was brief, and was not extended much beyond the end of 101—the time needed to prepare, in concert with the senate, a great expedition against Dacia with an army of eight legions, a force which, with the auxiliary contingents and the ten prætorian cohorts, amounted to at least 100,000 men. In the spring of 101, when these preparations were complete, Trajan declared war on Decebalus. The history of the great struggle which followed is far from clear. We know that Dacia was invaded by three armies, that the Dacians defended themselves with energy and skill, that Trajan won a signal but extremely costly victory at the Iron Gates (Tapæ), but that this victory was not enough to compel the enemy to make peace. The emperor had to pursue his advance and threaten the heart and capital of the kingdom. Then, but not till then, Decebalus accepted the conditions imposed by Trajan. He declared himself a vassal of Rome, abandoned the territories he had conquered at the expense of the neighbouring peoples, handed over his war material and demolished his fortresses (102).

In the following year the emperor returned to Rome to solemnize his triumph, but the peace with Decebalus turned out to be merely a truce. This new Mithridates restored his fortresses, prepared new munitions, received Roman deserters into his armies, and concluded new alliances including, it is said, one with the far off Parthians. At the end of 104 the senate was again faced with the necessity of sending an expedition—this time on an even larger scale, and war with Dacia again broke out in 105. The second campaign was no easier than the first. Abandoned by his allies and by part of his own people, Decebalus retired slowly into the interior of the country, offering resistance in the mountain passes, burning the crops and the towns, and compelling the Romans to undergo terrible hardships and to make very great sacrifices. In the end, after a strenuous defence, the king and the nobility of the country either committed suicide by the sword or by poison, or were massacred, or contrived to escape across the frontier, and Dacia was proclaimed a Roman province.

As the greater part of the population either had been slain or had fled or had been reduced to slavery the country was half deserted, and Trajan, who did not wish to have a depopulated province on the frontiers of his empire, conceived a vast plan of colonization. Settlers were invited to come to the new conquest from all parts of the empire, companies of *entrepreneurs* hastened to organize the exploitation of the Carpathian mines or the transport of the grain grown in the fertile plains on the banks of the Danube. The State assisted the development of the new province in every possible way by building towns and constructing roads, and the plan on which no expense was spared had a rapid success. The result was that where there had been a Germanic kingdom there was now a Roman province, the majority of the population of which were a Mediterranean race of medium stature with dark eyes and hair contrasting strangely with the tall survivors of the native population with their blue eyes and flaxen locks. The language of Rome is spoken to this day in this country, which is none other than the Greater Rumania dreamed of by their brothers across the Danube who pant to deliver their fellow countrymen from German and Hungarian oppression. The Roman Empire in the West had been enlarged by a vast province which for several generations was to be what we now call a "new country" offering a free field to the resolute immigrant, full of dangers but presenting many opportunities of making a fortune.

**85. The Civil Administration of Trajan (106–114 A.D.).** In the same year in which Trajan completed his difficult conquest of Dacia A. Cornelius Palma, one of his lieutenants, acquired another province for the empire, namely Arabia Petræa, the country extending from the Red Sea to the west of Palestine as far as Damascus, and including practically all Sinai and the wealthy cities of Petra and Bostra. The new conquest was immediately styled the province of Arabia (106) and the emperor, ruling in accord with the senate, had in a few years increased the empire by two provinces, one in the West, the other in the East.

From this time began a series of nine peaceful years during which the new nobility might well believe that the most glorious epoch of the republic had returned. "At last the nobles," says the younger Pliny in his famous *Panegyricus*, "instead of being overshadowed by the Prince, received renewed splendours from him every day. At last there was a Prince who did not fear the illustrious descendants of heroes, the latest heirs of liberty. On the contrary his only desire was to hasten the day when they would take office. . . . Wherever there was to be found a branch of an ancient stock, the remnant of an ancient glory, he protected and revered it and used it for the good of the republic. Great names, snatched from oblivion by the generosity of the Prince, whose merit lay as much in restoring as in creating an aristocracy, were restored to honour and to their rightful fame."[1] There

[1] Plin., *Paneg.*, 69.

was an end of trials, scandals, delation, and suspicion, and the republican tradition was again honoured. Titinius Capito, one of the emperor's secretaries, put the images of Brutus, Cassius, and Cato in a place of honour in his house and wrote verses in praise of these illustrious citizens which he read in public to an audience composed of all that was best in Roman society. The emperor himself struck coins bearing the effigies of Sulla, Brutus, Cicero, Cato of Utica, and even of the genius of Liberty. The senate and the magistrates of the republic were treated by the Spanish emperor with a respect of which the old Roman nobility had long been incapable. Trajan even introduced secret votes in the senate in order to free its members from the oppressive control of the princeps. The activities of government were multiplied in every sphere. Grandiose public works were ordered in all parts of the empire in order both to provide for the exigences of public utility and to commemorate the glorious achievements of the time. The harbours of Italy on the Adriatic and on the Tyrrhene Sea such as Ancona, Ostia, and Centumcellæ (Civitavecchia) were improved. At Rome public libraries were opened, and from the plans of Apollodorus of Damascus was built the Forum of Trajan, from the midst of which still rises the column recounting in its bas reliefs the history of the Dacian Wars.

Italy was now invaded by enriched and Romanized families from the provinces, who wished to serve the empire and to be admitted to the nobility by which it was governed. Trajan renewed one of the rules made by Tiberius, which was that every provincial who wished to become a candidate for office at Rome must invest a third of his capital in real property in Italy.

This was a clear intimation from the Spaniard who had become emperor to all provincials whose ambition it was to follow his example, that for all those who aspired to be her governors Italy must be an abiding city and not a caravanserai. Like Augustus, Trajan did not wish the Italic population to diminish; he took pains to check emigration, and developed the orphanages which Nerva had scarcely had time to form.[1] Fixed sums were assigned to the municipia by the treasury to be lent at moderate interest to private persons on the security of their property. The interest thus paid was to be used to bring up and educate poor boys, legitimate or illegitimate, and, to a less degree, poor girls, to whom at a certain age Roman citizenship was to be granted. The object of these institutions was twofold. On the one hand, they were intended to increase the number of the lower class which furnished soldiers for the legions, and on the other to help Italian agriculture by means of loans on specially favourable terms. They were, or seemed to be, so necessary and beneficial that they were immediately imitated by many of the great families of the empire each in proportion to its power. The aristocracy now adopted the new principle that its privileges were to be counterbalanced by equally important duties towards the lower classes and towards the State, that, in the words of Pliny "the truly generous man should give to his country, to his neighbours, to his poorer friend. . . . He should go in search of those whom he knows to be in need, should succour and support them, and make of them as it were a second family."[2]

[1] Plin., *Paneg.*, 27–28; cf. *C. I. L.*, ix., 1455; xi., 1127.

[2] Plin., *Epist.*, ix., 30. The best commentary on these words of Pliny is to be found in the number of charitable institutions

The restoration of the republic, for which Augustus and Tiberius had worked so hard seemed therefore to have been at last accomplished by the agency of a Spaniard. Rome at last had an emperor who used his supreme power of control in the manner dreamed of by Cicero, with full respect for the rights of the senate and the magistrates, a senate which, without envy or jealousy, had recognized the necessity of this supreme Officer of State and supported and obeyed him loyally. If, however, Trajan may be viewed in one aspect as the restorer of ancient Rome, he was in another sphere, namely finance, a representative of the spirit of the new age. Ancient historians praise his success in providing for public expenditure without increasing taxation, and indeed while reducing certain imposts. But, though this is true, it is also the fact that his finance was not the old traditional parsimonious finance of the republic, of Augustus, and Tiberius, which was averse to all new expense. It was the finance of Vespasian required by the new era, and it was accordingly lavish of expenditure. Trajan's government spent without counting the cost on public works, on what we should now call outdoor relief, on colonization, on intellectual culture, and on war. If he was able to keep up so profuse an expenditure without increasing the taxes, the explanation must be that the spoils of war, the lands, and the mines of Dacia, and above all the natural increase of the revenue, owing to the increase of population and riches, gave him what he required without compelling him to resort to new ways of raising money. In other words, Ves-

---

founded by private benefactors which were scattered all over the empire. Cf. *C. I. L.*, ii., 174; v., 5262; viii., 1641; x., 6328; xi., 1602; xiv., 350.

pasian's new fiscal system brought in its maximum return under Trajan, thanks to the favourable character of the times. It is certain that, in order to meet that part of his expenses for which the increased resources of the empire did not suffice, Trajan like his predecessors had recourse to the dangerous expedient of coining silver equal in weight to that of Nero but of a much baser alloy. In other words, Trajan, instead of regulating expenditure in accordance with the real wealth of the country, provided a fictitious prosperity for his contemporaries, not only consuming the fruits of that wealth but also encroaching on the capital of the empire, and impairing its future reserve. This financial policy, though it helped to pave the way for the catastrophe we shall have to relate, was one of the reasons for the success of his reign, and for the immense admiration which he excited. Trajan could spend profusely the funds of the State without harassing the empire with taxation, and hence he could appear as a sort of special providence and be hailed in the words of an inscription which has come down to us, as *locupletator civium*.[1] The empire had long dreamed of a government which should give much and take little. It had not been particularly grateful to Augustus and Tiberius for the moderation of their exactions because they had been niggardly in their expenditure. The generosity of Nero and Domitian had been equally little appreciated because, in the end, these princes had been compelled to recur to violence and extortion in order to procure the means of meeting the cost of their enormous prodigalities. Trajan, owing to the happiness and prosperity of the time, was able to spend like Nero and Domitian while he treated the

[1] *C. I. L.*, vi., 958.

taxpayer like Augustus and Tiberius. Thus every one thought that he could make the State a fountain of universal prosperity, and his prodigal finance enabled him to reap a harvest of glory for which others were destined to pay dearly at a later day.

**86. Trajan and Christianity.** Trajan, so far as we know, was the first emperor who had to take official notice of Christianity. This fact is too important to be passed over without full consideration.

Christianity had made great progress, especially in the East and among the most numerous classes in the community. This could not but be the cause of a profound perturbation. Christianity was not merely a new religion to be added to the many which were already professed in the East; it was a new religion which aimed at supplanting all others. Pliny the younger indeed, writing to Trajan at this time from Bithynia, of which he was governor, says that the temples of other cults were beginning to be deserted, so widely had Christianity been propagated.[1] But we have only to consider the importance for the State and the individual which religion had in the private life of the East to understand how innumerable were the reactions of threatened interests which the propagation of Christianity inevitably produced. Where Christians began to be numerous governors were constantly pestered to hear informers who accused

[1] Plin., *Epist.*, x., 96 (17), 10. Though the authenticity of this letter has been long and uselessly debated, there is no serious reason to doubt its genuineness. *Cf.* G. Boissier, *La lettre de Pline au sujet des premiers chrétiens*, in *Revue d'archéologie*, 1876; Ramsay, *The Church in the Roman Empire before 170 A.D.*, London, 1893, pp. 196 ff. V. Allard, *Histoire des persécutions pendant les deux premiers siècles*, pp. 145 ff. A. Marmaresi, *L'impero romano e il cristianesimo*, Torino, 1914, pp. 105 ff.

them of all sorts of imaginary crimes. Pliny was soon convinced that these charges were unfounded, and that, though the Christians professed what appeared to him to be a perverse and extravagant superstition (*superstitio prava et immodica*), they did nothing wrong at their gatherings. There was one point, however, on which the Christians were at the mercy of their enemies, and that was the worship of the emperor. This cult was now diffused throughout the provinces, and among the infinite variety of religions professed by the peoples subject to Rome it represented the religious and political bond which held the whole empire together. In every city there was now an altar to the emperor, on which sacrifice was made on solemn occasions. When a charge was made that the Christians did not sacrifice to the emperor the governor was bound to investigate it, and, as the charge was easy to test and often proved to be true, the Christians very soon acquired the reputation of being rebels. That their refusal to worship the images of the emperor was compatible (as it in fact was) with the truest loyalty and obedience to the imperial authority, was a thing that the Roman authorities could neither understand nor admit, as the exclusive religious spirit which inspired the Christians was entirely strange to the Græco-Latin spirit. But indeed the position of the Christians was still very confused and uncertain, both from the political and the legal point of view, and therefore a time came when Pliny from the depths of his province asked Trajan for instructions. Trajan replied by laying down a rule which was rough and ready but very mild, considering the times. The Christians were not to be sought out nor were anonymous accusations against them to be permitted. But if they were denounced and refused to venerate the imperial images and confessed that they were Christians they were to be punished.[1]

This is what has (very improperly) been called the persecution of Trajan. The truth is that Trajan gave the enemies of the Christians who called for the application of the utmost rigour of the law, the least and mildest satisfaction that he could. In a certain sense his decision was rather a defence of the Christians than a persecution if the concessions it made are compared with what the enemies of the Christians demanded. The imperial authorities, in fact, did Christianity a service by bringing it to a legal trial, for they thereby saved the Christians from the extermination which the popular fury of their enemies in every country had vowed against them, and would probably have accomplished had it not been checked by the authority of the empire which was independent of local influences.

**87. The Wars in the East (114–116 A.D.).** About the end of 113 or the beginning of 114, the senate honoured the emperor with the solemn title which paganism had attributed to Jove, the title of *Optimus*.[2] The nine years of peace which had now passed had not been an end in themselves. They had served for the preparation of a great warlike enterprise in the East analogous to the conquest of Dacia in the West. Trajan's purpose was to resume and enlarge the great design of Cæsar and Antony and to advance like Alexander the Great to the conquest of all the East from the Euphrates to the shores of the Persian Gulf. Oriental affairs, always in unstable equilibrium,

[1] Plin., *Epist.*, x., 97 (98).

[2] Plin., *Paneg.*, 2.

required a new intervention on the part of Rome about the year 114, because Chosroes, King of Parthia, had placed his nephew Parthomasiris on the throne of Armenia. Parthia was at this time distracted by civil war. Chosroes was one of three kings who were fighting for the throne and, this being so, it would not have been difficult to fight Parthia with Parthian aid if Trajan had desired to continue the policy of Augustus and Tiberius. Trajan, however, was a great soldier and, like the new aristocracy whose hero he was, he wished to cover the Roman arms with new glory on every frontier of the empire. He thought that the time had come to cut the Gordian knot of the Eastern question with the sword, instead of complicating it still further with new schemes of negotiation. The disorder of the Parthian Empire seemed to present favourable opportunity for action. In the spring of 114, therefore, Trajan left Antioch at the head of a great force to conquer Armenia. In vain Parthomasiris presented himself unarmed in the Roman camp begging that he might be invested with the Kingdom; Armenia was proclaimed a Roman province (114). Mesopotamia was invaded in the following year and its upper portion was also declared a province (115). But the real attack on the Parthian empire was not commenced until the spring of 116. In that year, having crossed the Tigris, Trajan occupied Adiabene and Assyria, which were also reduced to the status of provinces. He then marched again on the Tigris and entered Ctesiphon whence he continued his triumphal progress to the shores of the Persian Gulf (116). This, at any rate, appears to be the general effect of the confused accounts given by ancient writers.

Trajan had now reached the very summit of his renown. It seems that for a moment he even imagined that he had finally solved the oriental problem and had accomplished what Cæsar and Antony had failed to do by making Rome into a vast empire half Asiatic and half European. If we may believe the ancients he went so far as to dream of an expedition to India and a glory greater than that of Alexander himself. But if such an illusion dazzled him for a moment it did not last long. In his rear while he was roaming through Asia the fanatical nationalism of the countries he had conquered by surprise had again awakened. In 117 Mesopotamia and Assyria revolted, and it proved such a difficult and sanguinary task to repress this movement that Trajan at Ctesiphon found himself obliged to bestow the Parthian crown on one of the three contending candidates, a certain Parthamaspates, hoping thus to prevent the Parthians from joining the insurrection. But the revolt spread beyond the Euphrates. The Jews, relentless in their hatred, seized the opportunity and rebelled in Palestine, Cyprus, Egypt, and Cyrenaica. Meanwhile the Mauri resumed their raids on the province of Africa, the Bretoni were in a state of unrest, and the Sarmatians threatened once more to break the line of the Danube.

And, at the very time when the empire needed all the energy and intelligence of Trajan, he was carried off by a sudden illness, dying at Selinus in August, 117, leaving behind him a sea of fire and blood, the tragic heritage of a glorious reign.

## CHAPTER XI

### HADRIAN, THE GREAT REFORMER (117–138 A.D.)

**88. The Adoption of Hadrian, its Causes and its Significance.** Under Trajan and after their experience of him the senatorial aristocracy, or at any rate the wiser among them, had come to the conclusion that adoption as practised by Nerva was the legitimate principle of succession to the imperial dignity. Such adoption was to be carried out with the consent of the senate, and the choice of a colleague who seemed likely to be a worthy successor was to be made without any regard to relationship. The younger Pliny states this explicitly in an important passage of his *Panegyricus*.[1] This procedure, while it excluded the hereditary principle abhorred by the aristocracy, seemed to preserve the choice of the emperor from the two dangers which had vitiated so many elections —violence on the part of the soldiers and hesitation and discord in the senate. Trajan, however, being a man full of physical and mental energy, had never felt in need of the assistance of a colleague. It was not until he became suddenly aware of the approach of

[1] *Cf.* Plin., *Paneg.*, 7: *Nulla adoptati cum eo qui adoptabat cognatio* . . . etc. Tacitus (*Hist.*, i., 15 and 16) about the same time expresses the same idea which he puts in the mouth of one of his characters.

death that he remembered this last duty which he had still to perform for the empire and the senate. Having neither the time nor the means to consult the senate he carried out without further formality a plan he had long meditated, and on his deathbed adopted P. Ælius Hadrianus, one of his officers who was also his cousin and his nephew by marriage.

**89. The Renunciation of Trajan's Oriental Conquests.** Like Trajan, Hadrian was of Spanish origin, and belonged to the provincial nobility. He was a good general whose merits Trajan had recognized by entrusting him with important commands in all his wars. Shortly before his death, at the moment when he had decided to return to Italy, Trajan had handed over to Hadrian the supreme command of the army of the East. Like Trajan again, Hadrian was an enthusiastic believer in the great aristocratic and republican tradition. His first thought on receiving at Antioch the news of his adoption was to recognize the rights of the senate. He reminded the troops, who had at once acclaimed him, that it was for the senate alone to elect emperors, and he hastened to write to the senate requesting the confirmation of his imperial authority and excusing himself for having exercised the power in the meantime on the ground that the empire could not be left without a head in these critical times. Soon afterwards he repeated the promise made by Trajan that he would not condemn any senator, and he lost no opportunity of affirming that the State belonged not to him but to the people.[1] Nevertheless his first acts as emperor were the abandonment of all Trajan's oriental conquests except Arabia Petræa and the withdrawal of the fron-

[1] [*Hist. Aug.*] *Hadr.*, viii., 3.

tiers of the empire to the Euphrates. He gave back Assyria and Mesopotamia to the Parthians, recognized Chosroes, and restored Armenia to its ancient independence.

Hadrian sought to justify these acts by the traditions of the old republican policy, quoting the example of Cato and other great statesmen of ancient Rome who had so often renounced opportunities of ruling over subject peoples in order not to enlarge the empire unduly.[1] It cannot now be denied that his decision was wise, but it is certain that it greatly displeased the upper classes at Rome who were intoxicated by Trajan's enterprises. This was so much the case that some of Trajan's old generals, among them Cornelius Palma, the conqueror of Arabia, took advantage of the public discontent to form a conspiracy for the overthrow of the new emperor. This conspiracy was discovered and suppressed by the senate in Hadrian's absence, but the malcontents were not far wrong in seeing in his actions an indication that a new direction was to be given to imperial policy and one contrary to that of Trajan. Hadrian was not merely a good general and a Roman senator imbued with the spirit of the ancient aristocracy. He was also a passionate cultivator of literature and philosophy, of the fine arts, and of science so far as it was then known. He was so ardent a Hellenist that he spoke Greek better than Latin, and before he became emperor this had procured him many enemies who had given him the nickname of *Græculus*. In his foreign policy he wished to tread the path of Augustus and Tiberius, and to keep the empire on the defensive, not only because he would live more securely within restricted frontiers

[1] [*Hist. Aug.*] *Hadr.*, v., 3.

but because he would thus be able to use part of the funds expended by Trajan in wars and conquests for the embellishment of the capital, for the spread of education, and for reforms which would make the administration more efficient, more uniform, and more just, and the laws more humane, more reasonable, and less severe. In a word, he wished to reconcile Hellenism with its mastery of all forms of culture to Romanism with its skill in war and administration, in an empire which should be half oriental and half occidental, strong in arms, wise in its government, and splendid in the arts of peace. This reconciliation was the supreme object pursued during his long tenure of power by this Romanized Spaniard. Owing to the extreme uncertainty of the chronology, we are obliged to deal with his principal acts in groups.

90. **Hadrian's Administrative Reforms.** It has been repeatedly said that Hadrian was the founder of an absolute monarchy. It would be more true to say that he created the civil bureaucracy which was afterwards to become the instrument of absolutism. An emperor like Trajan, whose chief preoccupation was to enlarge his borders by war, had no motive for modifying the main outlines of administration, because Rome had a complete mastery of the military art. This was not the case with a prince who wished to perfect what we should now call the civil service, which was rudimentary in the republican constitution. As a matter of fact up to that time, and more especially from the days of Claudius, the emperors, in order to correct as far as possible the defects of certain branches of that service, had made use of freedmen who were not actual public functionaries, but who depended entirely on their patron and were responsible

for their acts to him alone. Too often this had meant that they were uncontrollable and irresponsible. Hadrian made all these collaborators of the emperor public officials, choosing them usually from among the members of the equestrian order, and giving them salaries and a career. The most important equestrian officials were those *a libellis*, who formed something comparable to a general imperial secretariat, those *ab epistulis*,[1] or the department of the imperial correspondence, and those *a rationibus*, the most important of all, who managed the finances controlled by the emperor.[2] Nor did he limit himself to reinforcing in this way the agents under the control of the emperor. In order to make good the defects in the administration of the republic he created new offices, not elective and gratuitous but salaried and filled by the emperor. Hadrian seems to have been responsible for the appointment of *curatores rerum publicarum*, who were charged with the administration of cities in Italy in cases where the local authorities were guilty of maladministration. It is certain that, with a view to improving the administration in Italy, he appointed four *iuridici* or supreme judges, each with a definite district, but this most important office could only be filled by men of consular rank.[3] His predecessors had already had a *consilium*, which each emperor had filled as he chose with his most trusted friends, which assisted him to come to a decision whenever he thought

[1] [*Hist. Aug.*] *Hadr.*, xxii., 8.

[2] *Cf.* Hirschfeld, *Untersuchungen auf dem Gebiete der römischen Verwaltung*, Berlin, 1876, p. 32.

[3] [*Hist. Aug.*] *Hadr.*, xxii., 13. It is not clear whether they were already known as *iuridici* under Hadrian, or whether they were given this name when re-established by Marcus Aurelius.

proper to consult it, but which had never had any official character. Under Hadrian this council from being a gathering of private friends became a public body. Its members were no longer to be chosen merely by the emperor, but had to be approved by the senate. They received a salary and were required to possess certain qualifications. One of the most prized of these was a knowledge of jurisprudence.[1] Finally it appears that under Hadrian the prætorian præfects began to assume judicial functions and to decide civil cases on appeal from decisions of the proconsuls in the provinces.

**91. Judicial Reforms.** Hadrian, therefore, attempted to combine the oriental bureaucratic principle of paid permanent officials controlled by the emperor with the aristocratic principle of the republic which required that only senators and knights should have a right to participate in the government of the empire. That is to say he set up a paid bureaucracy, directly dependent on himself, but reserved all the appointments for members of the two privileged orders in the State. In substance the reform rather limited than enlarged the powers of the emperor. All historians, in fact, admit that under Hadrian the occult power of favourites, of freedmen, or of women was a thing unknown. It is therefore natural to find side by side with the oriental and bureaucratic principle the beginnings, especially in the organization of the *consilium principis*, of the democratic principle of

[1] [*Hist. Aug.*] *Hadr.*, xviii., 1. On the *consilium principis* may be consulted E. Cuq, *Mémoire sur le consilium principis d'Auguste à Diocletien*, in *Mémoires presentées par divers savants à l'Académie des inscriptions et des lettres de l'Institut de France*, Paris, 1884, vol. ix.

individual capacity recognized in the form of legal knowledge. That this form of ability should have been the first, and perhaps the only, form admitted by Hadrian is a fact worthy of notice because it throws light on another side of his government. Hadrian was a "juristic" emperor; with him begins in the empire the epoch of the jurists and the great attempt to substitute for traditional and case law a reasoned system of jurisprudence. Hadrian introduced many novelties into the law as then in force,[1] but his greatest achievement in this field was the *edictum perpetuum*, whereby for the first time an attempt was made to codify the Roman law. Hitherto at Rome the sources of what we call civil law had been various. There had been laws passed by the people and *senatus consulta* by the senate, while the various magistrates, in virtue of their power to supplement law by making rules which had to be obeyed as if they actually were laws, had from time to time issued edicts or *interdicta*. The injunction of an American judge may be referred to as a modern parallel which gives some idea of the nature and working of the Roman *interdicta*.

In civil law, the most important edicts had always been those of the prætors, who had thereby been able to fill the gaps in the laws and *senatus consulta* by means of their rules in particular cases which had not been contemplated by the law. Like the English chancellor, the Roman city prætor could not theoretically make law, but he could (and did) provide new remedies. These were of three kinds: New actions, exceptions (new defences), and *interdicta* (injunctions).

Unlike the chancellor, the prætor announced in

[1] These reforms are enumerated in Duruy, *Histoire des Romains*, Paris, 1883, vol. v., pp. 113 ff.

assuming office what remedies unknown to the civil (= common) law he proposed to give, and this programme was set forth in his *edictum*.

He usually (and in the later times invariably) republished the edicts of his predecessor with such variations or additions as were suggested by the jurists whom he had drawn into his council. In this way, the Roman began to speak of the *edictum tralaticium*—the "handed along" edict.

The development of this new body of law came to an end, practically, at about the beginning of the Christian era, just as the development of English equity practically came to an end at the close of the eighteenth century.

In the early empire, the chief agency of legal reform was the *Senatus consultum*, which in the time of Tiberius wholly replaced legislation by the assembly; just as in England the chief agency of progress in the nineteenth century was the act of Parliament. The edict had long before the time of Hadrian become practically *perpetuum* and was so described. Hadrian charged Salonius Julianus, an African who was one of the best jurists of the time, with the duty of collecting and arranging in the *edictum perpetuum* the series of edicts which could still be of use as rules of law and to edit these in an authoritative and final text, and in 131 the senate was asked to approve this collection and to give to it formally the force of law.

**92. Hadrian's Travels. The First Series of Journeys, in the Western Provinces and Africa (119–122 A.D.).** Hadrian's policy explains why he was the first emperor who spent the greater part of his time in travelling in the provinces. A certain nervous restlessness, his insatiable curiosity, and his desire to see and know everything may have helped to impel him to these incessant peregrinations, but with these motives was associated a lofty political idea and an important reason of State. This man who understood and admired at the same time both the Roman and the Greek genius could not limit his activity to Rome and Italy. He was bound to extend it to the provinces, which were now the strength of the empire since they supplied most of the money, most of the soldiers, and most of the new families of the senatorial, and equestrian aristocracy. His travels were, so to speak, journeys of inspection made in order to supervise civil and military administration in every part of the empire and to promote everywhere the development, the embellishment, and the progress of cities. For Hadrian was also the greatest builder of cities that ever governed the empire and the prince who had their extension and adornment most at heart. Since the chronology of these voyages can be conjectured with at least a certain probability we propose to relate them one after the other in the order which seems most likely, taking the opportunity of giving a short description of the provinces at this, the most prosperous moment in the history of the empire.[1]

Hadrian began his travels in 119 with a journey which took him in the first instance to Gaul. Gaul had followed the path of Romanization which had been opened to her in the age of Augustus. Not only did she furnish Italy with excellent agricultural and mineral products such as timber, skins. cattle, cheese,

[1] The chronology of Hadrian's journeys is very uncertain. A special study of the subject, the conclusions of which, however, are not always acceptable, is given by Dürr, *Die Reisen des Kaiser Hadrian*, Wien, 1881

ham, salt fish, iron, copper, and lead, not only did she supply to Italy and export to Germany manufactured articles,—for the most part rather rough imitations of oriental products,—glass and pottery, linen and woollen stuffs, clothes for the lower classes; but she also sent loyal legions, generals, and statesmen for the service of the empire. The country which Cæsar had conquered now boasted great cities, such as Lugdunum (Lyons), Vienna (Vienne), Massilia (Marseilles), Narbo (Narbonne), Tolosa (Toulouse), Burdigala (Bordeaux), which were rich in palaces, monuments, theatres, baths, villas, libraries, and flourishing schools. In these cities trade and industry were very active, the most important industries being the manufacture of glass, pottery, and textiles, shipbuilding, the making of purple, armour, and metal work. As in Italy the towns were invaded by the most various Greek and oriental influences. At Lyons even Christianity was beginning to gain a foothold. What Hadrian did for Gaul during his first journey we do not precisely know, for it is difficult to distinguish his first acts from those which must be referred to a later period. But, however this may be, one of his biographers bears witness that in the course of this journey "he aided all men by his liberality," and a significant comment on this assertion is to be found in the legend on certain coins struck for the occasion which celebrates Hadrian as the "Restorer of Gaul."[1]

From Gaul Hadrian went to Germany where, both in the upper and the lower provinces, Roman ideas were making progress. The fortresses which had been built for the defence of the frontier were gradually developing into little cities and were becoming centres

[1] Cohen, *Monnaies*, *Hadrien*, 1065, 1067.

of an active trade between the semi-savage populations of independent Germany and the more civilized provinces of the empire. There can be no doubt that in this province the inspection carried out by the prince had above all a military character. Hadrian restored the discipline of the armies which he found somewhat relaxed, improved the system of training and the service generally, and perhaps gave a new impulse to the construction of the *limes*.

From Germany Hadrian crossed to Britain. Roman civilization was penetrating even this most recent conquest, more especially in the south. Latin was beginning to be spoken and teachers of rhetoric were in request for Latin and even for Greek studies. Trade with the empire was developing. Britain exported slaves, corn, cattle, pelts, leather, and fish, and was beginning to exploit her mines of tin, copper, and silver which had long been known to the Phœnicians, thus offering many occasions of profit to speculators from more civilized countries. The conquest was however so recent and the tribes still so incompletely subdued that Britain could not yet produce much revenue, and the country was accordingly regarded at Rome as a passive province.[1] Hadrian, therefore, having, after some fighting, struck terror into the mountaineers of the north, decided to rectify the frontier here as he had done in the East by drawing it back to a more easily defensible line. This was the line from the Solway Firth to the mouth of the Tyne, on which he built the famous *Vallum Hadriani*, of which the superb ruins remain to this day.

In the winter of 121–122 the emperor was in Spain.

[1] App., *Proem*, 5.

Spain was no longer the barbaric province against which the republic had had to carry on a sanguinary struggle for centuries. The ancient Celtic and Iberian languages and customs had practically disappeared. Latin alone was spoken. The worship of the emperor was at its height. There was an intense municipal life in its flourishing cities such as Tarraco (Tarragona), Corduba (Cordova), Nova Carthago (Cartagena), Italica (Old Seville), Salmantica (Salamanca), Cæsaraugusta (Saragossa), Augusta Emerita (Merida), which were all rich in temples, amphitheatres, and fine streets, and all resembled the cities of Italy in being full of the most varied manifestations, of spiritual life and in possessing centres of study, of pleasure, and of busy labour. The most flourishing industries were agriculture and mining, and among the products by which Spain was enriched the most important were cereals, oil, and wine which was exported and sold even to the Rhine countries, silver, gold, and copper, which here also had been first discovered by the Phœnicians. There was a corresponding commercial activity which was favoured by the system of roads, harbours, great markets, and numerous urban centres. We know little of what Hadrian did in Spain. Here also he received the title of Restorer,[1] but it appears that he did not stay long in the country, as an insurrection among the Mauri compelled him to go to Africa in the spring of 122.

Africa also had developed marvellously during a century of peace. Except for Mauretania, the ancient realm of Juba which had remained barbarous and

[1] [*Hist. Aug.*] *Hadr.*, xii., 3-4; Cohen, *op. cit.*, *Hadrien*, 1069-1075.

rebellious, the country had grown rich by agriculture, mining, and industry of all kinds. It supplied Rome, Italy, and all the empire with wild beasts for the arena, ivory, precious marbles, grain, oil, perfumes, and costly stuffs. Carthage had become once more a great and flourishing city, and many smaller towns had grown up which by their architecture and their manners reminded the visitor of the cities of Italy. But the Numidians, the Lybians, the Lybophœnicians, and in general the lower class in the cities, and the agricultural labourers in the country, had continued to speak the local dialect and still preserved their confused and violent indigenous religions. The upper classes, on the other hand, spoke, wrote, and studied Latin as in Gaul and Spain, and had already furnished several families to the senatorial aristocracy. The Romanization of Africa, however, was not so complete as that of Gaul and Spain, and certain local elements proved too strong to be assimilated.

In Africa as in Britain Hadrian had to occupy himself chiefly with military matters. In addition to a vigorous offensive campaign in the Atlas he appears to have taken in hand a series of fortifications which are strongly reminiscent of the British *vallum*. In this case, however, the principal defensive system was not an artificial rampart but an actual mountain chain. Here also he loaded the cities of the various provinces with benefactions, and once again received the title of Restorer.

**93. Hadrian's First Journey to the Oriental Provinces.** From Africa Hadrian crossed Egypt and went to the East to which he seems to have been called by the threat of a new war with Parthia. An accommodation with Chosroes, however, averted this danger, and peaceful relations with the Parthians were re-established.

Hadrian could now visit in peace and quietness Asia and Greece, the two countries to which he was naturally most attached. He had known the East as a soldier under the command of Trajan. He was now returning thither in more tranquil times not merely, as in the case of the occidental provinces, in order to provide for the needs of the empire, but also to satisfy his insatiable intellectual curiosity. With what admiration must the soldier who knew Greek better than Latin, who not only loved Hellenic and Hellenistic art but wished to be himself an artist, have contemplated the work done by the empire in all Asia Minor! Here were the richest, the most industrious, the most cultivated, the most populous of all the provinces. Here Romanization had made little progress, except perhaps in the countries of the interior and among the groups of colonists who had come from the West. The Greek language reigned supreme; the imperial edicts were published in Greek; Greek was the language of the courts of justice. Yet even in these provinces the influence of the metropolis made itself felt. Italian merchants were numerous in the principal cities. Roman law was insinuating itself among the varieties of the local codes. Numerous Asiatics were acquiring Roman citizenship, and architecture in the construction of baths, aqueducts, bridges, and amphitheatres was acquiring a partially Roman character.

Few countries in the world could then compete with Asia Minor in the variety of their productions. In the interior there were splendid forests and fertile plains covered with grain; stock rearing prospered, and timber in abundance was exported by sea. Phrygian and Galatian wool formed the material of an extremely active trade and industry. The cities of the southern and western coasts from Cilicia to the Hellespont were flourishing centres of manufacture, more especially of textiles. These manufactures prospered greatly because they found new and valuable markets throughout the vast empire which was now entirely open to them, and accordingly they rapidly developed even in some of the districts of the interior, for example in Cappadocia, where they were particularly stimulated by the exertions of the Semitic element in the population. It was a strange country in which Hellenism had been superimposed on the varieties of national traditions and customs, and where the Roman spirit had joined itself to Hellenism. Through all this complexity, however, Asia Minor preserved an oriental character under its Hellenistic veneer. Its literature was characterized by the softness, the fantasy, the verbosity, and the frivolity of Asia. Its religion was a chaotic miscellany of Greek mythology, and of Ægypto-Phœnician, Jewish, and Christian cults, while there was also an admixture of purely Asiatic religions, such as those of Mithras, Cybele, and Attis.

In these provinces Hadrian stayed some months, but he returned on subsequent occasions for longer periods and there were few places which did not retain the traces of his passage and his plans. Cities destroyed by earthquakes were restored from their ruins; others which were needy or shabby were succoured or embellished; and great harbours, roads, and other monuments of public utility rose out of nothing, encouraged by his help and advice.

In the spring of 123 the emperor crossed the Ægean,

where the Cyclades were now for the most part scenes of ruin and abandonment, and reached Greece, where he intended to make a long stay. Greece, alas, was no longer the Greece of Pericles or Demosthenes. Even the peace imposed by the empire had helped her less than other provinces, which were naturally richer or better situated. The population was sparse; many districts were either abandoned or infested with brigandage. Only the maritime cities and a few inland towns which were situated on busy trade routes had regained something of their ancient splendour or acquired new prosperity. Such were Thessalonica, Philippi, Nicopolis, Mantinea, and above all the restored Corinth, which was the capital of Roman Greece. As for Athens, it was now a flourishing centre of study to which rich youths were sent from all parts of the empire. Yet for the city which had seen Æschylus, Sophocles, Thucydides, Pericles, Socrates, Phidias, Plato, and Demosthenes within its walls, it was a great fall to be reduced to the status of a mere university town!

Hadrian stayed long in Greece (123–126) and spared neither pains nor expense in his endeavour to benefit the country. At Corinth he built baths in several quarters of the city, and an aqueduct to bring water from Lake Stymphalos. At Nemea he constructed a hippodrome, at Mantinea a temple to Neptune, at Argos he offered in the temple of Juno the favourite bird of the goddess, a golden peacock whose tail blazed with precious stones. He encouraged the resumption of horse races at the Nemean Games and improved the narrow and dangerous road on the Isthmus between Corinth and Megara. Athens, however, was the chief object of his care. It was apparently his wish to revive in fancy the bygone age of Miltiades and Isocrates. He assumed the Greek dress, became an Athenian citizen, and served the offices of Archon and Agonothetes. Every day he discussed with architects and sculptors the plans of the buildings with which he meant to adorn the city. With the philosophers, whose schools he freed from the shackles imposed by Vespasian, he talked of their teachings, with the learned of the memories of the past. The Athenians of the second century saw gradually rising in honour of Hadrian a new town in the plain of the Ilissus over against the ancient city of Theseus, a Hadrianopolis adorned by countless monuments in which were concentrated all the beauties of a less severe but more grandiose art. Here the Greeks were to erect a Panhellenion, a temple to Jupiter and Hadrian, near which games were periodically to be celebrated in the presence of an audience collected from all Greece.

94. **Hadrian and Christianity.** It seems to have been in Athens that Hadrian wrote his famous letter to Minucius Fundanius, which concerns the Christians. It was in more general terms than the letter of Trajan to Pliny, and the emperor did not lay down that Christians were to be condemned if they refused to worship the images of the emperor. He said that they should be condemned only if they were convicted of having done something against the law, and he strongly urged his correspondent not to listen to unfounded charges and calumnies due to hatred. Milder than Trajan's rescript, Hadrian's letter is even more decided in confirming the Christians in their right to the protection of the imperial authorities against the fanaticism of their enemies.[1]

[1] Justin., *Apol.*, i., 68; Euseb., *H. Eccl.*, iv., 9.

**95. Hadrian's Return to Rome (126–128 A.D.), and his Great Buildings.** Towards the end of 126 Hadrian came back to Rome and his capital also received its share of his attention. At Rome also, though he gave his mind to every branch of the administration, he laboured chiefly to adorn the city with new monuments and new institutions. He commenced the construction of the splendid temple of Venus and Rome near the Flavian Amphitheatre and put in hand the gigantic mausoleum for himself and his successors, the ruins of which now form the castle of S. Angelo. At Tibur (Tivoli) he planned for himself a splendid villa in which were to be reproduced the most splendid buildings in the empire which he had seen during his travels. It was probably in these years that he founded on the Capitol the Athenæum, which was to be the first great public institution in the capital of the empire for the teaching of philosophy, rhetoric, and jurisprudence, and which contained public reading rooms and lecture halls. The companies of lyric and dramatic poets the so-called *synodi dionysiaci*, the Pythian and Olympian competitions under the patronage of the emperor, were in universal favour; suitable schools of music were established and musicians and artists were much more largely recompensed than in previous times.[1]

**96. Hadrian's Travels. Second Series (128–131 A.D.).** On this occasion Hadrian stayed only two years at Rome and early in July, 128, he was again in Africa at the camp of Lambæsis, where he made a speech to his soldiers of which some fragments are

[1] C. Barbagallo, *Lo stato e l'istruzione pubblica*, pp. 167 ff. and the sources there cited.

still preserved.[1] Thence he returned to his favourite Greece and afterwards continued his journey to Asia on his way to Syria and Egypt.

Hellenism had penetrated western Syria very early but the country still seemed to have inherited much more of the Phœnician than of the Greek civilization. The people had remained Syrian in character and spoke the local dialects; the industries which made the prosperity of the country and for which it was still famous were as of old the Phœnician manufactures of wool, silk, purple, and glass. The Syrians, who were very skilful traders, imported their raw materials from China and India and exported them either raw or manufactured to Italy, Gaul, and Britain. Life there was easy, opulent and active, sensual and refined, and pleasures were plentiful. Antioch seems to have been the first ancient city which illuminated its streets by night, and all the Syrian towns were celebrated for the ease and pleasantness of their ways of life. The country was full of Hebrews who had emigrated after the fall of Jerusalem and lived apart, encamped, as it were, in the country of their enemies.

From Western Syria Hadrian passed to the more easterly part of the country. Here the scene was changed. There were no more industrial cities or lands under intensive cultivation; the scenery was for the most part rude and even wild, and the country was infested with brigands. The Roman conquest, however, had, as time went on, effected many changes. One immediate result had been the immigration of a numerous Semitic population bringing with them into these regions a more thoroughgoing form of agriculture and the first elements of urban civilization,

[1] *C. I. L.*, viii., *Suppl.*, 18,042.

whereby the deserts were already beginning to be crossed by main roads and aqueducts, and towns were growing up out of nothing as if by magic. The most distant city to be visited by Hadrian in this district was Palmyra, and Palmyra like the rest received a gift of magnificent buildings, and was raised to the rank of a colony.

The emperor then visited the new province of Arabia. Here also the upper classes might be regarded as Græcized, and the growing immigration from the interior and the complete awakening of their material and spiritual life demonstrated how much they had benefited by the imperial rule. Hadrian's chief task was to provide a system of roads, and having done so he received the reward of his statesmanship. The province struck medals in honour of the Restorer of Arabia, and Petra, its capital, assumed his name.[1]

From Arabia Hadrian proceeded to Egypt. The land of the Pyramids and of the ancient hieroglyphs was no longer the country of lonely temples excavated in the rock and adorned with colossal pillars and the monstrous countenances of sacred animals. After its conquest by Alexander, Egypt had become a kind of busy Cosmopolis, rich and always restless, where all the elements of the Mediterranean world were mingled. Such it had remained under the empire. There Romans, Egyptians, Greeks, Hebrews, and Asiatics of all languages and races met together. The villages and the country districts remained irreconcilably Egyptian, while the large towns were Greek, the ruling classes Greek with a Roman infiltration, and among all these there was a clash of opposing tendencies, religions, passions, and social prejudices. It was a scene

[1] Cohen, *op. cit.*, *Hadr.*, 1057.

of intense activity. The population was extremely dense; property was much subdivided; there was a complicated bureaucratic system; the minds of the people were full of unrest, prone to mockery, sarcasm, and sedition, but, above all things, greedy of gain.

Hadrian, the serene Greek prince, did not love this second Antioch. He busied himself with the local educational institutions, especially with the Museum, and conversed with their teachers. But some years later he wrote to one of his friends: "You praise the Egyptians. I know them as an unstable and frivolous people, prone to be excited by the most trivial rumour. They are a most seditious, vain, and insolent race. Their capital is rich; everything abounds there and everything nourishes its prosperity. No one is idle. Some work at glass making, others make paper or weave linen. Every man has a trade—the halt, the lame, and the blind all work. But the one god they worship, Christians, Jews, and all alike, is *money*. . . . It is much to be desired that the manners and customs of this great city should be more in harmony with its great position as the capital of Egypt."[1]

**97. The Renewed Insurrection in Judæa (132–135 A.D.).** About the end of 131 Hadrian was again in Rome, where he consecrated the newly completed temple of Venus and Rome. In the same year, as we have seen, he promulgated the *edictum perpetuum* after securing its approval by the senate. The following year was disturbed by grave events in the East. During his most recent journey Hadrian had ordered the reconstruction of Jerusalem, the ruins of which appeared to an emperor so much attached to peace and to the arts to be a relic of a barbarous age that

[1] [*Hist. Aug.*] *Saturn.*, 8.

should be effaced. His idea, however, had been that it should be rebuilt as a splendid Græco-Roman city, symbolizing in Palestine the union that he had effected, there as elsewhere, between the Greek and the Roman genius. To the Hebrews this appeared to be the supreme insult to their race. Was the sacred city of Judaism to be transformed into a Græco-Roman metropolis with grandiose buildings and pagan sanctuaries, baths, and theatres, and to assume the sacrilegious name of Ælia Capitolina? There was a new outburst of religious fanaticism and the Jews rebelled under the leadership of a popular Messiah, a certain Simon Barkokeba or Barcosiba (Son of the Star) (132).

Hadrian, with less insight than Nero, did not, at first, attach much importance to this movement. But in 132, while he was resuming his peregrinations through the oriental provinces of the empire, beginning with Greece, Rome was losing the province of Judæa and the Roman armies sent there sustained repeated and serious reverses. It was necessary in the end to send thither Sextus Julius Severus, one of the best Roman generals, who had already distinguished himself in Britain, and who carried on the war with implacable severity. It is said that he tortured the leaders of the revolt to death, that he destroyed fifty fortresses and nearly a thousand villages, and that in the war there perished not less than 600,000 Jewish combatants! (134). It was not until after this carnage was over that Hadrian was able to betake himself to Jerusalem and give orders for the resumption of the work of reconstruction.

98. **Hadrian's Last Years** (135–138 A.D.). This was destined to be the end of the great emperor's

journeys. He returned to Rome for the last time, and divided his attention during his final years between his artistic tastes and the cares of State. In these years he completed his villa at Tibur—a town rather than a villa—which, in addition to a wonderful assemblage of gardens, fountains, shady groves, porticos, galleries, rotundas, baths, basilicas, libraries, theatres, and temples glowing with precious marbles and metals, was to contain miniature reproductions of all the finest things which the prince had admired.[1] But the man who, like Ulysses, had travelled so much was now overcome by a weariness of life which was perhaps aggravated by the commencement of the malady which was to prove fatal to him. Feeling that his strength was declining, he understood that, like Nerva and Trajan, he must think of his successor and again apply the method of adoption, that ingenious combination of the principles of selection and election whereby the senatorial aristocracy flattered itself that it had solved the tremendous problem of the transmission of the imperial dignity. Hadrian's first choice, for reasons unknown to us, fell on L. Ceionius Commodus Verus, a wholly unknown personage. But Verus died on January 1, 138, and the emperor then adopted T. Aurelius Fulvus Antoninus, who assumed the name of T. Ælius Hadrianus Antoninus, and made him his colleague in the empire, with the tribunician power and the *imperium proconsulare*. He required Antoninus to adopt the son of the Ceionius Verus who had first been chosen as his successor, and Marcus Annius Verus, a youth of seventeen, for whom Hadrian had a great affection and who was the future

[1] On Hadrian's villa at Tivoli *cf.* Boissier, *Promenades archéologiques*, Paris, 1887, pp. 202 ff.

Marcus Aurelius. We do not know for what reason Hadrian insisted on this adoption which, to some extent, limited his successor's power of choosing his own successor. Six months later on, July 10, 138, the emperor died at Baiæ.

**99. Characteristics of Hadrian's Government.** We know that on Hadrian's death the senate for a time resolutely opposed his successor's proposal that divine honours should be paid to his memory, that they threatened to withhold approval from his acts, and that they were only with great difficulty induced to desist from this opposition. This fact, no less than the conspiracy which was formed immediately after the adoption of Verus, proves that among the aristocracy there was a current of opinion strongly averse to the person and policy of the emperor, though this opposition was not so strong as that directed against almost all the emperors of the Julio-Claudian house. The reason for this opposition is undoubtedly to be found in Hadrian's attempt to reconcile the Greek and the Roman spirit. Ancient Rome, with her military spirit and her pride of power, was jealous of her supremacy and in the renewed traditionalist spirit of the new nobility she found a final force of resistance to this Hellenistic and juristic emperor, the protector of the provinces, the patron of art, literature, and philosophy. His long absences from Rome, his administrative reforms, his literary and artistic leanings, his lavish gifts to provincial cities, his enormous building operations, his passion for adorning the empire with all the splendours of Hellenism, and, finally, his cautious foreign policy, and his aversion to conquests, offended the ancient prejudices which still survived in the Roman world.

Moreover, in order to find the money for the great expenses of his government, Hadrian had had to make the machinery of taxation more efficient. Though he began his reign by remitting arrears of taxes he afterwards appointed an *advocatus fisci* to defend the rights of the imperial treasury against the subterfuges of the individual taxpayer. Further, the development of his vast endeavour to reconcile so many contrasting elements could not but be characterized by contradictions, gaps, and imperfections in which, as always, contemporaries found plenty of material for grievances. These considerations may help us to understand why Hadrian's government had so many enemies in spite of—and perhaps because of—its merits. But, since his policy corresponded to the needs of the time and went neither too fast nor too slow, it may also be seen why this opposition was impotent and, though it hampered the emperor, did not succeed in spoiling his work.

Hadrian did no more than bring to perfection the policy begun by Vespasian and continued by Trajan. In his system Rome was to be the political and military, and Hellenism the intellectual and moral, bond of union between all the peoples subject to the empire. While, therefore, he did his best to perfect the army by means of reforms, some of which became permanent, he promoted the increase and adornment of cities. These cities, the magnificence and the pleasures of which they were the scene, the interests which they controlled, and the opportunities for making money offered by the growth of so many urban communities, were now the chief bonds which kept succeeding generations attached to the unity of the empire. An immense population protected by well-defended frontiers, longing more and more to enjoy the advantages of flourishing and civilized city life—such was the Roman Empire in the time of Hadrian. Its prosperity was destined to last as long as it maintained the equilibrium of the two elements, the Roman which provided its military and political strength, and the Greek on which the prosperity of its city life was based.

# CHAPTER XII

## THE CLIMAX OF PROSPERITY AND THE BEGINNINGS OF DECLINE—FROM ANTONINUS PIUS TO DIDIUS JULIANUS (138–193 A.D.)

**100. Antoninus Pius (138–161 A.D.).** Antoninus Pius belonged to a family which originally came from Gaul. He was fifty-two years of age, had been consul, proconsul of Asia, a *iuridicus* in Italy, and a member of the imperial Council. He was a conscientious and upright man and fulfilled with unshakable firmness his duties to the memory of his father by preventing the senate from venting on Hadrian's memory the hatred which they had been compelled to suppress while he was alive. The attitude adopted by the senate on this question was, however, a hint of their real feelings, and another was conveyed by a new inclination towards imperial expansion and a tendency to demand a return to the policy of Trajan.[1] Antoninus, a man of mild, equable, and conciliatory temper, distinguished rather by moral qualities than by energy or intellectual power, quite understood these hints and made it his aim to preserve scrupulously the work done by Hadrian, rather than to continue his complex and

[1] The coins struck by order of the senate in 139 reveal a tendency to regard Parthia and Scythia as Roman provinces. *Cf.* Cohen, *Monnaies rom.*, ii., *Anton.*, Nos. 701, 825.

indefatigable activities, seeking at the same time to placate by opportune concessions the hostility prevalent in senatorial circles.

Such, in fact, was the double aim pursued by Antoninus throughout all his government. The grandiose achievement of Hadrian was left practically intact. The *concilium principis*, the organization of the imperial chancellery and of the *advocatus fisci*, the military reforms, the religious policy, the direction of social legislation and of foreign policy were maintained as they had been established by his predecessor. The only new institution set up by Hadrian which Antoninus abolished was that of the Italian *iuridici*. But on the other hand he gratified the senate with lavish compensations, both formal and constitutional. He was never weary of repeating that towards the senate he meant to behave as he had wished the emperors to behave to him when he was himself a senator. He pardoned those who had been condemned for political offences during the last years of Hadrian's life and established a rule of unlimited indulgence towards those who conspired against him. He tempered the exactions of the *fiscus*, reduced the taxes, and, in 147 or 148, even went so far as to renounce solemnly all arrears of taxation for the three preceding lustres. He did his best to make men forget the ardent Hellenism of his predecessor by bringing back old traditions and the ancient republican symbols to honour at Rome and by restoring the old forms of the state religion. For this, like Vespasian, he was honoured by the senate *ob insignem erga cærimonias publicas curam ac religionem.*[1]

In him Rome saw, instead of a restless monarch like

[1] *C. I. L.*, vi., 1001.

Hadrian, a prince who hardly ever quitted the capital, whatever might happen on the frontiers of the empire. His predecessor's luxurious mania for building was checked. In every branch of administration Antoninus did his best to reduce expenditure; he diminished the salaries lavished by Hadrian on artists, particularly musicians, though he was generous, on the contrary, to rhetoricians and philosophers. He avoided war with Parthia; but, notwithstanding his love of peace and his attachment to the principles laid down by Hadrian, he yielded to the expansionist party so far as Britain was concerned, and reoccupied the frontier line as fixed by Agricola. Thus, when he died after ruling for about twenty-three years he was sincerely mourned by all those who upheld republican and traditionalist principles at Rome. In him and in Trajan the Roman genius irradiated the vast empire with its last sunset splendours.

Amid the glories of that sunset, however, storm clouds were already gathering. The emperor who had reduced the taxes left the Roman coinage more depreciated than even Trajan had done. He had increased by one third the alloy of the *denarius* which was a state of matters worse than had obtained in the days of the last civil war. The prince who, from love of Rome and deference to the senate, had never inspected a province or a frontier, died in ignorance of what the barbarians were doing beyond the Rhine, the Danube, or the Euphrates, in Africa, or in Britain. He left the army impaired by a prolonged peace, by the laxity which had followed the ceaseless vigilance of Hadrian's supervision, and by the hasty and too numerous enrolments of barbarians turned without consideration into Roman citizens. And finally, on every frontier he left the defence of the empire weakened and its enemies made more audacious by the remissness of his policy.

**101. Marcus Aurelius, the Imperial Philosopher (161–180 A.D.).** As we have already seen, the election of the new emperor may be said to have been decided in the time of Hadrian. He had willed that Antoninus should adopt as his sons Marcus Annius Verus (who then styled himself Aurelius, the name of his adoptive grandfather Hadrian) and Lucius the son of the other Verus who had first been chosen as the successor to the empire. Marcus Aurelius had received tribunician and proconsular powers in 146 and had therefore become the colleague and presumptive successor of Antoninus, who at his death explicitly chose him as such, though his choice as emperor, which events proved to be well inspired, ultimately goes back to Hadrian. On the death of Antoninus, Marcus Aurelius, mindful of Hadrian's intentions, appointed as his colleague in the empire his adoptive brother Lucius Ælius Verus and the two princes presented themselves jointly to the senate, the prætorians, and the people.

Marcus was a passionate student of philosophy, and a fervent follower of the Stoic sect. Philosophy he understood after the fashion of his time as a rule of thought and action and not merely as an intellectual pursuit. For the first time the Roman empire, hitherto governed by an aristocracy of politicians and soldiers, had for its head a philosopher whose highest ambition was to realize the ethical ideal of the Stoic school. Hellenic intellectualism had never won a greater triumph. With Marcus Aurelius the philosophy which Rome had more or less distrusted for so many centuries and which Vespasian had banished from Italy, rose at a bound to the government not of a small State but of the greatest and most powerful empire to which men had ever yet paid homage. Plato had said that men and States would be happy on the day when philosophers became rulers. How far did Marcus Aurelius prove or disprove the bold theory of that great thinker?

**102. The Oriental War (161–166 A.D.).** The new emperor's trials were destined to be serious, for stormy times were ahead. Immediately after the death of Antoninus, who was better at adroitly postponing than at dealing firmly with difficulties, the effects of his policy became apparent. In Britain there was an incursion of the Picts against the new *Vallum*, while the Roman troops stationed in the country threatened to proclaim another emperor. In Germany on the upper Danube and on the Rhine the Catti and the Cauci were in a state of unrest and were making raids into Roman territory. In the East, Vologeses III., King of Parthia, having completed the military preparations he had been making in the reign of Antoninus Pius, invaded Armenia, and drove out the king placed by the Romans on the throne of that country. From Armenia he broke into Syria where the vassal sovereigns and even the Syrian cities rose in rebellion against the Roman dominion (161).

The gravest danger was in the East. Marcus Aurelius ordered a levy, sent enormous reinforcements to Syria under competent generals, among whom was his own colleague L. Verus, and began a war which in length and importance was destined to be comparable to the great campaigns of Trajan. In the years 162–163 the Roman general Statius Priscus succeeded in reconquering Armenia and in replacing its exiled monarch on the throne, but in Syria Avidius Cassius had not at once been able to take the offensive. The discipline and moral of the troops in that region were at their worst. It was necessary first to train them over again from the beginning and break their seditious and rebellious spirit. Finally Cassius was able to take the offensive and, after initial successes which broke the cohesion of the enemy, he managed to advance vigorously if not rapidly. His progress was such that, apparently in 165, he penetrated into the heart of the Parthian empire and burned Seleucia, and even Ctesiphon the capital of the kingdom. Lucius Verus, who appears to have been up to this time occupied with the munitionment of the armies in Antiochia, now invaded Media, and the triumphs of Trajan's expedition were renewed. Then, and not till then, the King of Parthia made up his mind to sue for peace. This time the conditions were less favourable than on previous occasions, and he had to cede upper Mesopotamia, which was the first conquest which the Romans had made and had succeeded in holding in the region of the Tigris and the Euphrates since the days of Pompey the Great (166).

**103. The First Germanic Invasion (167–175 A.D.).** Thus after five years the emperor philosopher brought to a successful termination one of the most difficult oriental wars which the Romans had ever undertaken. His legions, however, on their return from their victorious campaign brought back with them to Europe the terrible scourge of bubonic plague which claimed more victims than the war itself had done, and which for years desolated more especially the Balkan peninsula and Italy. And, as if all possible misfortunes were fated to occur simultaneously, a new danger threatened the empire now that the East had been quieted, this time from the North.

In 166 all the provinces north and south of the Danube—Dacia, Pannonia, Noricum, and Rhætia—were invaded by a variegated coalition of Germanic tribes which swept aside every obstacle and penetrated as far as Italy. They besieged Aquileia, burned Opitergium (Oderzo), and pushed on as far as the Piave. This was in fact the advance guard of the German expeditions which in subsequent centuries were destined to overwhelm the empire. Who or what was the cause of this new scourge? In the absence of positive information we are reduced almost entirely to hypothesis. It is possible that at this moment there was a great movement of German and Slavonic tribes from the East to the West which had caused unusually severe pressure on the barbarians settled on the frontiers of the empire. The chief reason for what happened, however, is to be found in the new conditions which had arisen in Germany itself. The Germanic peoples when they were brought into contact, no longer with little Celtic states which were practically barbarous, but with a great civilized community like the Roman Empire, gradually acquired a certain amount of civilization themselves. They learned many things, good and bad, from the empire, which was at the same time their model and their terror, among others greater skill in defending themselves against the Romans by the adoption of Roman methods of warfare. It is easy to see, therefore, how the old untamable spirit of rebellion against discipline and the old habit of internecine warfare gradually disappeared among the Germans owing to their being in contact with the empire, and how, even in Germany, the scattered tribes began to form themselves into great monarchical states which were crude imitations of the Roman Empire and attempts to form a political and military organization. For this purpose, however, they needed money, and the Germans, who were ignorant and idle, had very elementary ideas of how to exploit their land. On the other hand it is not improbable that such principles of civil order as were introduced among the barbarous Germanic peoples favoured the growth of the population. This led to an economic crisis which was bound to drive them to invade richer countries and more fertile lands. Their natural objective was Southern and South-Western Europe, civilized and enriched as it had been by the Roman government, the Europe of great cities, flourishing marts, and fertile plains and hills. While the Roman armies on the frontier were numerous and well trained, the Germans kept quiet; but for several years the greater part of the Western legions had been in the East fighting against the Parthians in a war news of which probably reached the countries beyond the Rhine and the Danube in a very distorted shape. Naturally enough, therefore, a numerous body of barbarians, chiefly Germanic, among whom were the Marcomanni, the Hermonduri, the Quadi, the Jazigi, the Sarmatians, the Scythians, the Victuali, the Rossolani, and the Alani, seized the opportunity of hurling themselves in accordance with a preconcerted plan on the frontiers of the empire which they knew to be ill guarded.

We do not know what the object of the invaders was, or even whether they had any special object beyond plunder. It is certain that their sudden attack terrified Italy, all the more because the empire still had so large a part of its forces involved in the East. The gravity of the danger is demonstrated by the fact that this time Marcus Aurelius put his books aside and went in person to defend the frontiers of his empire. The history of the war is so fragmentary that it would be impossible to reconstruct it chronologically. We know that it lasted till 175, that it was a very violent struggle, that new legions had to be raised, that this was no easy matter, that the Romans did not rely wholly on their military power but endeavoured by diplomatic means to break up the Germanic coalition, that the conflict had various vicissitudes, and that at one time a horde of Custoboci broke out of Dacia and penetrated the very heart of Greece, getting as far as Elatea in Phocis. Whatever the actual course of events, the horrible conflagration appeared in 175 to be under control. The enemy seem to have been compelled to cede a strip of territory on the left bank of the Danube, to admit Roman forts and garrisons, to promise to use only certain Roman provincial markets at certain specified times, and to bind themselves to furnish soldiers for the Roman army. At the same time it appears that they received certain compensations for these concessions, and that, for the first time, barbarians were admitted within the imperial frontier, even into Italy itself, where they were distributed as *coloni* or cultivators among the landed proprietors of the province. This was the first beginning of a policy destined to have grave consequences.[1]

[1] On the introduction of the barbarians into Roman territory may be consulted E. Huschke, *Ueber den Census und die Steuerverfassung der früheren Römischen Kaiserzeit*, Berlin, 1847, pp. 149 ff.

In a word the peace seems to have been a skilfully disguised compromise.

**104. The Revolt of Avidius Cassius (175 A.D.).** The effects of this costly, sanguinary, and only partly victorious war were many and serious, both in Italy and in the provinces. Southern Spain was disturbed by an incursion of the Mauri, Egypt by an insurrection provoked by the so-called "Bucolici" about whom nothing definite is known. The finances were gravely embarrassed and a further deterioration of the coinage, both gold and silver, became necessary. What was more serious was that in the very year in which peace was concluded with the barbarians the empire ran the risk of a great civil war, this time owing to no fault of the senate. The senate was extremely well satisfied with the emperor's policy. The prince had not only followed the example of his immediate predecessors in renouncing the right of penal jurisdiction over senators, but had laid it down that capital cases in which senators were charged should be conducted with closed doors. He continued the useful practice of appointing *Curatores rerum publicarum*, but invariably chose them with scrupulous care from the senatorial order. Once more finance and foreign affairs were submitted to the supreme direction of the senate, to whom also was given the control of treaties, and to whom the right of appeal was transferred from the emperor. "Nothing," he frequently said, "belongs to the emperor. The very house in which I live is your property." This time, as at the beginning of the reign of Hadrian, the signal for revolt came from the military element. The leader of the revolt of 175 was Avidius Cassius, the conqueror of the Parthians and the greatest general of his time, to whom Marcus

Aurelius during the Germanic wars had entrusted the supreme command in the East. What this soldier thought of the philosophic emperor is expressed in an extant letter of his on the authenticity of which doubts have of course been cast by contemporary German scholarship: "Alas for the country which must endure this tribe which is so greedy of riches and which has sated its greed! Alas for the country! Marcus is certainly an excellent man but, desirous of being praised for his clemency, he allows many men to live whose conduct he reprobates. Where is that Lucius Cassius whose name I bear so vainly? Where is Cato the censor and the old school of manners? That which has long been lost is now no more desired by any one. Marcus philosophizes, studies natural science, the soul, everything that is right and proper; but he has no clear idea of what is required by the State. You in Rome see well what kind of energy and action is necessary to restore its ancient character. I see it here when I observe the governors of the provinces. But can I call proconsuls and presidents these men whose one idea on receiving a province from the senate or from Marcus Aurelius is to lead a disorderly life and amass riches? You know our philosopher's prætorian præfect. Three days before his appointment he was poor and needy. Now he has suddenly made his fortune. . . . How, I ask, if not out of the very entrails of the State and at the cost of the fortunes of the provincials? . . . ."[1]

In this letter are manifest the anxieties inspired in a soldier brought up in the old Roman tradition by the ever more pronouncedly intellectual and civil character which had been assumed by the policy of the imperial

[1] [*Hist. Aug.*] *Av. Cass.*, 14.

government since the time of Hadrian. Secretly but tenaciously the military element was resisting the transformation of the State commenced by the great emperor who had been a scholar and a jurist, in order that they might hark back to the glorious memories of Trajan. It would be difficult to say how it came about that this discontent broke out into open rebellion. It seems that Cassius thought he ought to be the successor of Marcus Aurelius and that in 175, on a false rumour of the emperor's death which was spread abroad in the East, he too hastily proclaimed himself, relying on the favour of the legions and the support of the Eastern governors. When, however, it became known that the news was untrue and that Marcus Aurelius was coming to the East, the sense of order and discipline which still reigned in the empire triumphed. Cassius was slain three months after his *pronunciamento* by two junior officers, and when Marcus reached Antioch and Alexandria there was nothing left but the ashes of what had threatened to be a dangerous conflagration.

105. **The Persecution of the Christians and the End of Marcus Aurelius (175–180 A.D.).** All these wars, epidemics, and revolts had profoundly agitated and distressed the peoples of the empire, and the consequence was a gigantic growth of popular superstition produced by terror. The humbler classes, having vainly appealed to all the gods of the old religions to save them, turned furiously against the Christians. Marcus Aurelius, as a good Stoic, could not be much inclined to this "superstition,"[1] but his natural and constant mildness would certainly have prevented him from being severe had not his hand been forced

[1] *Meditations*, xi., 3.

by public opinion throughout the empire, which became ever more fierce against the growing Christian minority. Already between 163 and 167 the martyrdom of St. Justin had taken place at Rome, although he had been freely allowed to defend Christianity in the time of Antoninus. This had been followed by a persecution which had gradually grown more intense as the position of the empire had become more serious, and it had been, so to say, authorized by a decree of the emperor in which torture and death were threatened against Christians as such, and not merely in so far as they were guilty of ordinary offences.

On his return from the East, Marcus Aurelius celebrated a splendid triumph at Rome for the victories over the Germans and the Sarmatians (December 23, 176). It was on this occasion that the senate voted him the fine equestrian statue that is still admired on the Capitol, and on the Campus Martius the column which still rises in Rome from the square that bears its name (Piazza Colonna), and which is adorned with bas-reliefs representing the struggle with the peoples of the Danube. The column and the statue were well earned, for the philosophic emperor had done his duty as a general and had spared no pains to defend the empire.

At this point Marcus Aurelius took a decision which no one would have expected of him. His colleague, L. Verus, having died some years previously, the emperor adopted in his place L. Aurelius Commodus, Verus's son, and caused him to be invested with the tribunician power in 177 after having conferred on him the title of imperator at the end of 176. Commodus was then fifteen years of age, and it is difficult to explain how it was that the Stoic philosopher so suddenly abandoned the method of adoption to which he himself owed the empire and which had been so successful, or why he resorted to the dangerous dynastic principle of heredity, in favour of a boy of fifteen, thus repeating the experiment which had such disastrous results in the case of Nero. This act of Marcus Aurelius is alone sufficient to show that Avidius Cassius may not have been altogether wrong in his estimate of the emperor which is quoted above. Be that as it may, the adoption of Commodus was destined to have consequences which were all the more serious as Marcus did not long survive that event. In 178 he had once more to go to the Danubian frontier where there was renewed unrest among the Germans. He had been there for about two years, busy with battles and negotiations when death overtook him in 180 at Vindobona (Vienna).

In his civil administration Marcus Aurelius, constantly occupied as he was with war, could not do great things like Hadrian. Yet he continued Hadrian's traditions so far as times and circumstances permitted. He built little, for he lacked money. He re-established the *iuridici* for Italy abolished by Antoninus. He protected rhetoricians, jurists, and philosophers. He appears to have assigned a salary of 100,000 sesterces to the members of the imperial *concilium* and 60,000 to the council's legal advisers. He developed charitable institutions by appointing a *præfectus alimentorum* of consular rank. He pursued the policy of mitigating the severities of the civil and criminal law and of making both more rapid and more humane in their action. In a word, if the world was not particularly happy under his rule, it must be admitted that the emperor philosopher did his duty amid circumstances and difficulties by no means congenial to his temperament. The one mistake which—so far as we can see—he might have avoided, was his mistake about Commodus. Ancient writers tell us that according to the general opinion there was one man who would have been a worthy successor—Pompeianus. Why did Marcus not choose him? And if he had chosen him would Pompeianus have been able to avert the grave crisis which we shall shortly have to relate? These are terrible questions which history cannot answer.

**106. The Empire at the Death of Marcus Aurelius. Its Splendours and its Weaknesses.** The reign of Marcus Aurelius closed the golden age of the Roman Empire. The second century after Christ was in fact the age of the greatest prosperity and happiness which the countries governed by Rome were ever destined to enjoy. This was the effect of many causes, immediate and remote: of the profound peace which with some insignificant exceptions prevailed in the interior; of the natural process of repair which had begun in the provinces in the preceding century, and of which the beneficial effects were now mature; of the imperial administration which was in general efficient. The grandiose system of roads, the diminished variety of languages, weights, measures, and coinage, the assimilation of manners, the canalization of rivers throughout the empire, the efficient policing of the seas, the closer relations with Rome, the army itself—all these created and favoured new currents of exchange which brought into mutual contact the most widely separated regions and in each produced knowledge of new habits and new commodities, and at the same time new wants and new activities.

Everywhere were opened factories for textiles, weapons, and dyes. The industries of the East, the manufacture of purple, of glass and jewellery, flourished exceedingly, having found new and rich markets in the less civilized provinces of the West. Even the parts of Europe which had remained longest barbarous, such as Northern Italy, Gaul, and Spain, began with some success, although not without imperfection, to imitate the products of oriental industry. Innumerable merchant ships ploughed the Mediterranean, great commercial expeditions explored new rivers and coasts, and pushed as far as remote India and China in search of silk and pearls, of rice which was then used as a medicament or a highly luxurious article of food, and taking with them in addition to the gold and silver which these very remote countries accepted in payment for their goods, the few products of the Mediterranean such as wine, which were consumed there. Like commerce and industry, agriculture was at the height of its prosperity and the cities great and small which were rising everywhere were surrounded with smiling orchards and gardens.

The population also was increasing, especially in the larger cities, which were developing very fast while the lesser centres were losing their importance, as always happens in very large states which are prosperous and provided with rapid and secure communications. Riches, culture, luxury, industry, and commerce tended to become concentrated in a few rapidly growing centres of population, opulence, and beauty, like Carthage, Alexandria, Antioch, Ephesus, Thessalonica, Milan, Verona, and Lyons, not to speak of Rome. Of this phenomenon, which has been repeated in so many other States, there are conspicuous traces in ancient writers, but an indirect proof is afforded by the growing solicitude of the emperors about the administration of the smaller towns. In this tendency of imperial policy has been seen merely one of the usurpations produced by absolutism, but it is more just to regard it as one effect of the decline of the lesser towns in favour of the great cities. There, little by little, the richer families and the more cultivated individuals tended to congregate, and in the lesser places the social elements which supplied the materials for local administration in the ancient city were no longer to be found. The result was that local administration failed more and more and the imperial authorities had to supply its defects.

Intellectual progress kept pace with material improvements. The second century was distinguished by the widest diffusion of public education throughout all the countries of the empire although great masterpieces in art and letters were rare. "The empire is crammed with schools and scholars," exclaimed the Roman poet Juvenal and the Greek rhetorician Aristides with one voice. Literature, philosophy, and science ceased to be the exclusive preserve of little cliques of choice spirits and became popular. Culture was no longer to be so profound but it was much more universal; intellectual activity was less fertile but more widely diffused. A love of philosophy pervaded all classes, and good taste spread from the capital to the remotest townships, where private liberality vied with official energy in beautifying the streets and imitating Rome. The most striking proof of all this splendour was that for a moment the ancient world was on the point of abandoning its pessimistic doctrine of corruption and of regarding this great transformation of the world as we regard it, that is to say, as progress. "The world," said Tertullian, a Christian writer, "is every day better known, better cultivated, and more civilized than before. Everywhere roads are traced, every district is known, every country opened to commerce. Smiling fields have invaded the forests; flocks and herds have routed the wild beasts; the very sands are sown; the rocks are broken up, the marshes drained. There are now as many cities as there formerly were cottages. Reefs and shoals have lost their terrors. Wherever there is a trace of life there are houses and human habitations and well ordered governments."[1]

All this, as has too often happened in the world's history, was no more than a fleeting semblance of prosperity destined to disappear at the first gust of misfortune. At this moment indeed begins a period which, by reason of its contrast with what went before, presents a tragic enigma to the historian. The mischief did not come from without. Had it been so, the crisis would have been shorter and more easily overcome. Nor does the responsibility for the melancholy era which was now dawning rest entirely with the men who now rose to power and who certainly were better than they have been represented by tradition. The evil was internal and was latent in a certain want of balance between the forces which governed the empire. The empire was now ruled by a senate in which was gathered the very flower of the rich and cultivated families of the provinces from Gaul to Africa and Syria, an aristocracy whose equal for culture, refinement of taste, nobility of aspiration, and variety of view the ancient world had never seen. In

[1] Tertull., *De anima*, 30.

this aristocracy the austere and difficult virtues of the Roman character were tempered by the influences of the loftiest Greek culture. In its ranks all forms of human genius and activity were brilliantly represented. There were generals, administrators, jurists, men of letters, philosophers, patrons of art and literature. They aspired to preserve the military vigour of the empire while they gave it a humane, intelligent, and splendid government which shed about it all the benefits of civilization and peace. Trajan, Hadrian, Antoninus, Marcus Aurelius, all attest the zeal and devotion with which they discharged this task. But, as the aristocracy of the empire became more refined, cultivated, splendid, and humane, as their aspirations became ever higher and nobler, the army became more barbarous. Under Claudius and Nero, the provincials made their entry into the army, and they became more numerous in the ranks under the Flavians. But with the advent of the Antonines, especially the two last of the line, foreigners and actual barbarians were received into the legions.[1] True, these barbarians, when they entered the army, were made Roman citizens, but the mere title of citizen was not enough to change their disposition. Even more serious was the fact that the prætorian guard, once the repository of the purest Roman spirit of all the troops, was invaded, though more slowly, by the same process of deterioration, for the number of Italians among them declined as the growing riches of the peninsula more and more disinclined its citizens to military service.[2] Between these two forces—the senate and the army—interposed what we should now call the administration, the nu-

[1] *Cf.* O. Seeck in *Rheinisches Museum*, 43, 611–613.

[2] Dio Cass., lxxiv., 2; cf. *C. I. L.*, vi., 2375–2402.

merous body of magistrates who exercised the civil and military functions of the State. This body, at any rate so far as the higher posts were concerned, was still recruited on the aristocratic principle from persons possessing the rank and education of senators and knights. Above them all stood the emperor, the first and most powerful of the senators, the head of the army, of the nobility, and of the administration, the symbol of empire and of authority, invested with powers which had never been any more clearly defined than the legal principle from which those powers emanated. It was clear that while the emperor, the administration, and the senatorial aristocracy were agreed they would have the power to keep the legions in order. The reigns of Trajan, of Hadrian, of Antoninus Pius, and of Marcus Aurelius are a sufficient proof of this. But what would happen on the day on which this accord was broken? This was the question now to be put to the empire at the moment when it had reached the zenith of its prosperity—a question to which a tragic answer was given by the terrible century the history of which is now to be related.

**107. The Reign of Commodus (180–192 A.D.).** The choice of Commodus as his successor which had been made by Marcus Aurelius showed, after a hundred years of almost unbroken concord, how fragile a thing the agreement between the emperor and the senate was. Since Titus and Domitian, Commodus was the only case in which a son had succeeded his father in the supreme office, and the fact that he was only nineteen years of age aggravated the situation. The senate, which had never acknowledged the principle of hereditary transmission of the imperial dignity, and which favoured the candidature of Claudius

Pompeianus, regarded the accession of Commodus as a usurpation. It was not long, therefore, before there was a rupture between the emperor and the senate, the consequences of which were all the more serious as Commodus was a young man who resembled Nero much more closely than Domitian to whom his contemporaries more frequently compared him.

After a brief apprenticeship he abandoned the affairs of state to his prætorian præfect, and gave himself up to enjoying the empire, thus aggravating the discontent and hatred of the senate. This negligence and the suspicion with which the senate regarded him afforded an opportunity greedily seized by many low-class adventurers to rise to offices hitherto reserved for men of senatorial and equestrian rank. Under Commodus repeated attempts were made to deprive senators of the exclusive privilege of occupying high positions in the State. Obscure and unworthy persons insinuated themselves everywhere and often succeeded in placing themselves above the highest and noblest in the empire. At the same time the young prince sought to multiply the outward and visible signs of his supremacy over everything and everybody. He set himself to revive in his person all the adulatory titles which the senate had abhorred in the case of Nero and Domitian. The inevitable consequence of such conduct was a renewed opposition and a multiplicity of conspiracies, and in a few years this bitter struggle between the emperor and the senate disorganized the whole administration.

We know little of the policy of Commodus. It is therefore difficult for us to estimate it, to judge, for example, whether the peace which he concluded with the Germanic tribes which had given his father so much trouble was honourable and profitable or the reverse. It is certain, however, that during his reign, which lasted twelve years, there were frequent revolts in many of the provinces, that there were grave symptoms of disorganization in the armies, that there were enough deserters in Gaul to form the makings of a rebellion, and that the finances went from bad to worse. Such a reign could have but one end. As in the case of Nero and Domitian, Commodus, in his turn, became more and more suspicious and violent and raised about him such an atmosphere of hatred and fear that his own friends finally became convinced that they must rid the empire of his presence. On December 31, 192, a group of courtiers, fearing for their own personal safety, and certain of being supported by a large measure of public favour and applause, successfully combined to assassinate the emperor.

**108. Pertinax (Jan. 1–March 28, 193 A.D.).** The end of Commodus recalled that of Domitian, as his reign had recalled that of Nero. The great question now was whether his death would be followed by the outbreak of a crisis such as had followed the fall of Nero, or whether a new Nerva would at once arise to lead the empire back to happier days. A great effort was made to avoid a revolutionary crisis which for a moment seemed to be successful. The senate chose as emperor Publius Helvius Pertinax, a man who might truly be described as a new Nerva, and they intimated their choice with so much firmness and resolution that the prætorians accepted it. Pertinax was a *homo novus*, for he was the first of his family to enter the senate, but he had gained the *latus clavus* by services in the army. His character was simple and austere, and as a soldier he impersonated like Trajan all the traditions of Roman militarism. He hastened, therefore, once more to recognize all the rights of the senate and to concede to them all the honours which were their due. He dismissed from office all the adventurers introduced by Commodus, he recalled the exiles, and immediately took in hand the restoration of the finances and of the discipline of the armies, especially of the prætorian guard which had been vitiated in the bad days of Commodus, in all things acting in concert with the senate. But in attempting to re-establish the former discipline of the prætorians he presumed too much on his own authority and on that of the senate. Even that body was now too much contaminated by low-class provincials. On March 28, 193, three months after his accession to the Empire, the prætorians revolted and killed Pertinax in his palace. His death was followed by a great panic in Rome, in the midst of which two senators, Sulpicianus, who was the father-in-law of the murdered emperor, and Didius Julianus, one of the richest of the senatorial body, seized the opportunity to persuade the prætorians to acclaim them emperors. Sulpicianus, whom Pertinax had directed to calm the mutinous prætorians, succeeded in entering their camp while Didius Julianus remained outside. But the prætorians well knew how to exploit the situation, and through deputations which they sent to Sulpicianus and Julianus they put the empire up to auction, asking each in turn what donations he would give in exchange for his election. Didius Julianus offered most and was made emperor.

The empire, however, was not yet a thing which could be sold to the highest bidder. When the legions in the provinces heard what had happened at Rome, they refused to recognize the bargain and revolted against the emperor of the prætorians. The legions of Britain proclaimed their commander, D. Clodius Albinus; those of Pannonia, L. Septimius Severus; those of Egypt, C. Pescennius Niger. After 124 years the outbreak after the death of Nero was repeated. The uncertainty of the legal principle governing the succession to the supreme authority had once more driven the legions to intervene and their intervention produced a civil war.

# CHAPTER XIII

## THE ABSOLUTE MONARCHY: SEPTIMIUS SEVERUS

(193–211 A.D.)

**109. The Civil War and the Victory of Septimius Severus (193–197 A.D.).** Of the three pretenders the most acceptable to the senate was Pescennius, an Italian probably of noble family. It does not appear that he was a man of much education, but he was a good soldier and by his courteous manners he ingratiated himself with everyone, including the troops, on whom, however, he imposed the most rigid discipline. Clodius Albinus, on the other hand, was, like Severus, of African descent, having been born at Hadrumetum of an ancient and noble family. He had many adherents at Rome, and many friends in the senate. Septimius Severus, who sprang from a rich and well known family of Leptis, was the most cultivated of the three competitors, for he had received a very brilliant education both in Latin and in Greek. He had studied at Athens, and as a young man had devoted himself to literature. He was, however, the first of his family to become a senator and a magistrate, and he was, therefore, a *novus homo*. Whether for this reason or for some other that we do not know, he was the candidate least favoured by the senate.

But, though he was the least favoured candidate, Septimius Severus, as governor of Pannonia, was the one who happened to be nearest to Italy and he had enough resolution and intelligence to profit by this geographical advantage. Without loss of time he marched on Italy and descended with his army into the valley of the Po. Didius Julianus, having no troops but the prætorian guard which had been unable to bar the passes of the Alps, defended himself as best he could. But the disparity of force was too great. He was abandoned by his soldiers and by the fleet, and on the approach of Septimius Severus the senate deposed and condemned him to death, electing the governor of Pannonia in his place.

The circumstances of his election were such that the new emperor could be under no illusion as to the sentiments entertained towards him by the senate, which had accepted him under compulsion. But Septimius Severus knew that he had to contend with two powerful rivals, and therefore did his best to make a favourable impression. He punished the accomplices of Didius Julianus; he caused the apotheosis of Pertinax to be decreed; he promised not to condemn any senator to death, and even made the senate pass a law declaring any emperor who did so a public enemy; he declared that his reign would be guided by the example of Pertinax and Marcus Aurelius. He did not hesitate to disband the prætorian guard which had slain Pertinax and put the empire up for sale, dismissing all the soldiers who composed it, and filling their places by the best that could be chosen from the other legions. Finally, in order to immobilize Clodius Albinus and to please the senate, he declared him his colleague in the empire and his presumptive heir, giving him the supreme command of the western provinces.

Having taken this precaution and having given these pledges of his intentions to the senate, he turned to the East to attack Pescennius, who had already secured for himself Asia and Egypt, the neutrality of Armenia, and the alliance of several oriental sovereigns among whom the most important was the King of Parthia. Severus was determined that Pescennius should not, like Vespasian, be allowed time in which to prepare to attack him, and, knowing that rapidity of action was the best means of success, he remained only a month in the capital and then immediately left for the East at the head of a great force. Having repulsed the enemy and blockaded a large part of his force in Byzantium, Severus, or rather his generals, defeated the remainder first at Cyzicus, then at Nicea, and finally near Issus. The fighting was very severe but in the end his most dangerous rival was beaten and, in the course of a tragic flight, captured and beheaded (194). It appears that the partisans of Pescennius were severely treated, but no senator was condemned to death. Those who were most seriously compromised were punished by the confiscation of the whole or part of their patrimony.

But, although Pescennius was dead, the war was not over, for Byzantium still resisted desperately. Moreover Septimius Severus could not flatter himself that his victory would increase the goodwill of the senate. He therefore decided to give his government a more secure and legitimate tenure, and in 195 he celebrated his own adoption by Marcus Aurelius! To cause himself to be adopted by the act of a dead man was from the legal point of view an extremely bold, not to say extravagant, proceeding. But by offering violence in this way both to law and common sense he was able to represent himself as the continuator of the Antonines whose name was so much venerated throughout the empire. Further it appears that Septimius made use of this adoption to secure for himself the vast fortune left by Commodus.[1] At the same time, while pressing the siege of Byzantium even more closely, he made provision for the complete subjection of the East, and sent an expedition to Adiabene and Osroene, the sovereigns of which had supported Pescennius. The whole of 195 was occupied with this expedition and with the siege of Byzantium, which finally capitulated in the spring of 196. The East might be said to be conquered and Septimius Severus hastened back to Italy.

There was a strong opposition in the senate, which since the death of Pescennius had fixed its hopes on Clodius Albinus. The latter had only accepted the position of colleague to Septimius in order to have time to prepare an army against him in Gaul and Britain. He had now openly raised the standard of rebellion, had convoked a counter-senate, and threatened, like another Vitellius, to make a descent from the Alps.[2] As usual Severus lost no time. Immediately on his arrival in Italy he caused Clodius Albinus to be declared a public enemy by the army and by the senate,

[1] Dio Cass., lxxvi., 9.

[2] [*Hist. Aug.*] *Clod. Alb.*, 8, on the other hand, attributes the beginning of this war to Septimius Severus, but the account given is so full of romantic stratagems that it inspires no confidence. The concatenation of events shows clearly that the war was begun by Clodius Albinus, who had a strong party in the senate behind him.

and persuaded the senate to proclaim his own son Septimius Bassianus (the future Caracalla) Cæsar, thus designating him heir to the empire. Bassianus was made to assume the venerated name of Marcus Aurelius, perhaps in order to compensate for the violence with which the hereditary principle was thus asserted. Septimius then left Rome to carry on the war. His task was no light one. If we may believe Dio, Albinus had collected not less than 150,000 men and Severus opposed him with as many more, that is to say, counting auxiliaries, about fifteen legions, a force larger than had ever been employed against the Great King, and a really enormous army for antiquity.

The events of this war are little known. It appears that Albinus was at first successful and that this caused great joy to the senate at Rome. But in a decisive battle at Tivurtium (Trévoux) not far from Lyons the new pretender was finally defeated (February 19, 197).

This time Septimius declared to the senate that the severities of Sulla, Marius, and Augustus were preferable to the weakness which had ruined Cæsar and Pompey.[1] Twenty-nine senators were condemned to death, a great number of rich Gauls and Spaniards who had supported Albinus were also executed, and their property confiscated. The product of these confiscations was immense. Part was divided among the soldiers, part paid into the treasury, and part taken by Severus, who thus laid the foundations of his colossal private fortune, destined to be the greatest which any of the emperors had hitherto possessed.[2]

[1] Dio Cass., lxxv., 8.

[2] Herod., iii., 15, 3.

**110. The Reign of Severus and its Characteristics.** The God of War had pronounced final judgment. Like Vespasian, Severus at the head of his victorious legions was now master of the situation. What could the senate do but submit? But Severus, unlike Vespasian, was not an Italian but an African, on whom (as we have seen was the case with Africans) the Roman spirit sat like a thin and lightly adhering veneer, beneath which seethed all the passions and the instincts of his race. Severus had none of Trajan's filial respect for the senate and the institutions of the aristocratic republic, he had none of the admiration of a disciple or the gratitude of a beneficiary. Not that he was an enemy of the senate or deliberately wished to humiliate and belittle it. In quieter times, as himself one of many senators, he would probably have been no less jealous than any other of the privileges of his own order. But fortune had permitted him to win the empire, at the cost of terrible dangers, against the will of the senate who had preferred Pescennius Niger and Clodius Albinus to him. Having won it he was determined to keep it and to enjoy it—herein appeared the African—as the possession of himself and of his family. Even before he conquered Albinus he had, as we have seen, appointed his son his colleague and had conferred great dignities on his wife Julia Domna, a Syrian lady of illustrious family and high intelligence. Further he had openly shown that the imperial authority was to be used to make his fortune. He was, in fact, the first emperor who set up a system of administration for his private fortune and appointed *procuratores privatarum rerum.* He was well aware that, little as the senate had liked his triumph, they would like still less a government animated by this spirit. It was inevitable, therefore, that he should distrust the senate, and, without open antagonism, he sought support for his government, not, as the Antonines had done, in the prestige, the sincere admiration, and the willing co-operation of the great council, but in the energy and intelligence of a small group of trusted and devoted servants whose origin and rank were matters of indifference to him, in the army which rivalled the senate in being the source of the supreme imperial authority, and in the classes below the senatorial order, more especially the knights. Hence, under his rule, there was an increase in the authority and consideration of the imperial functionaries, particularly in that of the *advocati fisci*, of the head of the *fiscus* who took the title of *rationalis*, and of the prætorian præfect. For the first time the prætorian præfect was admitted to the senate, and for the first time after so many years and in spite of the presence of the emperor in Rome, we are confronted with a new Sejanus in the person of C. Fulvius Plautianus, who for some time, until disaster overtook him, had as much power as the emperor himself and even more. This was no exceptional case. The prætorian præfect now became not only the head of all the prætorian troops but also the director of the whole *personnel* of the imperial administration. His judicial powers were extended, for it appears that in addition to appeals from the provincial authorities, he controlled the penal jurisdiction for all Roman territory within a hundred miles of the capital. Similarly in the provinces the governors were deprived of the right to levy taxation, and the senate of the duty of carrying out the census, which was now entrusted to imperial functionaries drawn from the equestrian order. With a view to increasing the prestige of the knights Severus not only allowed them to occupy offices hitherto reserved for senators but he granted new titles of honour, such as *vir egregius* or the higher distinction of *vir perfectissimus*, to knights who distinguished themselves in the posts to which they were appointed. These honours made a knight the equal of a senator without admitting him to the senatorial order, and the result was to reduce the prestige of the senate.

The strongest measure, however, which Severus took to consolidate his power was his attempt to please the army. He was in very truth the soldiers' emperor, both in virtue of the manner of his election and the methods of his government. The army was increased by three new legions. The pay of the legionaries was raised. They were given the right to contract regular marriages or something similar,[1] and also the right to promotion by merit into the ranks of the prætorians which were now reserved for them alone. To the veterans was granted the right of being dispensed from all public burdens (*vacatio a muneribus*). Ex-officers received new titles of honour and generals handsome gratuities. A more important reform was that equestrian rank was attached to the office of centurion, the highest to which a common soldier could be promoted, and which corresponded to that of captain in modern armies. Finally many civil posts were reserved for officers on half pay. It is clear that Septimius Severus was endeavouring to reinforce the equestrian order and the civil service by introducing elements taken from the army, thus

[1] Herod., iii., 8, 5. But the passage is obscure and the exposition of the remainder is also far from lucid and full of gaps.

creating, over against the senatorial nobility, a new social order, loyal and devoted to himself, from which he chose the men who were to create an administrative system which should regard the emperor as its benefactor and its head.

**111. Severus in the East: the Parthian War (197–198 A.D.).** An emperor who relied on the army was bound to concern himself much with the glory and prestige of the Roman arms. While Severus was fighting Clodius Albinus in Gaul the King of Parthia invaded Mesopotamia and laid siege to Nisibis. Mesopotamia, the new conquest of M. Aurelius, and perhaps also Syria, Armenia, and Cappadocia, seemed once more to be in danger. Severus could not tolerate such an affront. In 197, immediately after he had pacified Europe, he turned his attention to the war with Parthia. His preparations were on a great scale, and adequate to the occasion. Vologeses was beaten and for the third time the way to Ctesiphon was opened to the Roman legions. The emperor entered the city which was handed over to the troops to plunder, and 100,000 Parthians, citizens and soldiers, were made prisoners. The return march, however, as always happened, was by no means such an easy matter, and the army suffered terrible hardships in the desert from hunger and thirst. If Trajan had found it impossible to keep the Parthians in subjection, Severus was still less in a position to do so, for the empire had certainly grown weaker since Trajan's time. Having therefore inflicted a profound humiliation on the King of Parthia he made peace in 198 or 199, on the basis of the *status quo ante bellum*, securing perhaps some advantageous rectification of the Mesopotamian frontier.

Severus did not immediately return to the West. Whether because the oriental situation seemed to him to require his presence or because he preferred to remain at a distance from Rome, and from the senate, in order to emphasize the fact that he was the emperor of the provinces, solicitous for the interests of them all and not merely the head of a narrow oligarchy, Severus remained in the eastern provinces until 202, strengthening the military defences, distributing crowns to the feudatory princes, restoring the discipline of the legions and the government of the various countries, and—what was most characteristic of his policy—establishing Roman colonies everywhere. He visited Palestine and Egypt, and from Palestine issued an edict on the subject of the Christians which practically confirmed those of Trajan and Marcus Aurelius.[1] But the times were unquiet and a spirit of fear and superstition was abroad. The edict was enough to let loose the latent anger of the populace throughout the East against the Christian minority which was constantly growing and insinuating itself everywhere. Once more in many provinces the governors had to yield to public opinion, and once more there followed a series of denunciations, trials, torturings, condemnations, executions, and martyrdoms.

**112. The End of the Reign of Septimius Severus (202–211 A.D.).** In 202 Severus returned to Rome, where he was received with great festivities and with most flattering decrees from the senate which voted in his honour the erection of the triumphal arch which still stands on the Via Sacra opposite the Capitol. Severus refused most of the proffered honours and even a triumph. He thanked the senators, begging them

[1] [*Hist. Aug.*] *Sever.*, 17.

to preserve in their hearts the affectionate sentiments they had expressed so profusely in the solemn decrees of their assembly, and turned his attention to the peaceful government of the empire.

A contemporary who was no admirer of Severus thus describes the virtuous day of the new Augustus:

"He was at work by dawn and discussed affairs of State while he walked up and down. When the hour of the sittings of his tribunal arrived he went thither, unless it was a day of solemn festival, and gave his most careful attention to his duties. He gave up to the litigants as much time as they asked and to us senators who sat in judgment with him he allowed great liberty of opinion. He remained in court until midday. Thereafter he went out riding for as long as he could, or took part in some other form of physical exercise before going to the bath. He dined abundantly either alone or with his sons. After the meal he usually slept, and after taking his repose he conversed, walking up and down as before, with Greek or Latin men of letters. In the evening he took a second bath and supped with those who happened to be with him, for he never invited any one formally and only gave sumptuous banquets on days when they could not be dispensed with."[1]

At Rome Septimius Severus continued to develop his political and administrative system which shifted the centre of authority from the senate to the emperor and the army. Resistance now everywhere disappeared; even the senate in its impotence resigned itself to the inevitable. What could have been the result of a new conspiracy, even if successful, but to provoke another civil war among the legions, from

[1] Dio Cass., lxxvi., 17.

which another soldier would have emerged triumphant? Thus, without protest from anyone, Septimius Severus was the first of the emperors who was practically universally addressed as *Dominus*—a title which had for centuries been abhorred by the Romans. He was also the first emperor who administered justice not in the Forum but in his own palace, and the first who dared to put Italy on an equal footing with the provinces by using the title of proconsul in Rome itself and by stationing a legion in addition to the prætorians in the vicinity of the city. It was a wise provision, for the disaster which overtook Didius Julianus had shown that Italy, not having any military force besides the imperial guard, was at the mercy of the provincial legions if ever they chose to mutiny. But another of the cardinal principles on which Augustus had founded the government of the empire was thereby abolished.

Severus remained six years at Rome, energetically administering the empire and immune from conspiracies. His good fortune, his alertness of mind, and his energy secured tranquillity. In 208 he left for Britain because, according to one ancient authority, he was anxious about the tendencies shown by his two sons Bassianus and Geta. Having resolutely adopted the dynastic principle Septimius had given the elder the title of Augustus and made him his colleague during the Parthian war and had made the younger Augustus in 209. The young princes, however, resembled Commodus in caring for no company but that of gladiators and chariot drivers from the circus, and what was more, they hated each other. To distract them from their unworthy pursuits their father, according to ancient writers, decided on an expedition against Caledonia (Scotland) and perhaps on the conquest of that difficult country. As a matter of fact Britain had been in a state of unrest for a long time and the revolt of Albinus had not made matters any better.

The war was long and difficult. The terrain was mountainous, thickly wooded, and covered with marshes, among which the natives waged a ferocious guerilla warfare. At the cost of many sacrifices the Roman army reached the mysterious extremities of the great island, but on February 4, 211, Severus died at Eboracum (York). Shortly before his death he had not only ordered the recall of the legions from Scotland but also the abandonment of the most advanced line of forts established by Agricola and Antoninus Pius in favour of the excellent defensive system of Hadrian. The expedition, therefore, had led to no tangible result.

**113. Historical and Legal Importance of the Reign of Severus.** Septimius Severus was a distinguished soldier but he was not merely a soldier. He was also a man of great and refined culture. Round him and the Empress Julia Domna, the empress's sister Julia Mœsa, and his nieces, Julia Sœmia and Julia Mammæa, gathered a lettered court adorned by not a few of the brightest spirits of the age. Among these it will be enough to mention Ulpian and Paulus, the greatest lawyers in the empire, who were members of the *consilium principis*, and Papinian who was prætorian præfect. Thus, in the midst of the stir and bustle of his many wars, Severus like his predecessors continued the great process of developing the rational and humane system of law which is one of the greatest glories of Rome. Moreover it cannot be denied that he solidly reconstituted the authority of the State by putting an end, as Vespasian had done, to the anarchy produced by the mutinous legions, that he restored the prestige of the Roman arms, that he re-established the finances, though he also had recourse freely to the expedient of depreciating the coinage,—in his *denarii* the percentage of alloy rose to fifty and in some cases even to sixty. On the other hand he destroyed practically entirely the authority of the senate which Vespasian had rejuvenated, and which had for a century been the source of all legal authority. Surprised by the catastrophe of Commodus the senate had placed its hopes first in Pertinax, then in Pescennius, and then in Clodius Albinus. Deceived in all these it had been gradually degraded and belittled under Septimius Severus, leaving the way clear for the growth of military absolutism and surrendering practically all the rights and privileges it had claimed for so many centuries. Much has been written by modern historians in dispraise of the servility of the senate under Septimius Severus. But when it is remembered how completely the composition, the spirit, the very soul of an assembly may alter even in a few years under the pressure of circumstances, it will not seem so surprising that the Roman senate underwent this process of decline when confronted by Septimius Severus the victorious head of the legions—a force which must have seemed to them all the more invincible from the very fact that it had unexpectedly sprung on them as the result of a political convulsion. For the rest, if we may judge by its immediate effects, this diminution of the senate was beneficial. The government of Septimius Severus was more energetic and laborious than that of the last of the Antonines, owing to the very fact that it was no longer bound to take account of the wishes, the rights, the privileges, and the prejudices of the senate. This benefit, however, was counterbalanced by a grave danger. The senate being discredited, what was to be the legal source of power for the emperor's successor when he died? The hereditary principle, in itself, was not enough, both because it was not yet universally recognized and because the power of Severus was of too recent growth. The hereditary principle, therefore, had to find support in another factor—the will of the armies. When the senate was set aside the armies became as a general rule what they had hitherto been only occasionally and by accident—the power which chose or recognized emperors and legitimated their authority. But the armies were now nothing but a miscellany of all the races in the empire, and were full of barbarians with hardly a veneer of civilization. The terrible consequences of this revolution were not long in making themselves apparent.

We may safely date the beginning of absolute monarchy from Septimius Severus. He was the first of the wiser emperors who, with the support of the army, openly and without hesitation substituted their own authority and that of officials dependent on them for that of the senate. It would be impossible to say whether, if he had wished, he could have been a second Vespasian, and whether the change was made to gratify his ambition or under pressure of the inexorable force of circumstances. But whether it was voluntary or was forced upon him, it was this change that caused the appalling catastrophe which must now be related and for which Septimius Severus must bear his share of the responsibility before the tribunal of history.[1]

[1] One of the best accounts of Septimius Severus is to be found in the two chapters devoted to him by Duruy in his *Histoire des Romains*, Paris, 1883, vi., pp. 1–143.

# CHAPTER XIV

## THE GREAT CRISIS IN THE THIRD CENTURY

(211–284 A.D.)

**114. From Septimius Severus to Alexander Severus: Caracalla, Macrinus, Heliogabalus.** On the death of Severus the senate recognized as emperors his two sons, M. Aurelius Antoninus and Publius Septimius Geta who, as we have seen, were already colleagues of their father in the empire. Along with the principles of military monarchy the principle of hereditary succession was now so boldly affirmed that the empire was divided like a private inheritance between the two sons of the deceased emperor. But the first experience of the new order of things was not happy. The elder son, who from his favourite style of cloak was destined to be traditionally known as Caracalla, was a soldier and nothing more; he was passionately fond of war, greedy of supreme command, suspicious and arbitrary. He soon quarrelled with his younger brother, and, without wasting time by prolonging the controversy, had him murdered. Then, in order to efface the memory of this assassination, the first by which the imperial family had been stained since the days of Nero, he threw himself into the arms of the soldiers and exaggerated the policy of his father.

He still further humiliated the senate and apparently

excluded senators from all military command. He increased the taxes,[1] and further depreciated the coinage by reducing the *aureus* from 1/42 to 1/50 of the *libra*, that is to say he coined *aurei* which weighed not 7.8 but 6.54 grammes. He raised the pay of the legions and practically doubled at a stroke the expense of the army.[2] He introduced several measures of military reform, some of which were good, and gave himself up almost entirely to war. Of his campaigns in Germany, from which he derived the title of Germanicus, we know too little to pronounce judgment. It is certain that he did not suffer defeat, and that for several years Germany gave no trouble to the empire. But he occupied himself more with the East than with the West, and seems to have dreamed of repeating the exploits of Alexander the Great for whom he had an intense admiration. He began by annexing Osroene and Armenia and then turned against the Parthians. It appears that he asked for the daughter of Artabanus the new King of Parthia in marriage, perhaps under the delusion that by this means he might unite the Roman and Parthian empires. His request was refused, and he was making ready for a great campaign against Parthia, when, in the midst of the preparations, he fell beneath the dagger of one of his veterans, a victim either of a soldier's individual discontent, of the hostility of his prætorian præfect, or of a conspiracy of his generals. He left behind him nothing but the recollection of a harsh and violent reign. Amid many excesses, however, he carried out one most important reform, the act by which he gave

[1] Dio Cass., lxxvii., 9.

[2] *Ibid.*, lxxvii., 10, 24; lxxviii., 36.

Roman citizenship to all free men in the provinces.[1] It is said that his aim was chiefly financial. It may be so, but it is also possible that it was an audacious exaggeration of his father's policy in so far as that policy had sought to reduce the differences between Italy and the provinces. In any case this edict was a fact of capital importance, for it hastened the barbarization of the Roman governing class towards which the trend of the times had been driving the empire for more than a century.

On the death of Caracalla the legions acclaimed as emperor his prætorian præfect, Marcus Opellius Macrinus, another African of merely equestrian rank. Macrinus was the first knight to attain the imperial dignity. For a man of his obscure position, who was neither of noble birth nor illustrious by achievement, the acclamation of the soldiers was not a sufficient title, and election by the senate, though much impaired in value by the events of recent years, would have been a priceless support to his pretensions. Macrinus, therefore, spared no pains to ingratiate himself with the senate. He pardoned all the senators who had been condemned by Caracalla. He annulled many of the acts of his predecessor, more especially his fiscal measures. But it does not appear that he succeeded in inducing the senate to ratify his election. On the other hand he failed to compensate the legal weakness of his position by great military successes. He was beaten by the Parthians, and in order to obtain peace he was forced, for the first time in the history of Rome's oriental wars, to pay a war indemnity. This double weakness was not long in bringing about a catastrophe.

[1] Dio Cass., lxxvii., 9; *Dig.*, i., 5, 17; Aug., *De civit. Dei*, v., 17.

On the death of Caracalla, his mother Julia Domna had starved herself to death, while her sister Julia Mœsa, and her nieces Sœmia and Mammæa, had been banished by Macrinus and had gone to live at Emesa in the temple of Heliogabalus the Sun God, whose priest the father of Julia Domna had been. Each of these two ladies had a son; Sœmia's was Varius Avitus Bassianus, a youth of fourteen who was a priest of the Sun God like his grandfather, while Mammæa's was named Alessianus. Julia Mœsa, by taking advantage of the weakness and the failures of Macrinus, and by lavishly distributing the treasures of the temple of Emesa, succeeded in persuading a legion stationed near Edessa that Bassianus was the son of Caracalla himself, and in inducing them to proclaim him emperor against Macrinus (May 16, 218). Macrinus tried to resist, but the revolt spread among the discontented legions who were attached to the descendants of Septimius Severus. Macrinus, abandoned by his troops, was slain, and, twenty-three days later, the young priest of Heliogabalus was sole Roman emperor (June 8, 218).

The new prince, who on his accession assumed the name of Marcus Aurelius Antoninus, reigned for about four years until March 11, 222. With Heliogabalus, as the new emperor came to be known in history, the religions of the East triumphed over the opposition which for so many centuries had been maintained against them by Rome. This is a sufficient explanation of the legendary accounts, certainly exaggerated and in part untrue, that have been given about him and about his reign. Heliogabalus set aside the official Roman religion. Above the title of *pontifex maximus* he set that of *sacerdos amplissimus Dei invicti Solis Elagabali.* He celebrated a kind of mystic marriage between the Syrian divinity of the Sun and the Carthaginian Astarte, and introduced both into the official cult. The revolution, dreaded and avoided for so many years, was at last an accomplished fact. The priest of a Syrian religion under the guidance of women, was the supreme ruler of the Roman Empire! A still worse misfortune was that, while Heliogabalus represented the triumph of eastern religion, he was not the man to retain the assistance of the legions which had raised him to the summit of power. Under his weak and inept government whose sole cares were religious feasts and ceremonies, the empire declined still further. The discipline of the armies was impaired, and owing to reckless and growing extravagance the finances fell into almost total ruin.

It was not long before the priest of the Sun God turned Roman emperor was threatened by secret and increasing discontent. In order to strengthen his weak government, his mother, his aunt, and his soldiers compelled the emperor to adopt his young cousin Alessianus, then scarcely twelve years of age, as his colleague under the name of M. Aurelius Severus Alexander. Heliogabalus however was not well pleased to have a colleague who might well become a rival, and several times tried in various ways to get rid of him. Finally, on March 11, 222, when barely eighteen years old, he was murdered by his infuriated soldiers, who at the same time, slew his mother and his friends.

**115. Alexander Severus (222–235).** Modern historians, influenced by the German school of criticism, which is in spirit entirely monarchical and absolutist, are fond of repeating their conviction that the Roman senate was now a useless and a ruined institution. The senate, however, was the only legal source from which emperors could derive authority which was not conferred upon them by their own personal prestige, and at the death of Heliogabalus this was made very clear. Terrified by the growing predominance of the army, the family of Septimius Severus turned to the senate and begged its assistance in restoring a strong and respected government whose legitimacy would be beyond doubt in the eyes of everybody.

Alexander Severus was not yet fourteen years old. At first he seems to have been guided by his mother Julia Mammæa who was the Agrippina of this second Nero. Like Agrippina, and for the same reason, Mammæa began with a restoration of the republic. Inspired by his mother the young emperor, who was born in Phœnicia, resumed, and even exaggerated, the policy followed by Trajan, Antoninus Pius, and Marcus Aurelius. He refused the title of *dominus*, abolished ceremonial etiquette, treated the senators as his equals, and allowed the senate to choose the chief officers of State, including the prætorian præfect and the provincial governors. The *consilium principis* was again filled with senators; the *ærarium* was again set up side by side with the *fiscus;* even in the imperial provinces the governors were assisted by assessors, jurists for the most part, who belonged to the senatorial order; the consuls were designated by the senate, and the authority of the imperial procurators was reduced. Moreover the senate was purged of the worst elements which had been introduced in the previous reigns. The senatorial order, in a word, regained the position which had been lost to it since the time of Septimius Severus, and the equestrian order lost much that it had won. The prince and the senate entered into an alliance against the pretentions of the army as under Septimius Severus the prince and the army had combined to despoil the senate.

This senatorial restoration, however, was upset by a series of external events which were graver than any that the empire had had to face for a long time. About 224 or 227 there had taken place a revolution in the East which completely upset the equilibrium which Rome had established at the price of so much labour. Eight centuries had passed since the fall of the Median monarchy which had been brought about by Cyrus the Great. The consequences of that event had been both tremendous and varied. All western Asia had been united under the sceptre of the Achæmenidæ; there had followed the duel with Greece and the invasion of Alexander, the centuries occupied by the wars of the Diadochi and the Epigoni, the consolidation of the Hellenistic empire of the Seleucidæ, the insurrection of Arsaces, the first of the line of Parthian princes in the middle of the third century before Christ, and the foundation of the monarchy of the Arsacidæ. Then the star of Rome had suddenly risen, followed by the fall of the Seleucidæ, and finally came the duel, which lasted three centuries and was never decided, between Parthia and Rome. At this point the ancient Parthian monarchy, which had coquetted overmuch with Greek culture and had been found wanting as a champion in the contest with Rome and the occidental power, fell as the result of a Persian rebellion, a national movement which substituted a certain Ardeshir (Artaxerxes), who claimed to be a Sassanid like Cyrus the Great, for

Artabanus the last of the Arsacidæ who had been the opponent of Caracalla and Macrinus. But this was not merely a case of a change of monarch, such as the Romans had so frequently brought about and used for their advantage. The new Persian Empire represented a religious, political, and national reaction against the West, and therefore against the Roman Empire which was the representation of western civilization in the East. The new dynasty intended not only to restore to honour the ancient Iranian religion of Mazdeism whose prophet had been Zoroaster, not only to combat Greek culture but also to restore the Persian Empire to its old boundaries which included Asia Minor, the Cyclades, Greece, and Egypt.

Thus the Roman Empire was confronted by a new enemy who lost no time in taking the offensive. In 231 the new king threw himself on Roman Mesopotamia with the immediate object of conquering Asia Minor, and boldly launched his advance guards on Cappadocia and Syria. The Romans made some attempt to negotiate, but the Persian monarch declared that he considered as belonging to him all the territories which had been possessed by Cyrus, and this amounted to a demand for the total evacuation of Asia. Alexander was compelled to recall many legions from the Danube, to order and rapidly arm new levies and to proceed in person to the East at the head of strong forces. The plan of campaign formed by his generals was excellent. One column was to invade Media through Armenia which was also at war with the Persian King. Another was to cross lower Mesopotamia and threaten the heart of Persia. A third was to proceed more slowly between the two others across upper Mesopotamia, probably with the object of reinforcing the northern or the southern army as might be necessary. Before this great display of force Artaxerxes retired and cleverly regrouped his forces in such a way as to enable him to make a surprise attack on Alexander's southern army, before it could be reinforced from the centre. His plan succeeded. The southern army was defeated and forced to retire with great loss before the central army could come to its assistance. The northern army on the other hand had invaded Persia ravaging the country and making prisoners, but it also had to conform to the retirement of the other two forces. The Roman expedition therefore had failed if it is to be regarded as an attempt at an invasion. If on the contrary its object was to repulse the King of Persia from the territories of the empire it had been successful, because not only did Artaxerxes retreat but he admitted that the time had not yet come when he could reclaim the dominion of Cyrus.

In order to deal with the Persian danger Alexander, as we have seen, had had to recall many legions from the Rhine and the Danube. It appears that only four were left to guard the Rhine. The Germans did not neglect this opportunity. While Alexander was terminating the war in the East a coalition of Germanic peoples whom the ancients termed the Alemanni, succeeded in entering Gaul—a thing that had not happened for a very long time—while the Marcomanni crossed the Danube. Alexander had to transport his army to the West, to raise new forces and prepare for a second and not less serious campaign. But the empire had already made so great an effort in the East that Alexander decided in the second war to rely to some extent on negotiations and subsidies. His intention was prudent, but the troops had for some time been discontented with their prince who paid and treated them in a manner very different from that of Caracalla and Septimius, and they chose to regard this policy as treason to the empire. Discipline gave way; there was an outbreak of uncontrollable indignation and jealousy, and Alexander was murdered along with his mother in January, February, or March, 235. This was the result of a mutiny headed by C. Julius Verus Maximinus, a Thracian of obscure origin who by ability and valour had attained high promotion, who was devoted to the family of Septimius Severus and to the memory of Caracalla, but who spoke Latin imperfectly. He was proclaimed emperor by the soldiers at Mayence.

**116. Thirty-three Years of Anarchy—from Maximin to Gallienus (235–268 A.D.).** Thus fell the family of the Severi at the hands of the very army on which its power had been founded and which had been the instrument of its fortunes. This time there arose no Vespasian and no Septimius Severus to reduce promptly to order the legions who had arrogated to themselves the right of choosing an emperor and imposing him by force of arms. With the death of Alexander Severus began a period of civil strife complicated by foreign war which lasted for thirty-three years and was the most terrible that the empire had ever experienced. Its history is so obscure and so confused that it is impossible to relate it in detail. We shall try to give as clear and concise an account of it as possible.

Maximin (235–238), who had been raised to the empire by the power of the legions, cared for nothing but the support of the soldiers. He did not ask the senate to ratify his election, and ruled as if they did not exist, though he left them at their post—the worst way of abolishing an antiquated institution. The senate were not disposed to allow themselves to be treated as a useless survival from the past by a Thracian who had been put in power by a mutiny. The proconsul of Africa, M. Antonius Gordianus, a senator of great wealth who had many friends at Rome had been proclaimed emperor in that province as the result of certain local struggles. The senate hastened to recognize him and he took as his colleague his son of the same name, Gordianus II. The two Gordians, however, were defeated and slain by the governor of Numidia and the senate appointed two emperors, M. Clodius Pupienus Maximus, and Decimus Cætius Calvinus Balbinus. The former was a valiant soldier who had risen from a humble origin to high command, the latter a senator of ancient lineage who was much esteemed, though a mediocre personality. To these two was shortly added a third emperor in the person of a grandson of the elder Gordian who bore the same name. He appears to have been imposed upon the senate by a kind of popular *émeute* in Rome. However this may be the capacity of Pupienus, the prestige of Balbinus, and the authority of the senate were sufficient to create a government of some strength which energetically prepared troops and armaments for an attack on Maximin who meanwhile continued his war against the barbarians. When Maximin perceived that the new government was gaining force and that the loyalty of certain of the governors had become doubtful he resolved to march on Italy with his army. His advance was arrested by the fortress of

Aquileia to which he was obliged to lay siege. But the loyalty of his legions was shaken, partly owing to the resistance of the city, partly to the weakness of his authority which rested on no legal title, and partly to the revived prestige of the senate and the unanimous revolt of Italy, and Maximin was murdered by his own soldiers under the walls of Aquileia in the spring of 238.

The senate had triumphed, but its triumph was brief. Pupienus and Balbinus quarrelled, difficulties arose with the legions because the senate wished to make them feel its supremacy without having the power to impose it, and, in the end the two emperors fell victims to a military revolt (238). The soldiers acclaimed as emperor Gordian III (238–244). They had taken their revenge on the senate but what could be the authority of the new emperor who was very young and does not seem to have been very wise? Meanwhile grave events were happening. In this year, 238, the Carpi and the Goths crossed the Danube. In 241 the Persians under Sapor, the successor of Artaxerxes, invaded Mesopotamia and threatened Syria itself. Fortunately Gordian found in his prætorian præfect, C. Furius Sabinius Aquila Temesitheus, who was also his father-in-law, an intelligent, capable, and loyal servant. Furius Sabinius reorganized the army and, in a series of brilliant campaigns, succeeded in driving out of the empire both the Persians in the East and the Carpi and the Goths in the West. Unhappily Furius died in 243 and Gordian had to put in his place M. Julius Philippus a high official of Arabian birth. Philip was a good soldier but he had no intention of serving the emperor like his predecessor in the subordinate position of prætorian præfect. He instigated the soldiers to demand that Gordian should make him his colleague in the empire, and, as Gordian showed some reluctance in acquiescing, he had him murdered in the course of a military revolt.

Acclaimed emperor by the soldiers, Marcus Julius Philippus, known as Philip the Arabian (244–249), sought and obtained from the senate the confirmation of his authority. But the authority of the senate in its turn had now been too much shaken to be sufficient. Philip, who seems to have been a bad ruler, was soon faced by various pretenders set up in the provinces to express the discontent of this on that part of the empire with the government. Finally he was overthrown by a revolt which was particularly serious, owing to the reason which had provoked it. The Goths who had been repulsed under Gordian, had repeated their attempt to break the frontier of the empire, and with such great forces that the legions of the Danube considered the measures taken by Philip, whose chief care was to consolidate his position at Rome, to be insufficient. Wishing to have an emperor who would give them the means necessary to defend themselves and to defend the empire they proclaimed the governor of Dacia and Mœsia, C. Messius Quintus Traianus Decius. Decius went with his army to Italy and defeated and slew Philip at Verona (249).

Decius (249–251) had been elected to fight the Goths and accordingly made haste to recross the Alps, leaving behind him in Italy P. Licinius Valerianus invested with the old office of censor to reorganize the administration and reinvigorate the senate while he carried on the war against the Goths who meanwhile had thrown themselves upon Thrace. Fortune, however, did not favour him, for, after several combats, he himself finally fell in battle (251). He was the first of the Roman emperors to fall fighting the barbarians, and it is easy to imagine what a profound impression this event must have produced.

The legions at once proclaimed as emperor the governor of Mœsia G. Vibius Trebonianus Gallus (251–253), who, owing to his military reputation, appeared to be the man most capable of meeting the danger. But Gallus hastened to buy peace from the Goths with gold and then returned to Italy. The Goths did not keep to their bargain and once more invaded Mœsia. This time they were defeated by the governor M. Æmilius Æmilianus, a Moor, and the legions, to whom Æmilianus had promised as a donative the moneys formerly paid to the Goths, proclaimed him emperor (253). Gallus had him proscribed, ordered P. Licinius Valerianus the governor of Germany, who had been censor under Decius to march against the new pretender while he himself endeavoured to dispute with him the dominion of Italy against which his rival was marching. Before the army of Germany could arrive the two pretenders met in battle and Gallus was slain (253). The senate recognized Æmilianus. Meanwhile, however, the German legions had proclaimed their general Valerian, and Æmilianus having quarrelled with his soldiers, they slew him and recognized Valerian (253).

The times were terrible. A frightful plague was devastating the empire whose enemies, now encouraged by its internal discord, were attacking its frontiers on all sides. Between 254 and 260 the Goths renewed their attempts to invade Dacia, Macedonia, and Asia

Minor. The Alemanni and the Franks burst into Gaul. The Saxons, a new German tribe, appeared on the sea, coasting along Gaul and Britain. Grave troubles broke out in Africa and new dangers threatened in the East, where Armenia again fell under the influence of Persia, and the Persians invaded Syria. Valerian, who was a senator of noble family and some ability, did not feel that he had the strength to face all these difficulties alone, and took a step the effects of which were destined to effect a gradual revolution in the whole history of ancient civilization. He nominated his son P. Licinius Egnatius Gallienus (253-268), Augustus, and divided the empire with him, giving him as his share the occidental provinces while he kept the East for himself. The unity of the East and the West which had been the great work of Rome was beginning to break up. Nevertheless this measure was very helpful. While Gallienus did his best to arrest the incursions of the Germanic peoples into the western provinces Valerian attempted a great expedition against Parthia. It had little success and indeed in 259 or 260 he was made a prisoner by the Persians and died in captivity, when and how is unknown.

The disappearance of Valerian, who was the most powerful of the two Augusti, was followed by a general dislocation of the empire. In 258, the legions of Gaul, probably instigated by the local population who were discontented under Gallienus, had already proclaimed M. Cassianus Latinius Postumus emperor, while the legions of Pannonia and Mœsia had acclaimed Ingenuus. Postumus, who was a man of energy, succeeded in obtaining the recognition of Spain and Britain, and in founding a veritable Gallo-Iberian empire which lasted until 267 in spite of the attacks of Gallienus. In many things he was fortunate, for he vigorously defended his frontiers and restored a certain measure of security and peace to the provinces which he governed. Ingenuus on the other hand failed to maintain himself in Mœsia and Pannonia, was defeated by Gallienus, and committed suicide.

While this crisis was developing in the West, the East, which had been left to itself since the capture of Valerian, was defending itself as best it could against the Persians. M. Fulvius Macrianus, one of Valerian's generals, assisted by the rich and powerful city of Palmyra and by Odenathus its most powerful and influential citizen, by using the remains of Valerian's army had succeeded on his own initiative in driving out the Persians and saving the richest provinces of the Eastern Empire. Encouraged by this success, however, Macrianus decided to seize the empire for himself and his sons and caused them and himself to be proclaimed emperors. Odenathus on the other hand whom Gallienus had created *dux Orientis*, remained faithful to the reigning emperor and thus, while Gallienus was at war with Postumus in the West, a new civil war broke out in the East which ended in the defeat and death of Macrianus and his sons. But while the forces of the empire were being wasted in civil wars the boldness of the barbarians grew apace. In 261 the Alemanni succeeded in invading Italy and Gallienus did not succeed in defeating them before they were approaching Mediolanum (Milan). Shortly afterwards the Franks invaded Gaul and Spain and, it appears, crossed the sea and pushed as far as Africa. The barbarians of Eastern Europe—the Borani, the Goths, the Heruli, and the

Sarmatians—plundered all the coast of the Black Sea, forced the Dardanelles and even reached Asia Minor and Greece. In 267 the Heruli were encamped at Athens, Corinth, Argos, and Sparta. It is easy to imagine the despair of the unfortunate inhabitants and to understand why, feeling themselves abandoned by the central power, every district, every province rebelled in the vain hope of being able to defend themselves by appointing an emperor of their own. In the last years of the reign of Gallienus the pretenders known in history as the Thirty Tyrants[1] swarmed in all the provinces and were so numerous and so feeble that their history cannot be recorded. At last in 268 a conspiracy of generals proved fatal to Gallienus who was slain while engaged in besieging Aurelius, one of his numerous rivals whom the Rhætian legions had proclaimed in Mediolanum.

**117. Claudius the Goth (268–270 A.D.) and Aurelian (270–275 A.D.).** Of the three generals who conspired against Gallienus two, Marcus Aurelius Claudius and L. Domitius Aurelianus, were men of high character as was proved by the event. Claudius was in addition the most skilful and popular general in the whole army. These eminent persons, therefore, must have had a strong motive of public expediency for removing the legitimate emperor by violence. This motive must be sought in the new danger which threatened the empire—the Gothic peril. Encouraged by the growing weakness of the empire and grown skilful by experience, many Germanic tribes had united to form a powerful coalition under the joint names of

[1] Their names, with a brief notice of each, are given in the relevant book of the *Historia Augusta*, which is entitled *Tyranni Triginta* and is the work of Tribellius Pollio.

the Goths and the Alemanni, and had made great preparations for a formidable attack on the frontiers of the empire and for the conquest of a part of its territories. In the spring of 268 an army, which was said to consist of 320,000 able-bodied men and behind which flocked a multitude of double the number of women, old men, and children,[1] crossed to the right bank of the Danube and marched on Marcianopolis (west of Varna). Thence they inundated eastern Macedonia, Greece, the Cyclades, Rhodes, and Cyprus whence the flood recoiled upon the coasts of Asia Minor. At the same time another army, in which the Goths also predominated, entered Mœsia and thence invaded Macedonia by the valley of the Morava. Their plan was now made manifest in all its audacity. It was to interpose between the oriental and the occidental provinces, and to split the Roman Empire in two by conquering the Balkan peninsula. These were not times in which to sustain a weak and incompetent emperor. It was necessary to have a warrior at the head of the State. Claudius accordingly was recognized without dispute by the other generals, by the legions, and by the senate.

This time their choice was a happy one. Not far from the ancient city of Naissus (Nisch), Claudius surrounded and destroyed the bulk of the enemy's forces (269) and then waged a war of extermination against the remainder of the barbarian army. A year later the survivors were planted in Roman territory to till the soil for their conquerors or were incorporated in auxiliary cohorts to fight for the defence of the empire.

Once more the empire felt that it was governed by a

[1] [*Hist. Aug.*] *Claud.* 6 and 7.

firm and a strong hand. And assuredly, if Claudius had lived, he would have been able to render great services. But he died at Sirmium shortly after his victory about March, 270, a victim of the plague which had now been devastating the empire for fifteen years. Lucius Domitius Aurelianus, one of the generals, who had conspired against Gallienus, whom Claudius had himself designated as his successor, was proclaimed by the legions of Pannonia and became emperor. Aurelian, like Claudius, was a great soldier, and his selection was singularly fortunate for the empire, for the Goths defeated by Claudius were merely an advanced guard. Aurelian had hardly been elected when the Jutungi, the Vandals, and the Alemanni invaded Italy itself at the beginning of 271, and defeated a Roman army near Placentia (Piacenza). Shortly afterwards Aurelian succeeded in destroying them, but not before they had reached Pavia and Fanum Fortunæ (Fano), and the impression of the risk run by Italy was such that Aurelian resolved to make the first great sacrifice of territory to which Rome had resigned herself since the defeat of Varus, by abandoning the dangerous salient of Dacia, transferring the name of the evacuated province to the part of Mœsia which extended along the Danube (271) and creating a new Dacia Ripensis whose capital was Sardica (Sofia). Similarly, two hundred and fifty years earlier when the real Germany was lost, Germania Superior and Germania Inferior had been formed out of the territories of Gaul. It is clear that by concentrating his forces in a smaller space, Aurelian hoped to be in a better position to defend Italy. But this measure did not seem to him sufficient, for in the same year he began the construction of the gigantic circle of walls—eleven or twelve miles in extent—round Rome, which transformed the Eternal City into an enormous fortress, and which have survived to be admired even now in the twentieth century.

The empire which Rome had conquered in the West and which for two centuries had saved Roman civilization, was beginning to break up. Aurelius sought compensation in the East. There Odenathus, *dux Orientis*, who had saved Rome's Eastern Empire had died in 266 or 267. On his death his consort Zenobia and his son Athenodorus (Wahaballath) had seized the power which he had exercised. The office of a *dux Orientis* was not hereditary. Still less was it transmissible to a woman. But Gallienus had had to make a virtue of necessity, had recognized Zenobia as her husband's successor and had allowed her to give her position an oriental and monarchical character by assuming the title of Queen. Zenobia, however, had conceived even loftier ambitions, no less in fact than the constitution of a great Syrian State, even as Cleopatra of old, whom she took for her model, had aspired to the re-establishment of the empire of the Ptolemies. In 269 Zenobia had taken possession of Egypt, and Claudius, then occupied in fighting the Goths, had not been able to oppose her. Now she was endeavouring to extend her sway over the whole of Asia Minor. It was Aurelian who, when he had arranged the affairs of the West to the best of his ability, decided to rid the empire of this danger. In 272 he penetrated into Asia Minor and thence into Syria, successively storming Ancyra, Tyana, and Antioch, and overtaking the army of the Queen at Emesa on which she had retired. Here the pitched battle was fought. The Syrian army was beaten but not destroyed and was able to seek refuge in Palmyra which Aurelian took only after a protracted siege. Shortly afterwards Aurelian reconquered Egypt also (273), and all the East was once more under the sceptre of Rome.

These triumphs in Syria led to the inevitable reaction in Europe. The few pretenders who, like Tetricus in Gaul, still clung here and there to some scraps of territory, disappeared. The unity of the empire was, at least in form, renewed, and Aurelian might assume the title of *Restitutor orbis*. He then sought to use his authority to cure the innumerable wounds of the empire. But he went too far, and in a few years he was destined to fall a victim to his desire to reform everything. Towards the end of 275 he perished as the result of a conspiracy of generals, the reasons for which are most obscure.

**118. The Last Restoration of the Authority of the Senate (276–282 A.D.), the Last Emperors of the Third Century, Carus, Carinus, Numerianus, and the Election of Diocletian (282–284 A.D.).** The assassination of Aurelian was followed by a curious and unexpected occurrence. The legions refused to elect an emperor and referred this duty to the senate! This could only mean that the soldiers at last understood how weak were all the emperors who had been acclaimed by the legions and therefore lacked an indisputable title, however much this disadvantage might be compensated by great and glorious services to the State. Elected in this way the most capable no less than the most incapable princes, Aurelian no less than Gallienus, had been exposed to the danger of being overthrown by the very force which had set them up. The legions understood that the whole empire in its desperate desire for peace, order, salvation, was turning to the senate which for so many centuries had been with the comitia the sacred fount of legality at Rome. But the senate was old and weary, and at first, as if suspicious, tried to evade the request. Then, when compelled to act, they elected emperor the most eminent of their number, the *princeps senatus*, Marcus Claudius Tacitus, who in his turn, at first sought every means of avoiding the purple. Tacitus tried to govern like Trajan, but after a few months was murdered in the course of a mutiny by soldiers who were dissatisfied with the weakness of his rule. On the death of Tacitus, some of the legions proclaimed his brother M. Annius Florianus (276), others M. Aurelius Probus (276–282), one of Aurelian's best generals. Probus carried the day but, though he was a general, he continued the policy of Tacitus, invoked and recognized the authority of the senate, restored to that body the right of deciding appeals in criminal cases, the right to appoint provincial governors, and even that of ratifying the acts of the emperor. At the same time he vigorously carried out a gigantic frontier policy. The terror of anarchy which the policy of Septimius Severus had let loose on the empire must have been very real when even a soldier like Probus did all he could to reconstruct piece by piece the shattered edifice of the senate's power!

But it was too late. Probus was not much more successful with the new policy than Tacitus had been. After having had to struggle with several pretenders who had been elected in the provinces this brave emperor in 282 also fell a victim to the implacable violence of the legions, and anarchy broke out once more. The legions chose as his successor M. Aurelius Carus (282–283) who hastened to associate with him in the empire his two sons Carinus and Numerianus, and immediately undertook a war with Persia. The enterprise had been successful; he had already occupied Seleucia and Ctesiphon, when he was removed at the end of 283, after reigning a year, some say by a thunderbolt and some by a military conspiracy. The army was weary, as always, of the enormous difficulties of the Persian war. Numerianus who had accompanied and succeeded his father was a poet rather than a soldier and it was therefore decided to return homewards. But on the way Numerianus also perished. This time, his father-in-law, Aper the prætorian præfect, openly avowed having killed him. An inquiry was at once ordered and a tribunal of generals appointed who chose as emperor the commander of the bodyguard, G. Aurelius Valerius Diocletianus (September 17, 284).[1]

**119. The Economic Crisis in the Third Century.** The last attempt to restore order in the empire by means of the authority of the senate had failed. There had now been uninterrupted anarchy since the death of Alexander Severus, that is for half a century. It had become worse every year, and was more deep-seated and widespread than had ever been seen in the ancient world. The worst period of the civil wars of the republic had been a small thing in comparison; for then the essential elements of ancient civilization had not been destroyed. Now, on the contrary, the political crisis had become a crisis in the history of the world, for Greek culture as well as Roman, the two highest forms of ancient civilization, were mortally stricken during these fifty years and never afterwards recovered. Wars, invasions, general insecurity, uni-

[1] This is the date given by the *Chron. Pasc.*, i., p. 510, ed. Bonn.

versal impoverishment, and incessant epidemics had thinned the population. The persistency with which even the wisest of the emperors continued to transplant barbarians on to the territories of the empire, notwithstanding the obvious dangers of that policy, affords the clearest proof of the need of men from which the empire was suffering. The decline of the population had, as was natural, produced a crisis in agriculture and industry, and had further increased the general impoverishment which was itself one of its causes. Agriculturists—*coloni liberi*, slave labourers, and small landholders—disappeared in great numbers. The small landowner declined while the *latifundia* increased, and land went more and more out of cultivation. Industry, in its turn, which had been so prosperous under the Antonines, and even under the Severi, suffered severely partly because many artisans perished, taking with them the precious secrets of trades perfected by the labour of many generations, partly because the spread of poverty diminished consumption, and partly also because the means of exchange between the East and the West, between province and province, which had been so copious and easy during the first two centuries of the empire, were now seriously interrupted. Many mines, especially many gold mines, were closed either for want of labour or because the districts in which they were situated had been invaded by the barbarians.

The agricultural and industrial crises were, of course, accompanied by a commercial crisis. The little general security enjoyed by the empire, the difficulties of communication, the increased risk and cost of voyages, the badness of the coinage, and the reduction of consumption by the growth of poverty had paralyzed trade. All this was at the same time the cause and the effect of the universal economic crisis and the scarcity of capital. But, while the riches of the empire were thus declining, the number of public burdens was increasing. The rule of the financial policy of the State during the third century was the most odious form of fiscalism, the inevitable result of a multiplied bureaucracy, of the burdensome donations to the populace and the army and of the increase of military expenditure. The effect of the continual increase of taxation was aggravated by the monetary policy of the empire. Partly in order to remedy the growing dearth of gold caused by the barbarian invasion of the auriferous and argentiferous provinces of the empire, partly in order to meet the public expenditure without too much increasing the taxes, the emperors acquired the habit of lessening the weight and debasing the quality of the coinage. We saw how under Caracalla the weight of the *aureus* fell to 6.54 grammes. But after the time of Alexander Severus, it became so irregular that gold payments were made by weight. The silver coinage was in even worse case. The proportion of alloy in the *antonianus argenteus* issued for the first time by Caracalla had already grown immeasurably in the year which followed the death of Septimius Severus. But the *antonianus* under Claudius the Goth had no more than 4 or 5 % of silver, and was only distinguishable from the copper coinage by the colour imparted to it by being dipped in a bath of silver, or, for that matter, of pewter.[1] Even the copper coins were issued

[1] *Cf.* Lenormant, *Aureus* in Daremberg et Saglio, *Dictionnaire des antiquités*, i., 533 and 565; Macchioro, in *Revista di Storia antica*, 1906, p. 293.

light. The result was a tremendous rise in the price of commodities, a universal impoverishment aggravated by the desperate injunction of some of the emperors to their unhappy subjects to pay the taxes in gold. Thus the State refused the bad money with which it was inundating the empire!

**120. The Collapse of Greek and Roman Culture.** The economic crisis was therefore not less grave than the political crisis owing to which the empire had become the prey of the mutinous legions, or than the military crisis owing to which the frontiers of the empire were hardly defended; and all three together, acting in turn as cause and effect, combined to produce one of the most memorable crises in the history of human civilization. In it disappeared either through extermination, poverty, or dispersion, the aristocracy, and the opulent middle class which during the first and second centuries had grown up all over the empire and had been the foundation of all its social and political organization, and in which, after great efforts Greek and Roman culture had been fused in an equilibrium which represented the climax of ancient civilization. Such part of their riches as was not destroyed, together with the power which they had exercised, passed to a new oligarchy of moneyed men and high officials, civil and military, which the terrible vicissitudes of the time had brought forth from the lower classes and the more barbarous populations of the empire. Thus the civilization of the ancients received a mortal blow. After the crisis had passed not only had all the arts and industries, such as sculpture, architecture, and jewel work, in which Græco-Roman civilization reached such perfection become coarsened; not only had all forms of intellectual activity, philosophy, law, literature, become languid and enervated, but the religion of paganism which for so many centuries had been the foundation of political, social, and intellectual life in Greece and Rome was moribund. Eastern cults, long restrained by the resistance of the State, burst in from all sides and threatened to subvert morally the Græco-Roman world already severely shaken by so many wars and revolutions.

This phenomenon has been of such capital importance in the history of the world that we must pause for a moment to inquire why it was that at this moment the populations of the empire preferred oriental religions to Græco-Latin paganism. There were various reasons, two of which were more important than the rest. The first of these was the superiority of the eastern religions from the purely religious point of view, a superiority which was connected with the inferiority of the culture of the oriental peoples. The Græco-Latin world had reached such a degree of intellectual and moral development as to be capable of separating metaphysics and ethics from religion. Paganism was therefore reduced to a body of myths and ceremonies, outside of which had developed what would now be called a secular system of philosophic and moral life. It was not so with the oriental religions. Not only did they work upon the senses and excite the passions more strongly than paganism by the pomp of their festivals, by the splendour of their processions and their hymns, by the terrors, the hopes, and the ecstasies which the transcendentalism of their mysteries inspired; but they filled the place of the schools of philosophy which the eastern peoples had never known how to create. For these religions contained metaphysical systems of their own; they confronted the problems of man's destiny, of life, and of the universe, and claimed that they had reached a solution.[1] In an epoch in which philosophical culture had so much decayed these religions, offering, as they did, both a metaphysic and a system of morals which were alike positive, simple, free from doubts, and uncomplicated with excessive discussion, must have appeared to be—as in fact they were—superior to the formalistic and somewhat empty paganism which had to be supplemented by a high philosophic culture.

The other reason was that the oriental cults which arose in countries under absolute government almost all contained a mystical justification of a supreme authority, which amid the anarchy of the third century was well calculated to attract the attention of the governing classes of the empire. As the authority of the senate and the force of tradition gradually declined, these classes tended to seek in religion for a mystical principle of legitimism which gave the imperial authority a more solid foundation than the fickle favour of the legions or the caprices of the fortune of war.

The history of Mithraism is a remarkable instance of this phenomenon. Mithraism inherited the principles of the ancient Mazdeism of Iran combined with the principles of Semitic theology and with other elements of the indigenous religions of Asia Minor. It came, therefore, from a country against which Rome had maintained a tenacious struggle for centuries.

[1] *Cf.* Boissier, *La religion romaine d'Auguste aux Antonins*, Paris, 1892, i., pp. 354 ff; Cumont, *Les religions orientales dans le paganisme romain*, Paris, 1906.

Yet in the third century we find it diffused over the whole empire, especially in the frontier provinces, in eastern Gaul, in western Germany, in all the Danubian provinces, in Dacia, Numidia, and even in the very seat of empire, in northern and central Italy, more especially in Rome. Indeed, from the time of Commodus, the first of the Augusti to be initiated into the mysteries of Mithra, and throughout the whole of the third century, Mithraism was distinguished by ever growing imperial favour, until finally Aurelian, vindicating Heliogabalus, officially instituted the cult of *Sol Invictus*, which seems to have been Mithraism Latinized. For several generations after the reign of Aurelian the higher bureaucracy of the empire, both civil and military, may be said to have been adherents of Mithraism more or less Latinized so as to form a State religion. How can we explain the favour thus shown by the new absolute monarchy to a religion the origins of which might naturally have made it an object of suspicion? By its doctrine of the State, Mithraism taught that monarchs reigned by divine grace, and as such received from Mithras the superior attributes of divinity, which by his omnipresent influence became part of their substance.[1] The principle of legitimism was thus transferred from the senate to God!

121. **Christianity.** Along with Mithraism Christianity had also made great strides during the terrible crisis of the third century. It had spread over all the empire and in all classes; had penetrated into the armies, the senate, and the court; had made conquests among rich and poor, the ignorant, and the educated; had already produced a copious and profound theology,

[1] Cumont, *Les mystères de Mithra*, Bruxelles, 1902, p. 84.

and had evolved a simple but solid hierarchy based on rigorously authoritarian principles. Every church was provided with a numerous clergy composed of deacons who conducted the services, elders (πρεσβύτεροι) who formed an executive council, and a bishop (ἐπίσκοπος) who was the head and director of the church with practically absolute powers. The bishop was elected for life by the clergy with the assent of the assembled faithful. The elders and the deacons were chosen by the bishop, who, at the time of which we are now speaking, was already a person of importance in his city, not merely because in every city the Christians were numerous, but because the Christian body had already amassed immense riches and had created that marvellous system of works of charity and benevolence which was the great novelty it introduced into the world and one of the reasons for its triumph. Everywhere Christian communities provided not only for the expense of their services and the maintenance of their ministers but for the assistance of widows, orphans, and the sick, the impotent, the old, the unemployed, for the succour of those who had been condemned in the service of God, for the ransom of prisoners captured by the barbarians, for the building of churches, for the care of slaves, for the burial of the poor, for hospitality to strangers of the same faith, and for subsidies to Christian communities which were in difficulties or in danger.

The possessions of Christian communities were derived in great part from gifts made to them by rich members, many of whom during their lives or after their deaths transferred to them the whole or part of their fortunes. The church was therefore collecting to itself in a gigantic system of mortmain the property of a section of the moneyed class and was using it partly for the benefit of the church itself and partly for the benefit of the poor and needy. It is not difficult to imagine what a formidable instrument of power this patrimony, together with the institutions of public assistance and beneficence which were based on it, became amid the general misery and insecurity of the critical days of the third century. While the elect reached Christianity through their own trials and sorrows, or through the spectacle of the griefs of others, or through disgust with a disordered and contaminated world and a wild aspiration towards peace and happiness, many others were attracted to the new faith by the help so generously given by the Church in cases of need. If faith was the bond between the faithful and the Church, there were other and more material bonds which efficaciously reinforced the power and authority of religion, in the shape of charities, subsidies, assistance, ecclesiastical offices, and the advantages connected therewith, and, last but not least, the management and methodical development of the lands recently acquired which employed an ever increasing number of agents, slaves, labourers, and farmers.

Christianity, therefore, was now a spiritual and social power, but, unlike Mithraism, it enjoyed no imperial favour. It may be an exaggeration to say—as has been said—that all the emperors of the third century were against the Christians. But it is certain that Christianity had to endure the most terrible persecutions under some of them, such as Decius and Valerian, and that it was always looked upon by the authorities with a hostile distrust which contrasts with the favour shown to Mithraism. What was the reason for the attitude thus adopted by the empire towards the new religion? The reason was the very spirit of Christianity. From the point of view of the empire there is no doubt that Christianity was a force of dissolution. Little by little, as the times became more troubled, Christianity took courage to maintain, with more or less fervour according to the various sects, that a Christian should seek no public office or honour which compromised his faith. He must not maintain temples, arrange the games of the Circus or judge or prosecute his fellow citizens. He could not, therefore, except at the peril of his soul, become a magistrate. The world in which others lived and made merry was, as it were, an inn kept by a religion and a civilization which Christ had cursed, and neither its sorrows nor its joys were to be shared by the perfect Christian, who, on the contrary, should long only to leave, as soon as possible, this vale of sin and tears. Thus the duty of the Christian was to destroy the empire. If he did not do so it was—so Tertullian affirmed—because the Christian was thoroughly permeated with the doctrine of mildness.

The effect of such teaching at a time when public offices were becoming such a serious and dangerous responsibility can easily be imagined. Christianity was destroying the empire by the weapon of abstention which removed from its control and its municipal administration a great number of intelligent, cultivated, honest, and zealous men of the upper classes. Many citizens whose fortunes destined them to the management of public affairs preferred to give their patrimony to the Church and by poverty to escape from the grave responsibilities of power. Others evaded these responsibilities in different ways, of which some were deplored even by the Christian emperors.[1] Celibacy increased to a greater degree than at the end of the republic.

But the army suffered even more than the civil services. Even in the second century, Christianity had affirmed that "it is not right to be a man of the sword, for the Lord declared that he who taketh the sword shall perish by the sword," and that "a son of peace, whom it becometh not even to engage in a litigation, should still less take part in a battle," had affirmed the incompatibility of military service with Christianity, for "the Lord by disarming Peter clearly affirmed his will that every soldier should lay down his sword." It followed that there was nothing for the Christian soldier but "immediately to leave the army" or "to resolve to endure death for God."[2] The canons of the Church of Alexandria absolutely forbade volunteering, which was the foundation of the Roman army, and authoritatively laid it down that "it was not fitting for Christians to bear arms." Lactantius himself puts the impossibility of a Christian's taking part in a trial for a capital offence on the same footing as his taking part in a war, for it is "impossible to allow a single exception to the divine precept 'Thou shalt not kill.'" St. Augustine, finally, says that for the Christian it is indifferent under what rule he lives provided that the State does not compel him to commit impious and wicked actions.[3] It is not difficult to

[1] *Cod. Theod.*, xii., 1, 104, and 115.

[2] Tertull., *De corona*, ii.; *De idol.*, 19.

[3] Aug., *De civit. Dei.*, v., 17. On the relations between military service and the early Christians, *cf.* G. Adami, in *Bilychnis* (a review of religious studies), 1913, p. 169 ff.

see how much such doctrines must have weakened the empire in its defence against the barbarians.

On the accession of Diocletian to the empire the vital elements of Roman and Greek civilization were alike mortally stricken. The whole of ancient culture and paganism, the moral and political ideas of the ancient world were in their death throes. The social structure of the empire was in part already destroyed, in part seriously menaced. All that had been accomplished by centuries of Greek and Roman labour was tottering to its fall, some of it destroyed by foreign enemies, barbarian and Persian, some by the unbridled violence of the legions, some by Christianity, which, in order to make room for its loftier morality and its nobler conception of life, had to uproot the foundations of the constituted order of things. Against this dissolution, the effect at the same time of destructive and regenerative forces, the empire tried to react by pushing forward and bringing to the work of government its ruder populations and by renewing the ancient eastern religions with their mysticism, their metaphysics, and their absolutist spirit. When Diocletian donned the purple the Græco-Roman empire of Trajan and of Hadrian was already almost entirely transformed into an Asiatico-barbarian empire. The strange destiny of this empire which sought the way of salvation for the future in a distant past, in the religious and monarchical institutions of the Asia which had flourished before Greece and Rome attained their marvellous splendours, will form the subject of the last part of this book.

## CHAPTER XV

### THE REFORMS OF DIOCLETIAN

(284–305 A.D.)

**122. Diocletian and Maximian: the Partition of the Empire, 284–293 A.D.** The man whom the legion had elected as successor to Carus was also a Dalmatian like Claudius and Aurelian, but his birth was even more obscure. Some went so far as to say that he was the son of a freedman. He had been in the army from his earliest youth, had studied in the school of three great generals—Claudius, Aurelian, and Probus, and, though a barbarian, he was a great man. Immediately after his election he had to face a civil war with Carinus who in the meantime had been fighting with the Jazigi. Preparations were made on both sides which lasted several months, and in the spring of 285 the two armies met on the Morava. It appears that Diocletian would have been beaten if Carinus had not been murdered by one of his own officers. The death of Carinus led to the triumph of Diocletian, but the new civil war as usual brought about a crisis. The provinces, left to themselves for several months, no longer felt the controlling hand of the government and immediately began to proclaim new pretenders.

In Gaul broke out the rebellion of the Bagaudi, an

insurrection of ruined peasants and insolvent debtors. The barbarians renewed their agitations on the frontier and their piratical raids on the coasts of Gaul and Britain. Diocletian soon saw that one emperor could not cope with everything, and shortly afterwards—in the second half of 285, so far as we can make out—he summoned Maximianus, the son of a Pannonian farmer and one of his companions in arms, from the neighbourhood of Sirmium to share with him the fatigues of empire. Maximian was a good soldier but indifferently educated, from which we may infer that Diocletian's original intention was to make him not his colleague, but a faithful and trusted lieutenant. As a matter of fact Maximian did not receive the title of Augustus, but merely that of Cæsar, and while, in order to give a religious sanction to their authority, Diocletian assumed the appellation of *Jovius*, Maximian took that of *Herculius*. The relation of superior and inferior was thus maintained even in the divinities under whose protection the two heads of the empire were placed.

In a few weeks, however, Maximian stamped out the insurrection of the Bagaudi, and this piece of good fortune altered Diocletian's plan. In 286 he conferred the title of Augustus on Maximian and thus, at least in theory, made the powers of the two emperors equal, though he did not break the political and legislative unity of the empire. Each of the two Augusti had his own army, his own prætorian præfect, and his own treasury, though perhaps not his own *consilium principis*. But the laws and the coinage were common to both and the public acts bore both their names. Diocletian's came first, as his will predominated in all things, but this was due to his greater personal authority and capacity and not to his having a greater share of power. Administration and defence questions were divided between the emperors but even here no hard and fast line was drawn and, if there was any reason for doing so, neither hesitated to enter the territories entrusted to the other.

In a word, the empire was ruled no longer by one emperor, but by two, just as there had been for so many centuries two consuls at the head of the republic. The reform was indeed most necessary. Seizing the opportunity offered by the revolt of the Bagaudi, the Heruli, the Burgundi, and the Alamanni had recently crossed the Rhine and, what was worse, Carausius the commander of the fleet, who had been entrusted with the pursuit of the Saxon and Frankish pirates, had secretly entered into an understanding with them. Condemned to death by Maximian, he rebelled, assumed the title of Augustus in Britain, seized that island and also several coast towns of Gaul, and created a powerful armada which enabled him to defy the authority of the two legitimate Augusti.

Thus, the situation of the empire in the East remained as precarious as it had been for the previous thirty years since the days of Valerian, that is since Rome had lost Armenia, her most powerful bulwark against the new empire of the Sassanids. Two emperors, therefore, one in the East and one in the West, were not enough, but Maximian successfully repulsed the new Germanic invasion on the Rhine while Diocletian tried to recover a footing in Armenia rather by intrigue than by force of arms. The moment was favourable. The Persian empire was so much debilitated by a civil war that King Bahram had sent an embassy to Diocletian asking for his friendship. Armenia was weary and discontented with the Persian domination. Moreover, Tiridates the legitimate heir to the Armenian crown was living in voluntary exile at Rome. Diocletian secretly instigated and assisted Tiridates to recover the throne, and, a well-planned *coup de main* favoured by the embarrassments of the King of Persia and the discontent in Armenia, enabled Tiridates without much opposition to take possession of his ancestral realm. Armenia was once more under Roman influence, and the King of Persia, not being in a position to take the field, had to accept the situation and recognize the accomplished fact.

**123. The Tetrarchy and the Appointment of Galerius and Constantius as Cæsars.** This success improved the position in the East where, however, a new enemy appeared in the shape of the Saracens, who swooped down from their retreats in the Syro-Arabian desert to pillage Roman territory and where Egypt, for reasons which remain obscure, was in a state of unrest. There was no corresponding improvement in the West. There Maximian had not succeeded in disposing of Carausius who had raised a powerful force of Franks and Saxons. New agitations and migrations began to threaten Germany where Goths, Vandals, Gepidæ, and Burgundians were struggling among themselves. In eastern Europe Sarmatia was again active; in Numidia and Mauretania the natives were once more in a ferment. The two Augusti did their best to cope with all these difficulties. They flew from one end of the empire to the other, invested this and that general with full military and civil powers and made a virtue of necessity by recognizing Carausius, whom they could not conquer, as a third Augustus. But this difficult year was enough to convince Diocletian and Maximian that not even two Augusti were enough, and in 293[1] Diocletian decided to subdivide the administration still further by appointing two new official collaborators of inferor rank who were styled Cæsars. In this way several objects were secured. The defence of the frontiers was provided for; administration was improved; dangerous ambitions were assuaged and the question of the succession which had so long tormented the empire was solved by anticipation. On the death of one of the Augusti his Cæsar was to have his place, and was in his turn to nominate a new Cæsar. The two officers raised to this exalted rank were Galerius, who became Diocletian's Cæsar, and Constantius who was the Cæsar of Maximian. Galerius was a Dacian of a coarse but energetic disposition. Constantius, surnamed Chlorus from his pallor, was descended on his mother's side from Claudius the Goth; he was therefore a man of good family, gentle and cultivated—an aristocrat among the crowd of *parvenus* who then ruled the empire. The provinces were distributed among the four emperors as follows: Diocletian kept for himself the far eastern part of the empire including Bithynia, Arabia, Lybia, Egypt, and Syria; Galerius had Dalmatia, Pannonia, Mœsia, Thrace, Greece, and Asia Minor; Maximian ruled Rome, Italy, Rhætia, Sicily, Sardinia, Spain, and the remainder of Africa; Constantius, Britain and Gaul. Conformably to the reasons which had led to their appointment they were to reside not at Rome but on the principal boundary lines of the districts assigned

[1] On the chronological question *cf.* G. Costa, *Diocletianus* in De Ruggiero, *Dizionario epigrafico*, ii., p. 1805.

to each: Diocletian at Nicomedia in Bithynia, Galerius at Sirmium in Pannonia, Maximian at Milan, and Constantius at Treveri in Gaul.

**124. The New Absolute Monarchy and its Religious Character.** In spite of these arrangements the empire itself was not divided among the four emperors. Its political and legislative unity was preserved practically intact as before. The two Cæsars were subordinate to the two Augusti and between the Augusti, though Diocletian was the more important, there was perfect concord. Thus, though legislation was carried out in the name of the four sovereigns, the inspiring and co-ordinating mind was always Diocletian's. His reform, however, had an intimate and religious character to which historians have not always paid sufficient attention. As Maximian had been adopted by Diocletian as his son, so the two Cæsars were adopted by the Augusti and received their names. Further the two Cæsars repudiated their wives and married the daughters of the Augusti, who had adopted them as sons. And as, on the occasion of their being respectively raised to the empire, Diocletian had taken the title of *Jovius*, and Maximian the subordinate title of *Herculius*, so now the families of the two Cæsars came to be styled the *Jovii* and the *Herculii*.

There can be no doubt that in these arrangements concerning the supreme power, Diocletian was following the great example of the Antonines and the principle of adoption as practised in the second century, hoping to restore to the imperial authority the stability which it had then enjoyed. But he adapted the ancient principle to the needs of the time in which he lived. Thus he resolutely laid down once and for all the principle of the divinity of the emperors who were *a Diis geniti et deorum creatores*. The subject peoples and the army swore allegiance in their names as formerly they had sworn by Jove or Hercules, and the deity from which they and the empire drew strength and favour was no other than the Sun God who exercised his supernatural influence on monarchs, the Persian Mithras dispenser of thrones and empires.[1]

Moreover this new divine majesty of the empire was inculcated on its subjects by outward and visible signs. The sovereign wore on his head the diadem of the great oriental kings—a diadem with rays like those of the sun by whose special favour he was illuminated. His robes and his sandals glittered with precious stones. He was no longer, like Augustus, Trajan, or Vespasian, a mere mortal, accessible any day at any time. In conversing with him one had to observe the rules of an elaborate etiquette, and when admitted to his presence one had to make reverences which amounted to a kind of adoration. Oriental absolutism now finally triumphed, on the ruins of Greek and Roman culture which had been in such great measure destroyed by the great crisis of the third century, in an empire now to a great extent both populated and governed by barbarians. The fact that such great innovations excited no opposition except that which (as we shall see) the Christians offered to the adoration of the emperors, and that practically all of them persisted, demonstrates how thoroughly the age of absolutism was prepared during the profound revolution which was accomplished in the third century.

**125. The Reform of Provincial Government.** The Roman government was now in very truth an abso-

[1] *C. I. L.*, iii., 4413.

lute monarchy of the Asiatic type. Diocletian may have been careful to notify to the senate his own and subsequent imperial elections, and to respect many formalities which tradition had made august. But the senate, though a necessary part of the constitution, was treated as a body whose advice might be listened to but need not necessarily be followed. It no longer had any provinces to administer, for all had passed under the jurisdiction of the emperors. It was excluded from the direction of affairs, its place being taken by the *consistorium principis*, a new body which, like the ancient senate, examined questions of a legislative character and was composed of all the great officers of State.

By a still more important reform Diocletian finally severed the civil from the military authority. Every province was henceforth to have a *præses*, or civil governor in addition to a *dux* or military governor. This measure which may well seem in contradiction with the financial necessities of the empire, for while these imposed economy on the imperial treasury the partition of the administration demanded a notable increase of expenditure. But the political necessities which urged Diocletian to take this step were too strong to allow him to take account of financial considerations. On the one hand, by separating the civil from the military authority, he aimed at weakening both the *præses* and the *dux* and so making more difficult the proclamations of provincial governors as emperors which had been the curse of the third century. On the other, he was endeavouring to compensate for the deficiencies of the military element which, being recruited among the ruder peoples, did not possess the necessary qualities for governing the provinces of an empire which, however decadent, was yet the inheritor of an ancient tradition of civilization. Furthermore, there was a tendency to what we may call the breaking up of the provinces. To secure the better administration of the empire and to provide opportunities of promotion for his officials, Diocletian divided and subdivided the provinces as none of his predecessors had done. Thus we know that in the year 297 there were 96 civil governorships in the provinces instead of 57, as had been the case at the time of his accession. At the same time, in order to prevent this subdivision of the provinces from weakening the empire and the power of the central authority, he created the system of "dioceses." The diocese had hitherto been a financial or judicial subdivision of a province. Under Diocletian it became a group of several provinces in one inclusive district placed under the control of a new magistrate the *vicarius*. The dioceses were twelve in number: five in the East, styled Oriens, Pontica, Asiana, Thracia, and Mœsia, and seven in the West, which were known as Germania, Gallia, Britannia, Viennensis, Italia, Hispania, and Africa.

Thus henceforth, there were to be at the head of the State two Augusti with two Cæsars as their subordinates. Immediately under these came the twelve *vicarii*, and with these on an equal footing the proconsuls who were governors of certain specially privileged provinces. Below these again were the *præsides*, or, in some cases, the *consulares* or *correctores* as the governors of newly conquered provinces were variously styled. Side by side with this civil hierarchy stood the *duces*, with territorial powers limited to military affairs and not necessarily coterminous with the boundaries of the diocese or the province.

What place did Italy occupy in this new system? Italy was now no more than one province among other provinces, subject once more, as before the war with Perseus, to the land tax except for one last privileged corner, the Roman Campagna within a circuit of a hundred miles from the walls of the city. Thus fiscal uniformity between the provinces and Italy was complete. Italy, moreover, was itself divided up into provinces, the names of which are known to us, and the whole peninsula formed a diocese governed not as in other cases, by one *vicarius* but by two.

126. **Military and Financial Reform.** Diocletian had a great organizing talent and he did not put any of his reforms in practice without providing for the reactions which it was likely to cause, or without conceiving and carrying out all the consequential changes that became necessary. The increased number of heads of State, their removal to their strategically appropriate residences, and the separation of the military from the civil power were not in themselves sufficient to secure the more efficient defence of the empire. It was necessary to quadruplicate the imperial bodyguard, to add to the old prætorians new forces called *milites Palatini* and *Comitatenses*, and generally to increase the effectives of the army. Diocletian, therefore, increased his forces by about a third—from 300,000 to 500,000 men.[1] He increased the number of officers in even greater proportion, for in order to keep each legion better in hand and to counterbalance the powers of the *duces*, the

[1] *Cf.* G. Costa, in De Ruggieri, *Dizionario epigrafico*, ii., p. 1848.

number of men in the ranks of each was reduced, while the number of military tribunes was greatly increased.

But the augmentation of the staff of the central provincial bureaucracies and of the armies implied an increase of expenditure. For this also Diocletian made provision with much energy and ingenuity. He began by decreeing a general revaluation of lands —a new cadastral survey as we should now call it—and as this was completed he gradually introduced a new system of taxation which was uniform for all the provinces but which took strict account of the quality of the land and of its productiveness. With this object, he introduced a new fiscal unit denominated according to locality *iugum*, *caput*, *millena*, *centuria*, which included lands of various kinds and extent, but which were of identical value and were required to provide the same contribution. Thus, for example, five *iugera* of vineyard or twenty *iugera* of cultivable land of the first quality made up a *iugum*, while for the same unit forty *iugera* of the second and sixty *iugera* of the third quality were required, correspondingly more *iugera* being specified in the case of mountainous land and correspondingly fewer in the case of level plots.[1] The method of collection was regulated with great care. The sum assessed by the State on a complete fiscal unit comprehending a certain number of *iuga* was notified to the *decuriones* (the member of the little senate belonging to each city), who divided up the amount among the proprie-

[1] This information comes from a collection of laws of Syriac origin which belongs to the year 501, but which refers to Diocletian's reforms. *Cf.* Bruns-Sachau, *Syrisch-römisches Rechtsbuch aus dem fünften, Jahrhundert*, Leipzig, 1880.

tors and the tenants of the public land (*possessores*), excluding those who held insignificant portions, saw that it was collected and were responsible for paying it over to the Treasury. The system of tribute was thus perfect and the certainty that it would be received by the State placed beyond a doubt. But when hard times came it ended by ruining a whole social class, those, that is to say, who were in easy circumstances, and the municipal administration suffered severely, for no one could be found who would be responsible for it.

127. **The Great Reform of the Coinage.** Shortly after these reforms had been carried out Diocletian turned his attention to the economic cancer which had played havoc in the third century—the forced circulation of a debased coinage. He established the *aureus* at $^1/_{60}$ of the libra (*i.e.* at 5.45 grammes). He fixed the *argenteus minutulus* (now substituted for the old *denarius*) at $^1/_{96}$ of the libra (*i.e.* at 3.40 grammes) which was the average weight of the *denarius neronianus* and, as the proportion of alloy in each case was very small, their intrinsic values were respectively 17.75 lire ($3.43) and 1 lira ($.193). The *antonianus* disappeared. As however it was impossible to eliminate from daily transactions the use of the depreciated *denarius* to which the public had been accustomed since the days of the republic, Diocletian issued new *denarii* of the same shape and weight as the old, but of pure bronze, and fixed their value at 1/50,000 of the golden libra which was equivalent to .02 lire ($.00386).

This great reform was completed in 301, and Diocletian took in hand a supplementary measure on a grandiose scale which is unique in history. This was his *edictum de pretiis rerum venalium*[1] in which he fixed in minute detail maximum prices for all agricultural and industrial products throughout the empire. The object of this was to check the enormous increase in the price of commodities, the chief cause of which had hitherto been the bad currency and which had been a cause of loss to private persons but had more especially aggravated the expense of providing for the armies. Something of the sort had already been carried out in individual cases and may be hereafter, but so universal and rigorous a regulation had never yet been and probably will never again be seen. Diocletian's edict from the minuteness and variety of its provisions is indeed a unique monument of economic legislation. It is all the more to be regretted that we know so little of the circumstances of its composition and the effects that it produced.

**128. The Great Persian War** (296–298 A.D.). Thus the activity of the new government of the two Augusti was remarkable in the sphere of internal reform. It was scarcely less notable in military affairs. They succeeded in re-establishing the unity of the empire by recovering Britain. Carausius had been killed by one of his officers, a certain Allectus who flattered himself that he would take his place, but who was shortly afterwards defeated and also slain (296). An insurrection at Alexandria, where it appears that an attempt was made to set up a pretender against the rightful emperors, was promptly dealt with and very rapidly put down (296). On the other hand great difficulties had arisen with Persia. In 294 Narsetes or Narseus (Narsehi) had succeeded to the throne of that country. Under his rule there

[1] Given in *C. I. L.*, iii., pp. 1911–53; 2208–11.

came a reaction against the lax policy of his predecessor, and in 296 he profited by the circumstance that Galerius was in Pannonia and Diocletian much occupied in Egypt to throw himself on Armenia and threaten Syria at the same time.

Diocletian immediately recalled Galerius and sent him against the Persians, but that impetuous soldier made a serious blunder by attacking the enemy in the same region in which three centuries and a half previously, the legions of Crassus had found their grave, and he was defeated. The great emperor had to reconstruct the ruined army chiefly by enrolling barbarians from the West, more especially Goths and Dacians, and to repeat the attempt from another direction by invading the enemy's country through the mountains of Armenia. The new army was also entrusted to Galerius who was anxious to wipe out his previous disaster, and this time he was successful. By an impetuous night attack he not only overthrew the Persian camp but captured the entire royal family. Narsetes alone was able, though wounded, to save himself by flight. Emboldened by this exploit Galerius already dreamed of conquering Persia, and repeating the achievement of Alexander. But the barbarians were once more seriously threatening the borders of the empire. In this very year (297) Constantius had to go to Britain, and while the Germans, encouraged by his absence, were threatening Gaul, Maximian was forced to leave for Africa where a new rebellion had broken out. Diocletian, therefore, was disposed to make peace, and in the early part of 298 a treaty was concluded which was a new triumph for Roman diplomacy. The whole of Mesopotamia which had at one time been conquered by Septimius

Severus was again restored to the empire, and, in addition, the Persian king ceded five Armenian provinces in the upper valley of the Tigris which Sapor I. had conquered. Our sources of information disagree as to what these actually were.[1] Tiridates was confirmed in possession of Armenia as far as Zinta in Media Atropatene, and Iberia (the Georgia of today) became a vassal State no longer of Persia but of Rome. Finally Diocletian managed that all the trade of Persia with Rome should pass through Nisibis, an arrangement which completed and greatly simplified the excise system of the empire. In this way Rome secured an excellent strategic frontier, by which the defence of Asia Minor and Syria would be very much strengthened, and some extremely useful alliances in the Caucasus. In a word a peace had been obtained practically without fighting which was to last for forty years.

**129. The Persecution of the Christians (303 A.D.).** The great war with Persia was followed by several years of profound peace. Now that the finer part of the Græco-Roman intellectual tradition, and with it the republican spirit, had been destroyed, the empire seemed to have reached a kind of equilibrium in oriental absolutism, in the sentiments, the ideas, and the institutions by which Persia, Assyria, Egypt, and all the great empires of Asia had been governed. This half barbarous, half Asiatic empire with deified generals at its head appeared to have triumphed, and who knows what might have been the fate of the world, and of Europe in particular, if in place of the Græco-Roman tradition now almost exhausted, there had not arisen a new force in the shape of Christianity to combat theocratic absolutism? Though the whole

[1] *Cf.* Amm. Marc., xxv., 79; *F. H. Gr.*, iv., p. 189.

empire acquiesced in the adoration of the persons of the emperors as divine beings and accepted the new religious forms in which the sinking State sought new support for its authority, the Christians rebelled. They could not worship either Mithras or the Sun or the emperors who represented these divinities on earth, but only God whose Son had become a man in order to take away the sin of the world. And Christianity was now so widespread and so powerful that the barbaric Asiatic empire ended by seeing in it the mortal enemy which in fact it was. The persecution of the Christians was the logical conclusion of the whole political system of Diocletian, for the mere fact of being a Christian now meant a refusal to recognize the new régime.

The first anti-Christian edict was that of February 24, 303. It prescribed the destruction of Christian churches and books, the breaking up of Christian communities and the confiscation of their property, the prohibition of meetings of the faithful and their exclusion from all public offices. The edict was relatively mild, for it did not threaten Christians with the punishment of death; but they were now too numerous to be all zealous observers of the moral precept requiring that the other cheek should be offered to the smiter. This time they appear to have replied to violence with violence, to have set fire to the imperial palace at Nicomedia and to have formed a conspiracy against the emperors on a very large scale. In Syria, moreover, both in the army and among the civil authorities, there broke out an actual rebellion and an anti-dynastic movement.[1] Even in the face of

[1] *Cf.* Eus., *Hist. eccles.*, viii., 2 ff. The author very naturally relieves the Christians of all responsibility. The facts, however, speak for themselves.

resistance of this kind Diocletian hesitated to shed blood. He contented himself with a second edict whereby the bishops, priests, and deacons who refused to deliver up their sacred books were to be imprisoned. This edict was followed by a third which in a sense was a mitigation of its predecessors. On the occasion of the great public festival of the *Vicennalia* celebrating the twentieth anniversary of the accession of the two Augusti a general amnesty had been proclaimed. Of the Christian prisoners all were to be set at liberty who would openly return to the old religion. The rest were to be excluded from this favour, and, indeed, as a punishment for their insane obstinacy, they were to be more harshly treated.

These edicts are the most epoch-making documents in the history of the power of Christianity. The reluctance of Diocletian to take severe measures against an enemy now known to be too numerous and too strong to be put down is obvious. As always happens when a State finds itself in the presence of a danger with which it is not strong enough to cope, Diocletian had recourse to half measures which, then as in other cases, merely aggravated the evil. The resistance of the Christians became more bitter and the emperor was compelled to resort to severities from which at first he had abstained. Towards the end of 303–304, Diocletian fell seriously ill, and the government of the East was assumed by Galerius. It was then that the more decisive and uncompromising policy prevailed and Galerius and his colleague[1]

[1] The Christian tradition (Lact., *De mort. pers.*, xv., 4–5) throws the whole responsibility on the two princes of the East who are said not to have consulted their colleagues. This seems very improbable.

agreed upon the final edict, the most Draconian which Diocletian had been prevailed upon to sign. This edict made the obligation to sacrifice to the Gods universal and denounced the severest penalties against all who refused to comply.

This persecution lasted eight years; it was on a great scale and, as a whole, vigorous, though not so much so as ecclesiastical tradition would have us believe. It was unequal and the severity with which it was applied varied according to the district and the temperaments of the Cæsars and the Augusti. Constantius Chlorus, for example, did not put the persecuting edicts in force, no doubt because the Christian element at his court was too powerful and highly favoured.

**130. The Abdication of the Augusti (305 A.D.).** In 304 Diocletian reached the twentieth year of his reign and, though he was not yet sixty, he was weary. For years he had been meditating retirement from his long spell of government, a retirement from which he could serenely contemplate the various development of his reforms without having to direct it in person. For long too he had been building for himself at Salona in his native Dalmatia a retreat where he could rest in his declining years. Moreover it was his wish that in his retirement from public affairs he should not be alone, and that Maximian, the faithful companion of his labours should go with him. It even appears that he had made Maximian swear to him that he would do so. The great moment had come at last. On May 1, 305, on a hill rising gently from the plain three miles from Nicomedia at the foot of a column bearing a statue of Jupiter, on the spot where he had invested Galerius with the purple, surrounded by the great officers of the empire and the highest officers of the army, Diocletian laid down his diadem and his sceptre and put off his imperial robes, calling on Galerius to succeed him and giving him a Cæsar in his turn in the person of Maximinus Daius, one of the *protectores*. The same scene was repeated on the same day, and perhaps at the same hour, at Milan where Maximian yielded his throne to Constantius and placed the Cæsarian purple on the shoulders of Severus, another officer.

## CHAPTER XVI

### CONSTANTINE THE GREAT (306–337 A.D.)

**131. The New Civil War (305–314 A.D.).** A year had not elapsed from the abdication of Diocletian and Maximian, when Constantius Chlorus died in Britain. His death was enough to bring about the downfall of the tetrarchy. Diocletian, not wishing to establish the principle of hereditary succession, had excluded from sharing in the empire both Constantine son of Constantius and Maxentius son of Maximian. But Constantine was a young man of intelligence and energy, and was moreover very ambitious, so that, immediately after the death of Constantius, he caused himself to be proclaimed Cæsar by his soldiers at Eboracum (York)(July 25, 306).[1] This bold stroke was successful. In order to avoid a civil war Galerius, the elder and more powerful of the two Augusti, accepted the *fait accompli* by appointing Constantine a Cæsar and promoting Severus to the rank of Augustus. But the civil war which Galerius hoped to avert in Gaul soon broke out in a graver form in Italy.

Rome, the ancient capital, had taken very ill her

[1] It appears that, before the abdication of the two Augusti, Constantine had received assurances that he would be promoted to the post of one of the two Cæsars in the first vacancy. This promise would justify in part his proclamation in 306. *Cf.* Lact., *De mort. persec.*, 18–19.

reduction to the rank of a provincial town, and the populace and the prætorian guard, on the pretext of a new census decreed by Galerius, rose in rebellion and proclaimed Maxentius, son of Maximian, Augustus. Maxentius was living not far from the city and, since Constantine had been raised to the empire he too wished to be made a Cæsar (October 27, 306). To consolidate his authority he recalled his father Maximian, who was by no means contented in his retirement, and invested him also with the imperial title. The fragile system of the tetrarchy was shattered. The empire had six emperors, four Augusti and two Cæsars! Galerius charged Severus with the task of crushing the Italian revolt, but Maximian's name made him very formidable on his return to power. The troops of Severus refused to fight against their old general and preferred to go over to his camp. Severus fled and at Ravenna resigned to Maximian the purple which the latter had formerly bestowed upon him (307).

A second attempt against Maxentius made by Galerius in person had no better success. All Italy had declared for the cause of Rome and of Maxentius. The cities closed their gates against Galerius, who deemed it unwise to lay siege to Rome and left the peninsula, inviting Diocletian himself to meet him at Carnuntum in Pannonia in order that by his advice and authority he might help to discover a solution of the difficulty. Nothing could more clearly show the prestige which Diocletian retained even in his retirement. The conference at Carnuntum was joined by Maximian who had already quarrelled with his son Maxentius because after his successes he had tried to exercise an authority over his father which was much resented. But neither Galerius nor Maximian could persuade Diocletian to resume the imperial dignity, and the deliberations of the conference resulted in the decision that for Severus should be substituted another Augustus in the person of Licinianus Licinius, an elderly man and an old comrade of Galerius, who was to be governor of Illyricum (November, 307). Maximian was to return to private life and Maxentius was excluded from the empire.

The cure was worse than the disease. Maxentius maintained himself in Italy. Maximian did not lay down the purple but sought to make common cause with Constantine, to whom he gave in marriage his daughter Fausta, hoping to find in him the support for his ambitious schemes which Maxentius had withheld. The appointment of Licinius created new difficulties. Licinius had risen to the highest place in the empire without having passed through the intermediate grade of Cæsar, thus being promoted over the heads of Maximinus Daius and Constantine. The former at once had himself proclaimed Augustus by his troops; the latter demanded from Galerius a similar investiture for himself. Early in 308, therefore, the empire had four Augusti besides Maxentius and Maximian, and, what was more, these Augusti were no longer in any relation of subordination to each other. Diocletian's tetrarchy had fallen, and once more the uncertainty of the principle of succession to the supreme office—the mortal malady which since the days of Augustus had given the empire no rest—generated a crisis. The first victim was Maximian, the old collaborator of Diocletian, who disappeared in tragic and obscure circumstances. It was said that he conspired against his son-in-law; it is certain that

Constantine had him arrested at Massilia and that two years later he caused him to be finally removed (310).

In the midst of these disorders and intrigues three of the four legitimate emperors, Galerius, Constantine, and Licinius promulgated an edict in the year 311 which suspended the persecution of the Christians.[1] How are we to explain this sudden change of policy? It will be best regarded not so much as a retractation as a political measure suggested by the dangerous internal situation of the empire. It was clear that the balance of power between the five Augusti, among whom there was no preponderating authority, was unstable, and that there might be civil war at any moment. But Maxentius and Maximinus Daius were bound to the old pagan cult and were against the Christians. Maximinus Daius was in fact endeavouring to organize paganism on a more solid basis. It is probable therefore that by their decree the other Augusti were trying to secure the very powerful support of the Christian element for themselves with a view to future eventualities. In other words the Christians were profiting by the weakening of the imperial authority which had come about owing to the political crisis.

The decree of 311, in fact, was one of many premonitory symptoms of a new civil war. The outbreak seemed to have come when Galerius died shortly after the promulgation of the edict. Licinius and Maximinus appeared to be on the point of contending by force of arms for the succession. But after a little while they came to terms, the latter taking Asia Minor, Syria, and Egypt, and the former the remaining

[1] Euseb., *H. eccl.*, viii., 17, 1 ff.; Lact., *De mort.*, 34.

oriental provinces from the Bosphorus to the Adriatic. It was not in the East but in Europe that the great and imminent conflagration was destined to break out. For several years at least Constantine, who had already distinguished himself by successful campaigns against the Franks and the Alamanni, had been fixing an attentive eye on the affairs of Italy. Maxentius was consolidating his power there and was preparing great forces, intended—it was said—to wrest Gaul from Constantine and Illyria from Licinius. He was also making approaches to Maximin who, on the other hand, was vigorously carrying on the persecution of the Christians in Egypt, Syria, and elsewhere. Constantine was drawing nearer to Licinius, to whom he gave in marriage his sister Constantia, was preparing a powerful army, and was receiving secret intelligence from Italy. Early in 312, when he felt that he was ready, he crossed the Alps near the Mont Cenis with about 50,000 men of whom half were chosen and tried legionaries, easily overcame the resistance which was at first offered to him, and made himself master of the valley of the Po, whence he marched on Rome. Maxentius had not moved from the capital, trusting to the strong position of the city, to the numerous forces at his disposal, and to the many difficulties which had caused the failure of the expeditions of Galerius and Severus. But when he learned that Constantine was approaching the city at the head of a powerful army elated by a victorious march and favoured by a population which had grown weary of his government, he did not remain shut up within the impregnable walls of Aurelian, but issued forth to confront his enemy in the open field. The battle, which took place near the Pons Milvius, ended in the complete defeat of Maxentius who along with a great part of his army was drowned in the river (October 28, 312). On the following day the victor made his triumphal entry into Rome. He immediately turned with deferential words to the senate and practically promised them the restoration of their ancient privileges. He finally disbanded the prætorian guards and dismantled their camp. In recompense for this, the senate decreed him a triumphal arch which still stands where the ancient Via Sacra meets the road from the Porta Capena and which was adorned by the spoils of the Arch of Trajan.

The conquest of Italy dislocated the former relations between the three emperors, but it made Maximin's position even more difficult. Shortly afterwards, in the early days of 313, Licinius and Constantine had a meeting at Milan.

**132. The Edict of Milan (early in 313 A.D.) and the Downfall of Maximin (313 A.D.).** We do not know what was the course of the deliberations at the new conference. But we may easily suppose that, while Licinius consented to Constantine's new aggrandizement, he was given a free hand by the latter against Maximin, and that it was probably with this object, that is to say, the destruction of the foundation of Maximin's power, that they determined on a new edict of toleration for the Christians, an act which was destined to be one of capital importance in the history of the time, and which in the history of the world is held to mark the definite triumph of Christianity.[1]

[1] Euseb., *H. eccl.*, x., 5; Lact., *De mort. pers.*, 48. German criticism as usual has attempted to throw doubt on the very existence of an actual edict of Milan. But the text of Lactantius (*De mort. persec.*, 48) is too explicit and formal to be doubted by any his-

There was in fact no question of the triumph of Christianity in the sense of a solemn recognition of that faith as above all others, still less of the adoption of Christianity as the official religion of the State. The Roman State still had an official religion of its own and the emperor in that religion still held the supreme office of *pontifex maximus*. The edict declared that it merely confirmed the precedent set in 311; that is to say, it confirmed the religious toleration (τὴν ἐλευθερίαν τῆς θρησκείας) granted two years before, removed any remaining restrictions, and gave a new pledge of the purpose of the Augusti by ordering the restoration to the Christian churches of the premises and the property which had been sequestrated during the great persecution. The purpose of this enactment is clear. It aimed at a declaration of policy contrary to that pursued by Maximin in the oriental provinces. There, especially since the death of Galerius, Maximin had intensified the anti-Christian persecution and had clearly revealed his intention of leaning for support on the pagan element in his opposition to the policy inaugurated in 311 by the first edict of the three Augusti.

In other words, Christianity and paganism became weapons in the hands of the three emperors for use in the civil war, Constantine and Licinius aiming at raising the Christian East against Maximin, and Maximin at raising the pagans of the West against Constantine and Licinius. But, while Constantine and Licinius were then only thinking of carrying out

---

torian whose good sense has not been undermined by a passion for criticism. On all this question see T. de Bacci Venuti, *Dalle grande persecuzione alla vittoria del Cristianesimo*, Milan, 1913, Appendix, pp. 303 ff.

a skilful political move, the edict of 313, though they did not know it, marked an important moment in universal history—the moment at which the principle of the liberty of conscience was first affirmed. Fifteen centuries were destined to elapse before the principle which animated the edict triumphed and found a universal application in Europe and America. Maximin, however, soon grasped the intention of his enemies and did not hesitate to act. Before Licinius could leave Italy he invaded the Balkan Peninsula, stormed Byzantium, and then Perinthus at the first assault, and marched on Adrianople. Licinius had to hasten to the spot and at first assumed a defensive attitude; but, not far from Perinthus, about eighteen miles from Heraclea, a great battle took place in April 30, 313, which annulled all Maximin's previous successes. He was defeated and fled to Cilicia where he died.

**133. The New War between Licinius and Constantine (314 A. D.).** Shortly before this battle Diocletian had died at Salona after having witnessed the downfall of his system. He was fortunate at least in not living to see the acts of repression perpetrated by Licinius after his victory, among the victims of which were his daughter the wife of Galerius, and her son, who were guilty of no crime except perhaps that of living in the East. The new Asiatico-barbaric empire was animated by two passions, ferocity and suspicion. The fall of Maximin soon gave rise to a new civil war between the two surviving Augusti, for victory had enlarged the powers and the dominions of Licinius so much that Constantine took offence. A trifling pretext, Licinius's refusal to deliver up a certain Senecchio, who was said to have conspired against Constantine, was enough to cause an outbreak of hostilities. Licinius was defeated, first at Cibalæ on the Sava in Pannonia on October 8, 314, and again in Thrace in the plain called Mardiensis or Jarbiensis, but neither of these defeats was decisive. Constantine understood that in order to destroy his rival it would be necessary to carry the war into the heart of the East, uncovering the frontiers of the empire which were now ever in greater danger. He preferred, therefore, to come to terms with Licinius, who received Illyricum, Greece, part of Mœsia, Macedonia, Epirus, Dacia, Dardania, Dalmatia, Pannonia, and Noricum. But the most important clause in the treaty was that Licinius, who had no son, should renounce the right of naming a successor, while Constantine, whose son Crispus was nearly of age, should be free at an early date to name him his legitimate heir.

**134. Peaceful Years (314–323 A.D.). The New Reform of the Coinage and the Donatist Question.**

In any case the peace concluded in 314 or 315 gave the empire a breathing space at last. For about nine years arms were to be laid aside and many problems, new and old, were to be put in the way of being solved. One of these problems Constantine had taken in hand even before 314. In 312 he had commenced a new reform of the coinage by issuing *aurei* of a reduced but fixed weight, not $\frac{1}{60}$ of the libra as in the days of Diocletian, but $\frac{1}{72}$. The new gold coin was called by a new name—the *solidus*, and was apparently worth about three dollars or a little more. The reform, which could not be completely carried out until many years had elapsed, was destined to be more successful than that of Diocletian, and to last until the end of the Byzantine empire. As for the silver coinage Constantine maintained Diocletian's *argenteus* at the value of $\frac{1}{96}$ of the libra, but he added two new coins which facilitated exchange with the new gold money, the *miliarensis* equivalent to $\frac{1}{1000}$ of the gold libra, and therefore $\frac{1}{72}$ of the silver libra, and the *siliqua* (or κεράτιον) equivalent to half the *miliarensis*.

To the same year belongs an important innovation in financial administration. Completing Diocletian's work Constantine laid down that the census and the cadastral survey of the empire should be revised every fifteen years. The financial year was to commence on September 1st, and end on August 31st, at the close of the quindecennial period. The first year of the new era was 312. This periodical operation was called *indictio* and under the Byzantine empire was afterwards used in reckoning the years.

More serious, however, than the monetary and financial question was the religious problem. As we have seen, the edict of Milan had established toleration for all varieties of religion. The old idea, which runs through all classic paganism, that there is no separation between civil and religious society, that indeed all the functions of the latter are subordinate to those of the former, had not been abolished, and could not be abolished at one stroke. Strong as Christianity was, the State was still stronger and could not easily renounce a principle so useful and indeed so necessary in view of the endless variety of cults professed throughout the empire. But Christianity was an exclusive religion which claimed to be the only true one and therefore to be destined to supplant all the rest. Moreover it affirmed the supremacy of the religious over the civil element and held the view that civil society should be organized at the dictates of religious principle. It was therefore inevitable that this contradiction should give rise to difficulties of all kinds, the earliest of which were produced by the heresies, involved as these were with various local quarrels, political, economic, and municipal. The State could not disregard these conflicts because they disturbed the whole current of social life and often directly affected the public peace. But what authority had the State to decide religious questions in a church which in such questions recognized only the authority of its spiritual heads?

It was in Africa that Constantine for the first time made the disagreeable acquaintance of these difficulties. In that province there had arisen about this time an extreme sect which excluded from the ecclesiastical communion all who during Diocletian's great persecution had had any moment of weakness—the so-called *traditores lapsi*. And since, for example, the Bishop of Carthage had been ordained by one of these *traditores*, this sect set up against him first a certain Majorinus, and then, in 313, a man named Donatus. The name of the latter was given to a heresy known as Donatism. In a country so full of fanaticism and vivid social contrasts as the Africa and the Numidia of those days a schism of this kind could not but give rise to violence followed by reprisals. Constantine, therefore, had to take steps to deal with the situation. The two parties, moreover, the Cæciliani on the one hand and the Donatists on the other, appealed to him to decide between them. But how could he, a pagan, settle a question of this kind? Constantine caused the contest to be referred to a jury of Italian and Gallic bishops, sitting at Rome, who gave their decision against the Donatists. The latter, however, would not give in and refused to recognize the sentence. On this the emperor, the pagan *pontifex maximus*, convoked for the first time a Christian council which met at Arles on August 1, 314. The majority of the Council again decided against the Donatists but failed to subdue Donatism. Then, in conformity with the findings of the council, an imperial order was issued excluding the Donatists from the African Church. As the empire had by the edict of Milan affirmed religious toleration, it was necessarily drawn on by the necessity of maintaining public peace and order to intervene in the internal concerns of the Christian body as it did in the case of all other religions. The Donatists, however, who were in a majority, resisted, and, in spite of persecutions, riots, and conflicts, the Donatist heresy remained predominant in Africa. The empire in the case of a religion like Christianity had no authority but force in questions of faith, and for the settlement of such questions force is not sufficient.

135. **The End of Licinius** (319–324 **A.D.**). Until 319 the good relations between Constantine and Licinius remained undisturbed. After this year, however, they began to deteriorate. The reasons for this are not very clear, and were probably numerous. Licinius bore malice for the peace of 314. There was the mutual mistrust inherent in the system of multiplied emperors. Constantine's ambition made him desirous of substituting the hereditary principle for Diocletian's system of appointing emperors by the nomination of the Augusti which recalled the system of adoption under the Antonines. War was therefore inevitable, and both emperors began to make their preparations. Constantine collected material and

tried to conciliate the Persians who were the natural enemies of the Eastern Augustus. He promulgated new laws on the subject of debtors to the *fiscus*. He did his best to outdo the most generous governments of the empire and made great efforts to secure for himself the favour and support of the Christian element. Licinius on his side was preparing very powerful military forces. Without going so far as an actual prosecution he adopted a policy hostile to the Christians, which in many places did in fact degenerate into a persecution. He excluded Christians from the army and from the administration,[1] and even appears to have sought support from the Donatist faction against whom Constantine was fighting in Africa.

War broke out in 323 in a rather curious way. In that year there had been an incursion of the Goths which had penetrated into Thrace and Mœsia which were the European provinces assigned to Licinius. Constantine hastened to repel the invasion and Licinius chose to regard what might have been accepted as an act of friendly assistance as a violation of his territories. The swords which for so long had been sharpened were now openly brandished, and on July 3, 323, the two armies met in the plains of Adrianople. Licinius was defeated and, after a valiant struggle, shut himself up in Byzantium, the fortress which barred the way to Asia by land as his powerful fleet closed all access by sea. Constantine's armada, however, was commanded by his son Crispus, who, though still a very young man, had distinguished himself in earlier operations against the Franks and had received the title of Cæsar. Crispus defeated the fleet of Licinius at the mouth of the Hellespont,

[1] *Cf. Vita Const.*, i., 51–55.

whereupon Licinius abandoned Byzantium and tried to bar the way to Asia Minor against Constantine. He was surrounded, however, and compelled to give battle near Chrysopolis (the modern Scutari), where he was again beaten (September 18, 324). He then surrendered to his conqueror who, in spite of a promise to spare his life, had him murdered in the following year.

**136. Religious Complications. The Council of Nice (325 A.D.).** Christian apologists celebrate this victory as terminating the final duel between Christianity and paganism, and their view is nearer the truth than modern critics imagine. Constantine's victory was the victory of the Christians who throughout the empire had taken his part against Licinius. Constantine hastened to issue an edict in which he, the high priest of paganism, not only annulled the decrees of Licinius but described the religion of which he was the head as "a deplorable error," and even as an "impious opinion," a "power of darkness," and those who followed it as "wanderers from the truth," although by his sovereign grace he allowed them to keep their "temples of lies."[1]

The emperor who had succeeded in reconstituting in his person the unity of the empire had now given way to the exclusive spirit of Christianity, whose aim was to supplant all other religions including those which might be regarded as the moral basis of the imperial power, the worship of the emperors and Mithraism. In order to conquer the whole empire for himself and to found a dynasty Constantine, with the support of the Christians, had weakened the foundations of absolute power which Aurelian and Diocletian had

[1] Eus., *Vita Const.*, ii., 29, 56, 60.

sought to consolidate by the aid of oriental religions. This, in a word, was the sum of the political and religious work of Constantine. He does not seem to have clearly realized the scope and the consequences of his own policy. This is shown by the attitude which he assumed towards the Arian heresy which he found at its height in the East. A certain Alexandrian priest named Arius had for some time been maintaining that Christ had been created by God but not out of the divine substance, and therefore out of nothing, a doctrine which made the supposedly perfect identity between the three Persons of the Trinity impossible. The two chief dangers of this heresy were first that it threatened the Divinity of Christ, and hence the whole foundations of the new religion, and secondly that on the Arian hypothesis Christianity approximated to the schools of paganism, numerous in the third century, which admitted the existence of a single God as a superior spirit, the other deities being incarnations of His particular attributes. In the East, where philosophic culture was not yet wholly exhausted and the love of disputation was very much alive, such a doctrine was bound to make a commotion. Alexander, Bishop of Alexandria, supported by the vote of a Synod of a hundred bishops, had expelled Arius from the Christian community in 321.

Arius, however, was not alone. The simplicity of his doctrine made it accessible to the average intelligence and therefore popular. The sympathy which it encountered in the ranks of the Neoplatonists whose system was so widely diffused in oriental countries, the rancorous feuds and the passion for reprisals to which the earlier discussions and repression had given rise, soon gave him a large following. Altercations were as usual followed by violence and street fighting, and Constantine made up his mind to intervene. The letter which he wrote on the subject to the contending parties deserves to be read: "I had hoped," he wrote, "to unify the ideas which all my peoples have about divine things because I well knew that if I could secure agreement on this point as I ardently desired, the management of public affairs would be much simplified . . . But, alas, what is this news which has grievously wounded my ears, nay my very heart! I learn that there are among you more dissensions than there ever were in Africa. . . . And yet it seems to me that the cause is very trifling and indeed unworthy to be the cause of such a conflict. . . . You, Alexander, desired to know what your priests thought about a point of law—indeed on what was merely part of a question of no importance, and you, Arius, if that was your opinion, should have kept silence. . . . There was no need either to put or to answer the question, for these matters are problems which there is no necessity to discuss but which are suggested by idleness and are good for nothing but to confuse the mind. . . . Is it right that for the sake of vain words you should begin a fratricidal conflict? . . . These are vulgar matters fit for ignorant boys not for priests or wise men. . . . Restore to me, therefore, I beseech you, quiet days and nights free from anxiety, so that I too in future may taste the pure joy of life. . . ."[1]

It is quite clear from this letter that Constantine conceived Christianity in accordance with the pagan idea of religion as a political instrument for maintaining order in the State. The fury of these theological

[1] Eus., *Vita Const.*, i., 64–72; Socr., *Hist. Eccl.*, 1, 7.

discussions was in his eyes nothing more than a form of insanity which it was the duty of the State to suppress. Accordingly he caused a great council to be convened in order to compose the quarrel. At Nice in the spring of 325 more than 250 bishops, most of them from the oriental provinces, met together. Constantine opened the proceedings in a speech which was both modest and prosaic. By re-establishing concord in the church, he said, they would perform an act pleasing in the sight of God and "would render a great service" to the emperor.[1] The president of the council was the bishop Osius, one of Constantine's secretaries, who was opposed to Arianism, and the imperial influence was cast on that side of the discussion. Arius, accordingly, was once more condemned. The council decreed that Christ was not sprung from nothing, that He was in no way different from the Father but was generated from the *Essence of the Father*, *Very God of Very God*, and was consubstantial with the Father (ὁμοούσιος). Thus was drawn up the creed which is daily repeated by the Catholic Church at the principal of her services, the Mass. The question which was so subtle, and, in Constantine's opinion, so otiose, might it seemed be taken as settled. Christianity, however, was not a political religion like all the Eastern and Western religions with which statesmen had hitherto had to deal. It was the germ of a new and an immense world. It was a religion whose object was not to buttress the declining empire of Rome but to redeem mankind by preaching a loftier morality. So the Council of Nice which Constantine had convened in order to re-establish peace and harmony was destined to be the commencement of a

[1] Eus., *Vita Const.*, iii., 11–12.

formidable struggle which was to weaken the weary empire still further. It was now fated that everything which human wisdom thought it necessary to do to save the empire should help to precipitate its ruin.

137. **The New Organization of the Empire.** The very reconstitution of the unity of the empire which was accomplished by Constantine shows how much the State had been weakened since the time of Diocletian. Sole master of the empire after so many civil wars, Constantine was less secure of his power than Diocletian had been when he shared the supreme authority with another Augustus and two Cæsars. He became so suspicious that in 326, for reasons of which we are ignorant and on which we can only form vague conjectures, he caused his son Crispus, the conqueror of the Franks and of Licinius to be killed, together with his grandson who was called Licinianus and was still of tender years. Shortly afterwards Fausta, his second wife, the daughter of Maximian and the mother of his three younger sons, shared their fate. The court was still more orientalized. The pomp of the ceremonial, the complication of etiquette, the luxury of the courtiers, the mystery with which the emperor was veiled, all markedly increased. There were a series of great dignitaries under each of whom was a numerous and minutely graded and titled hierarchy. These were the *prætorian præfects* whom Constantine, following out the reform of Diocletian, deprived of all military power; the *magistri militum* or commanders in chief of the infantry and the cavalry; the *quæstor sacri Palatii* who received information and prepared and countersigned the laws to be discussed by the *consistorium* and promulgated by the emperor;

the *magister officiorum*, a kind of minister of the Imperial House, who directed the police, the palace guards, and the employés of the central administration; and finally the two ministers of finance—*comes sacrarum largitionum* and *comes rerum privatarum*. The new imperial council, the *consistorium*, also became more regularized than had been the case under Diocletian. Its ordinary members were the holders of the great offices above enumerated with the exception, it seems, of the prætorian præfects and the *magistri militum* who attended only on exceptional occasions. The great officers were supplemented by the *comites consistoriani* who were permanent members of the council selected by the emperor, and who we know were at a later date twenty in number.

Under the ministers of the imperial house and the *consistorium* who together formed the central organ of political and legislative control, was the ever increasing bureaucracy of the empire. The three officials of the imperial chancellery who under the earlier empire were known as *ab epistulis*, *a libellis*, and *a memoria*, now changed their names. Each was called a *scrinium*, and a fourth was added, the *scrinium dispositionum*, whose duty it was to attend to all the emperor's business in connection with journeys, inspections, etc. The change of name corresponded to a change of system. Instead of a single official we have now a whole department with a great hierarchy of officials. Nor were the *scrinia* limited to those above mentioned. All the functionaries of the empire had *scrinia* of their own, and each *scrinium* had its own hierarchy which was to serve as a model for the absolute monarchies in the earlier epochs of modern history.

The provincial arrangements were still ostensibly

those of Diocletian. The tetrarchy had disappeared; there was only one emperor. But the administrative divisions created by Diocletian remained in their entirety. The empire was regarded as divided into three, or possibly four, sections, at the head of which stood the prætorian præfects, who, now that the prætorian guards were disbanded, were merely great officers of State having judicial and civil functions. On these depended the *vicarii* and on the latter the *præsides*, the *consulares*, or the *correctores* as the case might be.

What, meanwhile, had happened to the old officers of State and to the senate? Ancient Rome had still her senate, her consuls, her prætors, her ædiles, and her tribunes, but they were now merely municipal officers, stripped of all their greatness.

Army organization retained the character impressed on it by Diocletian. The supreme directors of military affairs were, as we have seen, the *magistri militum*, under whose orders were the *duces* commanding one or more provinces or the frontier garrisons. This was an inheritance from Diocletian, but into the composition of the army itself Constantine introduced an innovation which exaggerated the precautions of his predecessor into positive errors to be expiated by bitter experience in after days. The effectives of each legion were still further reduced. Civil and military authorities were sharply separated from each other, as were the infantry and cavalry commands, the commissariat, the transport, and the paymaster's departments. All this had its advantages, but the forces could no longer be rapidly concentrated nor without the imperial will was it easy to bring about agreement between the different parts of the army.

These drawbacks were aggravated by the new regrouping of the forces. The army was divided into three great categories: (1) The palatine force (*domestici, protectores, scolares*) one fifth of the whole army, who were analogous to the old prætorian guard but now formed a kind of reserve army and followed the emperor on important expeditions. (2) Troops of the line, or *comitatenses*, recruited from citizens and barbarians, commanded by the military magistrates of the provinces (*comites* or *duces*) and scattered in small garrisons about the cities in the interior. (3) Lastly the frontier troops (*riparienses* or *castriciani* or *limitanei*) recruited in general among the barbarian peoples and the lowest class within the empire and held to a longer term of service at lower rates of pay. These troops had to remain permanently quartered in certain defined frontier zones, were installed in castles, fortresses and entrenched camps, and were in great part local *coloni*. This meant that the best part of the army (the *comitatenses*) was broken up into small units which lived in the towns of the interior where they oppressed the inhabitants and were themselves corrupted by the ease and effeminacy of city life. Finally it is to be noted that all three classes of troops were flooded with barbarian contingents.

These reforms are an evident proof of the growing weakness of the empire. It is inexplicable how a soldier and a statesman like Constantine came to split up his army by distributing so great a part of it among cities far from the frontiers, unless we suppose that the army had now to be used as much to maintain order in the interior of the empire, which was now threatened by so many possibilities of dissolution and discord, as to defend the empire against the barbarians. Again we cannot explain why he opened the ranks of the legions so easily to the barbarians unless we admit that he felt himself impotent to deal with the growing repugnance of the new Christian society for military life and all the other causes which were alienating his subjects from military service. The multiplication of military and civil offices which took place at this time can only be explained by the supposition that he wished for the support of a numerous bureaucracy bound to him and to his family by ties of interest and this was yet another sign of weakness. An even clearer proof of the growing debility of the empire was the foundation of the new capital. The reasons for this great change were undoubtedly many, and were above all military. The capital of an empire which in the East had to struggle with the Persians and in the West had to defend the Rhine and the Danube against the barbarians, an empire ruled by a single emperor who wished by himself to supervise the oriental and the occidental provinces and promptly repress any military revolt in either, was better situated on the Bosphorus than in southern Italy. There were also political reasons. The capital of the new absolute and Asiatic monarchy which was so well disposed towards Christianity could not be Rome, the most eminently pagan and republican city in the empire. Constantine therefore chose the ancient Byzantium, and, as the sequel proved, he chose well; but the transfer of the capital of the empire to the Bosphorus was nothing if not a declaration that the task of Rome in the West was fulfilled and that her great historic mission was at an end.

**138. The Last Years of Constantine (330–337 A.D.).** On May 11, 330, Constantine solemnly inaugurated the new capital of the empire,—Νέα Ρώμη or Constantinople. Two years later (332) we find him engaged in a successful campaign against the Goths and later (334) with the Sarmatians, who after his victory became colonists and soldiers of the empire.

In 335 the aged monarch performed another act which once more demonstrated, and more clearly than ever, the weakness of the political edifice which he had constructed. He partitioned the empire among his three sons. All three had been appointed Cæsars along with Dalmatius, his nephew. To his eldest son Constantine were assigned Spain, Gaul, and Britain; to Constantius, Asia, Syria, and Egypt; to Constans, Italy, Illyricum, and Africa. All three were given the title of Augustus. Dalmatius received Thrace, Macedonia, and Achæa with the title of Cæsar, and Hanniballianus, a brother of Dalmatius, was raised to the vacant throne of Armenia and the neighbouring regions with the style of King of Kings. What, it may be asked, was the use of having struggled so hard to overturn the tetrarchy of Diocletian only to re-establish it in a weaker and more precarious form by introducing into it the debilitated principle of hereditary succession which even yet had no firm roots in the empire? Not even Constantine had the strength to solve the tremendous problem of the legal principle of the supreme authority, and, towards the end of his long and laborious life, he split up the empire under the illusion that it would thereby be more easy to keep it in his own family, sacrificing the unity of the empire to this very hereditary principle which was sterile because the peoples of the empire did not acknowledge its legitimacy.

Finally (and this was an event of momentous

importance) Constantine, who had sought to re-establish the moral unity of the empire by means of Christianity, allowed himself in his last years to be dragged into the whirlpool of Christian quarrels by becoming a champion of the Arian heresy which he had caused to be condemned at the Council of Nice. After his condemnation at that Council, Arius had gone into exile, but Arianism was widespread and strong, and had powerful friends even at court among whom was Constantia, the sister of the emperor. Arius therefore did not lose heart. He profited by the errors of his adversaries. He mitigated and tempered his doctrines and in this way he and his followers succeeded in regaining Constantine's favour by persuading him that a reconciliation was possible. The efforts made by the emperor to effectuate this reconciliation and the opposition with which he met, more especially from Athanasius the new Bishop of Alexandria, drove him more and more into the arms of the Arian party. The sect derived new courage from the imperial favour and in 335 succeeded in securing the condemnation of Athanasius at the Council of Tyre. Athanasius was banished to Gaul and all the more important of his partisans were persecuted and dispersed. Arius returned to Constantinople. The court was invaded by the Arians who in all parts of the East became predominant in the Church. But the opposite party did not lay down their arms, though persecuted, and from this moment the empire was agitated by a new and implacable ferment of dissolution added to the rest. Christianity was to regenerate the world, but it could not buttress the empire.

The last enterprise undertaken by the indefatigable emperor was a great campaign against Persia where

Sapor II., the nephew of Narseus, was now king. The ever latent conflict between the two empires had of late years been exacerbated by a question which was both political and religious. Christianity had penetrated into Armenia where in 302, before Constantine's conversion, King Tiridates, had been baptized. It had also reached Iberia and Persia, thus giving the already half Christianized Roman Empire various points of support. In order to counteract these influences, Sapor had resumed in a more decided manner the propaganda of Mithraism, and Constantine had replied by demanding protection for his Christian subjects in Persia and by favouring at his court a certain Armisda who was Sapor's brother and probable rival. Sapor in his turn had dethroned the King of Armenia and Constantine had rejoined by assigning Armenia, as we have seen, to his nephew Hanniballianus. Sapor on this reclaimed the five provinces beyond the Tigris which Diocletian had torn from Persia. The Roman emperor was preparing to cross the Tigris in order to strike direct at Ctesiphon when he died suddenly on May 22, 337, shortly after having received baptism from an Arian named Eusebius of Nicomedia.

Constantine was certainly a sovereign of superior abilities. But he appeared at a critical moment at which an immense and decisive change in the history of the world was being accomplished, and, while he was no longer a pagan and a man of the ancient world, he was not yet a true and perfect Christian, and a man of the new world. His whole policy was influenced by this fact. It was wavering, violent, incoherent, confused and, in part at least, sterile. Compared with him Diocletian was powerful, coherent, vigorous, simple, and clear in his complete loyalty to the tradition of antiquity. Diocletian was the last great man of the ancient world, Constantine a restless figure typical of an age of transition.

# CHAPTER XVII

## THE GREAT RELIGIOUS STRUGGLES

## (337–363 A.D.)

**139. From the Death of Constantine to the Fall of Constantine II. (337–340 A.D.).** The death of Constantine was followed by several months of calm, but suddenly—it would seem between July and September, 337—a military revolt broke out at Constantinople in the imperial palace and in the city. The soldiers' cry was that they would have no rulers but the sons of Constantine, that is to say Constantine II. then twenty-one years of age, Constantius II. who was twenty, and Constans who was seventeen. They murdered Dalmatius, Hannaballianus and all the male descendants of Constantius Chlorus, their most distant relatives, and their supporters. None escaped but two boys, sons of a brother of Constantine, named Gallus and Julianus of whom one was twelve and the other barely six years old.

It is very difficult, in the face of positive accusations by contemporaries, to maintain that the sons of Constantine, and especially Constantius, had no responsibility for this murder. The revolt was directed by a faction on their side and in their interest. But at any rate it is certain that shortly after the murder on September 9th, the three Constantiniani received from the senate the title of Augusti, and that in the following year, at Sirmium in Pannonia, the three brothers met for the purpose of redistributing the empire. In addition to what he already had Constantius now received Pontus, Thrace including Constantinople, Macedonia, and Achæa. To Constantine II. was assigned Mauretania. Constans alone does not seem to have increased his share.

Asiatic absolutism had not been long in staining the new capital with the blood of its palace tragedies. Shortly after the murders an amnesty was declared in favour of the Athanasian party who were permitted to return from exile, and the religious policy of Constantine's last years was thus reversed. But the reason for this act will be plain when it is realized that it was due to the initiative of Constans and Constantine II. The East was predominantly Arian, but the Western provinces were, for the most part, Athanasian. The latent rivalry which for centuries had dominated the two parts of the empire, was now renewed in the Christian Church and especially in the two episcopates of Rome and Alexandria. The former sought to impose its supremacy, and with it the Nicene creed. The latter with its Arianism stood for all the ardent ambitions of the great Eastern churches—Cæsarea the most ancient and the most active, Antioch, Tyre, and now Constantinople—to be free and predominant. It is easy to understand, therefore, now that the empire had no longer a single sovereign, that the two Augusti of the West were interested in stopping the persecution of Athanasianism while it suited Constantius to continue it. But, though the two Western emperors agreed in their policy, it was not long before they were at war, the subject of their contention being (as is supposed) the possession of Northern Africa. Constantine II., taking advantage of the absence of Constans in Dacia, threw himself on Italy, hoping to drive out his colleague and thus to repeat the manœuvre of his father against Maxentius in 312, but he was defeated and slain not far from Aquileia (340).

**140. The Origins of the Catholic Church and the Schismatic Church of the East. The Councils of Sardica and Philippopolis (344 A.D.).** Constantius did not oppose the usurpation which doubled the power of Constans because he and the provinces already assigned to him had inherited from his father the whole burden of the Persian war which had just begun in 338. Each spring Sapor II., the Persian King, swooped down on the plain between the Tigris and the Euphrates, devastating the country, burning the crops, besieging the fortresses, sacking the open towns, putting the inhabitants to the sword, disturbing trade and industry, doing and suffering a series of small and never decisive feats of arms. Absorbed in this exhausting conflict Constantius could not intervene with much energy in the internal affairs of the empire. To the Persian war were added religious and civil disturbances. Constans no longer opposed the exclusive spirit of Christianity and initiated the systematic persecution of paganism; in 341 he prohibited pagan sacrifices.[1] But while he was involving himself in this final struggle against the immemorial religion of the Greeks and Romans, the heresies of the triumphant religion gave him no peace. Immediately on his return to Alexandria, Athanasius had to commence an intense agitation against Arianism, sum-

[1] *Cod. Theod.*, xvi., 10, 2.

moning to his assistance the two emperors of the West and, what was perhaps historically more important, the Western bishops, especially the Pope of Rome, in condemning the religious policy of the last years of Constantine and of his successor. Many of his followers who had also been amnestied followed his example, and religious agitations flared up in all parts of the empire. At the request of various parties, the Pope Julius had convoked a council at Rome in 340 to which he invited the Eastern bishops. Certain of these, however, including the bishops of Cæsarea in Cappadocia, of Antioch and Constantinople, replied in a letter from Antioch in which they laid down the principles of the schism which has continued to the present day. These were the equality of the rights of all churches and the denial of all pre-eminence in the Church of Rome. The council moreover was held in order to absolve Athanasius, but in 341 another council, entirely composed of oriental bishops was held at Antioch and reaffirmed, though in a somewhat attenuated form, the principles of Arianism.

The struggle between Arianism and Athanasianism was becoming a struggle between the East and the West which involved the two emperors, each side endeavouring to use to its own advantage the authority of the Augustus who was its ruler. Unhappily for Arianism, Constans, who had taken the provinces of Constantine II., was at this moment more powerful than Constantius who was involved in the long war against Persia. Thus when, towards the end of 342, or in 343, Constans proposed to his brother that an œcumenical council should be held at Sardica (Sofia) on the frontiers of the two empires, in order if possible to settle these differences, Constantius could not refuse.

It is probable that Constans was aiming at a declaration by the council of the supremacy of the Church of Rome, which politically would be very advantageous to him, rather than at settling the position of Athanasius in the Church or confirming the Nicene Creed. In any case it is certain that the great object of the oriental bishops was to evade the question of the Roman Church and in this they succeeded. On the pretext of the intervention of Athanasius and of other religious accused of heresy, they withdrew and met in a separate council at Philippopolis (344) protesting against the pretensions of the Western Church to reverse sentences of an oriental council, and excommunicating, not only Athanasius, but Pope Julius himself.

The excommunication was counterbalanced by a letter addressed to the excommunicated by the orthodox bishops of the East and the West. That letter, while it recognized that within certain limits the civil power had its rights in connection with councils, solemnly affirmed the deference of the writers for the See of Rome and "in honour of the memory of Peter" conferred on that See the right of deciding all appeals from condemnations pronounced by other bishops. The Church of Rome was thus declared to be the centre of orthodox Christianity. The Fathers of Philippopolis, on the other hand, declared in a circular letter, not only that they did not recognize the supremacy of the Church of Rome, but that they would recognize no other power in the spiritual governance of the Church except that of Councils. That is to say, they admitted no authority which could judge between the different churches and which was superior to theirs, except that of the emperor who was their protector. Thus came into being the schismatic Eastern Church.[1] About the same time all pagan temples were ordered to be closed and the old religion declared criminal and punishable.[2]

**141. Constantius Sole Emperor (353 A.D.). The Great Council of Milan (355 A.D.).** The decisions of the Council of Sardica, in spite of these declarations, applied to the East as well as to the West. Constans, taking advantage of the difficulties in which Constantius found himself, owing to the interminable war with Persia, succeeded in securing the reinstatement of Athanasius in the See of Alexandria and the cessation throughout all the East of the persecution of the partisans of the Nicene Creed. For a moment the unity of the Church seemed to have been re-established. But this result had been secured by political pressure of the West on the East, a dangerous expedient which contained the germs of a civil war between the two emperors. Chance alone prevented the world from seeing the sons of Constantine at war on a theological question. One day, while Constans was hunting, his *magister militum*, a certain Magnentius who was a barbarian of German origin and had an understanding with the *comes largitionum*, was proclaimed Augustus and the legitimate emperor was murdered (January 18, 350). Shortly afterwards in Illyricum, the province which still remembered that it had given the empire the greatest princes of the third century, another usurper named Vetranio followed the example of Magnentius (March 1, 350).

[1] On all this part of the history of Christianity the reader may consult Duchesne, *Histoire de l'Église*, Paris, 1911, vol. ii., chapter VI.

[2] *Cod. Theod.*, xvi., 10, 4.

This time Constantius determined to suspend the Persian war by concluding an armistice, and, at the end of 350 or early in 351, he moved against Macedonia with great forces. By means of bribery and intrigues, and by arousing memories of his father among the legionaries, he managed to win over the Army of Vetranio and to persuade Vetranio finally to renounce the purple. He then prepared to make war on Magnentius who appears to have tried to find support among the pagans who had been persecuted by Constans. Magnentius was a more formidable opponent than Vetranio, and Constantius had to fight for two years before he was overthrown. After the battle of Mursa (in Pannonia) fought on September 28, 351, the usurper was forced to retire on Aquileia, where he passed the winter, hoping to be able to bar the passes of the Alps against his enemies. These, however, were forced in the following year. Magnentius was thrown back on the Cottian Alps and from there into Gaul. At Lyons he was abandoned by his army and committed suicide. All his family was put to death and with them a great number of his partisans, real or supposed.

The unity of the empire was re-established, and this political event had an immediate effect in the religious sphere both Christian and pagan. The defeat of Magnentius was followed by an exacerbated persecution of paganism, those who practised the ancient religion being threatened with decapitation.[1] On the other hand the disappearance of Constans was a piece of great good fortune for the Arians. Before long their intrigues against Athanasius and the Bishops who upheld the Council of Nice, encouraged

[1] *Cod. Theod.*, xvi., 10, 6.

by the favour of the emperor, threw the whole Christian world into such confusion that Pope Liberius begged the emperor to convoke a council to compose the tumult. Constantius agreed and summoned a council at Milan but his intention was far from being the same as the Pope's. What he wished was to annul finally the council of Nice and to establish at any cost the supremacy of Eastern over Western Christianity. At the beginning of 355 fully 350 bishops actually met at Milan, practically all of them from the West, and therefore supporters of the Nicene creed. Constantius, however, now that he was sole emperor, felt himself strong enough to overcome the opposition and threw all the weight of his authority into the balance. He intervened personally and openly, and pronounced the famous words which marked an epoch in the early history of the Church: "My will must be considered as law. My Syrian bishops see fit that I should speak thus. Either you will obey me, or those of you who do not obey will be condemned to banishment. . . ."[1] This was no vain threat. Those who would not agree to the condemnation of Athanasius, including the Pope Liberius himself, were forced to go into exile, and Athanasius, condemned by the council of Milan, took refuge in the monasteries of the Thebaid. In the East and in the West alike all the bishops who remained faithful to the Nicene Creed were deposed, persecuted, and threatened. But at Constantinople, at Alexandria, at Rome, at Naples, and in Gaul popular insurrections broke out against the bishops substituted for those who had been banished and a new politico-religious war was soon raging between the West and the East.

[1] Athan., *Hist. Arianorum*, xxxiii.

**142. Gallus and Julianus Cæsars (351–355 A.D.).** The unification of the empire had produced another consequence, the necessity of finding lieutenants for the emperor. Constantius was not equal to ruling the empire as constituted by Diocletian and by his father, without assistance. Yet it was no easy task to find a competent and trustworthy collaborator in a court such as his. For want of better Constantius, who had no son, had recourse to Gallus the elder of his two cousins, who had miraculously escaped from the massacre of 332. Gallus and his brother Julian had hitherto lived in exile which bore a close resemblance to imprisonment, one at Ephesus and the other at Nicomedia. More recently they had both lived together at Macellum, a lonely spot in Cappadocia. Gallus, then 25 or 26 years of age was appointed Cæsar in 351 and was entrusted with the government of the East. But Constantius was a very suspicious monarch. After making Gallus swear fealty on the four Gospels he had imposed on him a minister chosen by himself for the purpose of keeping watch on him, had given him in marriage his sister Constantina, and had reserved to himself the appointment of all the chief officers and functionaries of Gallus's army and of the Eastern court. Notwithstanding all these precautions, or perhaps because of them, this experiment in collaboration ended in disaster. Gallus could not reconcile himself to this supervision and suspicion, which he could not overcome. Moreover he was a man of feeble abilities. His relations with the emperor became inflamed to such a pitch of distrust and hatred that after three years he was recalled and while on his return journey about the end of 354 was imprisoned and executed at Pola, together with many of his friends and supporters.

Meanwhile grave difficulties had arisen in the West, where, after the execution of Gallus at Pola in 354 and while Constantius was preparing for the great council of Milan, the eastern German tribes had seized the two Germanies and all eastern Gaul from the Lake of Constance to the North Sea, and had penetrated into the interior, devastating the country and dismantling two fortresses. Constantius had to find a general for the West also, and notwithstanding his misadventure with Gallus, whether because he had no choice or because of the intercession of his Empress, the gentle Eusebia, his choice fell on Gallus's brother Julian. After all, Gallus had been incapable rather than rebellious, and Julian, a harmless person of literary leanings, was intended merely to be the emperor's nominal representative. The actual power was to be in the hands of the persons whom Constantius meant to place by his side. Thus the exile of Macellum was created a Cæsar towards the end of 355, and was charged with the government of Gaul, Spain, and Britain.

**143. Julian in Gaul—the First Four Years (355–359 A.D.).** Julian was not yet twenty-five and had no political or military experience. His youth had been spent in enforced exile among books, in long, silent colloquies with Homer, Hesiod, and Plato, in the most humiliating observances of Christianity, in the memory of the blood which he had seen shed so profusely in the days of his boyhood and under the espionage of a thousand hostile eyes. And yet in his brain nourished on rhetoric and philosophy, in his heart which had been humbled by persecutions, in his frail and ailing body were concealed extraordinary will power and passionate energy.

The campaign which he conducted in Gaul was destined to be a revelation indeed. In the philosopher there was the stuff of which great soldiers are made. In a few months he had learned the rudiments of the military art. Real war with its perils and its surprises had revealed him to himself and to others. The generals of Constantius were cautious and methodical; they allowed the barbarians to lay waste the country under their very eyes rather than risk any enterprise in which they were not secured by a superiority of force. Julian saw at once that it was necessary to act, to take risks, and to exploit the local forces which were so valuable. In 356, hearing that Autun was threatened by the barbarians, he hastened to its assistance and raised the siege. Then by a rapid march he regained the valley of the Rhine, extricated Colonia (Cologne), and fortified both that town and Treveri (Treves), reoccupied Argentoratum (Strasbourg), and in mid-winter maintained vigorous siege operations before Sens. In all this he received no support from Marcellus, the general attached to his staff by Constantius. In the following year (357), though again badly seconded by his generals, he succeeded in taking prisoners a great number of barbarians on their return from an unsuccessful attempt on Lyons. Then having driven another barbarian force across the Rhine, he followed them by fording the river between a series of islets in the stream and defeated them with immense slaughter. Finally at Argentoratum, in the summer of 357, with only 13,000 men, he was faced by a German army of three times that number which a few days before had defeated 25,000 men led by one of the most experienced generals of Constantius. The legions of Julian who were now trained soldiers attacked and defeated the enemy after a day's battle.

Nor was his attention confined to military operations. He revived the ancient Roman flotilla on the Rhine, whose remaining vessels were lying idle, and caused four hundred new ships to be built. He completely cleared both the banks of the river of the surviving barbarians; he rebuilt the fortresses which had been destroyed, compelled the barbarians themselves to provide the materials and the necessary labour; repopulated with his prisoners the deserted districts of Gaul, reduced to a quarter the poll tax (*capitatio*) paid by the province, personally assumed the administration of the ruined districts, dismissing all the agents of the treasury and carrying out the collection of the taxes himself. In the second half of 359 he pushed far forward into enemy territory in upper Germany and there, like Julius Cæsar of old, he impressed on the minds of the population the lively conviction that Rome had still a sword.

At the end of the year he might, as he actually did in later days, sum up the results of his campaign in the very style of Napoleon. "I have three times crossed the Rhine. I have taken from the barbarians and brought back 20,000 prisoners. Two battles and a siege have made me master of 1000 enemies in the flower of their age. . . . I have recaptured not less than forty cities, and by the favour of the gods all the Gauls lie at my feet. . . ."[1]

**144. The End of Constantius (359–361 A.D.).** But in 359 the Persian danger reappeared. Sapor II.

[1] Jul., *Epist. ad S. P. Q. Athen.*, p. 280 c-d.

renewed his pretensions to Armenia and Mesopotamia, and this time, it seems, with greater forces and with better fortune than in previous years. He succeeded in capturing the fortress of Amida and, returning to the attack in the following winter, also those of Bezabda and Singara which he hastened to destroy.

Constantius even in this crisis was chiefly intent on imposing religious unity on the empire. In 359 the two councils of Rimini and Seleucia Isaurica, owing to imperial pressure, were induced to sanction in place of the Nicene Creed a vague and inexact formula whereby, under pretence of reconciliation, the Arians hoped to make themselves finally masters of the government of the Church. For the public at large theological formulæ were nothing but banners under which were grouped the interests or the passions of mankind. Thus, when Constantius insisted on imposing on everybody the agreed Arian formula, he found the whole empire ablaze with countless popular revolts. The new Persian attack, however, compelled him to turn his attention from religious disputes. He left Milan, sent Julian an order to send him part of his forces and left for the East. But this order to Julian was destined to be the spark which kindled a new civil war. Whether because the legions of Gaul were profoundly attached to their general or because they were for the most part men of Gallic race who felt they had been enrolled to defend their own country against the Germans and not to be sent to die in the depths of Asia, a military revolt broke out when the order of Constantius was promulgated and Julian was proclaimed Augustus. The youthful Cæsar hesitated for a time and tried to resist the acclamations of his soldiers. But his good genius did not allow him to persist in this impossible and dangerous attitude, and, after many hours of irresolution, he presented himself to the soldiers and declared that he was ready to share their destinies.

In spite of this, he not only insisted that the supporters and the emissaries of Constantius should receive no injury of any kind, but he loyally informed the emperor of what had happened and represented that it was the legions who demanded for him the title of Augustus. Constantius replied by making great preparations against the new Magnentius. But Julian was neither a Magnentius nor a Gallus, nor was his conciliatory temper to be confounded with inertia or incapacity. When he saw that the emperor was not to be moved, he decided to anticipate him and to raise against the Augustus of the East not only his own powerful legions but also the hitherto silent resentment of humiliated paganism. His offensive from Gaul was preceded by a manifesto, the so-called *Epistula ad Senatum Populumque Atheniensem*, the effect of which was to collect under his standards all the pagans throughout the empire. Leaving in Gaul as prætorian præfect his friend Sallustius, he took the offensive with lightning rapidity, dividing his army into three parts which were to reassemble at Sirmium in Pannonia. Constantius in great haste made an armistice with the Persians and set out on his way back to Europe. But at Tarsus he was seized with a violent fever and shortly afterwards, on October 5, 361, died at Mopsucrene.

**145. The Pagan Reaction. Julian the Apostate (361–363 A.D.).** When Julian reached Constantinople he was received with a perfectly delirious enthusiasm. The people, the ministers of Constantius, the whole court came out to meet him and to swear fealty to him with all solemnity. The Roman senate itself, which at first had hesitated, now hastened to send him the *senatus consultum* which conferred on him the usual imperial honours in all their fullness. Pagans and Christians were equally delighted. The orthodox rejoiced at the death of the man who for so long had trampled upon them. The Arians viewed the change with tranquillity in the belief that they were now strong enough.

The fact was that Julian had become emperor after about thirty years of a government which had damaged many interests and which, far from solving the problems by which it was confronted, had allowed them to grow more complicated. In these thirty years the Persian peril had become a chronic evil in the East. In the West, the barbarians of Germany had been allowed to overrun the most flourishing regions of Gaul without let or hindrance. On the other hand the provinces had begun to collapse with exhaustion under the enormous burden imposed on them by the system of tribute which now weighed on all departments of production, agriculture, industry, and commerce, and all the professions, even of the basest class, alike. The religious problem itself was unsolved. The anti-Christian persecution had been followed by the reaction against the pagans, and, what was worse, against all the sections of the Christian faith which were not orthodox, and had involved in its fury the substance, the good name, the very lives of those who professed such opinions.

Julian's accession, therefore, came at an opportune moment. All stood still to see whether the immense disorder of the empire could be dominated by a single man. Julian's aims were lofty and noble even to sublimity. Like Marcus Aurelius, his was to be the reign of a philosopher. Having lived in the midst of intrigue, violence, and injustice, he had by a sort of reaction made his public duty a cult, a mission to fulfil, a destiny to accomplish. "We should," he wrote, "in all things draw inspiration from the immortal essence which lives within us, and to this entrust the government of our private affairs no less than that of States. We should consider law as the application of universal reason. . . . A prince, who after all is a man, needs to spiritualize his sentiments and to banish entirely from his soul all that it contains of mortality, all that he has in common with the brutes. . . . He should issue, therefore, not rules for the moment, the work of a man who has not lived according to reason, but laws worthy of men pure in heart and spirit, who have not limited their consideration to the evils of today and to present circumstances alone. He should legislate, not merely for his contemporaries but for posterity, for foreigners, for men with whom he has not nor can ever hope to have any relation."

This account exactly fits Julian and never in the case of any other ruler did theory so closely approximate to practice. Immediately on his arrival at Constantinople he purged the court of all its innumerable parasites, barbers, cup-bearers, cooks, eunuchs, informers, ushers, secretaries, domestics, pages, gentlemen of the wardrobe, doctors. He reduced his staff to the limits of bare necessity and took the financial and judicial administration into his own control as he had done in Gaul. A contemporary not accustomed to hyperbole shortly afterwards wrote of him: "It might really have been supposed that Justice which, according to some poet, returned to heaven owing to the crimes of mankind, had once more come back to earth." The government again resumed a republican character. Julian refused the title of *dominus;* he again observed the ceremonies which were formerly carried out on the assumption of republican magistracies and he honoured the senate of Constantinople as Trajan had honoured that of Rome.

But the burning question, which was to be the touchstone not of his merit but of the possibility of coping with the growing disorder of the times, was the religious problem. Julian did not consider the question of Paganism and Christianity as a philosophical, but (being a soldier and a statesman) as a political and social problem. He could not know that Christianity was the sacred seed of a new world. For him, therefore, it was clear that the new religion was one more force of dissolution among the many which were already working for the disruption of the empire. In spite of the efforts made by the Church to minimize the contradiction, it was evident that the spirit of Christianity was in conflict with that which for centuries had sustained the Roman State. The need for conquest and dominion, the contrast between the barbarian and the Roman world, the great mission of Rome in the world, the sacred duty of marrying and having children, the subordination of the individual to the State, the civic and political consciousness—all these corresponded to sentiments and ideas which Christianity either openly combated or tacitly despised. Moreover, the ancient State had absorbed into itself so much religion as was necessary to consecrate its civil and political mission. Apart from this it was above all religions and exercised impartially over all a purely civil control. The Christian church on the contrary believed that the world was ruled by Providence, not with a view to its temporal interests but to higher and divine plans, that, if the citizens of the empire served the emperor, he was the servant of God and as such was subordinate to the Church which was God's representative on earth. Though the weakness of the new religion compelled it to recognize the supremacy of the State it cherished an inveterate aspiration to make the State its instrument.

This being so, there is nothing surprising in the fact that a Roman emperor who had received a thorough training in philosophy should have conceived it to be his duty to re-establish paganism and to reform the relations between the empire and the Church. Julian accordingly did not renew the persecutions, and resumed the old formula of the pagan State which in its essence had been reaffirmed by Constantine, viz., that paganism was the State religion, while all other religions were tolerated. But he interpreted this formula in its fullest sense, that is to say that the pagan State could not be indifferent to its religion, that it must have a religious faith beyond the reach of any philosophical criticism, not a system of dogma and mythology but a strong moral consciousness common to all who were associated with it. This was no new idea; the views and the practice of Augustus, Vespasian, and Trajan were precisely similar. The only difference was that, in the presence of an enemy now become much more menacing, Julian's work had to be much more energetic and concise.

In order to place the religions which lived under the shadow of the empire on a footing of equality it was in the first place necessary to abolish the privileges which had been gained by the Christian Church, to put an end to the persecution it was carrying on and to repair the damage it had done. Julian ordered that all property usurped by the church should be restored to the ancient organization which had been despoiled, that all ecclesiastics who had been banished as heretics should be recalled, and that the privileges of the clergy should be abolished.

This, however, was merely the beginning. In order to recreate the soul of Roman paganism it was necessary to invoke the help and collaboration of the men of letters, the schools and the clergy, of society as a whole.[1] Julian therefore claimed that pagan culture and education should resume their ancient mission while the pagan priesthood should adopt all the virtues and methods, which had been found in practice to be excellent, of Christian propaganda. He sought to give paganism an official organization and an equipment of philanthropic institutions in all respects similar to those of Christianity. Against an exclusive doctrine exclusion is a weapon to which its opponents must sooner or later inevitably have recourse. If the schools were to be a kind of temple of Roman paganism it was necessary to exclude Christian masters and to permit these to exercise their profession only in Christian schools.[2] If every office of State, and above all military offices, were to be carried out in entire corre-

[1] *Cf.* Liban., *Orat.*, xviii., p. 574. Sozom., *Hist. Eccles.*, v., 16; and Julian himself, *Epp.*, 49, 62 & 63.

[2] Julian's famous edict on education, as one might expect, is not included in the official codices but in the private collection of his letters (Jul., *Epp.*, 42). *Cf.* also Amm. Marc., xxii., 10, 7; xxv., 4, 20.

spondence with the emperor's plan it was necessary to return to Diocletian's policy of excluding Christians from the magistracies and from the army.

But was it possible that the new religion could have meekly tolerated all this? While a few pure and unbending Christians applauded the imperial restrictions which preserved Christianity from all contaminating contact with the infidel,[1] the mass of pagans, who were both weary and sceptical, disapproved of the fighting spirit of their prince. On the other hand the numerous band which represented the ideals, the passions, the interests, and the privileges of the Christians which were all alike threatened, rose in revolt. These first measures were followed, more especially in the East, by seditions, broils, conflicts between pagans and Christians and between Christians who differed among themselves. In spite of the lofty spirit of concord and pacification with which Julian was animated, his reforms would have kindled terrible discord throughout the empire had he been permitted by fate to continue his work for any length of time.

**146. The Great Expedition to Persia (March–June, 363 A.D.).** Julian, however, was not the man to give his whole attention to the religious question. Since 362 he had been preparing a military expedition on a gigantic scale which aimed at removing the Persian danger for ever, at reducing Persia to the status of a vassal kingdom like Armenia and at renewing to all intents and purposes the unsuccessful attempt of Trajan. For this purpose the emperor had got ready a powerful river flotilla, a perfected artillery, and a veteran army. He had 1000 transports,

[1] *Cf.* Socrat., *Hist. Eccl.*, iii., 16.

50 war galleys, 50 pontoons, and 100,000 men, besides auxiliaries from Armenia. His strategical plan was also a repetition of the old and excellent scheme devised by Trajan, an invasion of Persia from two sides and with two armies, which were to unite on the left bank of the Tigris and thence advance together to the conquest of the interior.

The campaign began well. All the forts on the Euphrates were either stormed or reduced to surrender, and the army was transported without mishap from the Euphrates to the Tigris, and from the right to the left bank of the latter river. In two months of constant and ever victorious fighting Julian had arrived practically at the gates of Ctesiphon. The other portion of his army, however, which with the Armenian contingents had marched through upper Mesopotamia and was coming south along the left bank of the Tigris, was still too far off. Julian, therefore, did not immediately attack Ctesiphon, which was the greatest of the Persian fortresses, but turned back towards the north-east, in order to meet the other expeditionary forces and to try to get behind the Persian army, thus giving occasion for a pitched battle. For this purpose it was necessary to get rid of the embarrassment of the fleet which would have immobilized a full third of the 60,000 men at Julian's disposal. He did not hesitate. The army having burned the ships turned towards the north, followed by the Persians who resumed the ancient tactics used by the Scythians against Darius I., which consisted in burning the surrounding villages and the face of the country, at the same time harassing the enemy and then retreating rapidly so as to be invisible and unattainable. On the 26th of June, during a new

Persian attack in the course of which the Roman troops repulsed the enemy with enormous loss, a dart launched by an unknown hand struck the emperor in the side, inflicting a mortal wound, while he was fighting as a common soldier among the rest without even the protection of a cuirass.[1]

[1] On the personality and work of Julian, *cf.* G. Boissier, *La fin du Paganisme*, Paris, 1907, vol. i., pp. 85–147; G. Negri, *Giuliano l'Apostata*, Milan, 1902; C. Barbagallo, *Giuliano l'Apostata*, Genoa, 1912; *Lo Stato e l'Istruzione pubblica nell' impero Romano*, pp. 239–280. Many fabulous accounts of the Persian expedition were circulated after Julian's death which have ended by giving it a tragic character. It is clear from the original sources that at the time of Julian's death the Roman army was in excellent condition and that the failure of the enterprise was entirely due to the emperor being killed.

## CHAPTER XVIII

### THE INVASION RESUMED

### (363–393 A.D.)

**147. Jovian, Valentinian, and Valens (363–375 A.D.).** On the death of Julian steps had to be taken to hold another imperial election. At first a council of generals was held in which there was a long and inconclusive discussion. Then suddenly a group of Christian soldiers fell to acclaiming one of the commanders of the imperial guard who was destined to be known in history as the emperor Jovian. Amid the general discord and uncertainty this solution was accepted. But the new prince had none of the qualities which were demanded by the critical character of the time. What was still more disastrous the death of Julian had struck terror into the legions who were already anxious, and on such an army and such an emperor Sapor had no difficulty in imposing a peace highly advantageous to himself. He secured the abandonment of the Roman conquests made in the time of Diocletian whereby the empire lost the five provinces beyond the Tigris, including the fortresses of Mesopotamia and Armenia, the advanced guards of the Roman power in the East.

Peace, therefore, had delivered Persia from the

dangers which might have arisen from the imminent junction of the army of the Tigris with the army of Armenia. That junction actually took place at Tilsafata in Lower Armenia, but Procopius, the general who had been so late in arriving, was immediately directed to convey the ashes of Julian to Tarsus. Some months later Jovian died at Dadartana in Bithynia without having been able even to bring his army home, and leaving behind him, beyond the melancholy disgrace of the peace with Persia, nothing but the memory of a new religious edict whereby he replaced the Christians in the privileged position which Julian had thought it necessary to modify.

The new council of generals which was held at Nicæa on February 26, 364, chose as his successor Valentinian, also a native of Pannonia, and another of the higher officers of the guard. At the request of the soldiers Valentinian nominated as a second Augustus his brother Valens and divided the empire with him, taking the West for himself and assigning the East to Valens (March 28, 364). He hastened to promulgate laws of religious toleration which, for their impartial character, may be compared with the Milan edict of 313. This time, however, the measure was not for the benefit of Christianity but of Paganism and in a measure it justified the policy of Julian. Valentinian deliberately took up the position of being above and outside all theological controversy, and his one object was to prevent either party from forcibly dominating the other.[1] He created a new magistracy, that of the *defensor civitatis*, whose chief duty was to protect the lower classes against the aggressions of the rich—

[1] *Cod. Theod.*, ix., 16, 9. Amm. Marc., xxx., 9, 5.

a plain confession of the growing impotence of the laws and of the State. Above all he made provision for the defence of the western provinces, which were now ever more seriously threatened, against the inroads of the barbarians.

In 365 the empire was subjected to a formidable German attack, evidently preconcerted. Gaul and Rhætia were simultaneously assailed by the Alamanni, the two Pannonias by the Quadi and the Sarmatians, Britain by the Saxons, the Picts, and the Scots, the African provinces by the Gætulians and the Mauri, and Thracia by the Goths. In 367 Valentinian succeeded in inflicting a serious defeat on the Alamanni on the *campi Catalaunici* (near Châlons-sur-Marne). In 368 he invaded their territory, did his best by intrigues to sow discord between the Alamanni and the Burgundi, and succeeded so well that he managed to conclude peace, granting the enemy the style of allies. On the other hand, in order to subdue the Saxons in Britain, the Picts and the Scots of Ireland, it was necessary to send a capable general in the person of the Spaniard Flavius Theodosius. After three years of war (368–370) Theodosius succeeded in re-establishing the frontier of Hadrian. He then went to Africa where he repressed the incursions of the barbarians, and also a rebellion attempted by one of the greatest landowners of the country who had managed to get himself proclaimed emperor. As for the Quadi and the Sarmatians they penetrated into Pannonia and massacred the Roman legions stationed there; but the situation was saved by the son of the victor of Britain and Africa who was *dux* in Mœsia and was named Theodosius like his father. The emperor himself also arrived on the scene but not for long, for, in

November, 375, Valentinian died suddenly in the plain of Brigetium in Illyricum.

**148. Gratian and Valentinian II.; the New War with the Goths** (375–378 **A.D.**). Conditions in the Eastern provinces had hitherto been less difficult. Valens had had to repress some attempts at civil war. He had had some trouble with the Isaurians and the Persians and in the years 367–369 had victoriously waged a little war against the Goths. But he had found time and means withal to sustain the cause of Arianism against the Orthodoxy of the West, and was heaping fuel on the flames of religious discord, when in 375 a grave danger arose in the East. Since the days of Claudius the Goth, the Goths, except for the brief war of 367–369, had left the empire in peace. They still held practically the same territory between Transylvania and the Don which had been theirs in the third century, and they were divided by the line of the Dniester into the Grutungi (the future Ostrogoths) and the Thervingi (afterwards known as the Visigoths). They had been converted to Arian Christianity, had attained a certain measure of civilization and had grown in numbers, riches, and power by the conquest of other barbaric peoples. They had moreover entered into commercial relations with the Roman Empire to which they had supplied soldiers. But in 375 these barbarians in their turn were visited by the scourge of a rival nation more barbarous than themselves—the Huns. The Huns were a people of yellow race, related to the Mongols of later days who scoured and devastated the face of Europe in the Middle Ages, and also to the Turks and Ottomans who came still later, and to the modern Chinese and Japanese. Terrible things are related of the Huns; it is at all events certain that they were a very numerous and a very warlike people. In their movement from the East towards the West they had first subdued the Alani of the Caucasus accompanied by whom they attacked and finally conquered the Ostrogoths. The Visigoths, despairing of their chances of successful resistance asked permission of the Romans to retire within the ring of fortresses on the right bank of the Danube (376). Valens did not think fit to reject this request; he merely required that the Goths should lay down their arms and undertake, henceforth without annual remuneration, to serve and defend the empire in any contingency that might arise. On the other hand, however, the imperial government had assumed the responsibility for feeding a very large population and in discharging this responsibility so many controversies and disputes arose that the Goths became exasperated and finally revolted and began to lay waste the whole of Thrace as far as the Balkans and beyond (377).

In the West, meanwhile, the officers of the army had raised to the empire Gratian and Valentinian II., both of whom were sons of Valentinian I., though by different mothers. To them or rather to Gratian, Valens at once appealed for aid. But Gratian was not in a position to respond to this appeal, for no sooner had the first cohorts begun to move towards the East, than the Alamanni swooped down on Upper Germany. Gratian, therefore, had to think of the defence of his own provinces and he was, in fact, able to inflict a severe defeat on the Alamanni. In the meantime, however, the upper portion of the Balkan peninsula fell into the hands of the Goths and—what was more serious—their success attracted other barbarians such as the Ostrogoths, the Alani, and the Huns themselves, to share in the booty. Some days before August 9, 378, a great council of war was held at which it was decided to risk a decisive battle with the enemy who had now for long been encamped on Roman territory, before the arrival of Gratian who, having conquered the Alamanni, was preparing to come to their assistance. This must have been the tremendous battle of Adrianople in which the Romans were defeated with terrible losses, their emperor himself being among the victims (August 9, 378).

**149. Theodosius and the Pacification of the Balkan Peninsula (378–382 A.D.).** The consequences of this defeat were very serious. While the victors overflowed all Thrace, carrying their attacks as far as Adrianople and Constantinople itself, and thence turned back on Illyria, the Sarmatians and the Quadi again crossed the Danube and the Alamanni prepared to repeat the attempt they had made several years before. It was a terrible moment. "The earth," exclaimed S. Gregory Nazianzene, "is covered with blood and corpses," and in 398 S. Jerome shuddered at the recollection of those days. "For twenty years and more, Roman blood is shed every day from Constantinople to the Julian Alps. Scythia, Thrace, Macedonia, Thessaly, Dardania, Dacia, Epirus, Dalmatia, the two Pannonias,—all are devastated by Goths, Sarmatians, Quadi, Alani, Huns, Vandals, Marcomanni. Everywhere there is pillaging and murder. . . . The Barbarians lord it over Athenians, Corinthians, Lacedæmonians, Arcadians—over all Greece in fact. . . . How many rivers are reddened with human blood! Antioch and all the other cities washed by the Halys, the Cydnus, the Orontes, the Euphrates, suffer the horrors of a siege.

Prisoners are driven off in flocks. Arabia, Phœnicia, Palestine, and Egypt are a prey to panic."[1]

In this terrible situation Gratian was happily inspired. He charged Theodosius, son of the valorous defender of Britain and Africa, with the task of saving the East, and Theodosius, then a young man of thirty-three, proved equal to this difficult undertaking. He hastily reconstructed the army, risked no great battle, but by a series of small and successful operations he began to defeat one by one and to exterminate the scattered bands of Goths which infested the Balkan Peninsula. The first result of this was that on January 19, 379, Gratian raised his general to the empire, thereby inaugurating a new dynasty. But this protracted and difficult guerilla warfare ended as was now usual in the struggles between Rome and the barbarians. Part of the Gothic horde was installed in the upper part of Dacia Ripensis, in Pannonia, in Thrace, Macedonia, and Mœsia as "allies," that is to say under the customary obligation of performing military service in defence of the empire (382).

**150. The Great Catholic Reaction (380–383 A.D.).** In the reign of Gratian, Valentinian II., and Theodosius, the East was governed by the West. All three emperors belonged to the western provinces and this meant that Orthodoxy once more began to prevail over Arianism, the Church of Rome over the Churches of the East. Gratian, indeed, was a fervent Catholic and a keen persecutor of the Arians. In 377 when he invited Theodosius to assume the purple, he had already relieved of most of the public burdens all the priests and servants of the Christian religion.[2] In the following year he had expropriated all premises used

[1] Hieron., *Ep.*, 60, 16. [2] *Cod. Theod.*, xvi., 2, 24.

for the worship of non-Catholics,[1] and shortly afterwards, immediately on the death of Valens, he had dismissed many Arian bishops, replacing them by Catholics. The most important religious measure of this time, however, was not passed until the two Augusti jointly assumed office. On August 3, 379, Gratian and Theodosius issued a very violent edict prohibiting all heresies.[2] Six months later, on February 27, 380, the two emperors affirmed in another edict that it was their will and pleasure to unify the faith of the empire, which was to be that of the Council of Nice and officially denominated Catholic. They further described the other forms of the Christian faith as not so much churches as "conventicles of madmen and disordered spirits," and threatened them not only with the vengeance of God but also with persecution by the government.[3] This threat did not remain a dead letter, for on January 10, 381, the Nicene Creed was imposed on the whole empire as the basis of the one permitted religion which was the Catholic faith.[4]

Laws, however, were not enough; they had to be enforced by the spiritual authority. In May, 381, therefore, Theodosius convened an œcumenical council at Constantinople at which the Nicene Creed was solemnly reconsecrated. The see of Rome received the first place among the great episcopal sees of the empire; the see of Constantinople, raised to the rank of a Patriarchate, came second, being placed above those of Alexandria and Antioch though the latter

[1] *Cod. Theod.*, xvi., 5, 4. On the date see the commentary of Gotefredo.

[2] *Ibid.*, xvi., 5, 5.

[3] Sozom., *Hist. Eccl.*, vii., 4; *Cod. Theod.*, xvi., 1, 2.

[4] *Cod. Theod.*, xvi., 5, 6.

claimed to have been founded by the Apostles. In the same year Ambrose Bishop of Milan and Gratian convoked another council at Aquileia. This council which marked a new triumph of Catholicism laid it down for the first time that it was the duty of the catholic clergy to pray daily for the emperors.

These two councils must have given a new impulse to the anti-pagan policy of the emperors. Towards the end of 381 Theodosius and Gratian threatened with severe penalties all who continued to perform acts of pagan worship.[1] In 382 they ordered the removal from the Curia Romana of the altar of Victory which had been placed there by Augustus after the Battle of Actium as a symbol of the power of Rome, which had been removed by Constantius and which Julian had replaced. It was decreed that all the privileges accorded to the pagan priesthood should be annulled, the revenues hitherto appropriated to the temples were suppressed, the property they owned was confiscated, and legacies in their favour were forbidden. Finally, in this same year or in the next Gratian and consequently also Theodosius, the first among the emperors laid down the ancient office of *pontifex maximus*. The exclusive spirit of Christianity was gradually becoming more manifest and was driving the State to extirpate all other cults.

In August, 383, however, Gaul was suddenly invaded by a new pretender, Magnus Clemens Maximus, a Spaniard like Theodosius, who seems to have been governor of Britain. Gratian, who had never been popular, was abandoned by his troops and his generals, and was assassinated on August 26th.

**151. The Arian Revival in the West (383–387**

[1] *Cod. Theod.*, xvi., 10, 7.

A.D.). Maximus had declared his intention of overturning Gratian only, as he was the more unpopular of the two Augusti and in fact he made peaceful overtures through St. Ambrose to Gratian's brother Valentinian II., promising not to cross the Alps. He also intimated to Theodosius that he merely meant to rule the provinces which had belonged to Gratian, that is to say Gaul, Spain, and Britain. Theodosius made no objection and recognized Maximus as Augustus, either because he did not think it opportune to embark on a new civil war or because he hoped to make Maximus his tool. Valentinian was still very young and his mother Justina, the second wife of Valentinian I., who was opposed to the uncompromising Catholicism of Gratian and Theodosius, governed on his behalf. It may be, therefore, that Theodosius hoped by means of Maximus to neutralize the influence of Justina. If that was his calculation Maximus fulfilled it even more completely than had been desired. Both Pagans and Arians were trying to profit by the death of Gratian, and Justina, who was a tolerant spirit, decided to do the Arians a favour by persuading S. Ambrose the Bishop of Milan to allow the Arians, who after all were citizens and soldiers like the rest, to have the Basilica Porcia outside the city (S. Vittore ad Corpus) for the exercise of their religion. This act of toleration was intended to conciliate the minority, but the Orthodox party rebelled and S. Ambrose found himself in a position to threaten and even practically to cause a revolt in Milan (Easter, 385).[1] The imperial authority was compelled for the moment to give way to this agitation but sought for an occasion to reassert itself, and in the following year Valentinian II. authorized the Arians

[1] *Cf.* Ambrose, *Epp.*, 20, an extremely important letter.

to practise their religion (January 25, 386).[1] Maximus now thought the moment had come when he could repeat against Valentinian the manœuvre which had succeeded against Gratian. Owing to their common zeal for the Catholic cause he was sure of Theodosius, and for the same reason of Italy where the great majority was Catholic. Accordingly in 387 he suddenly appeared in the plain of the Po as the champion of Orthodoxy against the Arian tendencies of Valentinian. The emperor with his mother and sister had barely time to embark and take flight to the East. Once more theological controversies had been made the tool of ambition.

**152. The First Conflict between Church and State (387–390 A.D.).** But Maximus had gone too far. Theodosius could not allow two emperors to be murdered before his eyes; still less could he permit the occidental Augustus to obtain such a great accession of power. In the face of a political danger religious considerations had to take the second place. The beauty of Valentinian's sister Galla finally turned the scale. The Catholic emperor, who had recently become a widower, was captivated and determined to make Galla his wife. Shortly afterwards Justina died, and when his mother was gone, Valentinian lost no time in being converted to Catholicism. The Western enterprise ceased, therefore, to be a danger and Theodosius, at the head of an army composed of Goths, Alani, and Huns, in which were serving among the chief generals the Franks Ricimer and Arbogastes, turned against Maximus. Beaten at Siscia (Siseck) in the valley of the Sava and again shortly afterwards

[1] Sozom., *Hist. Eccl.*, vii., 13; *Cod. Theod.*, xvi., 1, 4; Ambrose, *Epp.*, xxi., 13 ff.

at Petovium (Petau) in Pannonia, Maximus failed to defend, as he had hoped, the passes of the Julian Alps, was handed over by his own soldiers to the victor who had already reached the gates of Aquileia and was finally beheaded (summer, 388). Valentinian was therefore re-established in the plenitude of his powers.

The victory of Theodosius meant the triumph of Catholicism, a triumph so complete that it freed the Church from the pupillage hitherto imposed on it by the empire. In these years the great Archbishop of Milan openly formulated the doctrine, which had horrified Julian, that the State was subordinate to the Church, because the only object of an earthly society must be the eternal welfare of its members. The Archbishop therefore claimed an ever greater share of influence in the Consistorium and in the control of public affairs. The first conflict arose over the destruction of a synagogue in a little Asiatic town Callinicum on the Euphrates at the instigation of the local bishop. As no law forbade the exercise of the Jewish religion, Theodosius had decided that the synagogue should be restored at the expense of the bishop and that the incendiaries should be punished. St. Ambrose opposed this.[1] The emperor refused to yield and Ambrose suspended him from the enjoyment of religious ministrations.

Theodosius gave way, but worse followed. In 390 a great revolt broke out at Thessalonica in which perished the governor, several magistrates, and some of the officers of the garrison. Theodosius was very angry and by way of reprisal ordered a massacre in the circus in which innocent and guilty were alike slain in great numbers. Then for the first time the

[1] Ambr., *Epp.*, xl.–xli.

voice of a bishop—Ambrose again—was raised reproaching the emperor with his cruelty and Theodosius was punished by being forbidden access to the Church. The emperor had to yield a second time and, as the victims at Thessalonica could not be brought to life again, he expiated his guilt by abstaining from all the ceremonies of the Church until his next birthday. The logical consequences of this inexorably followed; the empire was weakened and the new religion went on with greater boldness than ever to seize the government of the world.

153. **The New Civil War (391–395 A.D.).** Such a surrender of the imperial authority could not fail to provoke a reaction in the pagan world. The first manifestations of this were in the East, and especially at Alexandria in Egypt, where, in 391, there were regular battles in the streets between Pagans and Christians. From Egypt the agitation soon spread to Italy where the pagan party were still very numerous. The Romanized Frank Arbogastes, a general whom Theodosius had brought with him from the East in the war with Maximus and who had afterwards driven a Frank invasion back beyond the Rhine by a lightning counter-offensive, picked a quarrel with Valentinian II., and caused him to be assassinated (May 15, 392). In Valentinian's place as Augustus he put a Roman noble named Eugenius, a man of great importance who had been elevated to one of the highest offices in the imperial chancellery. Recognized by Italy and the West and supported by Arbogastes, Eugenius commenced a regular restoration of paganism. The subsidies were restored to the temples. The altar of Victory was replaced in the Curia. The image of Hercules was substituted for the Cross on the banners

of the army. A suspension of public business (*iustitium*) for three months was ordained in order that the religious purification of the towns might be carried out and all the feasts inscribed in the pagan calendar were solemnly celebrated.

This was an open defiance which Theodosius could not overlook and he, therefore, set out from the East in 394 at the head of an army full of Goths, Alani, Huns, Iberians, and Saracens. A decisive battle was fought on September 5th beyond the Julian Alps on the banks of the Frigidus (the modern Vipacco, east of Gorizia). The first day's fighting was doubtful, but during the following night gold achieved what steel had failed to accomplish and part of the army of Arbogastes was induced to desert. The second day (September 6th) ended in victory for Theodosius. Arbogastes killed himself and Eugenius was beheaded. Immediately afterwards pagan worship was again forbidden; the temples were once more closed or destroyed and, as in the former persecutions, many masterpieces of ancient art perished.

**154. The Internal Crisis in the Empire at the End of the Fourth Century.** Five months later Theodosius died at Milan, being then only fifty years of age (January 17, 395). Following Diocletian and Constantine he was the last of the three great emperors who strove to reorganize the empire after the terrible crisis of the third century. Less than Constantine, as Constantine had been less than Diocletian he did what he could to cure the evils of the times, but, though his effort was great, its results were small. The ancient world was dying of the wounds received during the upheaval which followed the death of Alexander Severus, and no human power could restore it to health. Perpetual civil and foreign war, frequent invasion, growing taxation, the relentless exactions of the State now preyed too freely on what we call "acquired riches" or fortunes already consolidated. The reforms of Diocletian, especially those measures whereby the *curiales*, members of the *curiæ*, or little municipal senates by which the towns were governed, were made responsible to the State for the payment of the contribution of the whole district, had been a disaster for the middle class. As always happens in troublous times property had become extremely mobile and passed easily from one hand to another. The rich became rapidly impoverished and the poor as rapidly enriched. But this fluidity of fortune soon destroyed all that had survived the disasters of the third century of the brilliant municipal civilization which had been the glory of the empire at the summit of its power. That civilization, as we have seen, rested on a great number of solidly based fortunes. If we remember that in addition to this cause of disintegration, there was the great revolution in ideas and sentiments produced by Christianity, the confusion of races, the accession to power of the ruder populations of the empire, and the increasing influx of barbarians who established themselves in Roman territory, we shall easily understand how it was that the great work of the Antonines was now everywhere falling into ruin. Many cities were depopulated, their monuments decaying. The arts and the artists that had embellished, enriched, and delighted them were disappearing, the *curiæ* were deserted and public services disorganized.[1]

[1] Ancient writers afford many testimonies of this fact. It will be enough to quote an official document, an imperial rescript of

The wisest course perhaps would have been to bow to fate and to return to a simpler form of life. Christianity might have helped the empire to make this change. But the imperial authority had had too large a share in creating this urban civilization, had derived too much power and prestige from its splendours; too many political, economic, and intellectual interests pressed for the continuance of its brilliant and secular tradition, and the empire did what it could to arrest this decadence. The methods adopted were two in number and both equally dangerous—the grant of special privileges and coercion. Soldiers and veterans on the one hand and on the other artists whose work was necessary for the embellishment, the convenience, and the pleasures of the city, for instance, architects, sculptors, and painters, were given numerous privileges of all kinds, among others exemption from many public burdens.[1] The grant of these privileges, however, meant that so much was added to the burden which pressed so heavily on the rest. Life became very hard for many classes of the community, oppressed as they were by taxation and by the obligation to be at the charge of numerous public expenses. Great therefore must have been the temptation to enter the privileged professions and, for the more desperate, to live on the charity of the State or the still larger charity of the Church, or, finally to escape the infinite annoyances of civil life by entering the Christian priest-

---

the year 400: *destitutæ ministeriis civitates splendorem quo quidem nituerant amiserunt. Plurimi siquidem collegiati cultum urbium deferentes agrestem vitam secuti in secreta sese et devia contulerunt: Cod. Theod.*, xii., 19, 1.

[1] Cf. *Cod. Theod.*, xiii., 4, 2, where is given a very interesting list of the privileged artists; it includes all the luxury trades.

hood. Monasticism, which developed greatly at this time, was another refuge for the destitute.

In order to remedy this evil and to prevent a situation arising in which there should be a superabundance, say, of sculptors and painters but a deficiency of citizens and of bakers, the imperial government, after the reign of Diocletian in the course of the fourth century, adopted a resolute policy of compulsory organization. Several kinds of social condition and not a few forms of labour became hereditary and obligatory. Thus membership of the *curiæ* became compulsory on all who possessed a certain amount of property in land and the obligation descended to their posterity until all were ruined. No *curalis* could occupy any other official position; for example he was forbidden to enter the army. Many of the humbler occupations which were necessary for the pleasure or comfort of the city life were organized in compulsory associations. No man who became a member of such an association could leave it, and his sons were likewise compelled to join. In the course of the fourth century the same method was gradually applied to the *coloni*, who had hitherto been free peasants cultivating the lands of their master in accordance with a definite agreement, but who now became serfs of the soil, chained for generation after generation to the ground which they tilled. In the *Codex Justinianus* there has been preserved the decree introducing this form of servitude into Palestine,[1] which enables us to see how the plan worked in an actual instance. In places where there were too few peasants, owing to the attractions of less laborious or more profitable occupations, the proprietors appealed

[1] *Cod. Just.*, xi., 50, 1.

to the State, and the emperor issued a decree imposing hereditary compulsion on the country people of the district to cultivate the land there in the same way as the work of the *pistores* or bakers had been made compulsory at Rome.

It is easy to see what were the difficulties of such a system. It would only be carried on by means of a multiplicity of laws, and obedience could be secured only by great expenditure, much cruelty, and the services of an ever increasing bureaucracy. Discontent, resentment, and a spirit of revolt grew with the number of the victims. The natural reaction followed intensifying the cause of the evil which these measures were meant to cure by necessitating new expenditure and new taxes. Further the whole social organization of the empire acquired a rigidity which made it weaker and less capable of sustaining blows from outside. When so many persons were compelled, from father to son, to carry on the same trade a large proportion of them were condemned to pursuits for which they had no aptitude. It is probable, for example, that the prevention of the *curiales* entering the army was one of the causes of the increasing scarcity of officers owing to which the empire was more and more compelled to resort to the services of barbarians in the higher ranks and no longer merely as common soldiers. This was one of the most dangerous developments in the fourth century. The *curiales* in fact were the opulent middle class of the empire which could and should have been a recruiting ground for officers. Thus the internal crisis, aggravated by the very efforts which were made to deal with it, was destined to be one of the chief causes of the final catastrophe which must now be related.

# CHAPTER XIX

## THE CATASTROPHE (395–476 A.D.)

**155. The First Conflict between the East and the West (395–397 A.D.).** Theodosius on his death-bed divided the empire between his two sons Honorius and Arcadius. The territory in which the two portions adjoined each other was Illyricum, of which Dalmatia, Pannonia, and Noricum fell to the West while Dacia and Macedonia were assigned to the East. This time, as in the days of the tetrarchy, it was only the administration which was divided; the empire as before remained one and indivisible with a common system of law. The force of circumstances, however, was destined to prevail over human dispositions, and from the death of Theodosius began the final division of the ancient Roman Empire into two parts, Eastern and Western.

The two princes were both very young men. Theodosius therefore when he was dying had entrusted Arcadius, a boy of eighteen, to the care of Rufinus the prætorian præfect. His other son Honorius was only eleven and was put under the guardianship of Stilicho the *magister militum* or commander-in-chief of the armies of the East. Stilicho was a Vandal and a barbarian, but, like Arbogastes, was much more Roman in spirit and tendency than many of his contemporaries who were natives of Italy and Rome. Rufinus and Stilicho soon disagreed, and this came about the more easily as, since the foundation of Constantinople, the rivalry between the East and the West had been rekindled. Italy would not acknowledge that the new capital was the equal or the superior of Rome. Throughout the East, on the other hand, there was a growing tendency to regard Constantinople as a city which had eclipsed and supplanted Rome or which, at the very least, must not be considered as in any way subordinate to the ancient metropolis. This discord flared up into a rebellion of the Goths stationed in the East, the reason or the pretext being that Rufinus had failed to recognize some of their privileges. Having acclaimed Alaric as their sovereign they fell upon Thrace which they laid waste, and then invaded Greece (395). Stilicho immediately hastened to the scene of action with his army and reached Thessalonica, where, however, he was met by a message from Arcadius requiring him to dismiss the oriental troops which had been under his command since the time of the war of Theodosius against Arbogastes, to retire with his own and to take care not again to cross the frontiers of the Eastern Empire.

For the first time Constantinople explicitly affirmed that her sovereign rights were equal to those of Rome, and she did so in the face of the enemy and at the risk of precipitating a disaster. If Stilicho obeyed, the Roman Empire would be broken into two empires, independent of each other because possessed of equal rights. If he did not obey it meant civil war between the two parts of the empire. Stilicho, being a prudent and crafty person, devised a complicated expedient for avoiding this tragic dilemma. He pretended to yield, but placed at the head of the troops which were to be led back to the East a Goth named Gainas, an officer who was in his confidence. Gainas succeeded so well in exciting the anger of the soldiers against Rufinus and the separatist aims of the court of Constantinople that when they arrived at that capital they murdered Rufinus (November 27, 395),[1] an event which must have opened the eyes of the court to the dangers of a policy of separation.

This at first seemed to be the case and wiser counsels prevailed at Constantinople. Stilicho was allowed to lead his forces from Dalmatia into Southern Greece, where he barred the isthmus of Corinth and began the pursuit of Alaric's army through the hills and valleys of the Peloponnese. But no sooner had the Eastern Empire obtained a breathing space than the policy hostile to the West and to Stilicho got the upper hand once more, encouraged by the eunuch Eutropius who had succeeded Rufinus in the favour of the emperor. Profiting by the difficulties which prevented Stilicho from entirely annihilating the Goths,[2] his enemies succeeded in having him declared a public enemy of the Eastern Empire, in confiscating his property, and in concluding a treaty of peace with Alaric whereby Epirus and the eastern coast of Illyricum as far as Dyrrhachium (Durazzo) were ceded to the Gothic King who was appointed *dux* of the district (397).

This time Stilicho, who was unwilling or unable to embark on a civil war, resigned himself to retiring into

[1] *Cf.* Claudian in *Ruf.*, ii., 400 ff.

[2] The causes of the failure of Stilicho's campaign are very obscure. His friends blame the Eastern Court (Claud., *De bello Goth*, 516–517), his enemies blame Stilicho himself. It is wiser to remember the military difficulties by which he was confronted.

the occidental provinces to which he restricted his government. Thus the rupture between the East and the West was for the first time officially declared, and the great historic achievement of Rome, which was the union of the oriental and the occidental empires, was shattered.

**156. The New Invasions in the West and the End of Stilicho (397–408 A.D.).** To make up for this Stilicho devoted himself with renewed energy to the government of the diminished empire. The years during which he was at the head of affairs were, considering the time, by no means a period of bad government. The religious severities of Theodosius were mitigated. Finance, administration, and public safety were well looked after. Africa was reconquered for the empire, and the insurrection of its governor Gildo was suppressed. In spite of Stilicho's personal predilections, Christianity was ever more favoured at the expense of paganism; and by an edict dated August 20, 399, the abolition of the pagan festivals was decreed. But all these efforts were of no avail because the division of the empire into two parts had irremediably weakened the military power of the West. The empire had hitherto been able to resist all the attacks of which it had been the object because the legions of the East had hurried to the West, and those of the West to the East whenever the necessity arose. When the provinces and the armies were separated, the West had to face the same enemies with diminished forces and therefore with increasing difficulty.

The danger of the position was soon apparent. In 400 Alaric, encouraged by the weakness of the occidental empire and perhaps also by the secret advice of the court of Constantinople, invaded Italy at the head of his Gothic army reinforced by other barbarian tribes, and, having crossed the Alps, was able to threaten Milan itself, the residence of Honorius and his court (end of 401). It was a terrible moment which threw a strong light on the defencelessness of the Western Empire. In order to save Italy, Stilicho was compelled to have recourse to the disastrous remedy of recalling troops from Britain, from the Rhine, and from Rhætia, thus abandoning these provinces to their fate. Italy was, in fact, saved. Having raised the siege of Milan, Stilicho pursued the enemy as far as Pollentia (Pollenzo) on the Tanarus, and there inflicted on him a memorable defeat (April 6, 402) and a second in the following year near Verona (summer of 403). He was unable, however, to destroy Alaric's army, and the Gothic chieftain succeeded in evacuating the Venetian plain and in withdrawing the remnant of his forces.

Hardly, however, was the Gothic peril at an end when a new danger threatened. From the north of Europe a new and enormous horde of Germans under a pagan Ostrogoth named Radagaisus threw itself upon Italy. The invading masses were so great—it is said that they numbered more than 200,000 men[1]—that it was impossible to offer any immediate opposition (405). Honorius and his court repaired to Ravenna which possessed magnificent natural defences, while the enemy penetrated as far as Etruria. Stilicho once more took steps to reinforce the diminished army of Italy which had been severely tried by the Gothic

[1] *Cf.* Aug., *De civitate Dei*, v., 23; Oros., vii., 37, 4; Zosim., v., 26. On the two invasions of Alaric and Radagaisus *cf.* the valuable study of F. Gabotto, *Storia dell' Italia occidentate* (395–1313), Pinerolo, 1911, vol. i., pp. 82 ff., 112 ff.

war, by stripping the provinces, and by this means in the course of 405 was enabled to defeat and practically exterminate the invaders near Fæsulæ (Fiesole) in a battle in which Radagaisus himself was killed.

But, while Stilicho was triumphing at Pollentia, at Verona, and at Fæsulæ, Britain was becoming the scene of new usurpations, insurrections, and barbarian invasions. Gaul stripped of Roman troops had been invaded and laid waste by a combination of Vandals, Alani, Suevi, Franks, and Burgundians, while Alaric on the extreme eastern frontier was merely waiting until he had reorganized his army. On this Stilicho had recourse to the desperate expedient of suggesting to Alaric that he should leave the service of the court of Constantinople for that of the Court of Ravenna, and should be made præfect of Illyricum which should have the frontiers which the Western Empire claimed for this province but which were contested by the Empire of the East. Alaric was disposed to accept, but required the consent of the Court of Constantinople which was reluctant and protracted the negotiations. Irritated by the delay Stilicho finally decided to take reprisals by closing Western ports to ships coming from the East.[1] Meanwhile a usurper named Flavius Claudius Constantinus left Britain and landed in Gaul whence he began to threaten Italy. Alaric, ill-pleased with the delay in the negotiations, demanded a large indemnity for the expenses of his armaments of which no use was being made. Stilicho had the greatest difficulty in dealing with all these troubles which had the further effect of encouraging the ever increasing number of his enemies at court. His tolerant attitude in matters of religion, his inclination to

[1] Cf. *Cod. Theod.*, vii., 16, 1.

treat with the barbarians, and his policy of sacrificing the provinces for the sake of Italy had raised against him a bitter and implacable opposition, and yet he was blamed for the division of the empire. On the death of Arcadius in 408, his son, a boy of seven, succeeded him as Theodosius II., and it seemed as if the court of Ravenna might in the end succeed in acquiring that control of the East which all Stilicho's authority had hitherto failed to secure. But fortune betrayed the great general. His adversaries forced the situation which, they saw, might turn against them at any moment. While Honorius was at Pavia a violent mutiny, prepared with super-refined cunning, broke out among the soldiers stationed there, who demanded the head of Stilicho from their feeble sovereign. Stilicho might have resisted, for the great majority of the army was on his side, but he did not wish to provoke a civil war and allowed himself to be slain by the emissaries of the emperor (August 23, 408).

**157. Alaric (408–410 A.D.).** The consequences of this insane crime were incalculable. The death of Stilicho was the signal for the revolt or the defection of many of the barbarians allied to the empire who for the most part had been recruited by him for the defence of the declining Roman world. Worse still it brought about a rupture with Alaric. The Court of Ravenna had inevitably assumed an attitude towards the Goth which was the opposite of that of Stilicho, and replied to all his requests, whether just or unjust, by a curt refusal. The consequence was that in the same year (408) Alaric suddenly burst into Italy from Illyricum. This time, as Italy was soon to discover, Stilicho was no more. While Honorius took refuge in Ravenna, Alaric took and sacked Aquileia, Altinum,

Concordia, and Cremona. He left Ravenna on his flank, proceeded along the coast of the Adriatic and marched along the Via Flaminia on Rome without meeting any resistance. Since it was besieged by the Gauls, Rome had never seen a foreign foe beneath her walls. Surprised by this attack she did what was possible and defended herself within the circle of the Aurelian fortifications. But Alaric blockaded the city and by threats of starvation compelled it to come to terms. He demanded and received a considerable tribute which was to take the place of the indemnity denied to him by the official government. Further he pledged the senate to support at court a treaty of peace under which Alaric was to receive Noricum with the title of *magister militum* of the empire. These conditions were not excessive, but the court of Ravenna, which by its attitude had left Italy to its fate, refused to hear to anything of the sort. Alaric returned to Latium, occupied the port of Ostia, took possession of the magazines of corn from which Rome drew its provisions and threatened to starve out the city. By this means he compelled the senate to depose Honorius and to substitute for him a certain Attalus, the præfect of the city, who immediately after his appointment not only declared himself prepared to satisfy Alaric's demands but opened hostilities against Honorius by sending an expedition against Africa. This enterprise was a failure, whereupon Alaric deposed Attalus and, having carried him to his camp as a hostage together with Galla Placidia, the beautiful daughter of Theodosius I., he decided to negotiate.

The imperial court was again immovable, whereupon Alaric lost patience. In the night of August 24, 410, he stormed the Aurelian Wall by a surprise attack and entered the eternal city, which he had hitherto respected, which Hannibal himself had never dared to attack, but which was now given up to the spoiler for three days. Alaric, however, was not lacking in astuteness. His intention was not to conquer Italy where, in the very heart of the empire, he was, to use a military term, "in the air" and exposed to converging attacks from all the points of the compass. He wished to establish himself, with or without the consent of the empire, in a corner of the Roman world where he could live in peace. Having failed to secure that consent he considered where he could establish himself most securely by force with the means at his disposal and he seems to have cast his eye on Africa; not without reason, for Africa, though difficult to attack, was situated at one of the extremities of the empire, and was easy to defend. Moreover an invader could reckon on being assisted by its atrocious internal dissensions, and it was a rich country and the granary of Italy. Thus, if he got possession of it, he would have in his hands a powerful means of compelling the emperor to negotiate. Alaric therefore did not maltreat Rome too savagely, and on his departure turned towards Southern Italy with the intention, it appears, of conquering Sicily which was to serve as a bridge to Africa, as it had done for Rome in the days of the Punic wars. During his march, however, he died suddenly while still quite a young man. Subsequent legend relates that his Goths buried him in a golden tomb near Consentia (Cosenza) under the bed of the river Busento which was diverted for the purpose (410).

**158. The Final Loss of Western Europe (410–416 A.D.).** Alaric was succeeded in the command by his relative Ataulfus, who gave up the idea of conquering Sicily and Africa and once more opened negotiations with the empire. The attitude of the court had in the meantime altered, chiefly owing to the very grave events which had taken place in Southern Gaul. There, while Honorius was struggling with Alaric in Italy, a usurper named Constantine was confronted by the numerous barbarian tribes which had penetrated into the country since the year 406. Constantine had decided to free himself of their presence by directing them on Spain, and in fact the Vandals, the Alani, and the Suevi went on in 409 to the Iberian peninsula which they devastated and almost completely overran. The Suevi and some of the Vandals settled themselves in Galicia, the Alani in Lusitania and in the territories of Nova Carthago, while another section of the Vandals occupied Bætica which they called Vandalusia, a name which afterwards was altered to Andalusia.

This gave no breathing space to Gaul. After the barbarian invasions the civil wars recommenced. Against the usurper another usurper arose in the person of Jovinus. In 411 Honorius had to send Constantius, his new *magister militum* who was a great general, to the province and he was at last successful in placing Constantine *hors de combat*. Gaul, however, might be considered as lost unless the empire made a great effort, and in 412 Honorius offered Ataulfus the opportunity of taking his Goths thither to fight for him. Ataulfus accepted the mission and his arrival was the signal for new intrigues and conflicts between barbarians, pretenders, and Roman generals. For all that, after about a year and a half Jovinus was conquered with the help of the Goths and Southern Gaul was reoccupied as far as Bordeaux. This, however, did not serve to clear up the relations of Ataulfus with Honorius. The emperor hesitated, as he had done in the case of Alaric, to give Ataulfus the territory he wanted within the boundaries of the empire and to give him in marriage Placidia who was still a hostage in the Gothic camp. In the end Ataulfus, again like Alaric, tried to force the emperor's hand. About the end of 413 he attacked Massilia without success. He then took Narbona (Narbonne) and stormed Tolosa (Toulouse). At Narbona in 414 he solemnized his marriage with Placidia and again invested Attalus with the purple on condition of receiving from him Aquitania. Constantius then took the field against Ataulfus who was very soon compelled to retreat into Spain where he fell by the treacherous hand of a barbarian assassin (415). His death finally settled the Gothic question which gave no further trouble for about twenty years. The chief Vallia, who succeeded Ataulfus, after the very brief reign of Sigericus, succeeded in concluding the agreement for which Alaric and Ataulfus had striven in vain. Galla Placidia was restored to Honorius and Vallia was charged with the war against the barbarians in Spain and was promised Southern Gaul as a reward if he succeeded, on the understanding that he was to hold it as a vassal state of the empire.

Vallia completed his difficult task between 416 and 418, and in concert with Constantius drove back the barbarians into the extreme north-west of the peninsula. In the latter year or in 419 he obtained for his Goths and for himself as an independent prince a firm establishment in Aquitania and in several cities in the neighbouring provinces.

Four years later, on the 15th or, according to certain authorities, on the 20th of August, 423, the Western Emperor died after a reign of about thirty years. Terrible indeed was the state of the countries which his father had placed under his control! Britain and North-western Gaul were lost; the lands on the left bank of the Rhine near Magontiacum (Mayence) had been ceded to the Burgundians in the very year in which Ataulfus had been fighting in Southern Gaul. That region since 418 had been a Visigothic kingdom, while Spain was in the hands of barbarian tribes predominant among whom were the terrible Vandals. The occidental empire, which had been the great work of Rome, was half destroyed and one of the chief causes of this disaster had been the partition of the empire which followed the death of Theodosius.

**159. The Vandals (423–445 A.D.).** Honorius left no son, but had a nephew Flavius Placidus Valentinianus, son of his sister Placidia who on her liberation by the Goths had married the general Constantius. Flavius was a child of five and therefore the empire was once more united under the sceptre of the Emperor of the East, Theodosius II., the son of Arcadius, who meanwhile had grown to man's estate and had governed the Eastern Empire in comparative tranquillity. In the East the greatest difficulties had been as in the past the religious struggles, and, in the year 422, a Persian war which, however, ended in a truce destined to govern the relations of the two monarchies for nearly eighty years. The union of the distracted West with the tranquil and more prosperous East promised to bring advantages to both parts of the empire. Theodosius was accordingly proclaimed Emperor both of the East and of the West. Suddenly, however, a pretender arose in the West in the person of John the *primicerius notariorum* or chief of the imperial notaries, who immediately sent his general Flavius Aëtius to recruit auxiliary forces among the Huns for the civil war which was imminent. His revolt seems to have induced Theodosius to give up the idea of ruling the whole empire by himself, for he hastened to proclaim as Augustus the little Valentinian putting him under the guardianship of his mother and betrothing him to his daughter Eudoxia. He then prepared a great army and opened hostilities. John was defeated and slain, for Aëtius and his Huns arrived too late. The son of Placidia was invested with the purple with the style of Valentinian III., and as a reward for his intervention the Eastern Emperor received Illyricum, thus occupying all the eastern approaches to Italy, obtaining a direct outlet to the Adriatic and settling entirely in his own favour the dispute which had been so long and so bitterly contested with Stilicho.

The reign of Valentinian III. began with a disaster. The two principal personages in the Western Empire were Bonifacius the governor of Africa, who in 413 had conducted the defence of Massilia against Ataulfus and who had not recognized the usurpation of John, and Aëtius, who had made peace with the new government on his return from his mission to the Huns. Both had set their hearts on the office of *magister militum*. It appears that Aëtius succeeded in persuading the regent Placidia that Bonifacius was meditating an insurrection, by suggesting that she should summon him to Italy to test his loyalty, at the same time secretly warning Bonifacius not to come as the court was plotting against him. However this may be the regent finally dismissed Bonifacius who, thinking that he was ruined, had recourse to the desperate remedy of inviting the Vandals to come from Spain to Africa and carry out the design of Alaric.

The Vandals had seized the opportunity afforded by the civil war which broke out on the death of Honorius to seize and sack most of that part of Spain which Vallia and Constantius had reconquered for the empire. At this time they chose as their king a bold, cunning, and intelligent man named Geiseric or Genseric.[1] The chance was too good to be lost. In the spring of 429 Genseric landed in Africa with a force which seems to have amounted to 50,000 men. The event proved that if it had been difficult for the barbarians to set foot in Africa it was still more difficult to dislodge them when they were once established. It was in vain that the tragic misunderstanding between the Regent and the Count of Africa was cleared up, and that the latter did what he could to drive out the barbarians he had himself invited. The Vandals were now in force in African territory where they had found allies of inestimable value in the Donatists who had been persecuted by the empire. In 431 the greater part of the northern Coast of Africa, including the three Mauretanias and Numidia, were lost to Rome. After many centuries the Carthaginian danger had re-arisen in a new form.

This was a terrible, if not a mortal blow, and it was aggravated by a civil war which developed out of the disaster. In the following year, 432, Bonifacius returned to Rome and Placidia appointed him *magister militum* of the Western Empire in place of his rival

[1] On Genseric and the Vandals *cf.* the recent study by F. Martroye, *Genseric, la conquête vandale en Afrique et la destruction de l'empire de l'occident*, Paris, 1907.

Aëtius, who had been dismissed in spite of the military successes which he had been winning since 428 in Gaul, Rhætia, and Noricum. But Aëtius, refusing to submit took arms and the result was an atrocious civil struggle of which Italy was the scene and in which Huns were pitted against Goths. Bonifacius was victorious but soon afterwards died, and Aëtius, who after his defeat had taken refuge among the Huns, returned to Italy with a Hun army and forced the Regent to restore him to his old office (433). It was none too soon, for the civil war had encouraged disorder throughout the empire. Gaul was once more in flames. In the North-west the Armoricani had revolted; in the North-east the Burgundians were expanding; everywhere there were insurrections of peasants among whom now reappeared the ancient name of the Bagaudi; in the South there was renewed unrest among the Visigoths. With indefatigable energy Aëtius did his best to re-establish the situation. Between 435 and 437 the Armoricani and the Bagaudi were in fact subdued; the Burgundians, after a fierce struggle which lasted from 437 to 443, were removed into Sapaudia (Savoy) under the same conditions as the Visigoths in Aquitania who, in their turn, were brought back to a strict observance of the agreement of 418. But all these wars in the West compelled the government to make terms with Genseric in Africa. In 435 Valentinian III. concluded a treaty recognizing Genseric as possessor of the territory in his power, that is to say of all Mauretania and part of Numidia, on condition of paying tribute. But with a greedy and cunning barbarian such as Genseric, a treaty of this kind could be no more than a truce, and in 439 he in fact made himself master of Carthage by a surprise attack.

Great was the dismay caused by this event, not only in Italy but also in the East, and it was greater still when Genseric attacked Sicily in the following year. The Vandals were now threatening Sicily and South Italy from the coast of Africa as the Carthaginians had done seven centuries before. If their power were to spread Egypt, Syria, and Greece would also be endangered. The Vandalic peril became the common anxiety of the courts of Rome and Constantinople, and in 440 and 441 the two empires made great preparations for a joint expedition against Africa. These preparations alarmed Genseric who had recourse to negotiation. He affected modesty and docility, and promised not to repeat his offences. His proposals were successful in persuading the exhausted empire to give up the idea of war *à outrance* against him, and in 442 a treaty was signed whereby the map of Africa was readjusted. It appears that Mauretania and part of Numidia were restored to Rome, while to Genseric were ceded in exchange the Provincia Proconsularis and Bizacene.

**160. Attila and the Invasion of the Huns.** The significance of this rearrangement is not clear. It is difficult to see who was the gainer and who the loser by it. It is certain that after this peace had been concluded Genseric devoted himself to the formation, by every kind of intrigue, of a barbarian coalition against Rome. His conduct was undoubtedly connected with the rise of a new and graver peril to the empire; the peril of the Huns.

In 433 Attila had ascended the throne of the Hun nation. He was an active and energetic prince who had immediately taken measures to unite under his sceptre a great number of Hun, Slavonic, and Finnish tribes of the North and East as well as many Germanic peoples of Central Europe, thus forming a barbarian empire of vast extent. In 444 or 445 he became sole monarch on the assassination of his brother Bleda, and commenced an attack on the Eastern Empire with great forces. In 447 he laid waste Illyria, Thrace, the two Dacias, Mœsia, and Scythia, reaching the Propontis and the Ægean across Macedonia and Thessaly. It was a kind of avalanche and, after a vain attempt at resistance, Theodosius II., was compelled to buy peace at the cost of paying tribute to the barbarian. This shameful peace, however, was not of long duration. Theodosius II., died in 450 and his successor Marcianus refused to continue to pay the tribute. Attila, emboldened by his success in the East decided for the moment to attack thc occidental provinces where, a few months after the death of Theodosius II., Galla Placidia had also died and had been buried at Ravenna in the tomb which exists to this day. In 451, having collected a great army composed of Huns, Germans, Gepidi, Ostrogoths, Turcilingi, Marcomanni, Quadi, Heruli, and Franci Riparii, Attila invaded the Gallic provinces from Belgium to Metz. Metz was taken by storm and destroyed, and the invading army next threw itself on Orleans. Aëtius was despatched to check the advance of this horde. With his usual skill and energy he succeeded in opposing Attila's coalition with one of his own. He collected an army of Roman Gauls, Alani, allied Germans, Burgundians, Visigoths, Franks, Salii, and even Riparian Franks in which the meagre Roman legions were quite submerged. In the late summer the advanced guards of the two armies met on the way to Orleans. After a furious mêlée, Attila was repulsed and had to retire to the neighbourhood of Troyes where the plain begins which was ever afterwards famous under the name of the Campi Catalauni. Here decisive battle was joined. It was a terrible struggle which lasted for two days. Theodoric, the valiant chief of the Visigoths, was slain, but the fury of his tribesmen and the skill of his son Torrismondus decided the combat. Attila was compelled to retreat (451).

Attila's army, however, though defeated was not destroyed. He retired to Pannonia with the ruins of his forces, reorganized them and in the spring of 452 attacked Italy. At this moment the coalition made by Aëtius was dissolved. Fortunately Attila was checked before he had advanced very far by the fortresses which he encountered on his march, especially by Aquileia which he finally captured and destroyed. This delay soon bore fruit. Attila's army in the Venetian plain was wasted by hunger, fever, and the heat of the sun, while the army of the emperor Marcianus, hastening to the succour of the peninsula, threatened the audacious invader in the rear. It was at this point that the Western court organized an embassy to Attila under the direction of Pope Leo I. which easily persuaded him to retreat; but, in order to preserve the West from the tutelage of the East, allowed the worst enemy of the empire to escape (453). Fortunately Attila died suddenly in the same year and his motley empire went to pieces in a single day.

Shortly afterwards his conqueror followed him to the tomb, a victim to an intrigue similar to that which had destroyed Stilicho. At Rome one day while Aëtius was discussing affairs of state with Valentinian, the emperor, whose ear had long been poisoned against the great general, by courtiers, picked a quarrel with him and transfixed him with his sword (454).

161. **The Catastrophe (454–476 A.D.).** The death of Aëtius was not less disastrous than that of Stilicho. Valentinian III., did not long survive his victim, for on March 16, 455, he too succumbed to a palace plot. The dynasty of Theodosius was extinct, and he was succeeded by Petronius Maximus, a patrician and a Roman senator who had been the leader of the conspiracy. It was soon made clear what it meant to lack the firm hand of a soldier. A few months after the accession of the new prince the Vandals appeared with a numerous fleet off the mouths of the Tiber and, having landed a force, marched on Rome. Petronius was terror-stricken, tried to fly, and was torn to pieces by the Romans. Genseric took Rome which he plundered for fourteen days in a much more ferocious manner than Alaric had done. He then returned to Africa laden with booty. The Hun peril having disappeared, the danger of the Vandals re-emerged more threatening than ever, and this *coup de main* against Rome was the beginning of a new war in which Genseric aimed at making himself master of all Roman Africa and of the great islands of the Mediterranean—in fact at reconstituting the Carthaginian empire.

The necessities of the situation required that the whole empire, East and West alike, should make a great effort to destroy Genseric. The emperor Marcianus seems to have wished to do so. But in the West there broke out a new and critical quarrel about the succession to the empire. On the death of Maximus the Visigoths of Gaul induced their general M. Eparchius or M. Mæcilius Avitus to don the imperial purple either in July or August, 455. Shortly afterwards Avitus appointed as commander-in-chief of the forces in Italy one Ricimer, a protégé of Aëtius, grandson of Vallia, son of a Suevian chief and the last of the great barbarians of the West. Ricimer was then winning victories over the Vandals in Sicily and in Corsica, but Avitus, having been elected by the Goths, could not but be very unpopular in Italy and in Rome. The opposition found a useful but highly dangerous weapon in the new *magister militum*. Ricimer came to an understanding with the senate, and deposed and defeated Avitus; but as the senate and Ricimer could not agree as to who should be the new emperor, Marcianus at Constantinople remained the sole sovereign. Marcianus died on January 27, 457 and was succeeded by Leo I., who soon afterwards deprived the too presumptuous Ricimer of the office of *magister militum*, consoling him with the title of Patrician. For Ricimer he substituted Flavius Julius Maioranus, a general of great merit who was one of the most distinguished pupils of Aëtius. Ricimer for the moment had to give way, and some months later the troops acclaimed Maioranus emperor. This choice was ratified at Constantinople.

The Western Empire again had a capable man as its chief. His two chief aims were to reduce the administration to some kind of order and to destroy the power of the Vandals in Africa. He took the work in hand with great energy. Though he was hampered by many difficulties, and especially by a war against the Visigoths of Gaul into which King Theodoric had thrust Avitus, he managed to prepare a great expedition against Africa. Genseric, however, anticipated him and destroyed a great part of the Roman fleet while at anchor in the harbours of Spain before it could put to sea. This was a serious blow which badly weakened the authority of Maioranus. Meanwhile there had arisen an agitation among the administrative officers in the interior who were being compelled by the emperor to govern in a just and upright manner. The barbarian troops were discontented with his severe discipline and Ricimer was only waiting for a favourable opportunity for taking his revenge. Finally Ricimer once more put himself at the head of the malcontents and succeeded in slaying Maioranus (August 7, 461).[1]

Being a barbarian Ricimer could not himself aspire to the purple, but he imposed the choice as emperor of Libius Severus, an Italian who was destined to be a mere puppet. The death of Maioranus, however, raised against the new government several of his generals such as Marcellinus in Dalmatia and Ægidius in Gaul. The new emperor, therefore, found himself confronted by grave difficulties at home by which the barbarians did not fail to profit. The Goths, indeed, extended their sway as far as the north of Gaul and Genseric conquered Sardinia. The four years of the reign of Severus were disastrous, and, when he died in 465, there was an interregnum of two even more miserable years, the reason for which shows clearly how lamentably weak the empire had become. Genseric had pushed his audacity so far as to set up a candidate of his own for the empire, a certain Olybrius; and, as neither the Eastern Emperor nor the Roman senate (who did not want him) dared to refuse for fear of war with the Vandals, the throne remained vacant.

[1] On the political struggles during the reign of Maioranus the reader may consult R. Cessi; *Marcellino e l'opposizione imperiale romana sotto il governo di Majorano*, in *Atti del R. Istituto veneto di scienze e lettere*, 1915–16.

This pusillanimous conduct only increased the insolence of Genseric, who in 467 made a direct attack on the Eastern Empire and laid waste Greece and the islands in order to force Constantinople to accept his emperor. The Eastern Emperor on this decided to emerge from his inertia and nominated Procopius Antemius, a descendant of the ancient general Procopius and a son-in-law of Marcianus, to fill the throne of Italy. The power of Ricimer was again seriously shaken (April 12, 467).

Procopius, having been elected to defy Genseric, soon resumed the idea of a great Vandalic war in which the two empires should co-operate with united forces. Immense preparations were made, but owing to the incapacity, the disagreements, or the treachery of some of the generals, the enterprise, which began under favourable auspices, again failed (468). This failure enabled Ricimer to recommence his intrigues. He came to an understanding with Genseric and with Euric King of the Visigoths and succeeded in fomenting a war in Gaul between the Visigoths and Rome. Then taking advantage of this war he marched on Rome at the head of an army. Having taken the city and murdered Antemius (July 11, 472) he caused Genseric's candidate Olibrius to be proclaimed emperor (472).

The barbarians had triumphed, but neither Ricimer nor Olybrius lived long to enjoy their success. Both died of the plague in the very same year. The emperor Leo then nominated as Western Emperor Julius Nepos, grandson of the great general Count Marcellinus. The barbarian troops at once set up against him a certain Glycerius, but Nepos soon got rid of him, and in June, 474 he remained sole master of the last corner of what had once been the Roman Empire of the West. But now a new affliction was added to the many which tormented the empire. The triumph of Genseric, the growing power of the Visigoths in Gaul, the long predominance of Ricimer, the innumerable defeats sustained by the empire all immeasurably increased the pride and pretensions of the barbarians in the imperial service. There was now a barbarian party opposed to the party of the ancient Romans and each made its appeal to a different set of sentiments and interests. Nepos represented a reaction against the barbarians. But he soon quarrelled with the national party because in Gaul he ceded Alvernia to the Visigoths by whom it had been conquered and the legions of the north of Italy, which were composed of Roman citizens, revolted under the leadership of their general, a Romanized barbarian named Orestes an old officer of Attila's, who had transferred himself to the service of the empire. Orestes compelled the legitimate emperor to fly from Ravenna to Salina in Dalmatia (August, 475) and raised his son Romulus Augustulus to the throne. The barbarian party were not slow to take their revenge and demanded as the price of their acquiescence in this arrangement, the cession of one third of the great estates of Italy. Orestes could not accomplish so tremendous a revolution and accordingly refused. On this Odoacer, one of the barbarian officers of the imperial guard was elected king by his comrades, and, having summoned other bands of barbarian tribes from beyond the Alps, he attacked Orestes who had thrown himself into Pavia with the forces which still remained loyal, took the city, and overthrew and killed Orestes (August 27–28, 476). Romulus was deposed and imprisoned in Campania near Naples on the spot now covered by the Castel dell'Uovo. The conqueror sent to the Emperor of the East the useless ensigns of imperial power and declared that he would continue to govern Italy as his lieutenant.

Thus ended, in fact if not in law, the history of the western part of the Roman Empire, and also, as it is usually reckoned, the history of antiquity. Here therefore our narrative must end. In reality the West had still a legitimate, though a deposed emperor in the person of Julius Nepos, and after his death Italy was not an independent barbarian kingdom but a province of the ancient Roman Empire whose destinies were governed by its supreme head from Constantinople. The unity of the empire was not broken and Italy did not actually become a barbarian possession until after the Lombard invasion of the peninsula and after the Slavs had forced their way into the north-western portion of the Balkan peninsula, thus interrupting communications between the East and the West. Henceforth, however, the occidental empire was no more than a name. Rome's great historic achievement was destroyed, and a new era of history began. The Byzantine or oriental empire on the other hand was destined to last for more than another thousand years, preserving in broad outline the organization it had received from Diocletian and Constantine, until at last it fell under the blows of the Turks.

# INDEX

D

E

N

P

Q



R

T

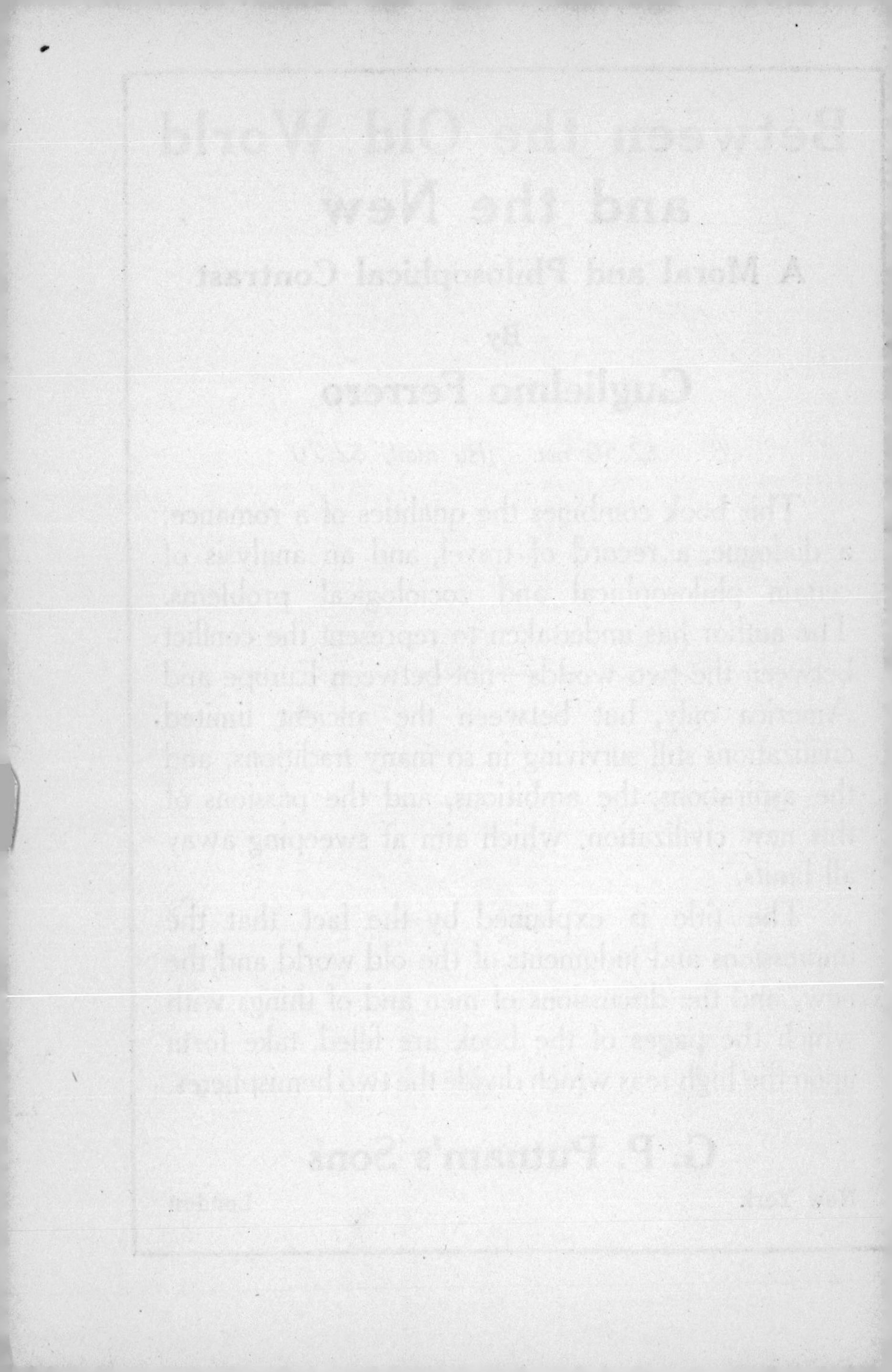